THE KABBALA

THE KABBALA
A TALE OF TWO TREES

The Tree of Life and The Tree of Knowledge

THEODORE J BALESTRERI

The Kabbalah

By Theodore J Balestreri

© Copyright 2017 to Nephilim Press and the individual Authors and Artists featured within this work

ISBN: 978-0-9987081-1-9

This Hardbound Edition is Limited to 500 Numbered Copies.

This Copy Being:

CONTENTS

Thank you to all who have taken the path before,
For they have left us with many clues to
Their earlier journeys.
And to those who are beginning their journey,
I dedicate this book.
For they who travel this path of truth,
Knowledge and Enlightenment
Remember
Knowledge is Truth
And
Truth is Enlightenment

Ha-Sad hu ha-yesod "Mystery is the foundation".
Says the *Zohar*. It is the foundation of everything.
The whole Kabbalah is called hokhmat ha-emet: "Wisdom of the truth".
ALEXANDRE SAFRAN: *Wisdom of the Kabballah*

PREFACE

At the time of this writing, if you were to make a search of the word Kabbalah or the Tree of Life in any of the current search engines available on the internet, you would find over a half million potential sites on these two topics. Many of these sites pertain to farfetched concepts ranging from pure fantasy to what many feel reflect absolute ignorance and lack of scholarly understanding of these topics. After sorting your way through, you will find the majority of reasonable references fall into one of two catagories. First, there are those sources that wish to promote a particular interpretation or direction on how one should use selected sacred works to attain "hidden knowledge". The other major grouping is advertising for support groups, books, Tarot decks and other items that promise to help the new student in their quest for wisdom. I have spent many disappointing research hours searching these sites. It is my hope that this publication will give the student a source for basic information and direction in their search of the "hidden knowledge" they seek.

I have taught the use of the Qabbalah for nearly forty years and during that time have found extremely dedicated students who knew every arcane term and function of the Tree of Life, Tarot and other tools of the trade, but did not know how to apply or use this knowledge in their daily life or toward the advancement of their studies. Most of the students who have attended my classes were there because of a curiosity about how to understand the mystical attributes of the Kabbalah. This latter group is generally made up of those who have honest open minds and are seeking knowledge that will help them improve their lives. They often have studied on their own, and have become confused by the vast number of books and articles that contain conflicting concepts. I always begin by explaining to the noviate that there are many paths to knowledge and they must pick one path, explore it, and then compare information to other sources they have encounted. I also explain they must be willing to abandon or discount beliefs that they had previously accepted as doctrine. I believe that this method of study develops a firm foundation upon which to build additional insight into their physical and spiritual relation to their fellow humans, the world, universe and God.

The reader needs to know that this is not going to be a book full of dry facts but will be a "story about" and an "introduction to" how the concepts of the various forms of the Kabbalah came into existence. It will also describe the two major forms of the trees described in the Garden of Eden, the Tree of Life and the Tree of Knowledge. With these explanations, I can provide both the novice and the advanced student a background for obtaining additional knowledge of a highly esoteric subject and a path forward discovering the breathtaking view of creation that only a few have experienced. As with all attempts to climb the mountain of knowledge, there are many ways to begin the ascent. There is not one singular path but many, and some paths are easier than others. It is my hope to give you, the reader, the necessary tools to begin you own ascent to a greater understanding of this important philosophy.

This book is not the result of a singular idea but the compilation of many questions by numerous people as to what is the Kabbalah. It is to these friends, students and aquanitances that I give thank. For without their curiosity and emotional support and encourgament this book would not have taken form.

I.

INTRODUCTION

B efore any coherent discussion can begin there must be a common understanding of key words. In the case of the word "Kabbalah", there are several definitions and spellings. The spelling varies for two main reasons. The first is who and where they where translated. The second depends of which type of "Kabbalah" is being discussed. Some basic guidelines can be applied. When the word begins with the letter "K" the subject is generally in reference to the Jewish based Kabbalah and or an "overall" discussion of the genre. When it begins with "C" the author is usually specifically referring to the Christian form of study. And finally when the word begins with the letter "Q" it is usually the case that the Hermetic version is being explored. There is even issues as to how many "b's" are used when spelling the various versions of Kabbalah/Cabballa or Qabbalah. It all dependes on its source. Unforantuntly these are not hard and fast rules and depend on the author of the text one is viewing.

The word "Kabbalah" has many meanings. The definition depends on the source. The traditional translation of the word is "to receive". The first use of the word was in a religious context, specifically to the Jewish rabbinical study of the *Torah*. The *Torah*'s teaching was initially verbal pertaining to God's creation of the Universe, and/or man's place within the creation process and the Universe as a whole.

The definition was modified by Christian, New Age and Occultist syncretic adaptations to become a term referring to a system of highly esoteric knowledge meant to explain the relationship between the finite man and the infinite God. The Kabbalah tries to define pathways by which man can reunite with the Divine due to his fractured relationship after his fall from grace at the time of his expulsion from the Garden of Eden.

Scholars of religious creation, trace the evolution of creation mythos as early as the Sumerians (1700 B.C.E.), to the Egyptian and Babylonian (1700–1450 B.C.E.) and followed by the Persian Empires around 500 B.C.E. These creation legends focused on trying to explain how the world was created, and man's place in that creation, and his place in the overall universe. The Kabbalah is viewed as a culmination of these scholars' ideas expressed in the terms of Jewish culture and law. By understanding man's relationship in the creation of the universe, and God intentions, a purpose is given to man in the scheme of that creation. The Kabbalah points to, and questions, this quest of knowledge, and most importantly man's role and purpose in life. Of course there is a great scholar debate as to these answers and it is often left to the aspirant to answer these questions for themselves. The teaching of Kabbalah provides many signposts to these answers but also leaves much to be explored by the individual.

Before delving into the topic of the Kabbalah a little basic background and history should be laid down to give a perspective of where the "tradition" is believed to have originated. I phrase it as 'believed' because there appears to be no single person or place of origin, and if there was it has been lost to history. The Kabbalah is not considered to be a religion as prescribed by a specifically organized group but more of a spiritual journey with God. Especially emphasizing one's relationship with God and mystical encounters that result from that relationship.

This book offers a brief summary of the basic history and extensive commentary on the development and principles that students of the Western Hermetic Qabalah should understand. As we progress you will note there are multiple spellings and translations of some of the most basic of works and words. This is generally the result of translations by various individuals and their interpretation as to what specific words meant in the vernacular of their current language versus what document source they were translating. An example is text that was translated from an ancient Hebrew and Aramaic scroll, to Modern Hebrew or Greek, there would be individual letters in translation often had more than one n meanings. Another example can be found in the Latin based language where words sometimes have regional variations. An example with Latin based languages is trying to explain to a non-English speaker that "hear" and "here" are two different words even though they sound the same. Other language issues occur due to a change in how words are used over time, such as the word "smug" which once meant "well-dressed" and now means "self-righteous".

We first begin with some basic building blocks in the world of the Kabbalah. In discussing the development and formalization of the Kabbalah from its apparently Jewish origin to the western form of the Qabalah, as well as the Christian Cabbala, you may note some basic differences such as how the knowledge gained from its study was not just for enlightenment, but to control individuals or groups of people.

II.

EARLY SCHOOLS OF STUDY

everyone who is called by my name,
whom I created for my glory,
whom I formed and made.

As stated earlier there is no single agreement as to how the Kabbalah came into existence. Rather it was over time in which the ancient scholars developed and borrowed the ideas represented in what we see today as the Kabbalah. There was a great deal of blending, refining, and incorporating of new of ideas between various Jewish, Arabic and mid-eastern teachers/scholars. This occurred because as many of the early empires grew they improved the means of travel through their empires by building roads and way stations to aid traveles. These improvements increased trade as well as helping their army's movements throughout their kingdoms which often involved tranversing large distance, by land or water. As these roads and sea lanes developed ideas traveled with the various merchants and emmisaries as they made contact with their neighbors. By traveling of these learned men began to have the means to of traveling with these groups between the various political, educational and trading centers of the ancient world.

When the schools of the Jewish Kabbalah were first established it appeared there were individuals and groups of men who were attempting to understand man's relationship to God, and God's involvement in creation. These schools were first documented in the first and second centuries. They were known as the *Merkabah*. *Merkabah* or *Merkavah* Mysticism were schools that studied what is referred to as "Chariot Mysticism". They were schools of early Jewish Mysticism, c. 100 B.C.E.–1000 C.E., and were centered on visions such as those found in the *Book of Ezekiel*, Chapter 1.

> *4 Then I looked, and behold, a whirlwind was coming out of the north, a great cloud with raging fire engulfing itself; and brightness was all around it and radiating out of its midst like the color of amber, out of the midst of the fire.*
>
> *5 Also from within it came the likeness of four living creatures. And this was their appearance: they had the likeness of a man.*
>
> *6 Each one had four faces, and each one had four wings.*
>
> *7 Their legs were straight, and the soles of their feet were like the soles of calves' feet. They sparkled like the color of burnished bronze.*
>
> *8 The hands of a man were under their wings on their four sides; and each of the four had faces and wings.*
>
> *9 Their wings touched one another. The creatures did not turn when they went, but each one went straight forward.*
>
> *10 As for the likeness of their faces, each had the face of a man; each of the four had the face of a lion on the right side, each of the four had the face of an ox on the left side, and each of the four had the face of an eagle.*
>
> *11 Thus were their faces. Their wings stretched upward; two wings of each one touched one another, and two covered their bodies.*
>
> *12 And each one went straight forward; they went wherever the spirit wanted to go, and they did not turn when they went.*
>
> *13 As for the likeness of the living creatures, their appearance was like burning coals of fire, like the appearance of torches going back and forth among the living creatures. The fire was bright, and out of the fire went lightning.*
>
> *14 And the living creatures ran back and forth, in appearance like a flash of lightning.*
>
> BOOK OF EZEKIEL 1:4–14

In *Ezekiel* (1:15–25) it continues and describes the throne of God and his multi-wheeled chariot.

> 15 *Now as I looked at the living beings, behold, there was one wheel on the earth beside the living beings, for each of the four of them.*
> 16 *The appearance of the wheels and their workmanship was like sparkling beryl, and all four of them had the same form, their appearance and workmanship being as if one wheel were within another.*
> 17 *Whenever they moved, they moved in any of their four directions without turning as they moved.*
> 18 *The rims of the wheels were covered with eyes.*
> 19 *Whenever the creatures moved, the wheels moved with them, and if the creatures rose up from the earth, so did the wheels.*
> 20 *The creatures went wherever they wished, and the wheels did exactly what the creatures did, because the creatures controlled them.*
> 21 *So every time the creatures moved or stopped or rose in the air, the wheels did exactly the same.*
> 22 *Above the heads of the creatures there was something that looked like a dome made of dazzling crystal.*
> 23 *There under the dome stood the creatures, each stretching out two wings toward the ones next to it and covering its body with the other two wings.*
> 24 *I heard the noise their wings made in flight; it sounded like the roar of the sea, like the noise of a huge army, like the voice of Almighty God. When they stopped flying, they folded their wings,*
> 25 *but there was still a sound coming from above the dome over their heads.*

These verses described what the prophet Ezekiel saw and were used as allegories to explain the mysteries of the Universe. The Merkabah's popularity lasted until around the tenth century when their teachings were incorporated into other schools that were emerging. These more "contemporary" schools of thought emphasized the study of the medieval doctrinal emergence of what would be called the "Kabbalah". This occurred primarily in southwestern Europe where the Muslim, Jewish and Christian intelligentsia merged. These Medieval schools became absorbed, not with just Ezekiel's visions but in a greater picture of creation itself. This idea of creation and man's place in this divine action caused many discussions/ debates, and meditation on these debates.

As scholars studied Ezekiel's prophetic visions another key mystic point became hotly debated, that being his description of the four supernal Universes. The word "supernal" refers to belonging to the heaven, to divine beings. These supernal Universes correspond to the Tetragrammaton, or the Name of God. The Tetragrammaton is represented in the Tree of Life in a vertical form. The form is a visualization of *Isaiah* 43:7, *"All that is called by My Name, for My Glory (Atzilut), I have created it (Beriyah), I have formed it (Yetzirah), and I have made it (Asiyah)"*. This verse describes one of the early versions of The Tree where the various levels of God's emanations is described. It describes four levels with the highest representation of God being the *Atzilut* (Closeness); the second level *Beriyah* (Creation); the third *Yetzirah, "I have formed it"* (formation); and the forth *Asiyah, "I have made it"* (making). The highest Universe, *Atzilut,* is found in *Isaiah* 43:7, and is called "My Glory". It is the Universe of the Ten Sefirot, the ten Divine Emanations, and in Ezekiel's vision, the "Man", who represents God, and who sits on the Throne as represented in his vision.

As scholars of Jewish Kabbalah intermingled with their Christian and Arab counterparts, new ideas were overlaid on older ideas and concepts. With this came newer ideas and new understandings of old beliefs. During these early centuries, these scholars attempted to conceal their perceived esoteric knowledge from those they deemed unworthy. For it was felt these inner workings of creation were too esoteric in nature to be exposed to those who were not trained to think and understand the concepts revealed. It was felt that if this knowledge fell into the "wrong" hands there would be great danger to the individual as well as others around them. It appears such words as "magic" or "esoteric" came into play both by those who were enlightened and those who were excluded from the special enlightenment. In many cases this was the result of those who believed themselves "possessors" of this knowledge having power over those who did not. This power was sometimes in the form of controlling natural events such as rain, lightning and the productivity of cattle, crops and harvests in general. This helped to establish the early initiatory practices of both in religious and secret societies.

As Europe emerged from the Dark Ages, many Christian scholars became aware of both the Jewish and Arab mystical thinking concerning creation process and God's hand in this process. As the concepts of the Kabbalah became known to non-Jewish thinkers other social currents were surging through Medieval Europe. One of these movements was the upsurge of religious zeal, where there was an emphasis by Christians to convert all other peoples to the "True Church" works, but more as spiritual works, and are now today accepted as enlightened scripts.

These observations must serve as cautionary signposts for the neophyte to not just take every word as a true doctrine. The student should view what they are studing in the historic context of how that information was revealed as well as the individual or schools reason for revealing that information. This skepticism must be balanced with the faith in the belief that additional knowledge and understanding will be revealed to the student. As you progress down the path of knowledge ayour comprehension will evolve to a higher level. And your ability to find even greater understanding of the mystic concepts revealed. This has been one of the big attractions to many of the schools in existence today. Some schools promise that IF you study hard you will gain the esoteric knowledge of the ancients, and with that knowledge comes power.

Trying to trace the historical lineage of the Kabbalah and its various forms can be very confusing, primarily due to the lack of any specific moment of creation. There are several schools of thought concerning when the Kabbalah came about, and by whom, as well as where the birth of the Kabbalah occurred. I will attempt to present some of the more popular thoughts on how, and what we moderns call the "Jewish Esoteric thought" development.

It appeared that much of the early Jewish mystic work was done as a means of understanding man's relationship to the world, both on the physical and spiritual plane. The early schools examined and tried to understand how God worked in developing the Universe as man understood it, as well as man's place in the greater scheme of that creation process. Most of this early study centered on Ezekiel's mystical encounter with the fiery Chariot, and to the spiritual palaces/temples described in the creation of the world. These discussions generally centered on 'what did these visions mean' and 'how one can replicate this experience' that the prophet Ezckiel reported.

Within these discussions, debates and meditations concering the meaning of Ezckiel's words, the early of Jewish Mystic thinkers had concerning as to what the *Book of Ezekiel* and his *Throne Vision*; *Ezekiel* 1:2: -2:1 should mean. Other discussion revolved around other visions of Ezekiel especially *Ezekiel 8:1*. New ideas emerged forming the basis for the understranding of how they thought the creative process occurred, mainly God's creative manifestation of the physical world.

As mentioned earlier there was a lot of confusion when it came to determining the origin of the Kabbalah. What most scholars do agree on is that there were several schools called *Beth Midrash* (also spelled *Beis Medrash*, or *Beit Midrash*). These schools concentrated on Ezekiel's vision and were intensely studied by Jewish scholars in hopes of following in Ezekiel's mystical revelations on creation.

MISHNAH (200–220 C.E)

Early evidence of the Kabbalistic philosophy dates to the pre-Kabbalah period of the Tannaim or what the "Sages" cited in the *Mishnah* or *Mishna*, meaning "study by repetition". It was the first major written Rabvinic literature that was an edited form of the Jewish oral traditions known as the "Oral Torah". The *Mishnah* appeared around 200–220 C.E. These early mystics studied and meditated on the divine *hekhalot* and *Merkabah* referring to the "Palaces/Temples" and "Chariot" respectively. Studies of the *hekhalot* and *Merkabah* can be found in the *Books of the Palaces and the Chariot*. Other reference points for this work can be found in a collection of works called the 3 *Enoch*, which comprised: *The Third Book of Enoch, The Book of Palaces, The Book of Rabbi Ishmael the High Priest,* and *The Revelation of Metatron*. These works described the mystic experiences of the ascent to the divine Chariot as described by Ezekiel and his visions of the supreme palaces/temples. These palaces/temples were described as being layered one above each other, like a ladder, to a mystic number of seven. This was one of the first written symbolic representations of the initiatory rites of the mystic realms. For it describes the climbing of this symbolic ladder until the aspirant reached paradise itself.

Ma'aseh Bereshit or Ma'aseh Merkabah

Another early work predating the Kabbalah was the study of *ma'aseh bereshit* which literally means *Work of Creation* and/or *Work of the Chariot.* Current scholars state this was not the work of a single individual but the work of a group of individuals whose thoughts concerned the interpretation of the first Chapter of *Genesis,* where God creates the universe. The *ma'aseh bereshit,* was compiled for the first time into a single text in the sixth century. It was the basis for the later work called the *Sepher Yetzirah* or *Book of Formation,* or *Book of Creation,* which describes the separation between the two worlds. The first world being the spiritual world of God and the other world, the material world of man. It explains that since God created everything including man, then it is only logical that man is by default a part of God and the human body itself reveals the presence of its creator.

Initially these early studies of many of these schools, as well as individual scholars, were still attempting to understand the great vision Ezekiel had described. This changed in the twelfth century, when the body of philosophical studies changed, to which today is referred to as the Kabbalah. There are three main branches of the Kabbalah. The first was the 'Kabbalah' in its original or Jewish form; and second, the Kabbalah was translated from Jewish to French, Greek, English and German. These forms of the Kabbalah developed into what is referred to as the "Cabbala" which is attributed to the Christian interpretation. The final major form is the "Qabalah" or "Hermetic Qabalah" or the New Age or Western version, which is currently the most popular in the Western world.

Kabbalah (Hebrew: קַבָּלָה)

The Kabbalah did not suddenly appear as part of the Jewish tradition. It developed over time and may have had its origins, at least first concepts, during the four times the Jewish people were held in captivity by King Nebuchadnezzar I in Babylonia, 605 B.C.E, 597 B.C.E., c. 587 B.C.E., and c. 582 B.C.E. During these periods of exile, it is speculated that there was exposure to the Zoroastrianism and idea of dualism. One concept introduced was the aspect of good and evil. Over the centuries these ideas were deeply guarded by the "chosen" and passed on orally only. Over time these ideas were refined and became the basis pillars of the early Jewish mystic tradition.

Early uses of the word *Kabala* or *Kabbalah,* refer to the common meaning of "tradition", or "receiving/tradition". It was an oral tradition where its tenents were taught initially from "mouth to ear". Much later symbols were introduced to help in the transmission and retention of the holy works. These symbols often had multiple meanings or even appeared meaningless when viewed by the uninitiated. This was done primarily as a means to assure that the sacred information would not get into the hands of the profane. The word "Kabbalah" at first referred to the study of the mystical awareness of the transcendence of God. The centers for the study of this transcendence became most prevalent during the twelfth and thirteenth century in Southern France and Spain, where there was a concentration of Jewish scholars. This concentration was often the result of expulsions from kingdoms throughout what is now modern Europe. The discussion of God's transcendence was part of the Jewish tradition of esoteric doctrine that could only be passed on to others after strict qualifications were met by the candidate, and then only transmitted verbally by symbol and metaphor. There were many additional restrictions set by various schools in an attempt to assure that the students were stable in their mental and emotional lives. Some historians state that the new students had to be proficient in Hebrew, the *Torah*, married and at least 40 years of age. Even though these qualities were stressed they were often over-looked, depending upon which school of study the student entered.

One must remember that in the twelfth and thirteenth century a "student" who was at least 40 years of age was past their prime, and was looked upon as elderly. Also by this time, his offspring should have been married and out of the home. It was then believed that when a child reached 13 years of age, they were viewed as adults and should be married by then or shortly thereafter. It was felt then that the 40-year-old "student" should be ready to set the material world aside and immerse himself in the world of esoteric studies. It was not the norm for students who had not reached the age of 40 to join the early esoteric schools of study because they were not mature enough to understand the inner workings of the material being presented.

Much of the scholarship and interest in the Kabbalah starting in the twentieth century was the result of the early works of Gershom Scholem (1897–1982) a German-born Israeli philosopher and historian. He was the first Professor of Jewish Mysticism at the Hebrew University of Jerusalem. Many of his lectures were published in *Major Trends in Jewish Mysticism* (1941). In his work, *On Kabbalah and its Symbo*lism (1965), many of his speeches and essays have been compiled and have helped to spread the knowledge of Jewish Mysticism not only to the Jewish world but also to the non-Jewish sector of academia.

EARLY PUBLISHED WORKS

SEFER HA-BAHIR

Several reference manuscripts were key to the development of what we call the Kabbalah. The oldest is the *Sefer ha-Bahir,* also known as *The Book of Brilliance.* It is stated by many scholars that this is the oldest and the premier work concerning the Kabalistic studies. The name "Bahir" literally means "brilliant" or "illumination". It was first published in Provence in 1176. It is thought to contain one of the earliest revealers of the ten Sefirot, the mystic aspects of the Hebrew letters, and the 32 paths of Wisdom as well as the mystical and true meaning of the opening verses of *Genesis.*

One of the earliest followers of the *Sefer ha-Bahir* was Isaac the Blind who was born in Provence, France, and is often identified as the first Kabbalist in Jewish history. His real name was Rabbi Yitzhak Saggi Nehor (c. 1160–1235). The term "Saggi Nehor" as an epithet was Aramaic for "of much light". Many scholars of Jewish Mysticism believe first, that Isaac the Blind was not blind, but had excellent eyesight, and second that Isaac was the author of the *Book of the Bahir.* This latter achievement is contested by Gershom Scholem, the first Professor of Jewish Mysticism at the Hebrew University in Jerusalem, and a leading expert on the Kabbalah.

Isaac the Blind and his followers believe man cannot understand God through rational thought. They believe that God can only be truly understood through symbols which He used in the creation of the universe. Isaac believed everything was a symbol for God's existence and that the *Holy Torah* was God's gif-t to man and was the very soul of man and nature itself. Within the *Sefer ha-Bahir* there is no physical picture of the emanations or spheres that represented the creation process. It is a discussion, mostly concerning the order in which these emanations occurred. Because there was only a discussion there was a great deal of creative licence taken in trying to make a visuall depiction of the Tree in the early centuries of its discussion. The following image of The Tree of Life is attributed to Isaac the Blind and his followers and appeared on the *Portae Lucis,* meaning *Portal of Light,* in 1516. This work was produced by Paolo Riccio (1480–1541), who was a German Jewish convert to Christianity in the first half of the sixteenth century. This work was some of the earliest written material that revealed Jewish mystic thought to the Christian world.

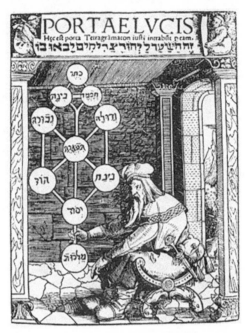

From *Portae Lucis* (1516)

ZOHAR

Another of the preeminent texts of Kabbalism is the *Zohar,* or *The Book of Splendor.* The *Sefer ha-Bahir* predates the *Zohar* and is often cited as the major work that influenced the *Zohar,* and is often quoted or referred to in the *Zohar.* Most scholars of the Kabbalah credit Rabbi Nehuniah ben ha-Kana, a Talmudic sage of the first century as the author of the *Zohar.* The *Zohar* itself is rather small in size, approximately 12,000 words.

This tome is alleged to be a collection of discourses by Rabbi Simeon ben Yochai, also known as Rashbi, who died at the time of Emperor Hadrian of Rome (76–138 CE). Hadrian was the fourteenth Emperor of Rome (117–38 CE). Due to Emperor Hadrian's persecution of the Jews in the Holy Land, Rabbi Simeon ben Yochai and his son Elazar hid from the Romans in a cave for 13 years. During those 13 years they studied the *Torah* continually and were believed to have discovered the deepest secrets of the Torah and God's secrets of creation.

Others believe, in accordance with Jewish tradition, that the *Zohar* is indeed an authentic document of the teachings of Rabbi Simeon ben Yochai, but feel only part, but not all, of the *Zohar* was written by Rashbi. The sections of the *Zohar* that are from Rabbi Simeon himself are described as "the First Mishna", while the *Zohar* as we know was authored over a span of many generations.

This tradition states that for 650 years these teachings were handed down verbally from one generation to the next until Rabbi Moses de León (c. 1250–1305), known in Hebrew as Moshe ben Shem-Tov, compiled them in a written form called the *Zohar* or *The Book of Splendor* around 1275. Rabbi Moses de León was born in Guadalajara, Spain, and he is credited with writing several mystical and cabalistic works in a short period of time. Many believe Rabbi Moses de León was the actual author of the *Zohar* while others attribute it to him as the compiler of Rabbi Simeon ben Yochai's earlier works.

The *Zohar* is made up of 22 literary parts. The main section deals with issues of the *Torah*. The term *"Torah"* means "instruction" and offers a way of life for those who follow it. It can mean the continued narrative from *Genesis* to the end of the *Tanakh*, or *Mikra* which is the canon of the Hebrew Bible. The *Torah* can even mean the totality of Jewish teaching, practice and culture. The remaining parts of the *Zohar* consist of comments and homilies.

But most importantly the prevailing view of the *Zohar* is that it describes the soul as consisting of three parts, called the "Tripartite Theory". This theory was first introduced in the Greek philosophical writing of Plato's *Republic* written around 380 B.C.E. According to the *Zohar* the first part of the soul is "nefesh", which is attached to the body and assures that the body is preserved and satisfied. It is the lowest section and is said to have no light of its own. The second section is "ruah" but according to the *Zohar* has no specific function except to illuminate the 'nefesh' and to sustain it with the light and influence that is coming down from "neshamah" the third part of the soul. Other scholars say that "ruah" is the home of the sensual desires and controls both good and evil conduct. "Neshamah" is described in *Zohar* in varied terms. It is said the "neshamah" provides the power to man to 'study the *Torah* and observe the commandments". Most importantly it is said that upon creation of the soul God "breathed into (man's) nostrils the breath (neshamah) of life, so that he might know and contemplate the mysteries of wisdom and gain a knowledge of the Maker's glory". It is with this knowledge that man would gain the perception of the divine and the soul would be reunited with the Sefirot and Shekinah. The Shekinah is the feminine aspects of God or more specifically the dwelling or settling of Divine Presence, thus making the connection to God more readily perceivable to man.

SEPHER YETZIRAH–SEFER YETZIRAH

No discussion about Jewish Mysticism would be complete without the *Sepher Yetzirah* or *The Book of Formation*, also known as *Sepher Yerirah* or the *Book of Creation* is brought into discussion. There is a great deal of controversy as to its origins. According to Jewish mystic tradition, known as the *ma'aseh* bereshit, it was the Patriarch Abraham who received it through divine revelation. Others attribute it to Adam, while still others feel it was passed down from Noah. According to modern historians the actual origin of the holy text is unknown. But most agree it emerged in stages between 100 AD and 600 AD. Some modern scholars believe it to be even an early medieval text.

The terms *Sefirot* and *Sephirot* are the most characteristic and recognizable symbols of the Kabbalah and are first found in the *Sepher Yetzirah*. It is one of the earliest texts to critically discuss the 22 secret paths of wisdom. Another key element concerning the understanding of the spiritual universe was the division of the world of God and the world of man. The description of the 10 emanations or attributes of deity are also first found in the *Sepher Yetzirah* and are the key to understanding the principles described in the Kabbalah.

The *Sepher Yetzirah* is very important in that it establishes two major components of study. The first is the understanding and description of the *Sephiroth* and second, the powers and virtues of the twenty-two Hebrew letters and the mystic aspects of the numbers. Any person who has shown any interest in the mystic Kabbalah will recognize that the majority of writing and study has to do with these three elements; the ten *Sephiroth*, the twenty-two Hebrew letters, and the numbers associated with the Sephiroth and Hebrew letters.

KEY CONTRIBUTORS TO THE JEWISH MYSTICAL TRADITION

ABRAHAM BEN SAMUEL ABULAFIA (1240–1291)

Abraham was born in Zaragoza, Spain and is the founder of the school of "Prophetic Kabbalah". His father died when Abraham was eighteen. Two years later Abraham began to travel in search of the Ten Lost Tribes of Israel. After returning from an unsuccessful trip to the Holy Land he stopped in Capua, Italy, studied philosophy and the *Moreh Nebhukhin* (Guide for the Perplexed of Maimonides), under the tutelage of Hill ben Samuel ben Eliezer of Verona. In 1271 he returned to Barcelona, Spain where he received visions while studying a form of the Kabbalah that was taught by Baruch Sheli'ah zibbur Togarmi, a cantor of eastern origin. Togarmi is known for his treatise called *Maftehot ha-Kabbalah* or *The Keys to Kabbalah*, which is a treatise on the *Sepher Yetzirah*.

Abulafia sought even deeper understanding of the creation of the world and man. Through his studies he came in contact with the writing of a German Jewish mystic, Eleazar of Worms. Eleazar was a great influence on Abulafia, and his study of the Hebrew alphabet, numerals, and vowel-points. These became important symbols of existence to him and led him deeper in his studies. These more intense studies included the Divine Names and in particular the consonants of the Tetragrammaton. Abulafia combined his studies with certain rites and ascetic practices which helped him gain a higher perception of the inscrutable nature of Deity, the secrets of creation, the miseries of humanity, and the purpose of precepts which would lead to the deeper meaning of the *Torah*.

Abulafia soon left Capua, Italy. In his travels, he taught his form of prophetic Kabbalah in cities in Spain, Italy and Greece. Abulafia established many schools where his students became inspired by him and began to write many manuscripts, not only about Abulafia's teachings and mystical experiences, but about their own experiences as well.

ELEAZAR BEN JUDAH BEN KALONYMUS, AKA, ELEAZAR ROKEACH, AKA ELEAZAR OF WORMS (1176–1238)

Eleazar Rokeach (Eleazar the Perfumer), was thought to be a descendant of the great Kalonymus family of Mainz, Germany. He was a leading

Talmudist and mystic, getting his mystical training from Judah ben Samuel of Regensburg, one of the first mystics in Germany. Eleazar wrote the *Book of the Perfumer* or *Sefer ha rokeah*. He was a mystic who had visions of legions of angels and demons. He developed and gave new emphasis to the mystical aspects of the letters of the Hebrew alphabet. He used the Gematria and Notarikon systems, which are methods of deriving different words using the same letters in different combinations to make those new words, to interpret the *Talmud*, and by using these new words Eleazar felt that miracles could be performed. Another way of using Hebrew Letters was to derive a word by using each of its initial or final letters to stand for another to form a sentence or idea out of the words. There are several variations; some use last and first letters of the initial word, often combining the middle letters as well. This difference between Notarikon and Gematria is that first, Gematria is a Jewish system of numerology, assigning to each letter, word or phrase, a numerical value; once this is done, one then compares that numerical value with other letters, words, or phrases of equal value. Second, that Notarikon is a method of deriving a word, by using each of its initial or final letters to stand for another, to form a sentence or idea out of the words created.

Judah ben Samuel of Regensburg (1140–1217) was a leader of the *Chassidei Ashkenaz*, a Jewish Mystic movement in Germany. It was thought to not be based upon kabalistic mysticism because it relied on a heavy emphasis on prayer and the following of the laws of moral conduct as prescribed in the *Talmud*. Regensburg's interpretation proved to be an early form of esoteric studies in Germany.

MOSES BEN JACOB CORDOVERO (1522–1570)
Moses Cordovero's place of birth is unknown but many scholars believed he was born in Spain or Portugal; other scholars believe he was born in Safed in northern Israel. He was also known by the acronym RaMaK. RaMak was a prolific writer while living in Safed, Israel, and was a considered a highly respected Talmudic scholar with deep insights into the meanings of the *Talmud*. He became the head of the Yeshiva, which is Hebrew for a university or place of study for Portuguese immigrants in Safed, which he ran for twenty years until his death. At his Yeshiva he was known for his views on the speculative and performative approaches to the Kabbalah.

Moses Cordovero was a mystic who used the Kabbalah to develop a framework of "cause and effect" from the Infinite to the Finite which reflects sequential logic and coherent approach to the Kabbalah. He produced his renowned book *Pardes Rimonim* (*Orchard of Pomegranates*) in 1548. In this work he systematically summarized all the various Kabbalistic thoughts that had developed over the years, from the various schools on the *Zohar*, to show that these schools formed an essential unity and self-consistent philosophical base to the Kabbalah.

Isaac ben Solomon Luria Ashkenazi (1534–1572)

Isaac Luria, aka Ha'ARI, meaning "The Lion" is considered the father of contemporary Kabbalah. His teaching is referred to as the *Lurianic Kabbalah*. Isaac was a rabbi and Jewish mystic born in Safed in the Galilee region of the Ottoman Palestine. He was not a major influence to the Kabalistic community in Safed as a writer or rabbi but more by his spiritual fame due to his strict adherence to authentic Halachah or Jewish Law.

ADDITIONAL SCHOOLS OF THOUGHT

Lurianic Kabbalah

Lurianic Kabbalah was named after the Jewish Kabbalist Isaac ben Solomon Luria Ashkenazi. Lurianic Kabbalah takes a different view of the Creation by examining it in an extremely rational way. Luria did not write down his ideas but expounded on them orally. Rabbi Hayyim ben Joseph Vital (1542–1620), of Calabria claimed to be the official interrupter and complier of Luria's oral and written works.

Lurianic Kabbalah places messianism as the central dynamic of its study. Luria applies many diverse ideas from the early kabalistic concepts to what will happen at "the End of Days". The ideas developed by Luria conceptualize and explain the Spiritual Worlds where God started the process of creation by "contracting" or limiting his infinite light to allow for a "conceptual space" in which finite and seemingly independent realms could exist. Luria called this Tzimtzum. Tzimtzum allows what is called 'empty space' to exist in which spiritual and physical Worlds and ultimately, free will can exist. Luria's three concepts of Tzimtzum, Shevirat HaKelim (the shattering of the vessels), and Tikkun (repair) describe the concepts of Divine exile and redemption. Additional aspects of the Lurianic mythology of theodicy or origin of evil as well as his description of the exile of the Shekinah (the Divine Feminine Presence). Luria goes on to explain that man's redemption is based on the persons's actions to redeem his own soul, through his daily activites.

Luria describes how from out of the *Ein-sof (the Infinite)* came the Yesh (something), and from its Ayin (nothing) Ein-sof performed an act of Tzimtzum, contracting and limiting its form from a point of allowing a metaphysical void to form. In this void Primordial Man, the Adam Kadmon and all the worlds emerged. From the Primordial Man came the ten archetypal values and the Sefirot plus the twenty-two holy letters (Otiyot Yesod) which became the building blocks of all physical things and the universe itself.

As the emanations or essences of God formed they developed the attributes of light. These lights formed into shapes which Luria called vessels (Kelim) that contained even more emanations of light of the infinite (or Ein-sof). But the vessels could not hold all the emanations and they shattered, an event which he called the Breaking of the Vessels (Shevirat ha-Kelim). The shattering caused the holy letters to become disorganized and became mere Babel rather than readable groups. This shattering also caused the balance of the universe to break creating opposites, especially between the masculine and feminine aspects of God and the Primordial Man.

The broken vessels did not lose all their light but retained small glimmers of light which were shrouded in darkness as they fell into the Sitra Achra or the "Other Side". The world was no longer made up of the ten pristine archetypal values of Wisdom, Understanding, Knowledge, Love, Judgment, Beauty and so forth, but became only a shadow of their previous splendor. They became "Kellipot" or "Husks". Because of these imperfect Husks of light, our world (Assiyah) became a world where there was still hope but only through the act of redemption.

Luria taught that it became the task of each individual to find the sparks contained within the Kellipots. It is his or her fortune to encounter, the sparks and then spiritualize them so as to reconstruct the Sefirot and the shattered Primordial Man, otherwise known as the Personalities of God. Upon this reconstruction, the universe will reach a state of equilibrium by balancing the masculine and feminine aspects of God, man and the world.

As we attempt to locate these sparks we will encounter people, events and things that are uniquely meant to help us obtain redemption. The sparks of light that comprise the Husks will help each person rekindle the sparks or life/light in their souls to aid in this process of redemption, called Restoration of the World (Tikkun ha-Olam). This restoration will help to overcome the evil and chaos that occurred with the shattering of the Vessels. For Luria the Ein-Sofis or divinity was not the just the beginning or forming of the world but a whole theosophical system which provided a way to gain insight about God. This insight would affect the world and how man functioned in his world through the restorative acts of mankind.

QLIPHOTH/QELIPPOT OR KELIPOT (קליפות)

In the discussion of the Lurianic mythology of theodicy (origin of evil) and exile of the Shekinah (the Divine Feminine Presence), the discussion of what is the nature of evil and its hierarchy is raised. In *Genesis,* there is mention of two sacred trees in the Garden of Eden, one was referred to as the Tree of Life and the other is the Tree of Knowledge of Good and Evil.

> Eden had two trees peculiar to itself. There was the tree of life in the midst of the garden. Of this man might eat and live. Christ is now to us the Tree of life, Rev. 2:7; 22:2; and the Bread of life, John 6:48, 51. 2. There was the Tree of the Knowledge of Good and Evil, so called because there was a positive revelation of the will of God about this tree, so that by it man might know moral good and evil. What is good? It is good not to eat of this tree. What is evil? It is evil to eat of this tree. In these two trees God set before Adam good and evil, the blessing and the curse. *Gen. 2:15*

In Western esotericism, there are have been two approaches to the occult and ceremonial magic developed; one is the right-hand path (RHP) which is associated with "white magic". The second is the left-hand path (LHP) that is generally associated with "black magic". Neither of these paths are good or evil. They can be used in a multitude of ways. The adepts of the RHP attempt to reconstruct the harmony that existed between man and God prior to the "Fall" when Adam and Eve were expelled from the Garden of Eden. This is in contrast to those who follow the LHP and attempt to descend deeper into the Abyss. The dark adept attempts to delve deeper into the aspects of the "Fall" from God to reach individual divinity. The followers of the LHP believe their quest to obtain what is promised, being the knowledge of the divine from the Tree of Knowledge, will lead them to a second birth, a spiritual rebirth as a god.

There have been many adherents to the left-hand path. Some of the groups often mentioned are: Satanists, Luciferians, Dark Pagans, LHP Occultists and the Church of Azazel. They propose that there is a Tree, though it is not mentioned as the "Tree of Evil" in the scriptures but as "Tree of the Knowledge of good and evil you shall not eat" *Genesis* 2:17. This symbolic Tree of Evil assigned various levels to evil spirits that populate the marial world. Like the Lurianic Kabbalah which assigns "husks", "peels" or "shells" as a way of describing the Tree so does the Qliphan/Kelipah Tree assign their evil or impure spiritual forces. This realm of evil is called Sitra Achra/Ahra. This kingdom that rose from God's wrathful and punishing nature exists in the Abyss that is symbolically below the Supernal Triangle of Kether, Chokman and Binah separating them from the lower or lesser Sephirot. The followers of the LHP believe that this kingdom exists as a separate world because of the sinfulness of man and will continue as long as man sins.

The Sitra Ahra is often described as a world with no goodness. Others say it is place of hidden sparks of life and holiness. Gershom Scholem's *On the Mystical Shape of the Godhead* describes them as the shards from the shattered vessels as described by Isaac Luria. He said this was necessary for creation. Scholem likened it to a seed's need to crack for it to flourish with life. Luria taught that when the vessels or shells where shattered 288 sparks fell into the Abyss where they are imprisoned. Qabbalists theorize these emanated from the lowest Sefirah, Malkuth.

The Tree referred to as the Tree of Evil gives mankind the potential of knowing all truth, good or evil, and supports the concept of duality in all things. This concept of good and evil or dualism follows similar tenets that were expressed by Zoroaster early in the sixth century B.C.E. which led to Zoroastrianism which also goes by the names of Zarathustraism, Mazdaism and Magianism, an ancient Iranian religion and a religious philosophy. Zoroaster's concept of dualism became one of the pillars of later development of the tenets of the Kabbalah and the description of the aspects of deity.

Qabbalists often describe the Tree of Life and the Tree of Knowledge as having a universal root base that they share. The big issue is that the knowledge that can be obtained from the Tree of Knowledge is detached from life as God created it. This results in a non-authentic or skewed perception of existence which could cause issues for those not strong enough to deal with that knowledge.

III.

THE CHRISTIAN CABALAH
CABALA, CABBALA

Like the spelling of the word "Kabbalah" there are numerous spellings of the Christian version as well. The Christian Cabalists view the interpretations of the Jewish Kabalistic doctrine in very different, uniquely Christian terms. It links Jesus Christ, His atonement and His resurrection to the ten Sephiroth. An example is the sixth Sephira or Sefira is listed on the Jewish Kabalistic Tree of Life as Tiferet, Tifaret, Tiphareth or Tyfereth which in Hebrew (תראפת) is "Adornment". Another version of the "Trees" is called the Qabalistic Tree of Life. In this version, the sixth Sefirah is referred to as "The Sun"; while on a Christian Cabalistic Tree of Life this same Sefirah is shown as the "Son". Below is one of the many depictions of a Christian version of The Tree of Life.

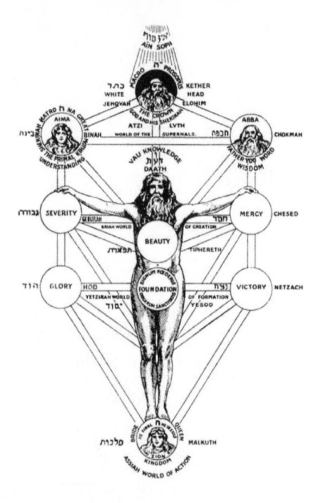

In the above figure, the three top Sephiroth represent the Trinity with Kether as the "Creator" or Spirit, Hokhmah as the Father and Binah as the supernal mother or Mary. The seven lower Sephiroth represent the lower worlds in which man resides. Note the masculine and feminine aspects of the two outer pillars. The *Zohar* established the correspondence of each of the Pillars due to the first Sefirah at the top of each pillar. The middle pillar is Equilibrium/balance and is made up of the Sephiroth of the *Crown* or "source", *Da'at* the "hidden center", which many say is not a true Sefirah but the culmination of all the aspects of the other Sephirot, which will be discussed in detail later. The image also places Yesod over Adam's sexual organ but it's traditionally associated with the knees.

Key Contributors to the Christian Tradition

Ramon Llull (1232–1315)

One of the early Christian Cabalists was Ramon Llull who was born around 1223 in Palma, Majorca, Spain, and died around 1315. He grew up on the Iberian Peninsula at the time when it was the center of the three great religions of Abraham, Jewish, Muslem and Christian faiths. The Catholic Church was to dominant the Christian religion. But a large part of the population was still under the rule of the Moslem Arabs since their overthrow of the Visigothic Kingdom around 718 AD. Spain, because of its tolerances at that time in its history, was the center of the European Jewish community in the middle Ages. Llull was a Catalan mystic and known for developing the "art of truth" that he used to support the Catholic Church's Doctrine. The time and place of his birth is very important because he used his thinking to help the Catholic Church's strong push towards conversion of the Catalan people. He is acknowledged as the first Christian to use the Kabbalah as a tool to convert the Jewish population to Christianity. Though he was not a scholar of the Kabbalah he saw that its fundamentals, when viewed as a Christian, were a means of converting Jews to Christianity by attempting to turn the concepts of man's relationship found in the Kabbalah toward a Christian interpretation and theology.

Llull was able to link the scientific principles he found commonly held as truths by Christians, Moslems and Jews as basis for his "art of truth". One of the principles, universally held by his contemporaries, was the theory of the elements; which are earth, water, air and fire. These four elements corresponded to the four elementary qualities of cold, moist, dry and hot. These elementary qualities extended to the seven planets and twelve signs of the zodiac. Each was assigned an elementary quality of cold, moist, dry or hot. The study of these principles as it pertained to the stars was called at the time "astral science".

Llull was most famous for his art. In his art he used visual representations of figures and trees to show the religious principles held by the three religious traditions concerning the Divine Names or Attributes. Llull took the Attributes of God, commonly held by all believers of the three monotheistic religions and made them a part of his art. These Attributes were *Bonitos* (goodness), *Magnitudo* (greatness), *Eternitas* (eternity), *Potestas* (power), *Spientia* (wisdom) *Voluntas* (will), *Virtus* (virtue or strength) *Vertas* (truth) and *Gloria* (glory). The figures and trees became known as the "Lullian Circle". They were drawn on a piece of paper in such a manner as to make a single sheet a "paper machine" that allowed the user to view the components of concentric circles. These circles were combined with his symbolic alphabet allowing the user to see different combinations to show all possible truths about whatever subject was inquired.

When Llull was around 30 he had a mystical vision of Christ, upon the Cross. This occurred while Llull was on Mt Randa and resulted in him entering the Franciscan Order. Around 1272, after another mystical experience on Majorca's Mount Randa, Llull stated that he had seen the whole universe reflecting the divine attributes. After this vision, he conceived the concept of reducing all knowledge to first principles and determining their convergent point was unity. This occurred one year before the *Zohar* was published. There were many resemblances between the Spanish Cabala and Llull's work. The *Zohar*, sometimes referred to the "Spanish Cabala", describes the Sephiroth and the doctrine of the twenty-two letters. In stead of the ten Sephiroth it mentioned 9 Dignities which are *Gloria, Sapientia, Virtas, Bonitas, Potestas, Vieritas, Eternitas, Splendor,* and *Fundementurm* which were very similar to Llull's attributes of God.

PICO DELLA MIRANDOLA (1463–1494)

Pico della Mirandola was born on February 24, 1463, to a noble Italian family. As a young man he was involved in the courts of Mirandola and Concordia which was near Modena, in the Emilia-Romagna region, north of Tuscany. At the age of 14 he left his home and traveled throughout Europe, including the centers located in Padova, Florence and Rome, Italy and Paris, France. Due to his many misadventures and criminal convictions for his misbehavior, he was often in conflict with Church officials. Because he was not in their "favor" the Church looked down and often condemned Mirandola's views on theology and politics. Pico died rather young at the age of 31 in 1494, with little of his works finished or published. Pico's fame came later from speeches which he was credited for, but never actually gave. In the work, *Oration on the Dignity of Man,* which he wrote in 1486, he introduced his *900 Conclusions*. In this work, he presented outrageous theological novelties including the claim that magic and the Cabala were the best proofs of Christ's divinity.

Pico was a very learned man and often interacted with fellow scholars of his time. He also studied the works of those many of the learned men prior to his time who published their thoughts on esoteric Christainity. These included the works of the Jewish Rabbi Menahem ben Benjamin Recanati (1250–1310), Abraham Abulafia (1240–1291), and other Cabalists whom Pico knew of through his interactions with other learned Italian Jews, including Elia del Medigo (1458–1493), born under the name Elijah Mi-Qandia or Elijah mi-Qandia ben Moshe del Medigo, also referred to in manuscripts as Elijah Delmedigo or Elia ben Moshe del Medi. Flavius Mithridates, a Jewish Humanist who converted to Christainty around 1466, as well as another Jewish Humanist, Philosopher and teacher Yohanan Alemanno (1435–1504). The Cabala was holier to Pico than the pagan wisdom which had been exposed by Marsilio Ficino, a fellow Italian humanist, who was born in 1433. One of Ficino's achievements was tracing the "ancient theology" or "tradition" that included Hermes Trismegistus, Pythagoras and Orepheus as pagan traditions so that they in fact confirmed and legitimized Christianity. Even though Pico studied Ficino's works it did not fall into Pico's overall philosophy of life.

Pico saw the holier Hebrew analog of the old theology as closer to the truth and in his *900 Conclusions* there were 119 dedicated to that concept. His last *72 Conclusions* were all very Cabalist in their view as written by a Christian. This was a simplified version of the Spanish Cabala but no less powerful. Pico attempted to connect all the world's wisdom traditions, from the primary doctrines of Christology and trinitarian theology, to the Cabala. In 1487, he explained in his work *Apology* that he divided the Cabala into two main branches, just as the Spanish Cabala had done. One was the *combinandi* or art of Hebrew letters which was similar to Llull's work. The other was about the spirits and angels. Through these works, Pico showed that he was one of the first western Christians to have expertise in the Cabala, thus legitimizing his claims that the Cabala was truly an extension and visual symbolic portrait of Christian theology.

JOHANN REUCHLIN (1455–1522)
Another prominent writer was Johann Reuchlin (1455–1522). Johann was a German who became one of Pico's most renowned followers. Johann found in the Cabbala a deeply profound study of God that would help man understand his relation to the deity through the Tetragrammaton, also known as

the pentagrammaton. He wrote two key books on the Cabala; in his first, the *De verbo minfico* he reveals how the name of Jesus is derived from the Tetragrammaton. His second book on the Cabala was *De arte cabalistica* (1517), which delved into Reuchlin's interest in Jewish Mysticism. The latter book was in three basic sections; the first was discussion on messianism, the second section was on the relation of the Pythagorean system and the Kabbalah and the third on the practical use of the Kabbalah.

Reuchlin took it one step further; he was continually searching for a deeper understanding of Jewish Mysticism which led him to Neo-Platonism with its bases of operative magic. Unlike so many of his day who thought operative magic as diabolical he saw Cabalist magic as a counter to the diabolical concerns. Reuchin considered Cabalistic magic, to be the study of holy forces, such as angels and the sacred names of God. Because of his view as to what Cabalistic magic was he changed the emphasis away from the intense study of such works by the Spanish Kabbalists Rabbi Isaac ha-Kohen. Rabbi Isaac's work *A Treatise on the Left Emanation*, had been one of the key manuscripts studied even though it had been published a generation before the *Zohar* had been produced. This work represents the earliest Jewish work presenting Lilith as Satan's consort. It detailed the concept of evil listing the princes of jealousy and enmity. Reuchlin shifted the study to those of the holy forces thus cleansing the evil and casting out the demons associated with the darker forms of magic.

Henry Cornelius Agrippa (1486–1535)

Henry Agrippa was born in Cologne, Germany and taught at the University of Dole in the Free County of Burgundy, a medieval county within the traditional province of modern France. Agrippa's work *De Occulta Philosophia Libri Tres;* were three books concerning the Elemental, Celestial and Intellectual aspects of magic. In the book, he described the 1) four elements, 2) astrology, 3) the Kabbalah, 4) numbers, 5) angels, and 6) the names of God. He also described how their relationships and virtues affected each other. He went on to describe how they affect the laws of medicine, scrying (predicting the future), alchemy, ceremonies, and where their origins were derived from Hebrew, Greek and Chaldean context. The *De Occulata Philosophia Libri Tres* became an essential piece of Renaissance Neo-Platonism combining period "Magia" and "Cabala" and bringing their teachings into the Renaissance consciousness.

Perhaps Agrippa's greatest gift to those studying the Cabala was his associating the Cabala as a means to not only attain the highest "super celestial" magic, but also guarantee the safety of the user against the demons. For at that time it was thought demons actively haunted humanity whenever man attempted to gain knowledge and power through deeper study into the occult. Agrippa maintained that the Cabala was white magic and thus protected those who sought the secrets of the occult sciences.

IV.

HERMETIC OR WESTERN QABALAH (HEBREW לבלה), QABBALAH, QABALA,

BIRTH OF AND HISTORY OF THE WESTERN HERMETIC QABBALAH

The term Qabalah or Qabbalah rose in relation to the Kabbalah during the French esoteric revival in the Nineteenth Century. The actual spelling is credited to the western spelling of the Hebrew letters of Q, B, and L that spell out Qa Ba Lah or Kabbalah.

Much of what is associated with the term Qabalah or Western Hermetic Qabalah is traditionally drawn from Eliphas Levi's book *Elements of the Qabalah*. Eliphas Levi, born Alphonse Louis Constant (1810–1875), was a French occult author and ceremonial magician. In this book he attempts, with a very simplistic view point, to establish an equilibrium between faith and science by establishing a "profound peace by means of tranquility of mind and peace of heart". He states that there are three occult sciences: Qabalah, Magic and Hermeticism.

According to Levi the Qabalah, or the traditional science of the Hebrews, formed the mathematics of human thought. It is the algebra of faith which solves the problems of the soul. He also states that the second esoteric science is Magic, and that magic is the science of the Magi who may have been disciples or teachers of the Zoroasterism. He goes on to state that this science consisted of the secret knowledge of nature that produced the hidden science of metals or the science of universal magnetism. The final of the three esoteric sciences was Hermeticism which is the study of hieroglyphics and symbols of the ancient world. Through the study and understanding of these symbolic keys it is the hope of the Adepts to accomplish the 'great work', that is the reproduction of man as a divine creature or micro version of God.

The above is a very cursory review of a very important and pivotal book that blended Jewish mystical study with that of the Hermetic schools. Many of the concepts of the Qabalah were coded by using symbols, by the use of tarot and by using the Qabalistic Tree of Life as a means of conveying information to its initiates. Eliphas Levi believed that these esoteric sciences should be kept from the profane or uneducated, not only to protect humanity from their misuse, but also from those not properly schooled in their powers. For this reason, he adopted the use of symbols and allegories to hide these working. As of the result Levi is credited with establishing a tradition of secrecy and mysteriousness of the Qabalah. This technique of hiding or confusing the uninitiated from the arcane asspects of the teaching of the Qabalah was later accepted by other fellow French authors and adepts.

This French esoteric tradition remained intact when it became popular in England where two dedicated adepts and authors, Samuel Liddell MacGregor Mathers (1854–1918) and Aleister Crowley (1875–1947), came into the picture. Mathers was instrumental in the establishment of the Order of the Golden Dawn and is credited with authoring the majority of the Order's critical teaching and the works of magic for the Order. He was also instrumental in the creation of what we today know as the tarot. Mathers produced the first English translation of the *Zohar* in a book called *The Kabbalah Unveiled* (1887). It was based on the *Kabbalah Denudata* by Knorr von Rosenroth (1631–1689) which states in his *Kabbalah Denudata,* Rosenroth writes that the Adam Kadmon, or "original man" of the cabalists is really Jesus, and that the three highest Sephirot represent the Christian Trinity.

Aleister Crowley was also known as Frater Perdurado or The Great Beast. He was one of the most influential English occultists, mystic and ceremonial magicians of his time. He is responsible for founding the religious philosophy of the Thelema. Because of his prolific writing and his renowned expertise and showmanship of ceremonial magic he is to this day credited with much of the working magic done by the tools of the Qabalah.

Much of today's scholarly discourse about the Qabalah is the result of Samuel MacGregor Mathers' personal writings as well as the writing from his students of *The Golden Dawn Order*, as well as Aleister Crowley's *Thelema*. This is not to minimize the work of other great mystics of this golden era such as Helena Petrovna Blavatsky's (1831–1891), pivotal work *Isis Unveiled,* which was published in 1877. Helena Blavatsky was an enthusiastic student of the occult and eventually, with the urging of her teachers who recognized her talents, she established a school in July of 1875. It was a philosophico-religious society, and in the fall of that same year, together with the aid of Colonel Henry Steel Olcott (1832–1907) and the mystic William Quan Judge (1851–1896) became the principal founders of *The Theosophical Society.* Like many of the earlier great esoteric schools *The Theosophical Society* became one of the premiere guardians of much of the early esoteric work.

Following Levi's tradition, those writing in the eighteenth and nineteenth century purposefully obscure their work with dead ends, blinds and misinformation to discourage the uninitiated from getting the esoteric knowledge from the published works. This was also a means to help increase membership in their specific schools or cults by offering to disclose the secrets behind the mysteries. Thus, the candidate had to join so the teacher could personally lead them into greater enlightenment.

Below is an earlier form of The Tree of Life. It is the result of the combination of thoughts of early scholars on what is described in the *Sepher Yetzirah* concerning the cosmology and cosmogony of creation. Cosmology is the scientific theory of the development of the universe whereas cosmogony is the study of the origin of the universe. Note that it is not colored and shows only the 10 *Sephiroth* and the 22 paths with their Hebrew letters. The Sephiroth had colors assigned to them (to be discussed latter) while the pathways have had various colors assigned to them by various schools of thought.

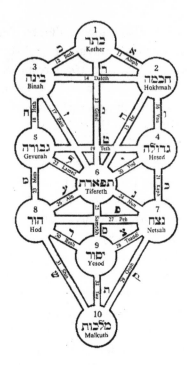

ISLAMIC SUFISM AND JEWISH KABBALAH

In order to understand the Kabbalah one must understand it is not a totally Jewish concept. As all great concepts of religion they are the result of the intertwining of many myths, traditions, customs, observations and interpretation of events and ideas. It is also the result of the blending of these ideas with other cultures and theologies. This is the case with the Kabbalah in that it came traditionally from the blending of ideas of the "three tribes of the Book".

Teachers, when talking about the Old Testament, often use the term "three tribes of the Book". The three tribes relate to those ethnic groups that trace their lineage to the monotheistic prophet Abraham, originally Abram, or Ibrahim in Arabic. The three groups are the Jewish tribes, the Christians and the Moslems. Abram is the first of the three Patriarchs of Israel, and is recognized by Islam as a prophet and apostle of God. The Jewish people affirm their descent from Isaac, the son of Abraham and his wife Sarah while the Arabs affirm their descent from Ishmael or Ismail, the child of Abraham's Egyptian slave Hagar.

The mystical traditions of the Islamic Sufi and Jewish Kabbalists are so close to each other that there is a presumption that they have a common origin. The transmission of these spiritual practices and doctrines are lost to history but indicate there was a two-way transmission of ideas, thus benefiting each. These ideas were not formalized but developed over time and influenced by external groups and historical events. This transmission or sharing of ideas was probably due to each group coexisting closely prior to the ethnic and sectarian upheavals after the death of the Islamic prophet Muhammad in 632 CE.

The reason for the schism between the Shia and Sunni was the dispute over the succession to Muhammad as caliph of the Islamic community. Those who became Sunni, meaning, "one who follows the traditions of the Prophet", believed that the heir to Mohammad should be determined by the community of elder Muslim clerics. To the contrary, those who became Shias, meaning "a group or supportive party of people" in this case The Prophet, felt Mohammad's successor should come from the Prophet's own family, namely Ali, his son-in-law, since Mohammad had no sons who survived into adulthood. The birth of Sufism as a mystic movement within the Islam community occurred sometime in the ninth or tenth century. There is speculation that its roots may be older than Islam and originated in Afghanistan and Iran and is connected to the dualism beliefs of Zoroastrianism.

In the *Qur'an*, they mention several forbidden trees in the Garden of Eden. This is not the Jewish Tree of Knowledge, but mixes elements of the Tree of Knowledge motif and the Tree of Immortality motif. Its primary function is as a metaphor of man's disobedience of Allâh. The tree symbol plays only a minor role in the *Qur'an* itself, yet among the mystics and in Muslim art and architecture it became one of Islam's most developed symbols. The *Shajarat al-Tûba*, or "Tree of Bliss", also referred to as the Islamic World Tree, does not appear in name or description in the *Quran*. Instead, there are several distinct supernatural trees. Only in the *Hadîth,* or "prophetic traditions", and among mystics are the various trees integrated into one consistent symbol.

There are, in the *Qur'an*, three distinct supernatural trees: first the Infernal Tree, or Zaqqûm, located in hell. According to tradition the Tree of Zaqqûm is found in the heart of Hellfire and its bitter and very nasty thorny fruit is eaten by the dwellers of Hellfire. This food provides neither nourishment nor a desirable flavor. It will only serve as a punishment for the dwellers of Hell. It is said that fruit itself resembles the heads of the devils that dwell in Hell. The tradition goes on to say the sinners who dwell in Hellfire will be denied forgiveness on the Day of Judgment and will be hungry, yet the only food they will find will be the frightening product of the tree of Zaqqûm. They will be compelled to eat this fruit for there is nothing else or anything better to eat. The fruit is so awful that when consumed it will scald and burn the insides of those who eat it, make them feel choked and increase their suffering and pain.

According to Islamic beliefs, the second Lote Tree of the Uttermost Boundary, *Sidrat al-Muntahâ*, in the Seventh Heaven which is the boundary where no creation can pass. The concept of the Seven Heavens is ancient, at least as old as ancient Babylonia. Originally, the number may have been taken from the celestial bodies that are nearest to earth, including those planets visible to the naked eye: the Moon, Mercury, Venus, Mars, the Sun, Jupiter, and Saturn. In Islam, the word for heaven does not refer to the planets but states that they are gardens. It is a place where all wishes will be fulfilled. The levels are separated by gates which can be opened if the person observed certain rituals on earth, such as jihad, charity, fasting, and pilgrimage to Mecca. The *Qur'an* briefly mentions Muhammad's journey through the Seven Heavens, while in a half-dream state. During this dream state the angel Gabriel appeared with Buraq, the heavenly steed of the prophets. Buraq took Muhammad to the Western Wall in Jerusalem, where Muhammad prayed and was tested. When he passed the tests, Gabriel and Buraq took him on a tour of the sevens heavens.

The *Sidrat al-Muntahâ* is a tree from the base of which issue rivers (al-kawthar) whose water is never brackish. The *Sidrat al-Muntahâ*'s water never changes in taste, color, or smell. It is the drink of those who reside in Paradise. It has the fragrance of musk. There are several rivers that flow, one of milk, whose taste does not change after it is drunk; a river of wine which brings only pleasure to those who drink it; and another river of purified honey.

On top of each leaf the *Sidrat al-Muntahâ* there are angels who covered it with colors which cannot be described. One version says the color would turn into sapphire and chrysolite the beauty of which it is impossible for anyone to praise according to its merit. On these leaves were beautiful moths of gold.

The third tree is the Tree of Knowledge, the forbidden tree in the Garden of Eden. The description of this Tree of Knowledge does not appear in the *Qur'an*. It does not even name this tree and it is always referred to as "the tree". It mixes elements of the Tree of Knowledge motif and the Tree of Immortality motif, but its primary function is as a metaphor of man's disobedience of Allâh. Muslims believe that when God created Adam and Eve, He told them that they could enjoy everything in the Garden but this tree. So like the Judaic/Christian depiction Satan appeared to them and told them that the only reason God forbade them to eat from that tree is that they would become angels or become immortals.

The fourth tree is mentioned in the Lamp Verse:

Allah is the Light of the heavens and the earth. The example of His light is like a niche within which is a lamp, the lamp is within glass, the glass as if it were a pearly [white] star lit from [the oil of] a blessed olive tree, neither of the east nor of the west, whose oil would almost glow even if untouched by fire. Light upon light. Allah guides to His light whom He wills. And Allah presents examples for the people, and Allah is knowing of all things.

SURANT AN-NŪR 24:35

The phrase "olive neither of the East nor West", has been subject to a great deal of debate. Some scholars feel it is the acknowledgment that the human being will have to admit his incapacity and inadequacy to perceive that Exalted Reality, which is the only Reality in the realm of existence.

The limited reach of the human intellect is not powerful enough to make judgements in the Divine sphere, or to unravel God's unfathomable secrets or to reach an understanding about such an Exalted Being.

As is found in Judaism, Gnosticism and other Hellenistic mystery groups/religions so do the Islamic mystics ponder the concept of climbing or ascending the Tree to reach heaven and/or reuniting with the Divine presence. It is often refered to as "Raising on the Planes" and "Path Working". Here is where the Lote Tree of Boundary (K.53:14) becomes the Tree of Life of the Qabalah, and the Perfect Man (al insan al karmil) becomes Adam Kadmon.[1]

---

1 *Isamic Mysticism*, Iban al-Rawandi, Prometheus Books, 2000, pg. 148

Raising on the Planes is using the middle pillar of the Tree and the spheres of sun and the Moon. If one is using the Tree for Path Work, then one utilizes the right and left hand pillars to ascend to heaven.

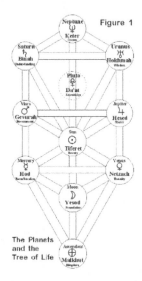

Figure 1

The Planets and the Tree of Life

When comparing the Jewish Kabbalah, versus the Sufi version, the Sufi version follows two general streams of thought. First is the "theosophical" which concerns itself with trying to understand the mystical content of the universe and man's personal relationship to God and God's creation of that universe. And the second is more spiritual in it nature, even "ecstatic" and seeks to awaken one's soul and develop a closer relationship with God.

This second stream of thought of seeking the spiritual is emphasized in one of the most loved passages of the *Qur'an*. It is the first section of the *Sura of the Compassionate* which continually links man's understanding of the Divine and how the Divine bestows existence and wellbeing to man. This passage is one of the foundations and sources of Sufi thought. It is composed of a question and answer between one individual proposing a question with two unnamed individuals responding. A Sura, also spelled surah or surat, is a chapter in the *Qur'an*. The *Qur'an* is comprised of 114 chapters, each sub-divided into verses.

In Islam, Adam is considered a prophet and is made Caliph, or ruler, of *Allah* on earth. When *Allah* announced his intention to create Adam as a regent by molding him out of clay and breathing His divine breath into

Adam, there was a great outcry by the angels. The angels questioned the creation of a being that will "corrupt the earth and spill blood". The Divine voice asks if they "know the names". The angels' reply that they only know the names they have been given by the Divine. Adam teaches them the names and they are commanded to prostrate themselves and assume the position of Islamic ritual prayer before Adam. As in most religions there is also evil, in this case it is called Iblis, one of the heavenly company who refuses to prostrate himself and is thus exiled from the Divine presence and later becomes known as Satan, ash-shaytan.

Unlike the character of Satan first described in the Abrahamic religions, who personifies evil and attempts to lead mankind astray, Iblis is described as an absolute monotheist. This is according to Mansur al-Hallaj, a Persian born around 858 and dying in 922. Hallaj goes on to say Iblis was the closest spirit-being next to Allah. When Iblis was commanded to prostrate himself before Adam he refused, saying he would never bow to any other being other than the one deity. For this he was expelled.

There is much scholarly debate as to the nature of these "names". Are they the "names" of the angels themselves or the "names" of all creatures of the world? There is even speculation they are the "names" of God. In Sufism the "names" are thought to represent the Divine names of the various manifestations of the forms of predications used in the *Qur'an*. The first sura of the *Qur'an* is the phrase "In the name of Allah, the Compassionate, the Caring". This phrase is repeated at the beginning of every sura of the *Qur'an* and is considered an integral part of the sura.

Ja'far ibn Muhammad al-Sadiq, (702–765 C.E.)

Ja'far ibn Muhammad al-Sadiq, the sixth Imam and spiritual successor to Muhammad was a descendant of Ali ibn Abi Talib, 607–661, the cousin and son-in-law to the Islamic prophet Muhammad, on his father's side. Ja'far was highly respected by both of the major Islam sects, Sunni and Shi'a, and was a scholar in the Islamic sciences including the *Qur'an* and *Hadith* or "the prophet's traditions". He was also a scholar of the natural sciences, mathematics, philosophy, astronomy, anatomy, and alchemy.

Ja'far used the Arabic script, called Arabic "abjad", which is a codified form of writing the Arabic language. An abjad is a type of writing system where each symbol always stands for a consonant, leaving the reader to supply the appropriate vowel.

Ja'far used the example of the first verse in the *Qur'an*, "In the name of God, the Merciful, the Compassionate". You would take the first letter of the phrase, less the vowels, and this would open up a possibility of various symbolic meanings. An example would be when Ja'far would associate the letter "A", which is in written in Arabic as a straight vertical line or column that goes through the shape of the letter not the key word that begins with alif. The column will become central, like the path ways on the Kabala's Tree of Life, for Sufi meditation. This letter symbolism is key to Islamic study even today. Most important it contains a fourfold hierarchy of interpretation that is very close to the hierarchies in the medieval Kabbalah and Christian Mystic thought.

DHU'L-NUN AL-MISRI (786–859 C.E)

Dhu'l-Nun al-Misri, whose full name was Dhul-nun Abu Faid Thawban idn Ibrahim, was born in Akhmin in Sohag Governorate of Upper Egypt in 786 and died in 859. (The city of Akhmin is referred to by the ancient Greeks as Khemmis, Chemmis and Panopolis.) Dhu'l-Nun al-Misri was considered the Patron Saint of the Physicians in the early years in Egypt. He is considered to be among the most prominent saints of early Sufism. Dhul-Nun al-Misri was a legendary miracle worker and alchemist, and was known for his sayings and poems which were very rich in mystical imagery. They reflect his great knowledge or gnosis (mafifah) versus fear (makhafah) or love (mahabbah) which are the other two major paths of Sufi spiritualism.

Dhul-Nun al-Misi means "Lord of the Nun" (Nun meaning fish), due to a legendary incident that occurred at sea where he was accused of stealing a jewel from a merchant. When he cried out "O Creator, Thou knowest best" a large number of fish rose from the sea, each bearing a jewel in their mouths. Dhul-Nun al-Misri was a great traveler and alleged to understand how to read Egyptian hieroglyphs. This knowledge earned him his nick name al-Misri which means 'the Egyptian' whenever he traveled outside of Egypt.

Because of his knowledge (or gnosis) Dhu'l-Nun al-Misri was credited with bringing the concept of Gnosis to the Islamic world. And because of this interest in Gnosticism he was viewed as one of the earliest Arab Sufis and was studied by later scholars, one of whom was Bahya idn Pakuda.

Bahya idn Pakuda (birth date
and death are not known)

Pakuda who was also known as Bahya ben Joseph idn Paquada or Bakudo was a Jewish philosopher and rabbi who lived in the eleventh century in Saragossa, Spain. He is often referred to as Rabbeinu Bachya. He was the author of the first Jewish system of ethics was written in Arabic in 1080. It is called, *Al Hidayah ila Faraid al-Qulub* or *Guide to the Duties of the Heart*. Little is known of him except that he had the title of dayyan or judge at the rabbinical court.

Bahya believed that the Jews of the day, like the Sufi, relied too heavily on the strict adherence to religious law. He believed that too many of the rabbis concentrated on only the 613 laws of Moses which dealt with the physical aspect of the body. Beyond following the laws there was no further thought as to their souls, or inner body. Bahya taught that in order to secure the perfection of the soul one must not only adhere to religious law but they also must personally commit their soul to God.

Around 1040 he wrote a Judeo-Arabic tome called *Chavot Ha-Levavot* or *Hobot Ha-Lebabot*, which translates to "Duties of the Heart". It was translated into Hebrew sometime between 1161 and 1180 by the Spanish translator and physician Judah idn Tibbon (1120–1190). It is here we find similarities to the Kabbalah where Bahya divides his *Hobot Ha-Lebabot* into ten sections which he calls "gates". Each gate relates to one of the ten fundamental principles that constitute man's spiritual life. The base of all spirituality is the recombination of God as the "sole maker" and designer of all things.

Bahya, like other Arabian philosophers and theologians before him, bases his arguments upon the Creation concept. He starts from three premises: (1) Nothing creates itself, since the act of creating necessitates its existence; (2) the causes of things are necessarily limited in number, and lead back to the "first cause" which necessarily has neither beginning nor end, because everything that has an end must needs have a beginning; (3) all created things have a beginning; and a cause must necessarily be created to justify their existence. He goes on to describe the world to be beautifully arranged and furnished like a great house, of which the sky forms the ceiling, the earth the floor, the stars the lamps, with man as the proprietor. Man as the proprietor uses the three kingdoms first of which is the animal; second is the vegetable; and the third is the mineral. Each of these kingdoms is composed of the four elements. There is a fourth kingdom called the celestial sphere composed of a fifth element, the "Quinta Essentia". According to Aristotle, it is composed of fire. These four elements are made up several qualities such as; matter and form, of substance and accidental qualities, such as warmth and cold, state of motion and of rest, and so forth. And because the universe is made up of all these various components, there must be a creative power as the prime cause of their existence. Nothing as complicated but organized as the universe can exist by mere chance of existence. Consequently, the universe, being a combination of many forces, must have a creative power as its cause. Bayan goes further to prove the unity of God by observing what the natural world reveals as to the existence of the Creator. He also attempts to prove that the Creator is a perfect unity and that it cannot, and is not made up of parts, for the Creator is Unity itself.

These are just a few of the contibuters to the birth and growth of what would later become today's Kabbalah, Cabalah and Qabalah.

V.

QABALAH

GROWTH OF MODERN HERMETIC QABALAH

There has been a great deal of debate as to exactly where and when the Hermetic form of the Western Qabalah originated. Some historians place it as far back as the time that the *Sepher Yetzirah* was introduced. The *Sepher Yetzirah* itself was written early in the formation of the Jewish Kabbalah. Some place its development as early as the second century B.C.E., to as late as the second century C.E. Like many concepts claiming esoteric or secret teaching many authors attempt to equate with much older traditions as a means to legitimize their claims. They seem to believe that if one links modern works to the ancient past there is a greater possibility of it being accepted as truly meaningful and esoteric in content. This linking to the past was extensively used in the eighteenth and nineteenth century when the western world was especially enthralled with anything Egyptian.

According to many others, the concept of the Hermetic Qabalah originated sometime during the Renaissance Period. This was the period when western European thinkers, who were just emerging from the lethargic period of the Dark Ages, blended the Jewish Kabbalah with the Hermetic mysteries. Around the same period the Roman Catholic Church was trying to consolidate their dominance over other non-Catholic groups. It was during this time of intellectual rebirth that philosophers were energized; they saw the tenets of the Jewish Kabbalah as a possible framework to prove the divinity of Christ thus supporting not only the Roman Catholic Church but Christianity in general.

It is believed that many of the earliest Hermetic texts were lost to the West during the period of Dark Ages. It was during this time that zealot churchmen were activity seeking out publications and/or books that they thought were Heretical in nature. Even after many of these incidents small numbers of scrolls or treatises survived and were rediscovered in the libraries and monasteries of the Byzantine Empire during the mid-1400s. These works revealed the blending of Egyptian spirituality with Greek philosophy. One account of "rediscovery" describes a Byzantine monk bringing these works to de' Medici court in the year 1460. The Cosimo de' Medici then introduced them to the west at his court in Florence, Italy in the form of thirteen tractates that had been translated to Latin by Marisllo Finico. Marisllo was a member of de'Medici's court, either in 1463 or 1471 depending on your source of information.

Important Works and Documents

During this period of enlightenment many important works were introduced, not only to the intellectual community but, at times even to the common people. As these works emerged the concepts of spiritualism, alchemy and philosophy changed. The important thing to remember is the Qabalah does not attempt to provide a complete magical language or an entire philosophy. Only by spiritual experience may the latter be acquired. But from the alphabet of Ideas, Numbers and the Symbols and the intimations which it presents, the student is enabled, with the aid of magical research, to construct a satisfactory edifice of high philosophy which will take him through life.

Corpus Hermeticum

In 1614, Isaac Casaubon (1559–1614), a classical scholar and philologist, who first wrote and studied in France, and then later in England, analyzed the famous Hermetic work, *Corpus Hermeticum*. He published his work in the *De rubus scaris et ecclesiasticis exercitions XVI — Sixteen Exercises on the Sacred and Ecclesiastical* while living in London. Casaubon, through his study of the *Corpus,* determined it was made up of a composite of many authors. The original work had been compiled at the earliest around the first century C.E. Up to this time the myth was that the fifteen tractates had come from Egypt and were originally authored by a mythical figure, Hermes Trismegistus around 172 B.C.E. The *Corpus Hermeticum* and the *Perfect Sermon* or *Asclepius* composes the basis for what today we refer to as the "Hermetic Tradition". The *Perfect Sermon* or *Asclepius* was a translation from Greek to Latin and is attributed to Lucius Aquleius of Madaura, (125 C.E.–180 C.E.). Madaura or Madaurus was in ancient Roman Algeria and is now M'Daourouch in the Souk Providence in Algeria. These two works by tradition and myth are attributed to the mythic figure of Hermes Trismegistus. Through time Hermes became a blend of the Greek god Hermes and the Egyptian god Thoth. No matter who was accredited as the actual author, these works were extremely important. The importance lay in the fact that at this time the literature coming from the intellectual centers in the Western world were trying to rationalize the impact of Platonic thought on the much older traditions of the Hellenized East.

These tractates were divided up into five groups of instructions for study. The first (CH I), called the "Poemandres", is the account of a revelation given to Hermes Trismegistus by the person of Poemandres or "Man-Shepherd", was a symbolic reference for the expression of the universal Mind. The next eight (CH II-IX), called the "General Sermons", are short treatises or lectures discussing various basic points of Hermetic philosophy. There follows the "Key" (CH X), a summary of the General Sermons, and after this comes a set of four tractates — *"Mind unto Hermes", "About the Common Mind", "The Secret Sermon on the Mountain"*, and the *"Letter of Hermes to Asclepius"* (CH XI-XIV). These four works touched more on the mystical aspects of Hermeticism. The collection is rounded out by the *"Definitions of Asclepius unto King Ammon"* (CH XV), which may be composed of three fragments of longer works.

The *Corpus Hermeticum* was the basis behind the development of the culture of thought on alchemy and modern magic starting around the time of the Renaissance, all the way up to the seventeenth century. It was during this time of early discussions in the various schools that the question of man's place in the natural world was debated. In an attempt to understand man's relation to the natural world that the famous documents of the Hermetic world were openly discussed and studied, one of the documents being the legendary *Emerald Tablet*. During these examinations of the *Corpus* there was much thought given to the concept that the treatises they were studying were an actual a record of the conversations between Hermes and his disciples. In fact, for over three hundred years the Catholic Church thought these ancient works lent support to their Christian doctrines and were required study by all Christian scholars. Hermes was held in such high esteem that many cathedrals thoughtout Europe have images of him, often in the company of Moses.

THE EMERALD TABLET

The *Emerald Tablet*, also known as the *Smaragdine Table*, or *Tabula Smaragdina*, is one of the oldest and most well know of all alchemical documents. Eric John Holmyard (1891–1959), who had interests in the history of alchemy, particularly in relation with Islamic science, discovered and later translated an Arabic version of the *Emerald Tablet* around 1923. Holmyard found the "Second Book of the *Elements of the Foundation*" attributed to Abu Mūsā Jābir ibn Hayyān (721–815 CE), who was also known by his Latinized name of Geber. Hayyān was a prominent Muslim polymath, with interests in chemistry, alchemy, and astronomy. He also was an astrologer, engineer, geographer, philosopher and physician. The Second Book was part of 112 books Hayyān wrote during the late ninth and early tenth century which were dedicated to the Barmakids, viziers of Caliph Harun al-Rashid. This group includes the Arabic version of the Emerald Tablet.

The actual origins of the *Emerald Tablet* or *Tabula Smaragdina* is shrouded in the mists of time. Because the earliest versions appear in two different texts in Arabic it is believed it first was published in or around Asia Minor. The first is credited to Abu Mūsā Jābir ibn Hayyān and known as Jarbirian *corpus*. The second version was discovered by Julius Ruska (1867–1949) in a book called *The Second Creation* ascribed to Apollonius. Apollonius of Tyana (15–100 C.E.) who was a Greek Neo-Pythagorean philosopher from Asia Minor. Jabir himself, when giving the *Tabular* says, that it he is quoting Apollonius.[2]

One of the earliest myths associated with *The Emerald Tablet* describes Hermes, who was a son of Adam, as having had written the tablet to show mankind how to redeem itself from the sins of his father. Another myth originating from Jewish mystics is attributing the tablet's authorship to Seth, the second son of Noah. According to this legend the tablet was saved by being brought aboard the ark during the great flood. The legend relates

---

2 *Alchemy, Holmyard, Eric John, Pelican Publication, 1968, Pg. 99*

how the *Emerald Tablet* was then hidden in a cave near Hebron where it was later discovered by Sarah, wife of Abraham. Another popular myth was that Hermes himself gave the tablet to Miriam, the daughter of Moses. And Miriam allegedly placed the tablet in the Ark of the Covenant, and it was lost to mankind to this day.

Some Hermetic historians believe that *The Emerald Tablet* was found in a secret chamber in the Cheops' Great pyramid of Giza sometime around 1350 B.C. There are also some who believe *The Emerald Tablet* was found in a cave in Sri Lanka by Hermes himself sometime in the fifth century B.C.E. After finding the tablet Hermes traveled throughout Asia and the Middle East teaching and healing. There are those who even state that Hermes was the great Buddha himself.

Some of the common elements of these and other myths concerning Hermes and *The Emerald Tablet* are that there are caves, corpses, ancient civilizations, ancient Egypt, and secret wisdom. They all describe the tablet as a rectangular green plaque with bas-relief lettering in a strangle alphabet that is similar to ancient Phoenician.

As with all myths there are those who challenge them and try to refute their authenticity. Further confusion occurred in 1614 when a Protestant scholar named Isaac Casaubon (1559–1614), declared these documents forgeries. He claimed they were written by 'semi-Christians' sometime between 200 A.D. and 300 A.D. This was done after a linguistic analysis of the writings on *The Emerald Tablet* which he felt appeared to resemble other writings from this period. Casaubon's rebuttal of *The Emerald Tablet* occurred around the same time that the Christian Church reversed its support of the *Corpus Hemeticum* as a supporting document from Christianity, thus causing both the *Corpus Hemeticum* and *The Emerald Tablet* to slip into the shadows of the esoteric world and becoming part of the legacy of such secret organizations as the Rosicrucian.

There are numerous translations of *The Emerald Tablet* from reportedly ancient sources. One of the most accepted versions is that of Isaac Newton (1642–1727) who was an accredited occultist of his time. The translation below is from a Rosicrucian study source:

> 1 *It is true, certain, and without falsehood, that whatever is below is like that which is above; and that which is above is like that which is below: to accomplish the one wonderful work.*

2 *As all things are derived from the One Only Thing, by the will and by the word of the One Only One who created it in His Mind, so all things owe their existence to this Unity by the order of Nature, and can be improved by Adaptation to that Mind.*

3 *Its Father is the Sun; its Mother is the Moon; the Wind carries it in its womb; and its nurse is the Earth.*

4 *This Thing is the Father of all perfect things in the world.*

5 *Its power is most perfect when it has again been changed into Earth.*

6 *Separate the Earth from the Fire, the subtle from the gross, but carefully and with great judgment and skill.*

7 *It ascends from earth to heaven, and descends again, new born, to the earth, taking unto itself thereby the power of the Above and the Below.*

8 *Thus the splendor of the whole world will be thine, and all darkness shall flee from thee.*

9 *This is the strongest of all powers, the Force of all forces, for it overcometh all subtle things and can penetrate all that is solid.*

10 *For thus was the world created, and rare combinations, and wonders of many kinds are wrought.*

11 *Hence I am called HERMES TRISMEGISTUS, having mastered the three parts of the wisdom of the whole world.*

12 *What I have to say about the masterpiece of the alchemical art, the Solar Work, is now ended.*

VI.

GROWTH OF MODERN
HERMETIC QABBALAH

ROSICRUCIANISM

Attempting to describe the Rosicrucianism movement is like trying to describe the weather, it depends with whom you are conversing. And like *The Emerald Tablet*, Rosicrucianism is surrounded by myth and emotional loyalties. These loyalties have been developed by numerous organizations and source documents. Everybody from the Freemasons to the Roman Catholic Church have their own spin on what, who and where the original Rosicrucian Order or Fellowship began.

According to one version of its beginning Henricus Cornelius Agrippa von Nettesheim (1486–1535) formed a cadre of scholars around 1506 in Paris. This group's initial efforts were the pursuit of scholarly studies of the occult mysteries. Many of the group were involved in more than just scholarly studies. Because these men were not totally dedicated to the occult sciences Agrippa became demoralized and eventually distanced himself from the group. Even though many of the original group were involved in political intrigues Agrippa continued to maintain correspondence with them. This original group of aspirants were drawn to Agrippa because of his knowledge and enthusiasm of the mysteries of magic and religion. This cadre of men eventually were seen as the prototype for what was later to become known "Rosicrucianism".

The term "Rosicrucianism" had at first no meaning before it appeared in the pamphlet published in Kassel, Germany in 1614 which at the time had two meanings. This often causes confusion as to which meaning is being used. The first meaning refers to works published anonymously in 1615 and 1616 called the *Rosicrucian Manifestos*. This work is attributed to the group that was associated with Agrippa. The second meaning refers to the formation of mystical groups in the nineteenth and twentieth century which claim their origin to be the ancestors of Agrippa's group who supposedly called themselves "Rosicrucians" early in the seventeenth century. According to some this later group had no evidence to support their claim to these earlier seventeenth century groups.

Legend is that early in the Seventeenth Century the *Rosicrucian Manifestos* made its appearance in Europe. It consisted of two documents announcing the existence of an unknown esoteric order called the *Brotherhood of the Rosy Cross*. At the time of the announcement the authors of these documents were unknown. The two documents are the *Fama Fratermitatis* and the *Confessio Fratemitatis*. The Fama Fratermitatis *Roseae Crucis Oder Die Bruderschaft des Ordens der Rosekreuzer,* is also known as the *Fama Fratermitatis Crucis* which was published in Kassel, Germany in 1614. It was translated into English in 1652 by Thomas Vaughan (1621–1666). Vaughan was a Welsh philosopher, Freemason and writer of works concerning "natural magic". The *Fama Fratermitatis* retells the story of a "Father C.R.", who was later referred to as "C.R.C.". The story describes C.R.C.'s pilgrimage to Jerusalem where he is tutored by the wise men of Damcar, Arabia. According to the narration he was instructed in the esoteric arts of the east including the study of physics, mathematics, magic and the Kabbalah. "Father C.R." later returns to Spain to study with the alumbrados, meaning the "Illuminated" who were the practitioners of a mystical form of Christianity in Spain in the fifteenth through sixteenth century. C.R.C.'s work is often referred to as the Great Work of transmutation by the occult world.

The *Confessio Fraternitatis* was formally known as the *Confessio Oder Bekenntnis der Societät und Bruderschaft Rosenkreuz,* or simply *The Confessio*. It was printed either in Kassel, Germany, or Frankfurt-am-Main, a year later in 1615, and is the second anonymous manifesto, or pamphlet, declaring the existence of a secret brotherhood of alchemists and sages who referred to themselves as "Rosicrucian". This work was a breviary about "the true

Philosophy" of the Order and was meant to complete the earlier work of the *Fama Fraternitatis*. Combined these two works promoted the concept of "Universal Reformation of Mankind" as Frances Yates rdescribed, in her book *The Rosicrucian Enlightenment* published in 1972.

Thomas Vaughan described himself as a member of the *"Society of Unknown Philosophers"*, and was responsible for translating into English in 1652 the Fama Fraternitatis *Rosae Crucis*. He claimed the translations to be the work of an "unknown hand" alleging that a "gentleman wiser than he communicated them to him". Later Arthur Edward Waite (1857–1942), the British poet and scholar of mystic, occult and esoteric matters, reprinted Vaughan's translations in his book *Real History of the Rosicrucians* in 1887.

A third pamphlet was published in Strasbourg, Germany, in 1616, called *The Chymical Marriage of Christian Rosenkreutz*. In the pamphlet, Christian Rosenkreutz claimed he was the founder of the Rosicrucian Order. Later Johann Valentine Andreae (1586–1654), German theologian, said he had written *The Chymical Marriage of Christian Rosenkreutz* earlier in his youth as an alchemical romance. He then published it under the mystical name of Christian Rosenkreutz prior to the publications of the *Fama* or *Confessio*. Some historians believe he revised his original work in hopes of profiting from the excitement raised from the *Fama* and *Confessio* publications.

The Rosicrucian Order was first formally established in the United States by Paschal Beverly Randolph (1825–1875) who was a medical doctor, spiritualist, medium, occultist and writer. In 1874 Randolph writes in his book *Eulis*, *"Very nearly all which I have given as Rosicrucian originated in my own soul"*. Both Randolph's work and the original *Fama* and *Confessio* manifestoes were alleged to have been included in the miscellany publications the Rosicrucians printed in Quakertown, Pennsylvania by Dr. R Swinburne Clymer (1878–1966). Clymer joined the Fraternitas Rosae Crucis in 1897, which he either reestablished or some believe actually created the Order. The *Fraternitas Rosae Crucis* is believed to be the oldest continuing Rosicrucian organization in the Americas. Clymer became the Grand Master of this Rosicrucian Order in 1905. Some claim that Clymer took this title after acquiring Randolph's extensive library on Rosicrucianism. Clymer had a number of conflicts with others in the occult field including; Harvey Spencer Lewis (1883–1939), a noted Rosicrucian author, occultist, and mystic, as well the founder of the Rosicrucian Order in the United States, and the first Imperator of the Ancient Mystical Order Rosae Crucis (AMORC); Aleister Crowley, and even the American Medical Association. All because Clymer had taken Randolph's original works and reworked their contents to reflect his own personal views.

When researching the history of the "Rosicrucian Order" as a fraternitythe term "Invisible" will frequently arise according to Paul Foster Case (1884–1954), a prominent member of the *Thoth-Hermes Lodge of the Alpha et Omega*, and founder of the *Builders of the Adytum*. This Lodge was formed by a group of men led by S.L. MacGregor Mathers (1854–1918) in 1906. Mathers formed his new lodge after the original *Hermetic Order of the Golden Dawn*, which he helped cofound, broke down earlier in 1903. Case claims, according to the manifestoes owned by the *Golden Dawn* that the Rosicrucian Order itself is "invisible" because it has no external organization. He claims one does not "join" the *Rosicrucian Order* but "*becomes a Rosicrucian*". Because of his statements there has continued to be a great deal of debate as to any group's claim of descent from "the original order" since all "true" members cannot be recognized by any physical marks by "ordinary eyes", thus the Order's members are "invisible" to the ordinary world.

Case, in his book *The True and Invisible Rosicrucian Order* says that there are many societies, both in Europe and America that follow the pattern of the Rosicrucian Order, but their members understand those societies are not the True Rosicrucian Order. They understand that some of the members of these societies that falsely claim historic connection to the Rosicrucians may themselves be true member of the *Invisible Order of the Rosicrucians*. With this said, what follows is a partial list of many societies, fraternities or Orders who claim to be historically linked the Rosicrucians. Over the years there were numerous schisms that occurred among the various groups when within the Order one or several of its higher "Adepts" clashed over some interpretation of ritual or in most cases due to a disagreement over the control of the organization. This generally comes down to power and individual egos of some of the members, and even to this day there is the occasional schism as one group breaks off from its founding order usually due to a disagreement resulting from a clash of egos.

The following is an attempt to follow the growth of the Rosicrucian and related esoteric groups in the nineteenth and twentieth century the importance of which is that these organizations were the vehicles that held, promoted and passed on what we today call the Western Hermetic Qabalah, both in its raw form and the many interpretations that are presented today. The list below is not a complete list but is an attempt to chronologically document the emergence and development of the Rosicrucian Order.

FRATERNITAS ROSAE CRUSCIS

This is one of several orders who claim they are the "authentic Rosicrucian Fraternity", claiming their birth in Germany in 1614. The order's "modern founder" was Paschal Beverly Randolph (1825–1875) in 1858. Randolph is also credited with introducing sex magic or occult sexuality to North America though what Randolph called The Eulistic Mysteries. This was a set of teaching that instructed the use of sex in ritual work. The term Eulistic comes from the Greek Eleusinian mysteries. Randolph's translation of these Greek mysteries and of his other writings while he was in Europe are alleged to be one of the sources that Aleister Crowley used to develop his rituals in his *Ordo Templi Orientis* (O.T.O.). There were one big differences between the two men's practice; Randolph advocated that sex magic only be practiced between married couples but Crowley professed more open practices.

Fraternitas Rosae Cruscis claims they existed in the Americas prior to the American Revolution with their great Council of Three, this governing body being composed of Benjamin Franklin, George Clymer and Thomas Paine. Their history states Marie-Joseph Paul Yves Roch Gilbert du Motier de Lafayette, better known as the Marquis de Lafayette having replaced Thomas Paine. Lafayette, had also been a member of the Paris Rosicrucian lodge *Humanidad*. The *Humanidad* Lodge is linked to the lodge called "La Parfaite Amitié" founded in 1723. It was founded to do research into the Divine Sciences. It also was known as the "Humanidad-Lodge". This was the same lodge to which Benjamin Franklin had belonged. In 1842 the Great Council of Three was revitalized by George Lippard (1822–1854), an American novelist, journalist, playwright, social activist, and labor organizer. During the Civil War under Lippard's leadership became known as a Christian organization that was extremely patriotical in nature. He did this to move it away from the *Martinism* professed in the tenets of the Humanidad Lodge which Louis-Claude de Saint-Martin (1743–1803) presented with its mystical tradition in which emphasis is placed on Meditation and inner spiritual alchemy. Lippard did this by installing new members to the Council. He installed: Paschal Beverly Randolph (1825–1875), General Ethan Allen Hitchcock (1798–1870), and Abraham Lincoln (1809–1865). The highest office in the Order is the Hierarch of Eulis.

BROTHERHOOD OF THE ROSY CROSS

The *Brotherhood of the Rosy Cross*, a.k.a *Brothers and Sisters of the Rosy Cross* also refer to themselves as the *Knights of the Rosy Cross* or the *Rosie Crucians*. According to their website, they were established in 1407 by Father Christian Rosenkreutz and a small group of his followers. They claim the exact date of their establishment of their Order was on October 13, 1407. This is the same date that King Philip IV of France arrested the Knights Templars. The Brotherhood did not become public knowledge until the publication of the *Fama Fraternitatis* and the *Confessio Fraternitatis*. It is from these two core documents that they received the foundation of Rosicrucian teaching and activity on which they basis their Brotherhood.

According to their history, they place themselves in the Americas around 1694 when 40 of their brethren congregated near Philadelphia. They were led by their Magister Johannes Kelpius (1667–1708), who was a German Pietist, mystic, musician, writer, who also had interests in botany, astronomy and the occult. Kelpius established his group of followers in Germantown, Pennsylvania and called the group *"Society of the Women of the Wilderness"*. This group's beliefs were based on an elaborate interpretation of the *Book of Revelations* 12:6. Kelpius later moved the group to Philadelphia which had a greater religious tolerance. He then changed the name to *"Monks of the Ridge"* or *"Monks of the Wissahickon"*. Kelpius and his followers spent a great deal of time searching the skies at night. They were looking for holy signs of the second coming.

The Brotherhood is still active in teaching hermetic wisdom, alchemical, mystical, theosophical and spiritual knowledge to their members.

SOCIETAS ROSICRUCIAN IN ANGLIA (SRIA)

The SRIA describes itself as a modern society of Rosicrucians. It was established by Robert Wentworth Little (1840–1878), a Freemason, after he claimed to have discovered manuscripts in the Grand Lodge of England's achives, sometime around 1865. The society has based its symbols and traditions on an earlier Society known as the *Fraternity of the Rosy and Cross,* which is supposedly had its origins early in the sixteenth centrury.

The society has many chapters located throughout the United States and Europe. These chapters provide their members a place to study, produce papers and deliver lectures as part of their College work. Their order's governing Grand College is located in England, with about fifty local chapters worldwide. There are also Grand Councils in Scotland that govern the *Societata Rosicruciana* in Scotland, and a Grand Council in the United States that governs the *Societas Rosicruciana in Civitatibus Foederatis*.

The Order has nine degrees. The First Order is made up of the degree Zelator, followed by Theoricus, Practicus and Philosophus. The Second Order, or Adept Grade, can only be reached by approval of the Supreme Magnus or Chief Adept. It consists of the three degrees of Adeptus Minor, Adeptus Major, and Adeptus Exemptus. The Third Order, which is the highest of their degrees is the ruling Order of the society is made only by the Supreme Magnus and encompasses the two degrees of Magister and Magus.

SOCIETAS ROSICRUCIANA IN AMERICA (SRIAM)

There is a degree of ambiguity as to when the *Societas Rosicruciana* in America officially formed. There is agreement that they were an offspring of the English SRIA that had chartered a group of Masons in Philadelphia in 1878 to form a new chapter. This group eventually reformed and reorganized itself to become known as the *Societas Rosicruciana* in the United States (SRIUS) in 1889. This group struggled until a local publisher, Sylvester Clark Gould (1840–1909) joined the group and began to publish various magazines about the group. One of Gould's interests was studying the historical aspects of the Rosicrucian tradition. Gould joined with George Wilson Plummer (1876–1944), another prominent Freemason and Rosicrucian, to establish what was to become the *Societas Rosicruciana of America* (SRIAm), 1907. In Gould's attempt to legitimize the *Societas Rosicruciana in the United States* as a true Rosicrucian Order, he contacted several established, known Europe Rosicrucian Orders in 1909 for help. Gould died before he could complete his dream of converting the *Societas Rosicruciana in the United States* (SRIUS) into the group he wished. Plummer took over the leadership as Supreme Magnus until after Gould's death in 1944, eventually incorporating the *SRIAm* in 1912. In 1916 they admitted women into their ranks and because of this action lost their charter from England and thus their sponsorship from the British mother-lodge or by any other Masonic organization resulting in the SRIAm becoming truly independent. With this independence came their ability to introduce new materials which were different than presented by the *SRIA*.

George Wilson Plummer was very active in the Rosicrucian community writing several books using the Plummer name as well as under the pen name of Frater Khei. His works included *Rosicrucian Symbology, Esoteric Masonry, Rosicrucian Healing, The Art of Rosicrucian Healing* and the *Principles and Practice for Rosicrucians*.

The current Order appears to have three levels of study, or Liber, each with twelve syllabuses:

Liber I Rosicrucian Series
Liber II Hermetic Series
Liber III Alchemical Series

ROSICRUCIANISM AND FREEMASONRY

Historically, from their conception, Freemason Lodges have been magnets for intellectuals, freethinkers, and educated men of their time both in the Americas and in its birthplace in Europe. Many of the names associated with the early Rosicrucian Orders were Freemasons. Some historians claim that Freemasonry grew out of the Rosicrucian furor sometime between 1633 and 1640. Unfortunately, there are just as many historians who claim that the Freemason's did not come from the earlier Rosicrucian Orders. No matter which came first historically many of the early Freemasons themselves were Rosicrucians, or became part of the "modern Rosicrucian" Orders.

The Rosicrucian influence can be seen with modern Freemasonry from the initial three "Blue Lodge" degrees of Entered Apprentice, Fellowcraft, and Master Mason Degrees, to the degrees offered by the Scottish Rite and York Rites. One statement in Masonry that hints to deeper, possibly esoteric roots is there are "circles within circles". This phrase can have many meanings. One is the deeper you search into Masonry the more you will find. It is like an onion, where there are multiple layers and each reveals a new layer below it. In Freemasonry, the more you delve into the myths, traditions and history of Freemasonry the more you will discover. The one universal Rosicrucian/Qabalistic symbol evident in the all Blue Lodges is the representation of three pillars upon which the Lodge is symbolically built. Depending on what interpretation as to what each pillar is called, they do represent the Tree of Life in their configuration. If a Master Mason goes on to join the *Ancient and Accepted Scottish Rite of the Southern Jurisdiction of the United States*, the new candidate will be exposed to the Tree of Life in the 4th Degree, Secret Master. In this Degree, the candidate is encouraged to study the Tree of Life so he can discover for himself its deeper meanings. The Tree, or its pictorial symbol, is also is seen and/or mentioned in many of the degrees that follow the Secret Master Degree.

Within the Scottish Rite of Freemasons, which is often referred to as the "University of Freemasonry", there is a specific degree called the Rose-Croix Degree. The modern Rose-Croix Degree seems to have originated in Germany along with the *Rite of Strict Observance*. The *Rite of Strict Observance* was so named because of having its members adhere by oath to blindly follow unknown superiors of the Order. The Order itself was said to have originated with C. G. Marschall von Bieberstein (1842–1912), a German politician, who had founded two Masonic Lodges in Germany, one in Dresden and the other in Naumber. Von Bieberstein died in 1750 and Karl Gotthelf, Baron von und Altergrotkau (1722–1776), a fellow German Freemason had founded the *Rite of Strict Observance* in 1751. This Rite had several degrees: The Entered Apprentice, Fellowcraft, Master Mason, Scottish Master, Novice and Knights Templar Degrees. The Order did not become widly known due to the confusion and social unrest as a result of the Seven Years War (1756–1763) that raged throughout Europe. According to historians studying the short history of the *Rite of Strict Obedience*, Rosicrucianism made its way into what would be the degrees of the *Ancient and Accepted Scottish Rite*. These Degrees were solidified by Albert Pike (1809–1891) to their current 28 Degrees practiced by the *Scottish Rite of Freemasonry of the Southern Jurisdiction*.

The *Rose-Croix Order* was developed by on Jean-Baptiste Willermoz (1730–1824) a leading Freemason in Lyons, France. This is according to records in the city achives that were researched by Madame Alice Joly (1730–1824), who wrote her findings in *Un Mystique Lyonnais et les Secrets de la Franc-Maconnerie,* in 1938. Her research revealed that Willermoz helped develop some 25 degrees around 1761, one of which was Knight of the Eagle, of the Pelican, Knight of St Andrew or Mason of Heredom. Up to this time most of these degrees existed in name only. Willermoz formalized them into actual rituals. During this time Willermoz was in contact with another prominent Freemason in the Metz Lodge, one Meunier de Précourt, who was in turn in contact with several other German Lodges. It is believed

Précourt received information from these German Lodges concerning the ritual which later became known as the Rose-Croiz Degree.

According to records Précourt wrote to Willermoz in 1762 concerning the German Rosicrucians who had a great many manuscripts containing secrets of what was called the *"Order of the Temple"*. Willermoz apparently obtained these manuscripts, and the secrets they contained, and based the Rose-Croix Degree on them. Willermoz completed this work on the degree in 1765. There is some debate to the accuracy of this account, with many believing that not all of Willermoz's material actually came from German sources but may have come in part from an earlier Masonic degree called the Knight of the Eagle that appeared as early as 1761.

Unlike today, the Rose-Croix Degree initially was not open to all Freemasons. In January of 1767, the Comte de Clermont, and the Grand Master of the Marquis de Gages, along with the Provincial Grand Master of the Netherlands, stated in letter that they only allowed seven Grand Masters, or Master of Lodges, into the "sublime Rose-Croix Degree in all its perfection". By around 1768 or 1769 there is mention of a Rose-Croix Chapter in Paris. By 1771 the degree was in the new world. Needless to say, Comte's restrictions did not last long.

Currently the Rose-Croix Degree is practiced in its current form as the 18th Degree of the *Ancient and Accepted Scottish Rite of the Southern Jursisticion of the United States*. It is called the Knight of the Rose Croix. Within this degree there is much symbolism that its current candidates are encouraged to interpert for themselves. The degree teaches the candidate to have "faith in God, mankind and in themselves". And they should have "hope in the victory over evil, and the advancement of humanity". Finally, it teaches charity in 'relieving the wants and tolerating the errors and faults of others.'

The Rite of Memphis-Misraïm

The Rites of Memphis-Misraïm, more commonly known as Egyptian Freemasonry, started out as two different Rites. The *Rite of Misraïm* originated in Venice, Italy around 1788. It combined Masonic symbolism with Egyptian and alchemical references and consisted of over ninety degrees. Joseph Balsamo (1743–1795), who went by Cagliostro or Count Alessandro di Cagliostro, introduced the secret degrees of *Arcana Arcanorum* into the *Rite of Misraïm* in 1788. The introduction of the new secret degrees to the *Rites of Memphis* occurred in Montauban, France, in 1815. The *Rite of Memphis* continued to develop and around 1838, it incorporated Templar and chivalry symbolism into the Rite. The two Rites were merged into a single order called the *Rite of Memphis-Misraïm* somewhere between 1881 and 1889 depending on which historical source one quotes.

What today is called the *Oriental Masonic Order of the Ancient and Primitive Rite of Memphis and Misraïm* or *Ancient and Primitive Rite of Memphis and Misraïm*, is a dual Masonic–Illuministic system which starts from the basic degrees of Craft Freemasonry, a term used by English Masons, and extends to the higher rituals of Rosicrucianism and Gnosisism. According to the *Oriental Masonic Order of the Ancient and Primitive Rite of Memphis and Misraïm* the higher rituals include the hermetic-philosophical-esoteric systems of the ancient Egyptian Hierophants and the Priests of Mithra.

According to their website they have four sections to their operative rituals; a Symbolic section; a Philosophical-cabalistic section, a Gnostic-hermetic section, and a Hermetic section. Each of these four sections has their own degrees and Ritual bodies which require practical ritual work and study. These differ somewhat from those revealed by John Yarker (1833–1913) around 1897 to A. E. Waite. Yarker was a member of Masonic Lodge called Lodge of Integrity, No. 189, in Manchester. He demitted from the Lodge and Freemasonry in 1862. In 1872 Yarker established the *Sovereign Sanctuary of the* Ancient and Primitive Rite *of Masonry* for England and Ireland under the authority of a Patent issued by the American Grand Master of that organization. Yarker provided a list of Degrees of the *The Rites of Memphis-Misraïm* to Waite. Waite stated prior to publishing them he confirmed them with other sources including to having 'verified with the Tyler of the Order'. Yarker's list starts at the 4th Degree and goes through to the 90th Degree. They resemble closely t the upper degrees of Masonry found in the Scottish Rite and York Rite in name only.

The first series is called the *Symbolic Section* is made up the first three degrees of Universal Freemasonry as overseen by the Masonic Community of the Grand Orient of Italy. The degrees listed below are from A.E. Waite's *A New Encyclopedia of Freemasonry* and may vary from other sources.[3]

---

3 *A New Encyclopedia of Freemasonry,* Waite, A. E., Wings Books, 1970, pgs. 342-345

Class I 1° Apprentice
    2° Companion
    3° Master

Class II 4° Secret Master
    5° Perfect Master
    6° Mastery by Curiosity
    7° Provost and Judge
    8° English Master

Class III 9° Elect of Nine
    10° Elect of the Unknown or Elect of the Perignan
    11° Elect of the Fifteen
    12° Perfect Elect
    13° Illustrious or Illustrious Elect

Class IV 14° Scottish Trinitarian
    15° Scottish Companion or Fellow-craft
    16° Scottish Master
    17° Scottish Panissiére
    18° Scottish Master (different from the 16°)
    19° Scot of the J.J.J.
    20° Scot of the Sacred Vault of James VI
    21° Scot of St. Andrew

Class V 22° Little Architect
    23° Great Architect
    24° Architecture
    25° Perfect Architect-Apprentice
    26° Perfect Architect-Companion
    27° Perfect Architect-Master
    28° Perfect Architect
    29° Sublime Architect
    30° Sublime Scot of Heredom

Class VI 31° Grand and Royal Arch
    32° Grand Axe
    33° Sublime Knight of Choice

The second series called the *Philosophical* or *Gnostic-Hermetic Section* is composed of 38 chambers in which only the 66th Degree is practiced by the Grand Consistory of Great Consecrator Patriarchs, where they study and research classical gnosis and its derivations. The "Classes" are:

Class VII 34° Knight of the Sublime Choice
    35° Prussian Knight or Knight of the Tower
    36° Knight of the Temple
    37° Knight of the Eagle
    38° Knight of the Black Eagle
    39° Knight of the Red Eagle
    40° Knight of the White East
    41° Knight of the East

Class VIII 42°Commader of the East
    43° Grand Commander of the East
    44° Architecture of Sovereign Commanders of the Temple
    45° Prince of Jerusalem

Class IX 46° Knight Rose-Croix
    47° Knight of the West
    48° Sublime Philosopher
    49° Chaos the First
    50° Chaos the Second
    51° Knight of the Sun

Class X 52° Supreme Commander of the Stars
    53° Sublime Philosopher (different than 48°)
    54° Miner
    55° Washer

56° Blower
57° Founder or Caster
58° True Mason-Adept
59° Elect Sovereign
60° Sovereign of Sovereigns
61° Grand Master of Symbolical Lodges
62° Most High and Most Powerful High Priest-Sacrificer
63° Knight of Palestine
64° Grand Knight of the Black and White Eagle
65° Grand Elect
66° Grand Inquisitor Commander

And *The Mystical* or *Hermetic Section* represents the end of the path for "Brother Master Masons". From this point the workers of the Royal Art journey through the immemorial and mysterious repository that is the Ancient and primitive *Rite of the Memphis and Misraïm*. In this section there are 24 Ritual Bodies in 6 Classes which are:

Class XI 67° Knight Beneficent
    68° Knight of the Rainbow
    69° Knight of the Banuka or Karnuka/Hanuka
    70° Most Wise Prince

Class XII 71° Supreme Tribunal of Sovereign Princes Talmudim
    72° Supreme Consistory
    73° Supreme Council General of Sovereign Princes Grand Haram

Class XIII 74° Supreme Council of Sovereign Princes Grand Haram
    75° Sovereign Tribunal of Sovereign Princes of Hasidim

Class XIV 76° Supreme Council of Governor Grand Princes Hasidim
    77° Supreme Grand Council General of Grand Inspectors Intendant

Class XV 78° Supreme Council of Sovereign Princes of the Seventy-Eighth Degree
    79° Supreme Council of Sovereign Princes of the Seventy-Ninth Degree
    80° Supreme Council of Sovereign Princes of the Eightieth Degree

81° Supreme Council of Sovereign Princes of the Eighty-First Degree
82° Supreme Council of Sovereign Princes of the Eighty-Second Degree
83° Supreme Council of Sovereign Princes of the Eighty-Third Degree
84° Supreme Council of Sovereign Princes of the Eighty-Fourth Degree
85° Supreme Council of Sovereign Princes of the Eighty-Fifth Degree
86° Supreme Council of Sovereign Princes of the Eighty-Sixth Degree

Class XVI 87° Supreme Grand Council of Grand Ministers Constituant
of the Order
88° Supreme Council of Sovereign Princes of the Eighty-Eighth Degree
89° Supreme Council of Sovereign Princes of the Eighty-Ninth Degree
90° Great Counsel of the Ninetieth and Last Degree

Many of these degrees correspond to modern Freemasonry Scottish
and York Rite Degrees, sometimes in name only. In addition, there are a
few more degrees that are not part of the Order but are offered. They are:

91° Grand Tribunal of Sovereigns Principles, Grand Defenders of
the Order and the Rite.
94° Gran Mystical Temple of the Sublime Patriarchs of Memphis.
95° Sovereign Sanctuary of Sublime Patriarchs, Grand Conservators
of the Order.

Like many of the Orders or Rites who claim their origins to the "first"
order there is confusion as to which group has the historic right of ancestry.
There are numerous Orders or factions of the *Rite of Memphis-Misraïm*
operating in countries throughout the world. This includes Argentina,
Brazil, Chile, England, Spain, France, Martinque, Mauritius, New Caledonia,
Scandinavia, Switzerland, Uruguay, USA, and Venezuela. They have many
similarities but many of them have customized their Degrees to meet their
own claims to authenticity.

In the United States the *National Sovereign Sanctuary Ancient and
Primitive Rite of Memphis-Misraïm for the United States and Jurisdictions*
traces its Grand Masters all the way back to General Joseph Garibaldi
(1807–1882) an Italian who is credited with starting the unification of the
two Rites in 1881, but died prior to its total merging could be accomplished.

SOCIETAS ROSICRUCIANA IN CIVITATIBUS FOEDERATIS (SRICF)

The *Societas Rosicruciana in Civitatibus Foederatis* is the Rosicrucian Society of the United States, first formed on September 21, 1880, by three Colleges chartered by the Society based in Scotland. The *Societas Rosicruciana in Civitatibus Foederatis* is also affiliated with two other similar societies in the world, the *Societas Rosicruciana in Anglia*, based in England, and the *Societas Rosicruciana in Scotia* based in Scotland. Membership Freemasons do not affiliate themselves with this Society.

The Society is governed by The High Council composed of Fraters of the Third Order. The Third Order is composed of two degrees; IXÂ° and VIIIÂ°, and any College Celebrant not a member of the Third Order. The head of the Order is The Supreme Magus, IXÂ° which is elected each triennium. The lesser bodies composing the Society are called "colleges". Each is governed by a Chief Adept, IXÂ° appointed for life by the Supreme Magus. There is a limit of only 72 members to each College.

According to the history of the Society as it relates to its presence in the United States, it was the result of three Master Masons traveling to England from Pennsylvania in 1878. These Masons were Charles E. Meyer (1839–1908) of Melita Lodge #295, Daniel Sutter of Phoenix Lodge #230 and Charles W Parker of Philadelphia Lodge #72, all in the Philadelphia, Pennsylvania area. They were admitted to the Zelator degree at the Yorkshire College while in England on July 25, 1878. A fourth member was admitted from Herman Lodge #1251, Mark Merckle, to the Metropolitan College in London the same year. They attempted to form a similar body in the United States as early as 1878 according to a Charter being given to Dr. Jonathan J French allowing him to organize a College in Illinois. Dr. French died before the College truly could be established. The original four Masons became the core of the Grand High Council of America, known as the *Societas Rosicruciana Republican Americae* on December 27, 1878. Other Colleges soon followed, with a total of nineteen Colleges recognized at a meeting of the High Council held in 1990. By 1996 there were 32 Colleges located in North America and one each in Hong Kong and Okinawa, Japan. In addition, the number of Colleges has grown in England to over 50 and Scotland has over 5 Colleges of their own.

The Colleges are composed of three Orders. The First Order has four Grades which are classified as "Learning Grades":

First Grade......... Zelator
Second Grade .... Theoricus
Third Grade........ Practicus
Fourth Grade........ Philosophuss

Second Order consist of Three Grades which are called the 'Teaching Grades'

Fifth Grade .... Adeptus Minor
Sixth Grade .... Adeptus Major
Seventh Grade....... Adeptus Exemptus

The Third Order consists of Two Grades, and is called the "Ruling Grades" and is only conferred by the Supreme Magus or his representative.

Eighth Grade........ Magister
Ninth Grade .... Magus

There are numerous other groups and sub-groups that have their membership qualifications as being Masonic or Orders that had separated from these initial groups. All these groups are important for without these societies much of what Rosicrucianism is would have been lost. These members of these various Rosicrucian Orders have greatly influenced and contributed to the inner working of most all the Masonic Fraternity and can be found with a little research and perseverance. The greatest danger is that there are many false sources or material that has been manipulated to meet someone's personal agenda. One needs to determine the true source and discover its pedigree. Many students often start their search with a very well know group such as *The Golden Dawn* which had a great influence on modern hermetic studies.

HERMETIC ORDER OF THE GOLDEN DAWN (HOGD)
The *Hermetic Order of the Golden Dawn* was founded in 1888 by three Master Masons who were also members of *Societas Rosicrucian in Anglia* (SRIA). The three Master Masons that established the *Hermetic Order of the Golden Dawn* were Samuel Liddel MacGregor Mathers (1854–1918) a British occultist and member of Hengist Lodge #195; William Robert Woodman

(1828–1891), who was appointed Grand Sword Bearer of the *United Grand Lodge of England*, and held high rank in many other Orders, including the *Order of the Red Cross of Constantine*. And William Wynn Westcott (1848–1925), another Freemason and member of the *Quatuor Coronati* research lodge. The English Branch of the Golden Dawn was called *Die Goldene Dammerung*. According to the Order's history the three Master Masons were initiates in the *SRIA* and also studied with a German adept named Fraulein Anna Sprengel (she died around 1891). According to Westcott she had in her possession some old cipher-manuscripts from her lodge. Sprengel existence as person has not been proven historically, and many believe she was invented by Westcott to provide legitimacy to his work. Westcott claimed Sprengel entered into voluminous correspondence with him claiming she was responsible for the foundation of the *Golden Dawn* around 1886. She is supposed to have held a Rosicrucian ritual and to have nominated Westcott as the head of the *Golden Dawn* in Britain. There are others who believe these ciphers that Westcott used came through or from one of the lodges of the *Frates Lucis*, or *Asiatic Brethren* which is a schism of the *Masonic Order of the Rosy Cross*.

According to Albert Pike (1809–1891), an American attorney, Confederate officer, writer, and Freemason, and the founder of the modern *Ancient and Accepted Scottish Rite of the Southern Jurisdiction*, the *Frates Lucis* or *Asiatic Brethren* were the successors of the German *Illuminati*. Pike goes on to say that the secret order was established by Moses Dobrushka or Dobruška (1753–1794) who was an alchemist, Freemason, writer and poet. Dobruška was later elevated to nobility in Vienna in 1778 and took the name of Franz Thomas Edler von Schönfeld. The *Frates Lucis*, also known as the *Brotherhood of the Light*, was chiefly comprised of Jews, Turks, Persians and Armenians who, according to Pike, were members of what was known as the *"Johannite Christians"*, a Gnostic Christian sect, who were rescued by the Templars. The Grand Master of the *Asiatic Brethren*, and leading member of the *Illuminati*, was Prince Karl of Hessen-Kassel, the brother of Wilhelm, and cousin to Frederick II the Great of Prussia.

There is little published about the current order which is based in South America. What is published is that there are five degrees:

Knight Novice of the Third Year
Knight Novice of the Fifth Year

Knight Novice of the Seventh Year
Knight Levite
Knight Priest

According to *Hermetic Order of the Golden Dawn* there are three basic levels or hierarchies similar to Masonic Lodges; Entered Apprentice, Fellow-Craft and Master Mason, except they allow women to participate on equal terms as the men within the *Golden Dawn*. The first level called the Operative or Outer Order is where study materials are based on the principles of Hermetic Qabalah. These materials are a primary source of teaching and include history of the original *Hermetic Order of the Golden Dawn*. This is the section of study were the initiate is to work on their personal development through the study and knowledge of the four Classical Elements; fire, air, water and earth, as well the study of astrology, tarot divination and geomancy. The more advanced operative levels are where special magical and *alchemical* practices are used for spiritual development. The Second Order or Inner Order is called *Rosae Rubeae Aureae Crucis* (Ruby Rose and Cross of Gold) and the members concern themselves primarily with the use of proper magic (theurgy) and alchemy, as exemplified by the earlier Rosicrucian Order, as well as scrying, and astral travel. The Third Order or Secret Chiefs today directs the activities of the two lower Orders.

The original function of the Third Order was to be capstone of the Order concerning enlightenment but this did not happen due to a group of Adepts, located in London, who rebelled before the Third Order ritual could be finished. Thus resulting in the Order's first schism. The London Adepts, who were against Mathers' leadership, formed a group which they called the *Hermetic Society of Morgerothe*, while Mathers' group took the name of *Alpha et Omega*.

The Morgerothe group had a very short existence before it too had a schism and broke into two new groups. Those who were interested in Christian Mysticism followed A.E. Waite. The second group took over what was left of the original Isis-Urania Temple group and made themselves independent of the mother group. They called themselves the *Rectified Rite of the Golden Dawn* which later became known as the *Fellowship of the Rosy Cross*. Those who were left in the Morgerothe group were more interested in occultism, and followed Dr. Robert William Felkin. Felkin was a British ceremonial magician who formed the *Stella Matutina*, meaning Morning

Star, to practice the traditional teaching of the *Hermetic Order of the Golden Dawn*. They were originally known as the *Mystic Rose* or *Order of the Mystic Rose in the Outer*, and their mother Temple was called Amoun. It was the rituals of the *Stella Matutina* that Israel Regardie released to the general public about the Golden Dawn Order.

Shortly after Regardie's disclosures, Edward Aleister Crowley published many of the Golden Dawn's rituals in *The Equinox*. The *Equinox*–"The Review of Scientific Illuminism" was a series of publications in book form that serves as the official organ of the A∴A∴, a magical order founded by Crowley. He left the Golden Dawn Order in 1905 and started the A∴A∴.

Today much of the hierarchical structure of the Golden Dawn came from the *Societas Rosicrucians in Anglia*. The First Order is made up of:

> Neophyte 0=0 (introduction)
> Zelator 1=10
> Theoricus 2=9
> Practicus 3=8
> Philosophus 4=7
> Portal Grade (intermediate)

The Second Order is made up of the following Grades:

> Adeptus Minor 5=6
> Adeptus Major 6=5
> Adeptus Exemptus 7=4

The Third Order is:

> Magister Templi 8=3
> Magus 9=2
> Ipsissimus 10=1

The paired numbers attached to each Grade relate to positions on the Tree of Life. In addition, the First Order Grades are related to the four classic alchemical elements, Earth, Air, Water and Fire respectively. These are not the physical forms but the symbolic and metaphysical aspects of the element. Once the Aspirant gains their proficiency of that Order and grade they would be allowed to progress, to the next grade and eventually the next Order. Before they can enter the Second Order they would need the approval of the Adepts of the Second Order

The Second Order was not, properly, part of the "Golden Dawn", but a separate Order in its own right, known as the *R.R. et A.C or Roseae Rubae et Aureae Crucis* ("Ruby Rose and Golden Cross"). The Second Order directed the teachings of the First Order as well as acting as the governing force behind the First Order. After passing the "Portal" of the Second Order, the Aspirant was instructed in the techniques of practical magic. After mastering these techniques, the aspirant faced another examination. After passing this examination the aspirant needed the approval of the other Adepts before the Aspirant attained the Grade of Adeptus Minor (5=6). There were also four sub-Grades of instruction for the Adeptus Minor, again relating to the four Outer Order grades.

As a member of the Second Order, they had the power and authority to initiate aspirants to the First Order, though usually not without the permission of the Chiefs of his or her Lodge.

Some of the more prominent persons who helped to establish the Golden Dawn were leading forces of not only western esoteric thought but also in the arts, theatre, literature and other fields. Some of the prominent individuals were: Arthur Edward Waite (1857–1942), Mina Bergson (1865–1928), Edward Munch (1863–1944), August Strindberg (1849–1912), Rider Haggard (1856–1925), Dion Fortune (1890–1946), Dr. R.F. Felkin (1853–1926), Alexander Edward Crowley "Aleister" (1875–1947), William Butler Yeats (1865–1939), Frederick Leigh Gardner (1857–1930), and Florence Farr (1860–1917), just to name a few of the more prominent founding members.

The *Golden Dawn* has centers all over the western world. They are considered one of the most prominent of the Rosicrucian Orders and have had and still do have a great influence on the modern western mystery traditions.

NEW VIEWPOINTS AND SCHISMS

A∴A∴OR ASTRUM ARGENTIUM

In 1906 or 1907 Aleister Crowley and George Cecil Jones (born sometime between the years of 1870 and 1873) joined together after leaving the *Hermetic Order of the Golden Dawn* to create a new magical order. They wanted to continue where the Golden Dawn had left off. The called their order A∴A∴. It symbolically has many meaning such as: Astrom Argon, Astrum Argentium, Argentium Astrum, Astron Argiron, Arcanum Arcanorum, Arikh Anpin, Anuttara Amnaya, Arcadia Academia, Alchemia Arcanorum, Alta Astra, or Angel and Abyss. The meaning of these Latin titles is believed by many to mean "silver star". The purpose of this Order was to be a means by which t Crowley could pass on his mystical and magical training system which is based on the principles of Thelma. The principal goal of this Thelemic Mystical fraternity as developed by Crowley is a complex mystical path with two interrelated paths. The first goal is for the initiate to learn what their unique True Will be and the second is to achieve union with the All. This path to mystical enlightenment was founded on Crowley's meditation techniques. These techniques were based on Crowley's understanding of Buddhism and the principles of the Qabalistic Tree of Life. The meditational techniques include the use of yoga, western ceremonial ritual of invocations and Eucharistic ceremonies, plus Qabalistic divination through the use of tarot and astrology. The motto of *A∴ A∴* is "The method of science, the aim of religion". The Orders "holy book" is *Liber AL vel Legis* or *The Book of the Law*.

A∴A∴ has three major grades. The first is the introduction made of 6 grades:

> Probationer Grade 0=0
> Neophyte Grade 1=10
> Zelator Grade 2=9
> Practicus Grade 3=8
> Philosophus Grade 4=7

Once the aspirant has shown mastery of Pratyahara and Dharana, which are stages of yoga and meditation they will gain the title of *Dominus Liminis*. Following this proficiency, they advance to *The Order of the R∴C∴* (Rosy Cross) where the following grades become available:

> Adeptus Minor (without) 5=6
> Adeptus Minor (within) 5=6
> Adeptus Major 6=5
> Adeptus Exemptus 7=4

The final grades are under the Order of the S∴S∴
  Magister Templi 8=3
  Magus 9=2
  Ipsissimus 10=1

Like the *Hermetic Order of the Golden Dawn* the A∴ A∴ is one of the premiere organizations that has led to the distribution of much of what today is called the Hermetic traditions. Without these two groups the traditions of these mysteries would have not become as well known through Europe and the Americas. Even today many groups trace their teaching back to these two great Societies and/or members who emerged from them.

EDWARD ALEXANDER CROWLEY (ALEISTER)
Edward Alexander Crowley (Aleister) is known as one of the greatest occultist of modern times. He was born in Leamington Spa, England on October 12, 1875. His parents belonged to a very strict fundamentalist Christian sect called the *Plymouth Brethren*. According to his biography this strict fundamentalist childhood resulted in Aleister's total disdain of Christianity in his adult life.

Crowley attended Trinity College at Cambridge University but left prior to receiving his Degree. Shortly after leaving Trinity College he met George Cecil Jones who was a member of the *Hermetic Order of the Golden Dawn*. Crowley was initiated into the *Golden Dawn* in 1898 and advanced rapidly through the various grades until the Order was shattered by schism. It was at that time Crowley left England and traveled throughout the East. During his travels he learned the discipline of yoga and Eastern mysticism.

In 1903 he met and married Rose Edith Kelly (1874–1932), and they went to Egypt for their honeymoon. While in Cairo in early 1904, Rose began entering trance states and insisted that the god Horus was attempting to contact Aleister through her. This was a unique experience for Rose because prior to this time Rose had no interest or knowledge with the occult. Aleister initially doubted his wife's affirmations. Aleister tested his wife by taking her to the Boulak Museum, in Cairo, where he asked her to point out an image or statue of Horus to him. After passing several well-known images of Horus she led him to a painted wooden funeral stele from the 26th dynasty, depicting the god receiving a sacrifice from the deceased priest named Ankh-f-n-khonsu. Upon seeing the stele, she claimed this was Horus. This really impressed Crowley because the artifact was numbered "666" by the museum, a number with which Crowley had identified since childhood. As a result of the experience at the museum, Aleister began to listen to Rose's affirmations.

Starting on April 8, 1904, at Rose's direction, he entered a chamber for three successive days, and wrote down what he heard spoken to him by a shadowy presence behind him. The result was the first three chapters of his *Liber AL vel Legis,* or *Book of the Law.* According to Crowley this book was heralding of the new aeon of Horus, which would be governed by the Law of Thelma. Thelma is Greek for "will". This Law of Thelma repeatedly proclaims 'Do what thou wilt' which became creed for Crowley as he tried to promote and spread his thelemic philosophy. Upon returning to England in 1906 he rejoined George Cecil Jones to establish A∴ A∴.

Crowley died in Hasting, England on December 1, 1947. He was both honored and despised for his teachings and his actions. He was honored for his great contributions to western magic and tradition and despised for his debauchery involving the use of drugs, alcohol and introduction and use of sex magick.

Ordo Templi Orientis (O.T.O.)

The official date of *Ordo Templi Orientis* formation is July 21, 1892. It was formed by Harry J Seymour, a past Grand Master of *Rite of Memphis-Misraïm.* The two Freemasons who established the basis of the Order were Carl Kellner (1851–1905), a student of Freemasonry, Rosicrucianism and Eastern Mysticism, and Theodor Reuss (1855–1923), who was an Anglo-German tantric occultist, Freemason, police spy, journalist, singer and head of the Germany based organization called *Ordo Templi Orientis* (O.T.O.).

In 1910 Theodore Reuss contacted Crowley. At the time *O.T.O.* was made up of high ranking Freemasons who claimed to have discovered the supreme secret of practical magic. Crowley became interested and agreed to join the Order. Crowley eventually rose to become the head of the Order when Reuss suffered a stroke in 1921. Crowley quickly changed the rites of the *O.T.O.* to conform to his views of the *Law of Thelma* and tasked the Order to establish Thelema throughout the world.

The other cofounder was Carl Kellner, who was a very influential Austrian Chemist and industrialist. Kellner had become a Freemason in 1873, being initiated at the Humanitas Lodge on the Austro-Hungarian border.

Kellner traveled throughout Europe, America and Asia Minor where he claimed to have met three Adepts, a Sufi named Soliman ben Aifa, and two Hindu Tantrics named Bhima Sena Pratapa of Lahore and Sri Manhatma Agamya Paramahamsa. These Adepts claimed to be members of the *Hermetic Brotherhood of Light*. During his esoteric studies Kellner claimed he had discovered a true understanding of the symbolism of Freemasonry which opened the mysteries of Nature. This secret or key was that sex magic was 'the Key' to all the secrets of the Universe and to all the symbols found not only in Masonry, but other secret societies or cults, as well as in religion itself. With this knowledge, Kellner wanted to develop an *Academia Masonica* that would allow Freemasons to understand the true meaning of their Masonic degrees and symbols.

In 1895, after discussing his ideas with Theodor Reuss (a.k.a. Frater Merlin or Peregrinus), Kellner decided to change the name of *Academia Masonica* to *Ordo Templi Orientis* or *Oriental Templar Order*. The Order would follow the lines of the *Rites of Memphis-Misraïm* and would teach the more esoteric doctrines of the Rosicrucians and the Hermetic *Brotherhood of Light,* as well as the esoteric inner knowledge of the Masonic symbols. Unlike Masonry, both men and women would be admitted into all levels of the Order. This meant they would have to pass through the various degrees of Craft and Higher Grader of Freemasonry as prerequisite to entry into the inner Cirlce of O.T.O. Kellner eventually separated from Reuss due to Reuss being too busy with his revival of the *Order of Illuminati* in 1902.

The membership into *O.T.O.* is based on passing through a system of initiations or degrees which use ritual drama that establish fraternal bonds and impart spiritual and philosophical teachings similar to Masonic degrees. There are certain of these degrees that must be obtained prior to their ordination as a priest or priestess in the *Ecclesia Gnotica Catholica* or *Gnostic Catholic Church*. It should be noted that the term "Catholic" refers to the "universality of doctrine" not the Roman Catholic Church.

The *Ecclesia Gnostica Catholica* (E.G.C.) is the ecclesiastical arm of the *Ordo Templi Orientis* devoted to promulgating the Law of Thelema, which was developed by Aleister Crowley's *The Book of the Law*. The chief function of the *Ecclesia Gnostica Catholica* is the public and private performance or the Gnostic Mass, a Eucharistic ritual written by Crowley in 1913. The church performed baptisms, confirmations, marriages (not limited to couples of the opposite gender) and the last rites. These rituals were said to be written by

Crowley when he was "under the influence of the *Liturgy of St Basil* of the Russian Church." This occurred to Aleister Crowley in 1913 when he wrote Liber XV, the Gnostic Mass, while in Moscow.

The *O.T.O.* has thirteen numbered degrees and twelve un-numbered degrees which are divided into three grades or "triads"—the Hermit, the Lover, and the Man of Earth. Each degree requires an initiation and swearing of an oath. The *O.T.O.* claims it is a similar practice as used by the Freemasons. Advancement through the Man of Earth triad requires sponsorship from ranking members. Advancement into the degree of the Knight of the East and West and beyond requires one to be invited by ranking members.

The Degrees are as follows:

The Man of Earth Triad

0°—Minerval
I°—Man & Brother
II°—Magician
III°—Master Magician
IV°—Perfect Magician & Companion of the Holy Royal Arch of Enoch.
P.I.°—Perfect Initiate, or Prince of Jerusalem

Outside all Triads

Knight of the East & West

The Lover Triad

V°—Sovereign Prince Rose-Croix, and Knight of the Pelican & Eagle Knight of the Red Eagle, and Member of the Senate of Knight Hermetic Philosophers.
VI°—Illustrious Knight (Templar) of the Order of Kadosch, and Companion of the Holy Graal. Grand Inquisitor Commander, and Member of the Grand Tribunal Prince of the Royal Secret.
VII°—Theoreticus, and Very Illustrious Sovereign Grand Inspector General Magus of Light, and Bishop of *Ecclesia Gnostica Catholica*.

The Grandmaster of Light, and Inspector of Rites & Degrees are the names of the next section which include the following Triads:

The Hermit Triad
    VIII°—Perfect Pontiff of the Illuminati Epopt of the Illuminati
    IX°—Initiate of the Sanctuary of the Gnosis
    X°—Rex Summus Sanctissimus
    XI°—Initiate of the Eleventh Degree (This degree is technical, and has
        no relation to the general plan of the Order.)
    XII°—Frater Superior, and Outer Head of the Order

The governing bodies of O.T.O. include:

1. International Headquarters

   - Presided over by the Outer Head of the Order XII° (O.H.O.— also known as Frater Superior)
   - Supreme Council
   - Revolutionaries

2. The Sovereign Sanctuary of the Gnosis of the IX°

3. The Secret Areopagus of the Illuminati of the VIII°

4. The Grand Tribunal of the VI°

5. The National Grand Lodge

   - Presided over by the National Grand Master X°
   - Executive Council

6. The Supreme Grand Council

7. The Electoral College

They have temples throughout the United States and the rest of the world.

Rosicrucian Fellowship aka Association of Christian Mystics (RF)

Max Heindel (1865–1919), who was born as Dane Carl Louis von Grasshof, founded The *Rosicrucian Fellowship* in 1909 in Seattle, Washington, with August 8, 1909 being its formal constitution date. Heindel was a Christian occultist, astrologer and mystic. Heindel unlike many who proceded or followed him did not claim that his group was a direct descendants of the earlier Rosicrucian groups but rather they as a "Fellowship" signify that they are inspired by the earlier Rosicrucians. The teaching of the RF is based on Heindel's writings which were influenced by his earlier meeting with an Elder Brother of the Rosicrucian Order.

According to Heindel, while he was traveling in Berlin, Germany, in the fall of 1907, he was visited by a Spiritual being who was clothed in a "vital body". This Spiritual being eventually identified himself as the Elder Brother of the *Rosicrucian Order.* According to this Spiritual being the Order was formed originally in the year 1313 and had no direct connection to the physical organization calling themselves Rosicrucians. It was from this Elder Brother that Heindel got his material for his writing. He was then directed to the Temple of the Rose Cross near the German Bohemian boarder where he received additional information and training from an Elder Brother of the Rose Cross. He was told that the *Rosicrucian Order* was made up of twelve Elder Brothers led by a thirteenth Elder who were the invisible Head of the Order. These Elders were human Adepts who had advanced beyond the cycle of rebirth.

Another influence on Heindel was Rudolf Steiner (1861–1925). Steiner was an Austrian philosopher, social reformer and esotericist who founded the spiritual movement of anthroposophy which has influences of Goethean science and Rosicrucianism. Heindel returned to America in the summer of 1908 where he at once started to formulate the Rosicrucian teachings calling them the Western Wisdom Teachings. He published them in a book entitled The Rosicrucian Cosmo-Conception in 1909.

The *Rosicrucian Fellowship* offers correspondence courses on esoteric Christianity, philosophy, "spiritual astrology" and Bible interpretation. They organized these teachings into seven grades or degrees. Its study is primarily based upon a system of three grades: Regular student, Probationer and Disciple. After a two-year term of being a Regular Student of the Fellowship, a person may apply to become a Probationer. When the Probationer meets the necessary requirements he may ask to become or "raised" to the Disciple grade. Once admitted to the Disciple Grade a subsequent Spiritual unfoldment of the advanced soul within the Order of the Rose Cross is conducted through the process of nine lesser initiations.

They have study groups and centers all over the world with their headquarters in Oceanside, California.

THE THEOSOPHICAL SOCIETY

The Theosophical Society was officially formed in New York City, United States, in November 1875 by Helena Blavatsky, Henry Steel Olcott, William Quan Judge and others. Helena Petrovna Blavatsky, born as Helena von Hahn (1831–1891), was a Russian occultist and author. Blavatsky did extensive research into the spiritual traditions of the world especially those of Hinduism and Buddhism. She published several key works that form what is known as the New Age Movement. The Secret Doctrine is considered her magnum opus and organizes the essence of her teachings into a comprehensive compiled source document. Blavatsky's other works include Isis Unveiled, The Key to Theosophy and The Voice of the Silence. *The Secret Doctrine* includes two volumes the first is named *Cosmogenesis* and the second is referred to as *Anthropogenesis*. It was an influential example of the revival of interest in esoteric and occult ideas in the modern age, in particular because of its claim to reconcile ancient eastern wisdom with modern science. Blavatsky claimed that its contents had been revealed to her by "mahatmas" who had retained knowledge of humanity's spiritual history, knowledge that it was now possible, in part, to reveal. Her second key work was *Isis Unveiled: A Master-Key to the Mysteries of Ancient and Modern Science and Theology*, published in 1877, a book of esoteric philosophy, Helena Petrovna Blavatsky's first major work and as the title indicates the "key" text in her Theosophical movement. *Isis Unveiled* is divided into two volumes. Volume I, *The "Infallibility" of Modern Science*, discusses Occult science and the hidden and unknown forces of nature, exploring such subjects as forces, elementals, psychic phenomena, and the Inner and Outer Man. Volume II, *Theology*, discusses the similarity of Christian scripture to Eastern religions such as Buddhism, Hinduism, the Vedas, and Zoroastrianism. It follows the Renaissance notion of prisca theologia, in that all these religions purportedly descend from a common source; the ancient "Wisdom-Religion". Another one of her books is *The Key to Theosophy* which was orginally published in 1889. This book expounds on the principles of theosophy in a readable question-and-answer format. It covers Theosophy and the Theosophical Society, Nature of the Human Being, Life After Death, Reincarnation, Kama-Loka and Devachan, the Human Mind, Practical Theosophy and the Mahatmas.

Colonel Henry Steel Olcott (1832–1907), one of the other co-founders of the *Theosophical Society* and was its first President, was an American military officer, journalist, and lawyer. Olcott was the first well known American to formally convert to Buddhism and is considered a Buddhist modernist due to his interpreting Buddhism through the views of a Westerner.

The third key figure in the establishment of the *Theosophical Society* was William Quan Judge (1851–1896), was born in Dublin, Ireland. When he was 13 years old, he and his family immigrated to the United States. He was a mystic, esotericist, and occultist. He was described as a vigorous, imaginative and idealistic young man, and was one of the seventeen people who first established the *Theosophical Society*. Like H.P. Blavatsky and Henry Steel Olcott, he stayed in the organization when others left. When Olcott and Blavatsky left the United States for India, Judge stayed behind to manage the Society's work, all the while working as a lawyer.

The *Theosophical Society* had a major influence on Buddhist modernism and Hindu reform movements, and helped to spread the modernized western version of these eastern religions in the west. Through the Society's teachings H. S. Olcott and Anagarika Dharmapala, (1864–1933) a Sri Lankan Buddhist revivalist and writer, with Blavatsky were instrumental in the Western transmission and revival of Theravada Buddhism. Theravada, the "Doctrine of the Elders" is the school of Buddhism that draws its scriptural inspiration from the Tipitaka, or Pali canon, which scholars generally agree contains the earliest surviving record of the Buddha's teachings. These three key founders hoped by establishing the *Theosophical Society* they would be able to promote the "study and elucidation of Occultism, the Cabala etc". After a few years Olcott and Blavatsky moved to India and established the International Headquarters at Adyar, in Madras (Chennai). They were also interested in studying Eastern religions, and these were included in the Society's agenda.

According to the Society their central philosophical tenets represented a doctrine of "The Intelligent Evolution of All Existence". This "Evolution" would occur on a Cosmic Scale, incorporating both the physical and non-physical aspects of the known and unknown Universe. It would affect all of its constituent parts regardless of apparent size or importance. The theory was originally promulgated in the *Secret Doctrine*, the 1888 magnum opus of Helena Blavatsky. According to this view presented by Blavatsky, "Humanity's evolution on Earth and beyond is part of the overall Cosmic evolution". It is overseen by a hidden Spiritual Hierarchy, the so-called Masters of the Ancient Wisdom, whose upper echelons consist of advanced spiritual beings. According to Blavastsky their Society was the current attempt by this hidden Hierachy to help guide humanity to evolve their Intelligent Cosmic Evolutionary scheme. This could only be done by having a formalized group. At this time of human evolution, humanity is offered the *Theosophical Society* as the group to aid in this human development. The control of the Society was by Blavatsky but held ultimately under the inspiration of a number of Mahatmas, or Adepts, who were members of the Hierarchy. Mahatma is Sanskrit for "Great Soul" or in Christian terms a saint such as Mohandas Karamchand Gandhi (1869–1948), Lalon Shah Lalon, a Bengali, who also known by the name of Lalon Sain, Lalon Shah, or Lalon Fakir (1774–1890). He was a Bengali Baul saint, mystic, songwriter, social reformer and thinker. Another was Jyotirao Govindrao Phule (1827–1890), also known as Mahatma Jyotibao Phule (1827–1890) was great activist, thinker, social reformer, writer, philosopher, theologist, scholar, editor and revolutionary from Maharashtra, India in the nineteenth century.

Blavatsky, was known from her writing to be a Renaissance Christian kabbalist. They were kabbalists who formulated their conception of the Kabbalah in a way accepted and further developed by many modern scholars of the Kabbalah: "*The Kabbalist is a student of "secret science", one who interprets the hidden meaning of the Scriptures with the help of the symbolical Kabbalah, and explains the real one of these meanings.*" (*Isis Unveiled*). Blavatsky did not consider herself a follower of the Christian Kabbalah (Cabalah) but she used it as key to symbolic understanding of esoteric concepts. Blavatsky differentiated between the Kabbalah as promulgated in the works of the Rosicrucian or Hermetic Kabbalah, and the Jewish and the Oriental Kabbalah. "*The Rosicrucian Cabala is but an epitome of the Jewish and the Oriental ones combined—the latter being the most secret of all.*"

After Helena Blavatsky's death in 1891, the group seemed to function harmoniously until Judge was accused by Olcott and Theosophist Annie Besant of forging letters from the Mahatmas. Judge ended his association with Olcott and Besant in 1895 and took most of the Society's American Section with him. The original organization led by Olcott and Besant remains today based in India and is known as the *Theosophical Society — Adyar*. The group led by Judge further splintered into a faction led by Katherine Augusta Westcott Tingley (1847–1929) who was a social worker and prominent Theosophist, and another associated with Judge's secretary Ernest Temple Hargrove (birth date is unkown-1971). While Hargrove's faction no longer survives, the faction led by Tingley is today known as the *Theosophical Society* with the clarifying statement, "International Headquarters, Pasadena, California". A third organization, the *United Lodge of Theosophists* or *ULT*, split off from the latter organization in 1909.

Another leading Theosophical member was Alice Ann Bailey (1880–1949) who was a writer and theosophist in occult teachings, "esoteric" psychology and healing, astrology and other philosophic and religious themes. Bailey was born as Alice LaTrobe Bateman. Bailey became active in the *Theosophical Society* and the work of Helena Petrovna Blavatsky in 1917. According to the Society Bailey became a member of the Esoteric Section of the society in 1918. She quickly rose to a position of influence in the American Section of the Adyar society, moving to its headquarters at Krotona Institute of Theosophy in Hollywood. She became editor of its magazine, *The Messenger*, and member of the committee responsible for Krotona Institute of America which is one of three important Theosophical "colonies" in the U.S. started during the early part of the 20th century. Originally built in Hollywood during 1912, the colony was eventually relocated to Ojai, California in 1926, where it operates today.

Following some of Bailey's writings the following Degrees/Initiations make up the work of the Society.

Initiation Zero

The vast majority of ordinary humanity lies on the probationary path (below the first initiation).

First Initiation ("birth" to the spiritual life)

According to Alice A. Bailey, at the first initiation one gains full control of the physical body. There are supposedly 800,000 members at this level.

Second initiation ("baptism")
Alice A. Bailey states that at the second initiation, one gains full control of the astral body.
A total of 240,000 members can potentially reach the Second initiation.

Third Initiation ("the transfiguration")
An individual who is at the level of the third initiation has acquired fully developed clairvoyance and clairaudience; there are between 2,000 and 3,000 members.

Fourth Initiation ("the crucifixion")
An individual reaching the fourth initiation is known as the perfected one, or an Arhat (Pali) or a Paramahamsa (Sanskrit). At this level, it is believed in Buddhism, one has the ability to remember all of one's past lives, and one also has various minor siddhis capable of affecting one's immediate environment. Symbolically the fourth initiation is denoted as the crucifixion initiation. An Arhat is supposed to be one who does not need to be incarnated again to develop spirituall.
Only 450 members have reached this level.

The seven choices before the "Perfect Human".
Having reached the threshold of the fifth initiation, a soul does not necessarily have to enter Earth's spiritual hierarchy proper as one of the "'Masters of the Ancient Wisdom". One has seven paths forward to higher levels that they can choose to go forward on, only one of which is to become a "Master of the Ancient Wisdom". These seven choices, called in Theosophical literature 'the seven choices before the perfect human' are:

1. "Remain with humanity as on official of the Hierarchy", i.e., become one of the Masters of the Ancient Wisdom.
2. "Remain with humanity as a Nirmanakaya", i.e., become a bodhisattva.
3. "Join the Devas".
4. "Join the Staff Corps of the Solar Logos", i.e., join the Masters living in etheric cities inside the Sun who supervise the activities of the Solar Angels that direct the process of evolution of the life waves (process of reincarnation) of the beings on all the planets of the

solar system (all of whom live except those on Earth live on the etheric planes of their planets).

5. "Prepare the work of the next Chain", i.e. join that subsection of the Staff Corps of the Solar Logos who are the solar planners, who plan the future development of planetary civilizations in this solar system.

6. & 7. "Enter Nirvana", i.e., become a Pratyekabuddha

Fifth Initiation ("the resurrection")

The fifth initiation, called the resurrection, comprises the first rung of beings designated in Theosophy as Masters of the Ancient Wisdom and in the Ascended Master Teachings as Ascended masters. Siddhis at this level include the ability to teleport and bilocate moderate distances and levitate within a localized area.

C. W. Leadbeaterharles Webster Leadbeater (1854–1934) was an influential member of the *Theosophical Society*, and co-initiator with J. I. Wedgwood of the *Liberal Catholic Church*, Alice Bailey and Benjamin Creme, (born 1922) a Scottish artist, author and esoteritis. C. W. Leadbeater state there are a total of 43 beings at this level of initiation; this figure is arrived at because all three have stated there are a total of 60 Masters in all—subtracting from the 60 the 17 Masters at level six and above identified by C. W. Leadbeater, leaves a total of 43 Masters of the Ancient Wisdom at the fifth level of initiation. Of these 43 Masters, a total of 12 have been identified by name, one by C. W. Leadbeater, nine by Alice Bailey, and two by Benjamin Creme. C. W. Leadbeater was named a Master and went by the title of "Master Jupiter" who lives in India. As a Master he was involved with overseeing the people, government, and development of India. Alice A. Bailey title was Master P., who is said to have helped St. Germain bring about the Age of Aquarius in the Americas, and two different English Masters. In addition to these three, she also identified the three Lords of Liberation — (they were called, Lord of Liberation #1, Lord of Liberation #2, and Lord of Liberation #3). According to Bailey, the three Lords of Liberation formulated the slogan Liberty, Equality, Fraternity. Finally, she also identified the three Lords of Karma (again giving them the titles of Lord of Karma #1, Lord of Karma #2, and Lord of Karma #3). These three beings are said to live in Shamballah and help Sanat Kumara decide where and when souls are going to incarnate in their next life. Benjamin Creme identified two additional Masters who were not previously identified Masters at this level in 2001—a Master in Moscow and a Master in Tokyo — but did not give their personal names.

Of the Forty-three potential Masters, twelve have been revealed leaving 31 Masters of the Ancient Wisdom that still have not been unidentified by name.

Sixth Initiation ("the ascension" or "masterhood")

The Chohans (Lords) of the Seven Rays — Morya (1st Ray), Master Koot Hoomi (2nd Ray), Paul the Venetian (3rd Ray), Serapis Bey (4th Ray), Master Hilarion (5th Ray), Master Jesus (6th Ray), and the Master Rakoczi (7th Ray) — are seven of the beings at the level of the sixth initiation, while their coordinator and communications director Djwal Khul is another, making a total of eight at this level.

All of these Masters are recognized by both traditional Theosophists and those adherent to the Ascended Master Teachings. In the Ascended Master Teachings, Master Rakoczi is referred to as St. Germain. Siddhis at this level include the ability to teleport, bilocate, or levitate to any place on Earth.

Seventh Initiation ("bodhisattva", "avatar", or "Christhood")

The seventh initiation is known as the initiation of the Bodhisattva (Buddhism) or the Avatar (Hinduism). The Maitreya or World Teacher (known as Krishna by Hindus, the Christ by Christians, Maitreya by Buddhists, Messiah by the Jews, the Iman Mahdi by Muslims, and the Peshotan by the Zoroastrians) is at this level. At this level also are said to be the Chakshusha Manu, the Vaivasvatu Manu and the Maha Chohan, thus making a total of four beings at this level.

In the Ascended Master Teachings, the Chakshusha Manu is referred to as Lord Himalaya.

Eighth Initiation ("Buddhahood")

Level eight is the level of the Buddha. At this level also, according to C.W. Leadbeater, are The Three Pratyeka Buddhas (the task of these three Buddhas is to focus the Seven Rays from Sanat Kumara through Djwal Khul to the chohans of the Seven Rays). Unlike Buddha, the three Pratyeka Buddhas do not interact with the human race except for fulfilling their function of focusing the seven rays.

There are four beings at this level, according to traditional Theosophy.

Ninth Initiation ("godhood")

Level nine is referred to as the "Lord of the World": Sanat Kumara — "The Eternal Youth" and "The Ancient of Days", the Nordic alien that is believed by Theosophists to be the "Lord of the World", that is the governing deity of Earth. The Society adds that the Sanat Kumara has a "twin flame" referred to as his celestial wife, named Lady Master Venus who he brought with him from Venus, as well as a daughter named Lady Master Meta born to them on Venus who they brought with them to Earth, both of them presumably also functioning at the ninth level of initiation.

Tenth Initiation ("planetary logos")

The tenth initiation is considered to symbolize perfection and is used to describe the Planetary Logos, also called the Spirit of the Earth, and specifically denoted as the Planetary Logos of Earth. In order to reach the status of a Planetary Logos, the being would have had to have been from a different solar system before it incarnated inside our planet at the time of the creation of the world. According to C.W. Leadbeater, the "Planetary Logos" is functioning at the tenth level of initiation and Sanat Kumara, in continuous telepathic rapport with the Planetary Logos, functions as its spokes-deity.

Levels of initiation beyond the tenth level

In the theosophical teachings of Alice Bailey, there is a powerful being living inside the sun serving as the Solar Logos called the Avatar of Synthesis. Its job is to transmit the seven rays from the heart of the sun through the seven spirits before the 'solar throne' to all the life waves of the solar system.

The Solar Logos itself must be at least several levels beyond the 17th level. The Solar Logos, the Sun God in Theosophy, is personified as the cosmic beings Helios and his twin flame (celestial wife) Vesta, the "God and Goddess of this solar system", in the Ascended Master Teachings.

Perhaps several dozen or a couple of hundred levels above the Solar Logos would be the Galactic Logos. In the Ascended Master Teachings, the Galactic Logos is personified as the cosmic being Averran.

These descriptions are sourced from numerous publications discussing the philosophy of Theosophy.

THE UNITED LODGE OF THEOSOPHISTS (ULT)

The United Lodge of Theosophists was founded in 1909 by a *Theosophical Society* member, Robert Crosbie (1849–1919). He was a Canadian who moved to Lomaland, Point Loma, California in 1902, where he helped in building a theosophical community. In 1908, he published a letter to all open-minded Theosophists about his thoughts on the *Theosophical Society*. In February 1909, he founded the *ULT* in Los Angeles. At the time the organization had no presidents or hierarchical structures. Crosbie's goal was to bring the group back to the orginal teaching of Blavatsky and William Q. Judge and the Founders of the Movement. He contended that over the years there had been numerous changes or "adaptations" made that altered the teachings of the society, thus obscuring the true teaching on which the Society was based.

With Crosbie's leadership, the *United Lodge of Theosophists* re-established its overall purpose to disseminate the Fundamental Principles of the Philosophy of Theosophy. To that end, the texts regarded as "straight line Theosophical Literature" by the ULT are generally those which are reproduced from the original plates, or are photographic reproductions of original documents. This literature is currently made available through The Theosophy Company, which is a non-profit publishing entity for the United Lodge of Theosophists. After Crosbie's death, the movement gained momentum under the leadership of B.P. Wadia (1881–1958). Bahman Pestonji Wadia or Bomanji Pestonji Wadia was an Indian theosophist and labour activist. He was first a member of the TS Adyar, which was the International Headquaters Olcott and Blavatsky established at Adyar, in Madras India. He later joined the *United Lodge of Theosophists*.

According to the Society it is not the goal of the *United Lodge of Theosophists* to attract more people to their society so they might call themselves "Theosophists", rather that the effects of the Movement will serve to "leaven the Race mind". They believe this effect lies in germ form deep within its cause. "Independent Devotion to the Cause of Theosophy" is the Policy of the *ULT*.

ANCIENT MYSTICAL ORDER ROSAE CRUCIS (AMORC)

AMORC was established as the American branch of the *Antiquus Arcanae Ordinis Rosae Rubae Aureae Crucis* in 1915 by Harvey Spencer Lewis (1883–1939). Others say Lewis established the Order officially in Florida in 1925. In 1908 Lewis met a Mrs. May Barkes-Stacey (1846–1918), who claimed to be a Rosicrucian who had been introduced to the Rosicrucian Order in Europe. Lewis was then brought before this same Rosicrucian Order where he received the approval to form a new Order by the *Supreme Council of the Rosicrucian Order*. This was only done after being 'tried, tested and finally initiated' into the Order in 1909 in Toulouse, France. He was given the mission to reestablish Rosicrucian ideas back in America after the Order had been dissolved during the early part of the seventeenth century. Lewis, as the first Imperator, set about writing what would become the basis of the teaching of the Order. These teachings comprised their lessons on mysticism.

Ancient Mystical Order Rosae Crucis' teachings have been expanded by incorporating the ideas of other major philosophers such as Pythagoras. Pythagoras believed in metempsychosis and in transmigration, the belief in the reincarnation of the soul. Another philosopher is Thales of Miletus (624–546 B.C.E.) who has been described as one the Seven Sages of Greece, and is known for being one of the first philosophers to try to explain the natural phenomena of the world without reference to mythology of folklore. *AMORC* also draws from the philosopher Solon (638–558 B.C.E.), who was remembered as an Athenian statesman, lawmaker and poet who attempted to provide legislation that would stop or slow down the political, economic and moral decline of ancient Athens. Heraclitus of Ephesus; (535–475 B.C.E.) works are also included. He was famous for insisting on the idea that the universe is in an ever-present state of change. He is also credited for saying "No man ever steps in the same river twice". Heraclitus also believed in the unity of opposites. And finally, Democritus (460–370 B.C.E') who is called the "father of modern science". This is because of his formulation of an atomic theory for the universe.

AMORC's teachings are divided in Degrees which are grouped in categories with titles such as Postulant, Neophyte and Initiate. The Degrees cover such topics as physical, mental, psychic and spiritual existences. During the course of studies, the student is taught healing techniques, alchemy, meditation, sacred architecture, symbolism and the "mystical state of consciousness relating to the experience of unity with the Divine".

The following is a list of their Introductory Lessons and Degrees:

Illusory Nature of Time and Space
Human Consciousness and Cosmic Consciousness
Rosicrucian Technique of Meditation
Development of the Intuition
Human Aura
Telepathy
Metaphysical Healing
Mystical Sounds
Spiritual Alchemy

After passing through these introductory degrees the candidate enters into a series of Atriums. They are:

First Atrium:
Structure and Composition of Matter
Power of Thought
The Creative Power of Visualization
Mental Projection and Telepathy
Law of the Triangle

Second Atrium:
Origin of Diseases
Influence of Thoughts on Health
Mystical Art of Breathing
Rosicrucian Healing Treatments
Perception of the Aura
Awakening of the Psychic Consciousness
Mystical Sounds

Third Atrium:
The Great Religious Movements
The Nature of Soul
Purpose of our Spiritual Evolution
Reincarnation and Karma

Good and Evil and Free Will
Intuition, Inspiration, and Illumination

After passing through these atriums the student is allowed to progress through the nine "Temple Degrees". They are as follows:

First Temple Degree:
Structure of Matter
Positive and Negative as Vibratory Polarities
Rosicrucian Definitions of Electricity, Magnetism, and Electromagnetism
Rosicrucian Classification of Elements
Material Alchemy

Second Temple Degree:
Cosmic Consciousness
Our Objective and Subjective Consciousness
Mental and Sensory Illusions
Imagination and Memory
Physical, Psychic, and Spiritual Influence of the Subconscious
Memory and Reasoning of the Subconscious
Psychology and Mysticism

Third Temple Degree:
Cosmic Purpose of Life
Rosicrucian Definitions of Living and Non-living Matter
Incarnation of the Soul
Transition of the Soul
Initiatic Aspects of Death

Fourth Temple Degree:
Vital Life Force and the Living Soul
Cycles of Life and Constant States of Flux
Time, Space, Infinity and Eternity
Symbols—Natural, Artificial, and Mystical
Sacred Architecture

Fifth Temple Degree:

The Fifth Temple Degree includes the works of the Great Philosophers such as: Thales, Solon, Pythagoras, Heraclitus, Democritus, Empedocles, Socrates, Plato and Aristotle.

Sixth Temple Degree:

Spiritual Dimension of Food
Breathing and Respiratory Health
Cell Consciousness and Cellular Health
Rosicrucian Therapy and Self-healing
Personal Treatment to Restore your Psychic Equilibrium
Physical and Mental Prevention of Disease
Emotional and Spiritual Prevention of Disease

Seventh Temple Degree:

The Psychic Body and Psychic Centers
Psychic Perception and Psychic Consciousness
How to Accomplish Psychic Projection
Nature and Symbolism of Dreams
The Physical, Psychic, and Spiritual Auras
Mystical Power of Vowel Sounds and Mantras

Eighth Temple Degree:

Universal Soul and the Human Soul
Divine Consciousness and Self Consciousness
Spiritual Evolution of Humans
Mastery of Karma
Reincarnation of the Soul
Memory of Past Incarnations
The Mystery of Birth and Death
Help to the Dying, Before and After Death

Ninth Temple Degree:

Macrocosm and Microcosm
The Four Principles: Earth, Water, Air and Fire
Symbolism of the Cross, Triangle, Square, Circle, and Rose-Cross
Mental Alchemy

Telepathy, Telekinesis, Vibroturgy, and Radiesthesia
Cosmic Protection, Mystical Regeneration
Attunement with Cosmic Consciousness

The current national headquarters and Egyptian Museum for *AMORC* is in San Jose, California. *Ancient Mystical Order Rosae Crucis* also controls and runs the *"Traditional Martinist Order"* (TMO) which was founded by Lewis and Augustin Chaboseau (1868–1946), and Papus. Papus was the pseudonym used by Gérard Anaclet Vincent Encausse (1865–1916), a Spanish born French physician, hypnotist, and popularizer of occultism, who founded the modern Martinist Order in 1888. The only way an aspirant can enter the *Martinist Order* is through being an active member of *AMORC*. The Imperator of *AMORC* is also the head of *TMO*. *Ancient Mystical Order Rosae Crucis* has an Inner Order that is highly restrictive in its membership and is called the *Milita Crucifera Evangella* (MCE).

Over the years there have been many schisms in *Ancient Mystical Order Rosae Crucis* which resulted in several related organizations being formed including the *Ancient Rosae Crucis* (ARC), *Order of the Militia Crucifera Evangelica (O.M.C.E.)* and the *ConFraternity Rosae +Crucis* (CR+C).

Ancient Rosae Crucis (ARC)

Ancient Rosae Crucis (ARC) was founded by several individuals who in 1990 left *Ancient Mystical Order Rosae Crucis* because of the so-called "Stewart-affair". They originally asked Gary Lee Stewart (1953–) to become their Imperator. This did not occur due to internal disagreement over finances resulting in Stewart being barred from the organization. *ARC* now functions under the leadership of its founders Paul Walden and Ashley McFadden (the author/editor of the "Rosicrucian Primer"). Around 1997 McFadden announced herself as Imperator, drawing on the authority from Walden, which he himself claims has his line of authority as the Imperator succession from Stewart. *ARC* is only located in the USA, but similar groups exist in other countries as well. Their teachings are based on the *AMORC* monographies from the fifties, and are hence older than those currently used by *AMORC*. *Ancient Rosae Crucis* builds on the tradition of *Ancient Mystical Order Rosae Crucis,* such as it was practiced during the time of Harvey and Ralph Lewis.

Order of the Militia Crucifera Evangelica (O.M.C.E.)

The *O.M.C.E* was first organized on July 16, 1990. According to their history they were established as a perpetuation of the Tradition of the original *Order of the Militia Crucifera Evangelica* which was reorganized at the *Cruce Signatorum Conventus* held on July 27, 1586 in Luneberg, Germany. That Convention was chronicled by Simon Studion (1543–1605) in his work *Naometria,* published in 1604. Simon was a German teacher of Latin, poet, historian, archaeologist, and author of apocryphal literature. In his book *Naometria* he stated the Papacy was corrupt and needed to fall which he prophesied in his book.

The purpose of the *Order of the Militia Crucifera Evangelica* at that time was to activate the surviving remnants of the Order of the Temple in Jerusalem, more popularly known as the Knights Templar, as well the *Ancient Rosae Crucis*. It was their purpose to actualize the mystical and spiritual doctrinal teachings and practices of both Orders to present to a world on the brink of religious crisis.

They describe their "outer purpose" is to protect the religious and mystical significance of the Cross and to prevent its use as an instrument of war. They were directed to peacefully promote religious freedom, freedom of thought, and freedom of inquiry throughout the societies of the world.

Their "inner purpose" as to establish an exoteric body of Servants of Light to direct and guide humanity towards mystical enlightenment. This "inner purpose", according to *O.M.C.E.* manifested itself in the Seventeenth Century establishment of Rosicruciansim. The *Order of the Militia Crucifera Evangelica* has two main functions: Self Development and Service to Humanity. Membership in the *O.M.C.E.* is obtained by interview, selection and invitation. All sincere seekers and workers, who are prepared to work in harmony with the existing membership and to adhere to the rules of the Order, are eligible to apply. Members are expected to be guided by their conscience in all matters including financing the Order. There are no set dues, as they rely on their members' contributions and fund raisers.

ConFraternity Rosae + Crucis (CR+C)

Another Order emerged as the result of Stewart expulsion from *Ancient Mystical Order Rosae Crucis*. It is called *ConFraternity Rosae + Crucis* (CR+C) and is headed by the former *AMORC* Imperator Gary Lee Stewart

(1953–). They work with original *Ancient Mystical Order Rosae Crucis* lessons and rituals, as well as some supplementary materials. One of these documents is *The Nodin Manuscript*. There is no concise history as to when or where *The Nodin Manuscript* appeared. According to *AMORC* in the fourth degree the student knows the *Manuscript Nodin*, supposedly the angular stone of the knowledge rosacruz of *Ancient Mystical Order Rosae Crucis*. There are no historical facts as to what is in the manuscript. The Hermetic Philosophica Library (BPH) of Amsterdam, founded on 1957 by Joseph R. Ritman considers the book of Nodin an apocryphal work, written up in language of principles of the twentieth Century. According to Gary Stewart he inherited the manuscript when he succeeded to Ralph Maxwell Lewis as Imperator of *AMORC*. The manuscript is passed down from one Imperator to the next to be used for the instructions of its *esoteric Order.*

The manuscript is divided into two parts. The first is revealed to the aspirant in the Fourth Degree while the second section as stated is reserved for Imperators only.

ConFraternity Rosae + Crucis is connected to and partly controlled by the *Ordo Militia Crucifera Evangelica* (OMCE), which also is governed by Stewart.

BUILDERS OF THE ADYTUM (BOTA)

In 1922 Paul Foster Case (1884–1954), founded the *Builders of the Adytum* after a disagreement with Moina Mathers who was the head of the *Hermetic Order of the Golden Dawn*. Case had advanced very quickly in the *Order of the Golden Dawn* and was part of the senior leadership until Moina Mathers (1865–1928), widow of MacGregor Mathers, one of the Order's founders, wrote Case about some of Case's teachings. According to the records Case was discussing the topic of sex magic to Golden Dawn members. At the time sex magic had no official place in the Order's curriculum.

According to histories about him, Paul was a talented musician, Freemason, and occultist. In his earlier life he embarked on a successful career as a violinist, and orchestra conductor. During his travels in 1900, as a musician playing at charity performance he met the occultist Claude Bragdon (1866–1946) a writer and stage designer. Bragdon asked Case what his ideas were of the origin of playing cards. After some contemplation and research Case discovered the link of today's playing cards to the tarot. This became a lifelong study for Paul which lead to the creation of the *BOTA*

Tarot deck which Case claims was the "corrected" version of the Rider-Waite deck. In 1916 Case published a groundbreaking series of articles on the Tarot Keys, titled The Secret Doctrine of the Tarot, in the popular occult magazine *The Word*.

In 1918, Case met Michael James Whitty (who died in 1920), who was the editor of the magazine Azoth. Whitty was also serving as the Cancellarius (Treasurer/Office Manager) for the Thoth-Hermes Lodge of the Alpha et Omega. This is the same lodge formed by S. L. MacGregor Mathers' in 1906 after the demise of the original Hermetic Order of the Golden Dawn in 1903. Whitty invited Case to join Thoth-Hermes, which was the direct American lodge under the Alpha et Omega mother lodge in Paris. Case did and quickly moved up through the initiations in the Rosicrucian Grades. He described these Grades in his book True and Invisible Rosicrucian Order. Case soon became the Sub-Praemostrator or Assistant Chief Instructor at the Thoth-Hermes lodge.

Between 1919 and 1920, Case and Michael Whitty collaborated in the development of the text which would later be published as The Book of Tokens. This book was written as a received text, in that the inspiration and contents came through meditation, automatic writing, or some other means. Paul later claimed that a Master R. was the source. On May 16, 1920 Case was initiated into *Alpha et Omega's* Second Order. Three weeks later, according to the Hermetic Order of the Golden Dawn's bio-page on Case, he was named Third Adept.

Sometime between 1909 and 1910 Case met a Dr. Fludd, a prominent Chicago physician. According to the young Case the Doctor hailed him by surname and claimed to have a message from a "Master of Wisdom". This Master offered him a choice of being a successful musician or dedicating himself to the "service of humanity". From that time forward Case began his study and formulated his lessons on the Qabalah and the study of the tarot which lead to the core curriculum of the *Builders of the Adytum*.

In the summer of 1921, Case claimed to have received a phone call from "The Master Rococzy" (Rakoczy, Rákóczy or Rákóczi), a mysterious personality for which actual records are scarce. Case later allegedly he met The Master R in person at the Hotel Roosevelt Hotel in NYC. According to esoteric lore "Master R" is one of the members of the Karmic Board for the planet Earth who represented the "First Ray". He is also known as the Ascended Master Saint Germain aka Comte of Saint Germain who was reported to be a member and Ascended Master of the *Great White Brotherhood.*

The *Adytum News* described this meeting as occurring in the following way: "One day the phone rang, and much to his surprise the same voice which had been inwardly instructing him in his researches for many years spoke to him on the phone. It was the Master R who had come personally to New York for the purpose of preparing Paul Case to begin the next incarnation of the Qabalistic Way of Return. ... After three weeks of personal instruction with the Master R, Builders of the Adytum was formed."

In 1922 Case left the *Alpha et Omega* to form his own Mystery School. In 1923 he formed *The School of Ageless Wisdom* probably in Boston. In a couple years after the school's founding he abandoned his career as a musician and moved to Los Angeles to establish a second school, which he called the *Builders of the Adytum.* Here he organized a curriculum of correspondence course covering the Western Mystery Tradition, occult tarot, Qabalah and Alchemy.

In 1944 Ann Davies (1912–1975) began classes with her sister in Case's school. Prior to this time Davis held many different the views of life from that of an ardent atheist, to an agnostic, and even as a skeptic, but claimed she was always a devotee of Hindu philosophy and practiced as a Buddhist. After attending class and talking with Case she changed her studies to the Holy Qabalah and the Sacred Tarot seeing them as her "Path of Return". That year she moved into the Case's house with her young daughter Bonnie where she helped prepare meals and mimeograph lessons. After Cases' death she became Prolocutor General until her own death in 1975. During her time with *BOTA* she expanded the curriculum of the school by amplifying and reworking Case's "Esoteric Astrology" and by authoring the courses on "Developing SuperSensory Powers," "Sexual Polarity," "Meditational Ascent of the Tree of Livingness," and "Qabalistic Doctrines of Rebirth."

Builders of the Adytum is organized using several layers. The *Builders of the Adytum* first layer is the indiviual lessons that are sent to their students. At the end of each set of lessons there is a written test that is sent in and commented on by a member at their headquarters. The first layer of group work is called a "Study Group". These "Study Groups" are located generally wherever there enough 'active' members are that wish to form one, with

Builders of the Adytum headquarers approval. These Study Groups are open to the public and allow any interested person to attend. The Study Groups are lead by *BOTA* members and discussions are focused on the initial teaching of *Builders of the Adytum.*

The next layer is what is called a "Pronaos" which is the first phase of group ritual work. The Pronaos is only open to active members of the *Builders of the Adytum.* The Pronaos ritualistic work occurs only after initiation which includes an oath of secrecy. There are three Grades or Degree in the Pronaos. The six officers perform the initiations as well as conduct the Pronaos in a group healing ritual. This healing ritual is not directed specifically at any member but as a channel for the higher spirits to send their energy down and out to the greater world.

The Pronaoians are referred to as members of the *Builders of the Adytum* Outer Order. There is a secret Inner or Second Order that is only by invitation and is called a "Chapter". The Second Order is composed of ten Degrees and is supervised by three Chiefs, and there are ten levels or Degrees that are obtained only after test and initiation. The work of this Inner or Second Order again is on universal healing. The Third Order is composed of three Great Adepts or Chiefs and is said to be part of the "Invisible Order". In Paul Case's book *The True and Invisible Rosicrucian Order* he lists the following Grades:

Grade of Zelator	1=10
Grade of Theoricus	2=9
Grade of Practicus	3=8
Grade of Philosophus	4=7
Grade of Lesser Adept	5=6
Grade of Greater Adept	6=5
Grade of Exempt Adept	7=4
Grade of Magister Templi	8=3
Grade of Magus	9=2
Grade of Ipsissimus	10=1

The headquarters for the *Builders of the Adytum* is in Los Angles, California.

SOCIETY OF THE INNER LIGHT OR THE FRATUERNITY OF THE INNER LIGHT

In 1922, after a falling out with Moina Mathers (1865–1928). She was an artist, occultist and the wife of Samuel Liddell MacGregor Mathers. Later Mathers organized a second group called the *Rosicrucian Order of the Alpha et Omega* which Moina took assumed the position of head of the Order upon her husband's death in 1918. Moina worked with Dion Fortune until they had a falling out. Dion Fortune, who was born Violet Mary Firth (1890–1946), was a prominent British occultist, author, psychologist, teacher, artist, and mystic. She was also a prolific writer of the supernatural and the occult in both novels and non-fiction works. As a psychologist, she approached magic and hermetic concepts from the perspectives of Jung and Freud.

Dion left *Alpha and Omega* in 1922, with Moina's consent. Dion claimed she was coming under magical attack from Moina. Dion Fortune and her husband, Thomas Penry Evans (1892–1959) also known as "Merlin" or "Merl", who is said to have brought many pagan ideas with him, formed the *Fraternity of the Inner Light*. When she left, Fortune brought many of the members of *Alpha et Omega* with her. Fortune later renamed her new group "*The Society of the Inner Light*".

With the start of the Second World War, Dion and her group lost several important members. In 1932, she had managed to interest Christine Hartley, better known as Christine Campbell Thomson (1897–1985), a British horror fiction author, to join Dion's magical movement. Soon after Christine's admittance into the Society, Dion quickly noted that her husband Thomas was developing a keen interest in Christine. Dion tried to nullify this interest by pairing Christine with Colonel Charles Richard Foster Seymour (1880–1943). Despite Dion's attempts to separate Christine from her husband, Thomas Penry Evans left Dion Fortune and the Society in 1939. Seymour and Christine became the Society's most brilliant magicians: their "dance of the Gods" remains one of the most impressive examples of evocatory magic in the twentieth century.

According to the *The Society of the Inner Light,* their philosphy is in keeping with Qabalistic teaching. The Society considers that the whole human being consists of three basic elements:

1. The Incarnationary Personality which is the normal human personality that we develop from birth and which is formed and influenced

by a variety of factors; hereditary, environmental, cultural, educational and so on.

2. The Evolutionary Personality (sometimes also known as the Soul, Individuality, or Higher Self) which encompasses the essence of experience of previous lives. Its influence may well be the positive demonstration of unique abilities at one or many levels, the downside of which may be the need for lessons in life yet to be learned.

3. The Divine Spark or Spirit which emanates both from the Incarnationary and Evolutionary Personalities, which should be its servants. Needless to say, direct awareness of this state may not be achieved immediately and the reality of its existence may seem imperceptible, even though our very existence depends upon it. Its full expression would be likely to produce sanctity or genius, and at the present stage of the world it's considered to be a somewhat rare condition.

The Society of the Inner Light's training center is based in London, England, and is geared towards those aspirants who reside in England and the European Union. Those aspirants who reside outside of this area do have access via correspondence as their form of study. Once the student is admitted they must pass through Three Degrees of the so-called "Lesser Mysteries" which are broadly based upon traditional Masonic symbolism. The Society states these Degrees are designed to develop and strengthen character, to give experience of ceremonial working, and to develop the visionary powers of the mind as a means towards attaining higher consciousness. With the Degree work there is additional academic course work which continues along with a meditation discipline and regular practical group working which takes place once a month.

Those who successfully pass through the Lesser Mysteries may then move on to the "Greater Mysteries", which are concerned with developing consciousness at the level of the Evolutionary Personality and ultimately the Spirit. This is the level of the adept as a natural progression from that of the Lesser Mystery Initiate. Here specialized work may be undertaken under the direction of the inner plane hierarchy. The *Society of the Inner Light's* prime purpose is to maintain and expand the bridge that exists between outer life in the world and spiritual forces upon the inner planes.

KABBALISTIC ORDER OF THE ROSE-CROSS A.K.A ORDRE KABBALISTIQUE DE LA ROSE-CROIX

Around 1850, the Viscount Louis Charles Edouard de Lapasse (1792–1867), a physician and the Chief of the *Order of Rose Cross* was one of the active esotericist in Toulouse, France region. Lapasse' group was the focal Order for the Rose Cross Tradition in this section of France. The Rose Cross Tradition emphasized the mystical and symbolic German tradition and several Mediterranean Hermetic traditions. In particular, the Hermetic heritage of the school of the Rose Cross Tradition was more focused on alchemy, astrology and Theurgic rituals.

In 1884 Stanislas de Guaita (1861–1897), a French poet, an expert on esotericism and a mystic, met with Joséphin-Péladan (1858–1918), a French novelist and Martinist, both active members of the *Rose Cross Order*. During their discussions on the current state of the Rosicrucian Order they decided to rebuild the Rosicrucian Brotherhood. In 1888, de Guaita founded the *Cabalistic (Kabbalistic) Order of the Rosicrucian*. According to de Guaita, he had received the transmission of the traditional teaching of the Hermetic sages as well as the initiatory rituals of the *Rose-Cross Order* and installed them in his new *Cabalistic (Kabbalistic) Order of the Rosicrucian*. He felt he was charged to form a new Order, utilizing the authentic *Rose-Cross* initiation he had been given. He combined it with a theoretical education centered on the traditional sciences, such as the works of the classical authors, as well as a precise, serious and rigorous ritual progression and practice. In 1888 Stanislas de Guaita, then 27 years old, founded "*The Kabbalistic (Qabalistic) Order of the Rose-Cross*" or in French "*Ordre Kabbalistique de la Rose-Croix.*" The date of its founding was not randomly selected. According to the Order, the *Fraternity of the Rose-Cross* follows a cyclic pattern of 111 years of activity and 111 years of quiescence.

There is very little know of the Order's inner workings or rituals due to the member's complete secrecy. The Order is governed by the Invisible College of six brothers and the Grand Patriarch Rose-Cross who directs that group. In respect to their tradition of a 111-year cycle of birth and rebirth, the inner Order time to be reactivated occurred 1999. In 2006, after the prescribed initial period of seven years the hermetic, Rose Cross and Martinist power was once again given to the "*Qabalistic Order of the Rose Cross*" known in France as the *Ordre Kabbalistique de la Rose-Croix*.

THE ORDER OF THE HERMETIC
GOLD AND ROSE + CROSS

As the one of the founding members of the *Ordre Kabbalistique de la Rose-Croix*, Joséphin-Péladan with de Guaita recruited o Gérard Anaclet Vincent Encausse (1865–1916). Gérard, who is often known by his esoteric pseudonym of Papus, was a Spanish born French physician, hypnotist, and popularizer of occultism. Papus is credited for founding the modern Martinist Order. In November of 1890, Péladan split with de Guaita and Papus and the *Ordre Kabbalistique de la Rose-Croix* over disagreements about strategy and doctrines. Péladan soon created his own Order called the *"Rose+Croix Catholique"*, which Péladan almost immediately changed to *"Order of Rose+Croix of the Temple and Graal"*. In June of 1890 Péladan left the *Martinist Order* and created a "quasi-Catholic" *Mystic Order of the Rose + Cross* which was tenets were based on Péladan's heavy Roman Catholic training. Péladan, as leader of the new Order, took the titles of "Imperator" and "Super Magician". Around this time Péladan recruited Emile Dantinne (1884–1969) who was a Belgian philosopher and esoterist. Dantinne later became the head of the Order and reorganized it to form the *Ordo Aureae and Rosae Crucis*. The traditional and authentic Latin name is: *Antiquus Arcanus Ordo Rosae Rubeae et Aureae Crucis* (AAORRAC), which translates to English as *"Ancient and Mystical Order of the Red Rose and the Golden Cross"*.

Dantinne was the leader, of several esoteric societies based in Belgium such as *"La Rose+Croix Universitaire"*and *"L'Ordre d'Hermès Tétramégiste"*. In 1934 he founded the *F.U.D.O.S.I.*, or *"Fédération Universelle Des Ordres et Sociétés Initiatiques"* (*Universal Federation of Initiatic Orders and Societies*). *F.U.D.O.S.I* was disbanded in 1951. By that time, he had adopted the esoteric name of Sâr Hieronymus.

The main Esoteric Order in the *F.U.D.O.S.I.* was the Ancient and Mystical Order Rosae Crucis also known as *A.M.O.R.C.,* to which Dantinne belonged since the days of his friendship with Grand Master Joséphin Péladan. Dantinne was never a member of AMORC; this is group that Harvey Spencer Lewis re-activated AMORC in the United States of America versus the European group known as Ancient and Mystical Order Rosae Crucis or *A.M.O.R.C.* Péladan was also not a member of the United States's AMORC. The latter was the founder and Grand Master of the *Ordre Rose+Croix*

Catholique. Dantinne was an enthusiastic disciple of Péladan and became the Imperator of the OR+CC when Péladan died in 1918. Dantinne changed the name of the Order to the *Ordre Rose+Croix Universelle.*

Course material for the Order covers the following subjects: Kabbalah, Rosicrucianism, Martinism, Alchemy, Magic and Theurgy. There appear to be three distinct divisions to the Order consisting of:

> Rose-Croix Universitaire which is composed of nine degrees
> Rose-Croix Universelle that is made up of nine degrees
> Rose-Croix Interioure which is the Inner Order and has four additional degrees

KABBALAH CENTRE INTERNATIONAL

The Kabbalah Centre was founded in the United States in 1965 as *The National Research Institute of Kabbalah* by two Rabbis. Philip Berg (1927–2013), an American Rabbi who was born as Feivel Gruberger and Rabbi Yehuda Ashlag (1885–1954) also known as Yehuda Leib Ha-Levi Ashlag. Leib was also known as the Baal Ha-Sulam (Hebrew: בַּעַל הַסּוּלָם, "Author of the Ladder") in reference to his magnum opus. They were orthodox rabbis and kabbalist born in Łódź, Congress Poland, in the Russian Empire, to a family of scholars connected to the Hasidic courts of Porisov and Belz. Rabbi Ashlag lived in the Holy Land from 1922 until his death in 1954. Rav Yehuda Tzvi Brandwein, was the Dean of Yeshivah Kol Yehuda in Israel which was the precursor of the *US Kabbalah Centre,* which was founded in 1922. After Brandwein's death, and after several years in Israel, Philip Berg and his wife Karen Berg re-established the *U.S. Kabbalah Centre* in New York.

The current headquarters of the *US Kabbalah Centre* in Los Angeles was opened in 1984. Karen and their sons Yehuda and Michael act as directors and spiritual leaders of the organization with over fifty branches worldwide, including major ones in Los Angeles, New York City, London and Toronto.

Kabbalah Centre teaches the Lurianic Kabbalistic with its concept of Klippot. The idea is that everyone has a direct and clear connection to the upper metaphysical-spiritual world of the Light called the Ein Sof, or Ayn Sof, (Hebrew אין סוף). This is a Kabbalistic term used to describe God prior to His self-manifestation in the production of any spiritual Realm. Ein Sof may be translated as "no end", "unending", "there is no end", or "infinite Unbounded God". But the path or channel is "blocked" by Klippot. Klippot are the scattered sparks of divine light, or "husks." These "husks" formed as of the result of Ein Sof attempting to fill the vessel of creation with its divine light, catastrophe struck, and the vessel shattered. *Shevirat ha-kelim* is the Hebrew name for the breaking of the vessel. The breaking of the vessel destroyed the ordered universe that Ein Sof had begun to create. Because of this breaking it restricted the spiritual energy from entering the physical body of man. It is through meditation and practice of Kabbalah teachings and Jewish law (which the *Kabbalah Centre* says is early Rabbinistic construction to aid in practicing Kabbalah without revealing its secrets) that one removes Klippot, and it is by violence and negative behavior that one adds Klippot.

The *Kabbalah Centre* also has a strong belief in astrology and asserts that astrology has been part of Judaism since its inception. The Centre claims astrology was lost in Jewish tradition as part of the suppression of Kabbalah by rabbis nearly 2000 years ago. This can be seen by ancient archeological finds of temple mosaics and zodiacal designed rings found at these ancient tells or mounds. This claim of being lost until their revival is historically inaccurate, as astrology was studied by Jewish scholars throughout the Middle Ages, though it was opposed by more philosophically inclined thinkers such as Maimonides.

There is a strong belief in the Kabbalah tradition that cosmic forces affect everything, and knowing how to understand them can prove to be valuable to the aspiring Kabbalist. Philip Berg, the founder of the *Kabbalah Centre*, is himself an astrologer and has written numerous books on astrology during his career.

It should be noted that the Centre has had a great deal of controversy and criticism due to the sensationalism resulting from many of its celebrity members. But they are still a good source of teaching to those students that do not have previous knowledge of Hebrew and Jewish texts.

LEFT-HAND PATH VERSUS RIGHT-HAND PATH (LHP VS RHP)

When exploring the various groups that use the symbolism and allegories of the Qabbalah the term "Left-hand Path" and "Right-hand Path" will appear. There are various definitions as to what the two sides represent. Some believe the RHP describes the ascension up the Tree of Life in the attempt to better know the universe through a struggle of growth and hierarchical seeking. While the LHP is said to find perfection right where we stand and that there is no need to ascend higher and that heaven has been reached while on this physical plane. They are also heavily involved with The Tree of Knowledge. (Refer to Section XII.).

Others view the terms "Left-Hand Path" and "Right-Hand Path" to refer to two opposing approaches found in Western esotericism. In some definitions, the "Left-Hand Path" is equated with malicious Black magic and the "Right-Hand Path" with benevolent White magic. Other occultists have criticized this definition, believing that the Left-Right division refers to different kinds of working and study, and does not necessarily denote good or bad magical actions.

When viewing the RHP one is said to be using Tantra which is described loosely as a spiritual expansion of oneself, is a Tantric. Tantra in itself is neither a religion nor an "ism". Tantra is a fundamental spiritual science. In more recent definitions are based on the term's origins among Indian Tantra. The "Right-Hand Path", or RHP, is seen as a definition for those magical groups which follow specific ethical codes and adopt social convention. While the "Left-Hand Path" adopts the opposite attitude, espousing the breaking of taboo and the abandoning of set morality. Some contemporary occultists have stressed that both paths can be followed by a magical practitioner.

TYPHONIAN ORDO TEMPLI ORIENTIS (TOTO)

The Typhonian Order, previously known as the *Typhonian Ordo Templi Orientis* (TOTO), is a degree-based self-initiatory magical order based in the United Kingdom that focuses on magical and typhonian concepts. It was originally led by British occultist Kenneth Grant (1924–2011) and his partner Steffi Grant (1946–2011). Steffi was an acclaimed occult artist and practitioner who provided Kenneth much artwork. Kenneth Grant was an English ceremonial magician and prominent advocate of the Thelemite religion. Grant was described as a poet, novelist, and writer, and with his wife Steffi Grant he founded his own Thelemite organization, the *Typhonian Ordo Templi Orientis*, later re-naming it *The Typhonian Order.*

Grant served in the British Army in India and after his tour returned to England and became the personal secretary of Aleister Crowley in 1904. Crowley took Grant as a personal student and taught Grant Crowley's version of esoteric practices. He initiated him into his two active ceremonial magic orders, *Argenteum Astrum* and *Ordo Templi Orientis* (OTO). When

Crowley died in 1947, Grant was seen as his heir apparent in Britain, and was appointed as such by the American head of the O.T.O., Karl Germer (1885–1962). Germer was also known as "Frater Saturnus", and was a German occultist who was also very close to Crowley, who appointed Germer his successor upon his death.

In 1954 Grant founded the New Isis Lodge after spending around 10 years perfecting his concepts and ideas about how to establish its teaching of the New Isis Lodge. These teachings centered on expanding Crowley's Thelemite teachings, blending extraterrestrial themes and influences Grant had found in the work of H.P. Lovecraft (1890–1937). Lovecraft was an American horror fiction writer. In 1955 Grant's New Isis Lodge was declared operational with Grant announcing his discovery of a "Sirius/Set current" in which he established a new manifesto upon which the lodge would be based. Karl Germer felt that this new manifesto was so out of line with OTO's teachings he expelled Grant from the O.T.O. Grant then responded by declaring himself the Outer Head of the Order, assuming the XII°, and taking his supporters into an alternative group called their new group the "Typhonian Ordo Templi Orientis". They absorbed the New Isis Lodge in 1962, around the same time that Germer died without formally naming a successor as Head of O.T.O.

In 1959 Grant began publishing on the subject about occultism, and proceeded to author the *Typhonian Trilogies*, as well as a number of other novels, books of poetry, and publications devoted to propagating the work of Crowley and Austin Osman Spare (1886–1956). Spare was a prominent English artist and occultist. Grant's writings and teachings have proved a significant influence over future British occultists.

- According to their website "*The Typhonian Order* (sometimes called *Typhonian O.T.O.*) is concerned with effective transmissions and communications from outerspace for the purpose of opening Gateways". The Typhonian deities denote specific operations of psycho-physical alchemy which involve essences or elixirs secreted (thrown out and/ or considered unclean) by the human organism. Its formula is that of the XI° involving kalas that are entirely absent from the masculine organism. Kalas are sometimes referred to as masculine and feminine fluids. In Grant's *Nightside of Eden* he describes 22 paths or Tunnels of Set. They are qliphotic attributes with the names of demonic entities of each path. The first letter of these names match the Hebrew letters to their corresponding paths according to the Golden Dawn.[4] They are:

Path	Key	Demonic Entity
11	Aleph	Amprodias
12	Beth	Baratchial
13	Gimel	Gargophias
14	Daleth	Dagdagiel
15	Heh	Hemethterith
16	Vav	Uriens
17	Zain	Zamradiel
18	Cheth	Characith
19	Teth	Temphioth
20	Yod	Yamatu
21	Kaph	Kurgasiax—
22	Lamed	Lafcursiax
23	Maim	Malkunofat
24	Nun	Niantiel
25	Samekh	Saksaksalim
26	Ayin	A'ano'nin
27	Peh	Parfaxitas
28	Tzaddi	Tzuflifu
29	Qoph	Qulielfi
30	Resh	Raflifu
31	Shin	Shalicu
32	Tav	Thantifaxath

There is no comparison to other *O.T.O.* versions, essentially because there are no group rituals or ceremonies of initiation at any stage of the degree structure. The basis of initiation is the assimilation of direct magical and mystical working. It follows that all initiation is in effect self-initiation. There is a small amount of set gradework in the *Typhonian Order*. However, the emphasis is on the initiate charting his or her own course. There is of course the experience of others to draw upon.

---

4 Approaching the Kabbalah of Matt, Karr, Don, Black Jackal Press, 2013, pg. 36

TREE OF QLIPOTH

When discussing the LHP the key symbol is the Tree of Qlipoth or the "Kingdom of Shells" which is described as the anti-structure or reverse to the Tree of Life. The Tree of Qlipoth is sometimes referred to as The Tree of Knowledge as well. The concept of Qlipoths refers to debris left over from when the all-encompassing divine force self-manifested into a limiting emanation. This "limiting" of something "all-encompassing" is like trying to put ten pounds of flour in a one-pound container. Each "Shell" or Qlipha is said to represents a negative, chaotic or adverse aspect of a particular Sephirot on the Tree of Life. In the left hand path occult systems, it is often identified with the Tree of Knowledge from the Garden of Eden.

They describe the Tree of Knowledge as the Tree having the fruit that if eaten by man, he is given the promise of godhood by the Serpent, which is sometimes named Samael and other times Lilith. Samael is sometimes referred to as the "poisoner" as well as "the angel of death". Lilith is the name of Adam's first wife who was banished from the Garden of Eden when she refused to be "submissive" to Adam. She is often described as being evil and a stealer of children. The promise of reaching "godhead" status is fulfilled when the adept accomplishes the initiatory journey through the particular qlipothic levels and reaches Thaumiel (the top of three or anti-pole to Kether). Below is one of the comparisons of the two Trees.

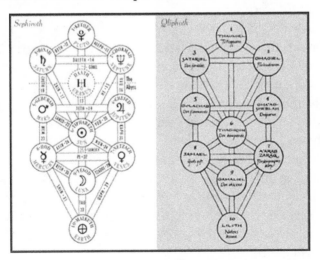

	Sephiroth				Husks	
1	Kether/ Keter	Crown		1	Thaumiel	The Twins of God
2	Chokhmah	Wisdom		2	Ogiel	Hinders
3	Binah	Understandin		3	Satariel	Concealers
4	Chesed	Mercy/Kindness		4	Gash'khalah	Breakers in Pieces
5	Gevurah/Geburah	Severity		5	Golachab	Flaming Ones
6	Tiferet/ Tiphareth	Beauty		6	Tagiriron	Litigation
7	Netzach	Eternity/Victory		7	Orev Zarak	Ravens of Dispersion
8	Hod	Splendor		8	Samael	False Accuser
9	Yesod	Foundation		9	Gamaliel	Obscene Ass
10	Malkuth	Kingdom/Kingship		10	Lilith	Woman of the Night

On the Tree of Life there is often depicted an 11th Sephiroth which is called Da'ath/Daath whose essence is called "knowledge". On many depictions is hidden for reasons that will be explained later.

WISDOM

Wisdom is said to be knowledge one has obtained, with the ability to apply that knowledge to one's life. This only comes from acknowledging that what one believes is truth. Except truth itself is only the truth of that time in which one is standing. For truth changes as we view what we think is truth from a different perspective and experiences. Even history's truth is changed depending who is viewing it with what knowledge they apply to that historic truth. A couple of classic examples are who "first discovered America" or "which culture produced our first civilization" depending if you are European or from Asia. Students start upon the path of knowledge and enlightenment for many reasons, knowledge of the unknown, curiosity of what is hidden, and sometimes even the promise of power. As the student follows their advances along what is called the "path of enlightenment" they will be presented with many options. They will be tempted with many paths leading to different supposed ancient sources of esoteric knowledge while alluding that with this advance special knowledge they will find themselves evolved over their uninitiated fellow humans. This often poses a great dilemma, for with this knowledge comes power versus the pure joy of self-enlightenment.

As you followed the development of the Kabbalah, the first students were attempting to understand and repeat Ezekiel's vision. As time progressed this became an attempt to understand their relationship to God and their place in the greater universe.

As the blending of ideas from different cultures and religious backgrounds occurred these studies became a quest for trying to understand man's place not so much in respect to the divine but to that of understanding the workings of the divine which eventually secularized to be called nature. Many groups simply attempted to understand the laws of nature and man's place within the great mosaic of the physical world. Others took the approach of attempting to understand nature as a means to control and manipulate nature through the use of alchemy, mental energies and magick. Each group claims with sincere convictions that knowledge will lead them to a greater wisdom and thus a greater perfection of mankind. Historically the Kabbalahist sought to perfect their own temples so as to gain a closer personal relationship to their God. Unfortunately, man has for the most part not perfected his own nature to the point of becoming wise or, as the Rosicrucian's say, enlightened.

During the Renaissance, many scholars of the Kabbalah began to show interest in religious and philosophical tradition based primarily upon pseudo-epigraphical writings attributed to Hermes Trismegistus. The Hermetic tradition claims descent from a prisca theologia, a doctrine which affirms that a single, true theology exists in all religions and was given by God to man in antiquity thus offering an addition source of knowledge to understanding man's relationship to God.

According to Hermetic tradition Hermes Trismegistus received the name "Thrice Great", derived from his work The Emerald Tablet, wherein it is stated that he knew the three parts of the wisdom of the whole universe. The three parts of the wisdom are alchemy, astrology, and theurgy which is Greek for the practice of rituals, sometimes seen as "magical in nature, performed with the intention of invoking the action or evoking the presence of one or more gods, especially with the goal of uniting with the divine, and perfecting oneself".

Around 1300 to 1600 A.D. these concepts of Hermeticism became the seed for the development of science, which included the idea of influencing or controlling nature. This led many scientists or hermetists to put Nature to the test by means of magic, alchemy, and astrology. From these and other pseudo-religious ideas many scholars began to formalize a corpus of ideas to support their schools of thought. Many of these scholars attempted to legitimize or differentiate their philosophies by attaching or alluding to their source as being from a more ancient lineage to that of what they called the great teachers, Adepts or Masters. Each claims they are the keepers of the knowledge which they obtained from special exclusive training. Unfortunately, men's egos get in the way and schisms occur. Thus, the list grows of the number of organizations that claim they are the true keepers of knowledge and wisdom.

Those who start the path must be cautious as to what their true motives are for seeking knowledge. When one reads that such and such a Master will teach you to control the four elements, earth, fire, water, and air, or that through such and such practice one can manipulate their world, be cautious. For there are many societies, cults and fraternities that currently seek only financial and/or emotional control of their students.

After over 40 years of walking the path I can tell you Wisdom comes from gaining the knowledge to see the truth of one's own existence. As that truth is glimpsed it will change for with that knowledge new wisdom comes and greater changes occur in oneself. It does not come from just the advancement through degrees or even the gaining of knowledge but from applying that knowledge to oneself to perfect the most precious of treasures—one's own essence. It is taking the lead of man and placing it in the crucible of life to perfect the gold of the Philosophers Stone.

Walking the path will change you; there are emotional and physical changes that do occur. The student can learn to control their passions, such as fear, lust, anger, and hate, through meditation. They can develop a keener sight in that they will start to see their physical world at different levels and perspectives. And the experiences they go through will add greatly to their wisdom of the universe and their place in it. Just remember that whichever society, cult or fraternity you join you WILL be changed. Choose wisely. And remember what one great teacher said you do not initiate to become a Rosicrucian your thoughts become that of a Rosicrucian.

VII.

THE TREE OF LIFE

According to a Jewish legend all souls that ever existed were with God before the creation of the universe. God kept them stored under his throne until the time of their birth. When the child is conceived by its earthly mother, God plants the soul in the mother's womb. On the journey from the divine realm to the earth God sends an angel to accompany the soul. During the gestation that angel instructs the soul in all the mysteries of the universe. At the time of birth the angel taps the child's forehead and the Child promptly forgets everything it had learned. Thus the child bursts into tears. "Life is the journey of the soul back to God, attempting to recapture forgotten wisdom on the way."

From *Archetypes on the Tree* by Madonna Compton

When studying the Qabbalah one of the universally acknowledged symbols is the glyph referred to as Tree of Life. Issues arise immediately because of this symbolic representation of creation as a written description with no visual portrayal in the *Sepher Yetzirah*. Because of this its portrayal is strictly a personal interpretation which is further confused due to language translations and cultural and religious perspectives. Since the revealing to the general public of the *Sepher Yetzirah* there have been literally hundreds of depictions of how the Tree should look. It is not the purpose of this book to provide a definitive depiction or description of the Tree. It is suggested that the student attempt to find a representative glyph that they are most comfortable with, for it is not important that as to the exact representation be historically true but that the concepts it represents resonate with the student to help them with their progress on the Path.

The Path of Enlightenment is not a singular set of footsteps but a path with many curves, dips and reversals. In describing the Tree of Life, we are trying to give the reader the middle path allowing for the individual to take the information and incorporate into their own perspective depending on their life experiences. Since everyone learns from different perspectives and tools I am including brief comments on components that may aid them. These different tools or aids are such things as sound, color, numbers, angelic lore and planetary associations to the various components of The Tree of Life. These components may give familiarity to an arcane topic and thus aid the student on his journey down their path.

The Tree of Life, or Etz haChayim (עץ החיים) in Hebrew, is a classic descriptive term for the central mystical symbol used by the Kabbalah of esoteric Judaism. It is traditionally composed of 10 emanations known as the "10 Sephirot" or Sefirot meaning spheres. Sephirot is the plural from of the word Sefirah, both of which have multiple spellings due to the result of converting Semitic language to Latin based. Its diagrammatic representation, arranged in 3 columns/pillars, derives from Christian and esoteric sources and its earliest form first appeared in the *Sepher Yetzirah* or *Book of Formation*, also called *Book of Creation*, sometime in the second century. In this book it described that the ten Sephirot were mythical and dynamic numbers emerging out of God and returning to Him, and together with the Hebrew twenty-two letters became instrumental in the creation of the universe.

Originally the term of Sefirot was used to denote "numbers" but the author of the *Sepher Yetzirah* seemed to allude to more metaphysical principles or to stages in the creation of the world. Later in Kabbalah literature the term became associated with the theory of emanation. The *Sepher Yetzirah* does not mention the first Sefirah which emanated from God and was not directly created by Him. The author vaguely alludes that it is part of the mystical quality of the Sefirot. According to Gershom Scholem the German-born Israeli philosopher, historian who is regarded as the founder of the modern, academic study of Kabbalah, the first four Sefirot emanated from each other. The first one is the "spirit (ru'ah) of the Living God". Gershom says the author of the *Sepher Yetzirah* goes on to describe the first Sefirah coming forth by way of condensation, "one Spirit from another". From ru'ah, the Hebrew word for "breathe" or "spirit", came the next Sefirot which was the primal element of air or ether. After this came the third and fourth Sefirah representing water and fire. Upon the primal air, God created or imprinted the 22 Hebrew letters; from the primal waters He placed the cosmic chaos and on the primal fire the Throne of Glory and the hosts of the angels. The last six Sefirot are different in their nature and represent the six dimensions or extremities of space. In short the Sefirot provide a span or bridge between the infinite God and the finite world of man.

Over time the kabalistic scholars attempted to quantify the concepts of the Sefirot and their relationship to each other. It was not until the teaching of Isaac ben Solomon Luria Ashkenazi (1534–1572), became know that the fully developed form of the Tree, as we know it, with its the twenty-two Hebrew letters to the twenty-two paths, as shown on the Tree below appeared in the sixteenth century.

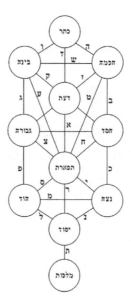

LETTERS OF CREATION— THE HEBREW ALPHABET

Luria divided the twenty-two Hebrew letters into groups of the three "mother letters", the seven "double letters" and the twelve "single letters". According to Luria, these represent the completion of the formal elements of the cosmic creation. Luria took a very rational approach to his interpretation not from *Sepher Yetzirah* but from the *Zohar* or *Book* of *Splendor* or *Radiance* which first appeared in Spain around 1275. The Lurianic Tree differed in not only the placement of the Sephiroth but the paths as well. His work became very popular due to his strict adherence to Jewish Law. This appealed to those Jewish scholars due to their zeal to hold on to the pure Hebrew teachings. Luria placed his paths of the Tree using three categories of letters; the three horizontal paths with the three mother letters, the seven vertical paths with the seven double letters and the twelve single, or simple letters with the diagonal paths. Thus the Tree of Life visually or conceptually represents as a series of divine emanations God's creation, the nature of revealed divinity, the human soul, and the spiritual path of ascent by man. In this way, Kabbalists developed the symbol into a full model of reality, using the tree to depict a map of Creation.

The Three Mother Letters

א מ ש

Aleph, Mem, Shin

The Seven Double Letters

ב ג ד כ פ ר ת

Beth, Gimel, Daleth, Kaph, Peh, Resh, Tau

The Twelve Simple Letters

ה ו ז ח ט י ל נ ס ע צ ק

Heh, Vav, Zayin, Cheth, Teth, Yod, Lamed, Nun, Samekh, Ayin, Tzaddi, Qoph

The three mother letters Aleph, Mem, and Shin correspond to the three root energies symbolized by the divine or magical elements of Air, Water and Fire. One must understand these are the primordial elements and not the literal description of fire like found in a camp fire. The Three Mother Letters described in the *Sepher Yetzirah*, represent Air, Water and Fire. Water is silent, Fire is sibilant, and Air derived from the Spirit is as the tongue of a balance standing between these contraries which are in equilibrium, reconciling and mediating between them. From these Three Mothers the heavens were produced from Fire; the earth from the Water; and the Air from the Spirit is as a reconciler between the Fire and the Water. The *Sepher Yetzirah* goes on and says the three Mother Letters are the primary forces in the universe—representing the Heavenly Fire, the Waters of the Abyss, and the Air (or Spirit) of God that moved upon the face of the Waters as described in the *Book of Genesis*, Chapter 1. The Water and the Fire are the polar opposites of the cosmos, and the Air is the reconciling force between them, forming the *Equilibrium* of Creation. They are the Thesis, Antithesis, and Synthesis that compose all things in created reality. As such, it is from the Three Mothers that the other forces of the universe are born.

The Seven Double Letters described within the *Sepher Yetzirah* are: Beth, Gimel, Daleth, Kaph, Peh, Resh, and Tau which each have two sounds associated with them, a soft and a hard pronunciation. They are referred to as Life, Peace, Wisdom, Riches, Grace, Fertility and Power. They are called Double, because each letter presents a contrast or permutation; thus Life and Death; Peace and War; Wisdom and Folly; Riches and Poverty; Grace and Indignation; Fertility and Solitude; Power and Servitude. This goes back to sixteenth century Cordoverian Kabbalah which utilized the conceptual framework of evolving cause and effect where a positive act brings forth a negative one such as wisdom defines folly, riches causes poverty and life itself brings forth Death.

The *Sepher Yetzirah* describes how these Double Letters represented the Seven Ancient Planets: Saturn, Jupiter, Mars, Sol, Venus, Mercury, and Luna. They also represent the Days of the Week, and the seven Gates of the soul in Man to name a few. From these Seven, God produced the "Seven Heavens, the Seven Earths, and Seven Sabbaths: for this cause He has loved and blessed the number Seven more than all things under Heaven (His Throne)".

The 12 Simple Letters are Héh, Vau, Zayn, Cheth, Teth, Yod, Lamed, Nun, Samekh, Ayin, Tzaddi and Qoph; they are the foundations of these twelve properties of Sight, Hearing, Smell, Speech, Taste, Sexual Love, Work, Movement, Anger, Mirth, Imagination, and Sleep.

In the *Sepher Yetzirah* God designed, and combined the letters to formed with them into the Twelve celestial constellations of the Zodiac, whose signs are Teth, Shin, Tau, Samech, Aleph, Beth, Mem, Oin, Qoph, Gimel, and Daleth. The Twelve are also the Months of the Jewish Year: Nisan, Yiar, Sivan, Tamuz, Ab, Elul, Tishri, Hesvan, Kislev, Tebet, Sabat and Adar. The Twelve are also the twelve organs of living creatures: the two hands, the two feet, the two kidneys, the spleen, the liver, the gall, private parts, stomach and intestines.

BIRTH OF THE SEPHIROT

The actual naming of the ten Sephirot does not appear until later. It first appeared in the *Bahir,* then later again in the *Zohar.* It was not until the sixteenth century that the Safed Kabbalists fully revealed the Sefirot and paths to the non-Jewish scholarly world. This was done when Moses ben Jacob Cordovero's (1522–1570) book *Pardes Rimmonium* or *Garden of Pomegranates* was published in Cracow, Poland in 1548. In this publication, he included a detailed commentary on the Sefirot and the channels with a diagram depicting them thus ending three hundred years of verbal allusions which derived from a 1516 publication of Paolo Riccio's or Paulus Rincius' (1480–1541). Paolo was a German Jew who connverted to Christianity and translated many works from Hebrew to Latin for the Holy Roman Emperor Maximilian I (1459–1519), including the *Talmud.* He published *De Portae Lucis* or *Portal of Light* which had many "eccentric proportions" which caused confusion and misdirection by those who tried to study the work.

Jewish Kabbalah usually refers to the Tree symbol as having 10 Sephirot or primal numbers. This is in contrast to non-Jewish Christian Cabala and Hermetic Qabbalah who generally use the term Qabalistic (Hermetic) Tree of Life. This metaphor derives from Judaic or Lurianic Kabbalah, which is less popular in the western world compared to the Hermetic Qabbalah. The Jewish Kabbalist view is, that there were two trees in the Biblical Garden of Eden, the Tree of Knowledge of Good and Evil and the Tree of Life. These Trees were alternative perspectives of the Sephirot.

The symbolic version of what we now consider the Tree of Life, like the Kabbalah itself, has been developed by scholars as they attempted to formalize their view of how the Tree should look. Here are a couple of versions of its development.

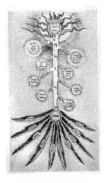

A version of Robert Fludd
Complete Works
1617

From *Porta Lucis,*
1516

It should be noted that the original diagrams of the Tree of Life did not have the ten Sephiroth with 22 lines connecting them to make the 32 paths of wisdom. There originally were only the verbal descriptions of the first three Sephirot with inference to "lower" spheres. Thus a definitive depiction of what the Tree looked like only developed over time.

GERONESE TREE

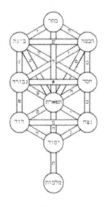

As the concept of the Tree developed so did the complexity and diversity of the physical diagram of the Tree of Life. During the early eleventh and twelfth century the general view of how the Tree was constructed. It became known as the "Geronese Tree", sometimes referred to as the "Jewish Tree" due to its origination in Gerona, Spain in the Jewish Talmudic centers of study.

History of the Geronese Tree

After Isaac the Blind (1160–1236) death, his commentary on the *Sepher Yetzirah* continued to influence and stimulate Cabalists throughout Spain. Though were numerous versions of the Tree a general consensus developed around accepting what became known as the Geronese Tree. Originally this version came about in Gerona, a small town in Catalonia, where the Cabalists began to consolidate their ideas as to the names and location of the Sephiroth on structure resembling a "tree". The Geronese theories were based on the writings of Rabbi Barzilai, Rabbi 'Ezra of Gerona, Rabbi Jacob ben Shesher, and Rabbi Asher ben David of Provence.

Rabbi Barzilai was also known historically as Yehudah ben Barzilai or Judah ben Barzilai of Catalonia, was born in 1035 and died in 1105. Rabbi Azriel (Ezra) ben Menahem (Ben Solomon) born in 1160 and dying in 1238, is often historically confused as being two people, an elder and younger. Historians are still debating this fact. Rabbi Jacob ben Shesher (1326–1408), also known as Rivash, was another Talmudic authority working in the Catalonia area. The third great Talmudist of this era was R. Asher ben David of Provence. He was the nephew of Rabbi Isaac the Blind and the first Provençal kabbalist who sought to explain and clarify the theosophical doctrine of the Sefirot in an unhindered and uncryptic manner.

At the time that the students of Gerona were writing and theorizing on the interpretations of the essence of the Sefirot their teachings were not unified, resulting in a great deal of debate as to which concepts were clearer and closest to *Talmud* teachings. Because of the debates that ensued Rabbi Isaac became displeased, especially with the degree of exotericization practiced by his students in Gerona. In order to rein in the Gerona students, he asked R. Asher ben David to serve as his diplomatic envoy to the Spanish kabbalists. The Geronese scholars had requested that R. Isaac himself make the journey, in order to clarify ambiguous matters of doctrine and heal the ideological rifts, but this proved to be impossible. Instead, R. Isaac appears to have selected R. Asher as his spokesman in Spain.

Another of the great leaders of the Gerona Schools was Rabbi Moshe ben Nahmanides (1194–1270). Rabbi Isaac the Blind and Rabbi Nahmanides tended to agree on the view that the mystical aspect of the Kabbalah should be concealed from non-Kabbalists. For the esoteric teachings contained in the Kabbalah discussed many of the mystical views concerning God, angels, the soul, miracles and life after death. They felt only those who knew and understood *Talmud* and the intricacies of its teaching could understand man's relationship to God. For the *Talmud* contained the essence of Jewish ethics, philosophy, customs, history and lore. And only by understanding these core values of Judaism can one hope to understand this crucial relatationship to the Divine.

It was Nahmanides who preached moderation when orthodox Rabbis met in 1232 representing the Jewish leadership of both Northern France and Germany in order to condemn Mosheh ben Maimon, (1135–1204), also known as Maimonides, for his heretical teachings. This is important to modern Kabbalist because Maimonides's teachings appealed to the Andalusian and Provencal Jews who had more of a secular and philosophic view of their religious beliefs. Because of this his "intellectual" views and concepts of the Kabbalah sprung forth out of the orthodox "traditional" schools to the non-Kabbalist world and the western European scholars.

At the time, the problem was determining, and agreeing about the essence of the Sephirot, and their relationship to the other Sefirah. At that time, most of the Trees were represented without connecting paths, which seem to have secondary value in any basic understanding of the structure of the Tree itself. Three major questions were being debated.

First was if the Sefirot were actually part of the Divine nature. And if they were would the Sephiroth possess the Divine essence of the Creator? Second if the Sefirot were not divine in essence how closely were they affiliated with the Divine? Were they merely tools or instruments that the Creator used to create with and govern the world? Or perhaps they were the vessels which the Divine used to present to the lower worlds. The third and final question debated was on the theory that the Sefirot were themselves Divine emanations.

These basic questions were essential in understanding man's relationship to God and his place in the creation of the universe. The debate continued until end of the fifteenth and the early sixteenth centuries, when these earlier positions presented as conflicting stands and thereby crystallized as independent perceptions. It was Moses ben Jacob Cordovero who unified the coexistence of the Sefirot as emanation from the Divine. In his mystical school in the Safed, Israel area he taught that the Sephirot were the vessels and instruments by which creation manifested itself. His teaching became the dominant factor in Kabbalistic theosophy.

The work of the mystics of Gerona took the Kabbalah from a secret work to one of active spiritual and intellectual discussions throughout medieval Jewish thought and the public forum. This was in direct contradiction to Rabbi Isaac the Blind "demanding" that the dissemination of the concepts of the Kabbalah be kept secret. Because of Gerona's refusal much of the terminology and basic ideas that prevailed in the Kabbalah during the next seven centuries was formulated.

According to these early Kabbalists the universe, with all its multifarious manifestations, was latent in the essence of the Ein-Sof. The En-Sof or Ayn Sof is a Kabbalistic term for God prior to His self-manifestation in the spiritual realm. It is God without any boundaries, it is "there is no end" or infinite. The Ein-Sof is of infinite variety, forming an absolute unit, just like the various sparks and colors that proceed from the one and indivisible flame potential in the coal. This act of creation did not manifest any specific new thing; it was merely a transformation of potential existence into realized existence. Thus there was really no creation, but a spark of Azilut. Azilut is the beginning of all existence. Kabbalists describe creation starting with the World of Azilut. It begins with the Kether (Crown) of Azilut, which is associated with the God name of *Ehyeh* ('I AM'). This was the name with which God revealed Himself to Moses in *Exodus* 3:14 *(Ehyeh Asher Ehyeh—I AM that I am)*.

Azilut is the eternal unchanging world symbolized by the "archetypal" Divine Sephirot. The root of the term Azilut means "to stand near", as Azilut is the "buffer" or "interchange" between the unknowable Ein Sof and the three lower worlds of Beriah, Yezirah and Asiyyah.

Azilut is also called the *"World of Divine Light"*, and the *"Glory of God"*, which passes through all four worlds which exist within Azilut. It is also called the *"World of Unity"*, as it is apart from the dimensions of time and space that exist in the lower worlds. Thus, Azilut is strictly a world of consciousness, and represents a stage of "pure Divine will." As time and space do not exist in this world, there is never any type of motion, therefore Azilut is always in perfect equilibrium. It existed before evil was manifested.

The effluence was effectuated through successive gradations from the intellectual world to the material, from the indefinite to the definite. This material world, being limited and not perfect, could not proceed directly from the En-Sof; neither could it be independent of Him; for in that case He would be imperfect. There must have been, therefore, intermediaries between the En-Sof and the material world; and these intermediaries were the Ten Sefirot. The first Sefirah was latent in the En-Sof as a dynamic force; then the second Sefirah emanated as a substratum for the intellectual world; afterward the other Sefirot emanated, forming the moral, the material, and the natural worlds. The Sefirot, according to their nature, are divided into three groups: the three superior forming the world of thought, the next three the world of soul, the last four the world of corporeality. They all depend upon one another, being united like links to the first one. Each of them has a positive and a passive quality—emanating and receiving. In this version the first Sefirah was not Kether but Azriel. Later cabalists thought that Azriel meant "Will" ('Ḥefeẓ') which is the highest dynamic force of the Deity. The second and third Sefirah were Hokmah and Binah; the fourth, fifth, and sixth, Chesed, Geburah and Tiphareth; the seventh, eighth, and ninth, Neẓaḥ, Hod, and Yesod 'Olam; and the tenth, Malkuth. For the *Sepher Yetzirah* says there are 'ten not nine' Sephirot. These Ten Sefirot were put by Azriel into correspondence to the ten parts of the human organism and to the ten different refractions of light.

As the debate continued as to how and what the Tree of Life looked like an eleventh Sefirah was considered. It was called Da'ath or Da'at. The psedo-sefirah, Da'ath, became recognized early in the thirteenth century by Joseph ben Abraham Gikatilla (1248–after 1305) who was a Spanish kabbalist, and a student of Abraham Abulafia. This psedo-sefirah was a culmination of all the Sephiroth and was seen as the total of "Knowledge". This additional "sphere" or "center" was firmly placed on the middle column above Tiphareth. And according to traditional views of the Tree of Life according to the *Sepher Yetzirah* there can only be ten Sephirot. Thus the number ten depends on the mutual exclusivity between Kether, the Crown, the first Sefirah and Da'at, Knowledge. Others like Rabbi Shlomo Yitzchaki (1040–1105) whose pseudonym is Rashi, a French biblical scholar, defined Da'at as *ruach hakodesh* or Divine inspiration. According to Rashi when the powers of Chokmah and Binah are combined, only then can Da'at be achieved. This contradiction as to the place of Da'at on the Tree of Life has long been debated amongst scholars.

Since the distribution of the *Sefer ha-Bahir* toward the end of the twelfth century rabbis have attempted to understand the homilies and commentaries on biblical verse that the *Sefer ha-Bahir* discussed. It was these writings that said it was impossible to reach God or understand God through rational means. It was believed that God's existence could be possibly understood from the symbols and traces He left throughout the Universe at the time of creation. It was these symbols that Kabbalist attempted to place in some rational relationship to each other.

As the Tree is the symbolic representation of the scholar's interpretations of the written description of the relationships of the Sephiroth to each other the structure of the pathways and Tree is always in flux.

UNDERSTANDING THE PATHS OF THE GERONESE TREE OF LIFE

As the commentaries on the Kabbalah moved from the esoteric studies of Talmudists to that of the non-Jewish scholars of biblical works so did vision of what and how the Tree of Life represented creation. Initially Jewish scholars tried to describe the process of creation. Once the Supernal Sephirot were determined as progressing from Kether, to Chokmah and then to Binah the other seven Sephirot were established in their order of creation. The concept of channels between the various Sephirot drew a great deal of discussion. The early Kabbalist attempted to rely heavily upon the *Talmud* for direction. They took a very philosophical approach to the creation of the universe. When describing how the creation occurred they used the Sephirot as a means to interlock not just the spiritual aspects of the Sefirah but also the essence of the Divine. They explained how God used the Hebrew letters in the creation of the Universe.

> 22 foundation letters. HE engraved them, carved them, weighed them, permuted them, combined them, and formed them, with them all that was formed and all that would be formed in the future.....HE engraved them with voice, carved them with breath, fixed them in the mouth in five places.....HE weighted them and permuted them with: *Alef* with them all and all of them with *Alef, bet* with them all and all of them with *bet, Sepher Yetsirah 2:2-5*

These early writers believed it was proper for all men to resemble his Creator in all their actions and for in that way they will become worthy of his "Godly image". This was most important to the Eretz Yisrael or

Jews in exile. For the Jewish sages taught that even though the Matrona or Shekhinah's first Temple was destroyed she would always accompany her people no matter what their Diaspora station.

In Venice in 1588, Moses Cordovero's book *Tomer Devorah* (*The Palm Tree of Deborah*) was published. It was a small text describing the "Imitation of God" by acquisition of divine qualities attributed and found in the Sephirot.

When meditating upon the Geronese Tree the student must consider not just the attributes of the individual Sefirah but the relationship to the other Sephirot and the Hebrew letter bridging them. This was very important to the early Jewish scholars as they attempted to humanize their understanding of an Infinite boundless concept of the Creative God. The only way they could rationalize the creative force was by limiting human qualities such as love, truth and punishment to an essence that in reality had no such confining limitations.

The descriptions of the individual Hebrew letters are presented in the context presented by rabbinic studies versus the later Qabbalistic and Cabbalistic Sages.

1 KETHER — 2 CHOKMAH

In the Geronese Tree Kether, the Crown, was connected to Chokmah, Wisdom, by the letter *Heh* ה.Kether is first Sefirah that God self-manifested from the Ein-Sof to the spiritual realm. It is God without any boundaries and contains all potentials. It is connected by the channel which is assigned to ה. One of the symbolic interpretations of *Heh* ה is that its three lines compose the three "garments" that represent the means of expression; thought, speech and action. If Chokmah is Wisdom then these attributes are very important for without them there is no ability for the Divine to express Itself. For Chokmah is said to look to god to impart of His knowledge to man. And it through this knowledge that man may attain a better and clearer perception of Godliness.

1 KETHER — 3 BINAH

Binah's pathway from Kether is attributed to the letter *Vav* ו the "nail" or "connection". It is said in the beginning of Creation, the Infinite Light filled all of reality, and God contracted His Light to create a "hollow" empty space that would allow for the existence of finite worlds. And into this void He drew His Light from the Infinite Source to a perceivable light of creation.

From this "connection" to Kether does Binah reflect the 'truth' of His Godliness and is nailed and held to its true form.

2 Chokmah — 3 Binah

This path is attributed to the letter *Shin* ש. *Shin* bridges Chokmah, Wisdom to Binah, Understanding. For it is said that Wisdom is of little worth if not understood. *Shin's* ש attributes reflect that this Wisdom and Understanding must fill man's soul. And the soul has three parts, just like *Shin* ש. The three parts of the soul are spiritual, the spirit and final part the bodily soul. Thus, to truly understand God's Divine nature, one must know it within the entire soul.

2 Chokmah — 4 Chesed

The path from Chokmah, Wisdom to Chesed, Love is *Beth* ב. Beth represents the power to manifest itself in ceaseless change but remain changeless. Thus, as Wisdom is manifested in its ceaseless forms revealing the reality, God's goodness and beauty is always present. This is especially important not just to the student but to everyone for no matter how bad something appears God's essence is present. One must look for the Divine in every form. This was important to the Diaspora Jew when he was exiled from the Holy Land and physically stripped from the Temple and all it represented.

3 Binah — 4 Chesed

Chesed is associated with love. The love of God and the love of mankind. This love comes from knowing God's greatness and the beauty of each man, woman and child. But how is this done, especially in a world of Chaos? That is where *Qoph* ק, the letter assigned to this pathway comes into play. ק represents the calling to God and God whispering back. If we call on the Divine the Divine will let Godliness of everyone and thing shine forth.

2 Chokmah — 5 Geburah

The path from Chokmah, Wisdom to Geburah, Restraint, is *Zaïn* ז Sword. This is the sharp sword of separation that divides the Wisdom into many realities. In particular, it divides the One unity into the Father and the Mother. This sword allows for choice of among many paths for the aspirant. And the restraint of Geburah will provide reward or punishment depending on the path of choice.

3 BINAH — 5 GEBURAH

Geburah represents restraint. The ability to hold back and to control the passions of action. From this restraint comes reward. The quality of free choice according to Maimonides is of great importance to the Jewish faith. According to Nachmanides/Nahmanides, who was also known as Ramban, and who was one of the Girona commentators, free choice was part of the physical world. And the choices of man reflect in this reality but are rewarded in the "world to come" which is also on the physical plane, which differs from Maimonides's concept. Maimonides felt the "world to come" was on the spiritual plane of existence.

Gimel ג according to Jewish Sages symbolizes the rich man running after the poor man to give him charity. The act of charity is one of the ultimate goals in order for the soul to merit and receive God's light. For in *Gimel* comes the balancing of the warring forces of restraint and reward. For as the camel travels the sands the rider must balance and strive to move forward toward the final destination, the unification with the Divine.

6 TIPHARETH

In the Geroness Tree Tiphareth seems to play a pivotal role. It is referred to as the Heart and as Beauty and at this phase of the Tree's development is where all paths lead. In fact, it is the only Sefirah to hold this distinction.

Tiphareth is the balance point between the upper and lower Sephirot and became more evident as the non-Jewish philosophers developed their concepts of the Tree and its interconnecting pathways. As students of the Tree this central key emanation demands more than a casual study. It is said this Sefirah is highest center to which our limited meditative powers can aspire. It is on the center column and symbolically represents balance between the two male and female pillars as well as the upper and lower Sephirot. The upper Sephirot would be Kether, Chokmah, Binah, Chesed and Geburah, while the lower Sephirot would comprise Netzach, Hod, Yesod and Malkuth.

1 KETHER — 6 TIPHARETH

Tiphareth is known sometimes as the "highest point of the lower Sephirot" that man can touch. The Jewish sages referred to as representing the symbolic "heart" of man in the Tree of Life. Being so it has a direct connection to the Crown Kether by way of *Dalet* ד. *Dalet* represents the poor lowly man and is characterized by the Hebrew word *shiflut* or "lowliness". For like man in general the aspirant must realize they possess nothing of their own. That even "free will" is a gift from the Divine. For He gives everyone the power to achieve success through Divine Inspiration. Thus, from Kether comes the Light of Divine manifestation that shines in the Heart of Man. And as the humble servant of God we must bow our heads to receive the gift of the Divine Act of manifestation.

2 CHOKMAH — 6 TIPHARETH
Teth ט is the inverted container that symbolizes the hidden, inverted good as expressed in the *Zohar* as "its good is hidden within it". This is the secret of the path that leads from the Wisdom manifested in Chokmah to that of the beauty that is Tiphareth. This teaches that within every form of manifestation, whether it be thought, word or action there is some Godliness.

3 BINAH — 6 TIPHARETH
The "eye" *Ayin* ע sees all of God's Glory. Its placement is on a path leading from the great Understanding, Binah to that of the Heart/Beauty of Tiphareth. For with opening of the spiritual eye of truth the Understanding of God's glory will become know. The important aspect is seeing the truth and not just what we imagine as true. This truth causes the heart to shine forth reflecting the Godliness not only upward but down to the lower Sephirot and to the manifested physical world of Malkuth.

4 CHESED — 6 TIPHARETH
Cheth ח is the letter of life. God's creative power ever permeates all of reality bringing forth the manifestation of life on all levels, spiritual as well as physical. As in the physical world when Chesed, Love permeates Tiphareth, the heart, life springs forth. This concept was not lost on the Sages and when they tried to conceive the idea of their deity bringing forth life they transposed their concept of birth to the Divine. As the farmer tends his fields and the shepherd tends his flocks both caring with love for their charges thus allowing or nurturing them in a maner that they would give birth to new crops and yearlings. So the Sages conceived God would do to his people.

5 GEBURAH — 6 TIPHARETH

The Sefirah that forces change by the very aspect is Geburah, and is linked to Tiphareth by *tzaddi* צ which lives "by his faith". This is extremely important for as the aspirant is tested not only on the new concepts to which they are exposed but also their ability to handle what they have learned. They need to have faith that the light of enlightenment will become clear even if at the time, it seems out of context and/ or confusing to the perceived reality the aspirant is comfortable with.

4 CHESED — 5 GEBURAH

Aleph א according to Jewish philosophers represents the two aspects of water. The upper is "wet" and is the feeling of oneness with the "exaltation of God". The second aspect or lower water is "cold" and relates to the separation and frustration and "lowliness of man" when not feeling the oneness with God. This sadness is due to the reality of the gap between the purification of God and the flaws of man.

This paradox is expressed in the extremes of the love Chesed holds and the pain of Geburah. This paradox is symbolically seen in the formation of *Aleph* א of the two *Yods* י representing the two waters of Love vs Pain and the *Vav* ו connecting them. The *Vav* is often called the "letter of truth" thus hinting that the balance between the two extremes may be the path or column of equilibrium and the truest path to the Divine.

4 CHESED — 7 NETZACH

Netzach, Victory, like its opposite Hod, Splendor, are the lower extensions of the Sefirah which are vertically above them; Chesed is above Netzach, and Geburah is directly above Hod. They are the limiting principles of the Sefirah above them. Netzach depicts the expansion of time and the "victory" is that of the Love maintained over a long period of time. In other words, the aspirant's ability to incorporate the Divine Love (Chesed) into their daily life.

Kaph כ, according to the *Zohar*, is "He is grasped within all worlds, yet none grasp Him". God is present in all the worlds and permeates every reality. This is the key to the aspirant that no matter what the apparent reality seems, whether it appears good, bad, divine or evil, God is there. This is the "victory" of understanding the Divine's true presence in all the realities that the student can experience.

5 GEBURAH — 8 HOD

Hod is the eighth Sefirah and when the word Hod is used as a noun its meaning is "echo". As a verb root, it means "resonate". These key words are the secret to this Sefirah. Hod resonates the splendor of the Most High.

Peh פ is "mouth". By the mouth of God came the first light when from the Creator's mouth came the words "Let there be light". From this light came actual creation. At the lower levels of the Tree the paths are showing or expressing how creation came into the limited vision of man. Here is where the concept of 'hearing' the word of God takes on form and substance so the Divine's reality takes on forms the aspirant can experience.

6 TIPHARETH — 7 NETZACH

Yod י is the "little that holds much". The "much" refers to the Infinity of what God is and it is hidden within this initial point of revelation. For *Yod* is the foundation and starting point of the other letters of creation-the Hebrew alphabet. From the heart, Tiphareth comes the victory which is Netzach. The victory is that which was hidden is now being brought forth.

6 TIPHARETH — 8 HOD

Sameckh ס circular shape, according to the Jewish philosophers, represented the fundamental truth at all levels of the *Torah*. To the nonJewish student it symbolizes that our consciousness should remain unaffected by the chaotic events of the world. For that consciousness should be anchored to the soul and consciousness splendor of the Divine.

6 TIPHARETH — 9 YESOD

Yesod as the ninth Sefirah means foundation. According to the Kabbalistic principle 'all is in heaven and in earth'; Tiphareth is heaven and Malkuth is earth. Yesod is the channel that functions to align heaven and earth. It is through Yesod, the foundation, which the heavenly realm shines on earth.

Resh ר is the beginning of "cognizant intelligence or wisdom". The Jewish sages taught that "the beginning of wisdom is the fear or awe of God". For the soul is ever ready to contain the new flashes of insight and knowlegde it is challenged with. But with these enlightened challenges comes an innate "fear" or "awe" of the revelation.

7 NETZACH — 8 HOD

Mem ם is water or the sea. Mem is the fountain in which the Divine Wisdom symbolically flows forth. It has two forms, the first is מ with its bottom open, and its final form ם with its bottom closed. The first shape is open at the bottom; it has a gap. This gap symbolizes the flowing wave made by the *Yod* through the ray of creation, the *Vav*. The closed shape represents creation, but in potentiality, not in activities.

7 NETZACH — 9 YESOD

This path is governed by *Nun* נ the "fish". The fish *Nun* נ swims in the hidden world symbolized by *Mem*, the sea. Creatures of this hidden world lack any self-consciousness. The fish acts as the nourishment to the soul as it digests it into totally new and higher levels of consciousness. For *Nun* is the creative energy that aids in the formation of consciousness in Yesod.

8 HOD — 9 YESOD

Lamed ל represents the aspiration of the truly devoted student to learn from the mouth of the master. For the literal meaning of *Lamed* is "to learn". The secret of *Lamed* ל is the heart ascending in aspiration to understand the knowledge that it is open to learn.

9 YESOD — 10 MALKUTH

Malkuth is the "kingdom" of our existence. It represents the world that we inhabit. This world is based on the realities that each individual makes based on their own interpretations of their experiences, emotions and desires. This reality changes as the interpretations evolve and are viewed differently because of these changes or perceived changes. These interpretations are the basis that the world and its reality are reinforced by our reactions to that reality.

The secreat of *Tav* ת is that it links all worlds and all generations together. Is from this link we are linked to the higher worlds and the higher worlds to Malkuth. It is said it is the final letter but it is also the first link to what is above and the gateway for those following the path to enlightenment.

The pathways on the Geronese Tree worked well when trying to understand the philosophical and spiritual relationship of God the Creator and the Universe of His creation. As the students of this Tree studied it appears as though they were seeking a way to understand the non-understandable and to find their place within that scheme. Later scholars moved away from this view of trying to reconcile man's fall from Grace to one of attempting to meditatively expand their understanding of the Divine as it related to the natural world.

VIII.

BIRTH OF THE CABBALISTIC AND QABALISTIC TREE OF LIFE

E lijah ben Shlomo Zalman Kremer, known as the Vilna Gaon or Elijah of Vilna, or Elijah Ben Solomon, (1720–1797) was a Talmudist, and Kabbalist. He was born in Vilnius, capital city of Grand Duchy of Lithuania. His view of the Tree moved Yesod upward and lettered the 22 paths according to the principle of the "mother" letters on the horizontal paths, the "doubles"; on the vertical paths and the "singles" on the diagonals. This seemed to be an attempt to deploy the naming of the paths as a means by which students of the Tree would relate to them in a more practical means of enlightened development.

This version came about in Gerona, a small town in Catalonia, where the Cabalists began to consolidate their ideas as to the names and location on the Tree of the 10 Sephiroth. This version was re-interpreted by a Christian scholar and German Jesuit priest named Athanasius Kircher, S.J. (sometimes erroneously spelled Kirchner; 1602–1680). His work and visual explanation of the Tree became the basis of many of the schools of Western Hermetic Qabbalah including the extremely influential *Order of the Golden Dawn.*

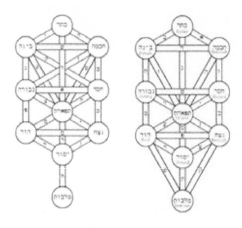

Jewish Tree of Life   Kircher's Tree of Life

The biggest physical, and most apparent, difference in the various Trees has been the placement of the paths between the various centers of energy. According to William Gray in his book *Qabalistic Concepts*, the paths or channels are the changing consciousness from one Sphere to another involving a flow of force or exchange of energies between concepts.[5]

With the Jewish Tree the first three Sefirah, Kether, Chokmah, Binah or the Supernal Triangle, had to have lines for the energy or "life breath" to flow. This "life breath" flowed from the higher Sephirot to the central Sefirah known as the "heart" of Tiphareth. The sixth Sefirah was referred to as the "heart" for its location on the visual display of Adam ha-Kadmon (the original man) or as the Kabbalists called the depiction Adam Kadmon (primordial man). In either case this was pictorial representation of the first man including within himself all future human souls before the sin of the Tree of Knowledge. The spiritual realm of Adam Kadmon represents the Sephiroth or Divine attributes of Kether, the crown, with the specific divine will and plan for subsequent creation.

The nature of a path is determined not only by which Sephirot they are attached to but also which Hebrew letter is assigned to it. As time progressed, other assets were associated with specific paths such as; astrological values, angelic personas, alchemical elements, colors, and musical notes, and other attributes were added by various scholars in hopes of further explaining and

---

5 *Qabalistic Concepts*, William G. Gray, Weiser Books, 1984, pg. 145

clarifying the individual paths' personalities. From the beginning, there has been a great deal of debate as to which letter and attributes should be assigned to which path.

The concept of the "life breath" appeared to be the result of interpretations of the *Sepher Yetzirah* which describes the first Sefirah coming forth by way of condensation, "one Spirit from another". From ru'ah, the Hebrew word for "breath" or "spirit", came the next Sefirot which was the primal element of air or ether and from it came the third and fourth Sefirah representing water and fire. Thus, the Sefirah have shown the source of the three primary elements; air, fire, water. The last six Sefirot are different in their nature and represent the six dimensions or extremities of space. In short, the Sefirot provide a span or bridge between the infinite God and the finite world of man.

THE KIRCHER TREE OF LIFE

The Tree of Life which is the basis for today's modern Hermetic Qabalists was first published by Athanasius Kircher, S.J. (1601 or 1602–1680) (whose name is sometimes erroneously spelled Kirchner). He was a seventeenth century German Jesuit scholar and polymath who published around 40 major works, most notably in the fields of Oriental studies, geology, and medicine. Kircher's work on the Qabalah was published in his work called *Oedipus Aegyptiacus* in Rome over a two-year period of 1652 through 1654. *Oedipus Aegyptiacus* was part of three folio tomes complete with ornate illustrations and diagrams which Kircher claimed had came from Chalerioddean astrology, Hebrew kabbalah, Greek myth, Pythagorean mathematics, Arabian alchemy and Latin philology.

In his first work, he attempted to hide some of the more esoteric information from the general public. This was a common practice at the time of using blind leads and false paths as a means of "protecting the information from the uninitiated".

Athanasius Kircher's Tree of Life

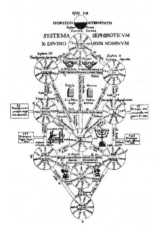

When he was challenged by his comtempories he published a corrected second version that appeared in 1653. This second version became the basis of today's Cabalistic and Qabalistic Trees. This version appeared in Kircher's *Oedipus Aegyptiacus* in 1653 as seen below.

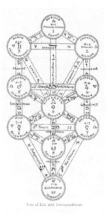

Oedipus Aegyptiacus 1653

Kircher was a firm believer in the influence of heavenly bodies on earthly happenings and phenomenon. He was also heavily influenced by Egyptian mythology and at his time was considered an expert in Egyptian mythology. He firmly believed that the temples of Egypt incorporated both the cosmology of the ancients as well as their advanced knowledge of physics or science. He saw in the temples of Egypt the story of Enoch as well as the concealed secrets of this tale all within the stone carvings that decorated those temples.

Kircher then took the Pythagoreans' belief that numbers were the key to understanding the order of the universe. According to the Pythagoreans the soul could ascend through the spheres, to eventual union with God, by means of mathematics. Kircher combined these ideas with sixteenth century Kabbalist, and Talmudist, Rabbi Isaac Ben Solomon Luria and his commentaries on the *Sephir Yetzirah,* to produce what would become the basis of Renaissance Hermetic occult science of the Tarot, claiming it came from Egypt. From Kircher's work the study of the Tarot and its relationship on the Tree became a focal point by which our association of the Tarot and the Tree of Life developed. From Kircher the Christian Cabbalah and later the Hermetic Qabbalah were born.

Kircher's Tree presented many different concepts. They included the first use of Tarot Keys, as they pertained to specific Hebrew Letters. Kircher also placed the elemental designations on several of the paths and Sephirot. One example is the Δ signifying the aspect of "elemental fire". Another idea attributed to him was incorporation of the concept of the four worlds of Creation.

> *Atziluth*-world of emanation which is made up of Kether
> *Briah*-world of creation, made up of Chokmah, and Binah
> *Yetzirah*-the world of formation, comprising of Chesed, Geburah, Tiphareth, Netzach, Hod and Yesod
> *Assiah*-the world of action which is Malkuth.

By attempting to show the pathways designated by their relationship to these "worlds" and how each expanded to the next level Kircher and his contemporaries redesigned the pathways to what is traditionally used today. Kircher numbered his pathways by placing the first Hebrew letters on paths leading from the lower numbered Sefirah such as Aleph leading to Kether and Chokmah. This configuration became the norm for non-Jewish Cabalists. Problems arose immediately because Jewish Kabbalists associated the Hebrew letters with different paths. This was especially difficult for Cabalists who were trying to traverse the Sephiroth in mystical visions or wishing to evoke the angelic powers associated with the Tree.

Another issue was that the Jewish mystics approached the Tree from the top (Kether), downward to Malkuth. By meditating on the Sephirot and Hebrew Letters they attempted to understand the Divine and the spiritual aspect of the Creation. If this could be understood, then, and only then there might be a chance of redemption. This was an important concept differentiating how the Tree was used by the Esoteric Mystic Jewish Sages and the non-Jewish scholars.

In the Geronese version the channels or paths seem to converge on the sixth Sefirah, Tiphareth. It is centrally located on the Tree and is the balancing Sefirah between the male and female columns, as well as the higher and lower spiritual powers. It is the manifestation of all that is sacred, balanced, strong, and filled with the love of first creation.[6]

Tiphareth is also referred to as the heart of the Tree. This concept is illustrated in the pictorial version of Adam Kadmon which is a term used by Kabbalists to mean "original man". This comes from an older mainstream rabbinic term of Adam ha-Kadmoni meaning "primordial man". The Jewish Encyclopedia provides this traditional image.

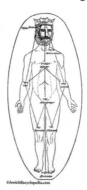

On the Geronese Tree the paths are assigned specific Hebrew letters. According to the *Zohar*, the Hebrew letters preexisted the act of creation. They were in their potential spiritual form and when their spiritual energy intelligence became manifested they would constitute the dimensions of life itself. These energies or dimensions were held within the Holy One. In

---

6 *Judaic Mysticism*, Dr. Avram Davis & Manuela Dunn Mascetti, Hyperion, pg. 199

time the Holy One organized the letter energy intelligences thus activating their spirit, thus the creation began.[7]

The post-Kircher mystics generally approached the Tree from Malkuth upward. The alchemists and cabbalistic mystics tended to try to reach a state of "Divine Grace" by traveling up the Tree. This concept is very familiar to those who study the Tree of Knowledge of Good and Bad. For they too attempt to gain a "Divine likeness" by transitioning *up* the Tree. Those who use the Tree of Life do not speak of reaching "Divine likeness" but only of basking in the presence of the Divine. But the directional approach to the use and study of the Tree seem to be the same.

The whole debate as to which labeling is correct is still raging with each new scholar's attempt to interpret what was said within the *Sepher Yetzirah*. This is because of the issues of so many translations of this and other early Jewish works that were written using the Hebrew alphabet. The Hebrew alphabet from the earliest times only consisted of consonants with no vowels. It was primarily a verbal alphabet. And because it was verbal there was a need to have someone familiar with what it truly meant. For the meaning could be different even between two native speaking Jewish scholars. Because of this a singular written Hebrew word may have had multiple meanings such as the Hebrew word "aph", spelled in Hebrew as אַף. This word could mean; a nostril, nose, face, or anger. Thus, when transcribing a Hebrew text to a Latin-based version, a single mis-translated word could make a big difference in the understanding of a particular verse. And with each "translation" comes "new insights" as to where and what is truly represented by the individual paths.

The pathways on the Geronese Tree worked well when trying to understand the philosophical and spiritual relationship of God the Creator and the Universe of His creation. The Tree was presented in this manner to allow those who where studying and meditating on its paths and Sephirot a means to understand the non-understandable and to find their place within that scheme of life, death and creation. Later scholars moved away from this view of trying to reconcile man's fall from Grace to one of attempting to meditatively expand their understanding of the Divine as it related to the natural world.

---

7 *The Inner Meaning of the Hebrew Letters*, Robert M. Haralick, Aronson Publishing, 1995, pg. 1

On Kircher's Tree the paths, though the same in number, have been altered with more emphasis on the lower part of the Tree. Also many of the paths have had different letters assigned to them. They also combined the attributes of the major arcana Tarot keys that are associated to the individual keys. For at around this time the Tarot and its pictorial aspects were seen to hold esoteric meaning "to those who could read them".

Whereas in the Geronese Tree the scholars were trying to describe a process of creation using the humanistic qualities attributed to the Hebrew letters, Kircher, and those who followed, were using the Tree and paths as a pictorial map describing the way for man to better himself and become re-connected to his spiritual creator.

This school of thought also had many breaks in tradition, one being when the Hermetic Alchemist took the concepts of the Tree to seek to understand and control nature and life itself. Even though esoteric alchemy was practiced before the birth of Christ, the use of Kircher's Tree was viewed as another tool in their attempt to discover the Elixir or Tincture. It was hoped by obtaining this magic elixir they could prolong life for an indefinite period of time. They believed it could only be "obtained by divine grace and favor". This led to a gradual development of a devotional system where the transformation of metals became a symbolic process in which the sinful man, through prayer and devotion, transformed himself to the will of God.[8] Thus, the ability to work the magic of paths and tap into the Divine essence of the Sephirot became a hidden goal of many alchemists.

The development of the Kircher Tree was a pivotal point as it came to the assignment of the "qualities" attributed to the pathways or channels. It also took a totally different presepective of the Tree of Life. Up to this time the Jewish consciousness looked at the Tree as a process. A process by which they could attain redemption for the guilt, for being expelled from the Garden of Eden. They also suffered from the collective guilt of loosing their home land and, the loss of their Temple, the symbolic heart of their religion.

When Kircher presented in discussions it generally centered on the concept whoses end will procedure a product. For some this product, the ability to use meditation to climb the Tree and attaining knowledge and grace. For others, it was to find the secrets of the Tree that will enable them to control nature or others. Others, especially secular achemests attempted

---

8 *Alchemy*, E.J. Holmyard, Dover Publications, 1990, pgs. 15-16

to discover the "philosopher's stone". They were looking to gain something while the pre-Kircher Tree scholars were attempting to find the means of redemption. They were using the Tree for more spiritual reasons vs. their post Kircher scholars who were using it to gain something.

While the Jewish scholars generally used only the attributes directly assigned to their Hebrew letters, non-Jewish started assigning many different attributions to them in an attempt to give "a more complete" meaning to the individual channels. With the re-distrubution of the paths between the two Trees additional confusions developed. Here is a comparative chart of the paths between the two trees.

Paths	Hebrew	Hebrew	Letter	Tarot	Astrological	Alchemical	Sephirot Connections	
Number	Letter	Letter	Meaning	Key	Sign	Sign	Kircher	Geronese
11	Aleph	א	Bull	The Fool	Uranus	Air	1st - 2nd	4th-5th
12	Beth	ב	house	The Magician	Mecury	Mercury	1st - 3rd	2nd-4th
13	Gimel	ג	camel	High Priestess	Moon	Silver	1st - 6th	3rd-5th
14	Daleth	ד	door	The Empress	Venus	Copper	2nd - 3rd	1st-6th
15	Heh	ה	window	The Emperor	Aries	Fiery	2nd- 6th	1st-2nd
16	Vav	ו	hook/nail	The Hierophant	Taurus	Earthy	2nd-4th	1st-3rd
17	Zain	ז	sword	The Lovers	Gemini	Airy	3rd-6th	2nd-5th
18	Cheth	ח	fence	The Chariot	Cancer	Water	3rd-5th	4th-6th
19	Teth	ט	Serpent	Strength	Leo	Fiery	4th-5th	2nd-6th
20	Yod	י	open hand	The Hermit	Virgo	Earthy	4th-6th	6th-7th
21	Kaph	כ	closed hand	The Wheel of Fortune	Jupiter	Tin	4th-7th	4th-7th
22	Lamed	ל	ox goad	Justice	Libra	Airy	5th-6th	8th-9th
23	Mem	מ	water/sea	The Hanged Man	Neptune	Water	5th-8th	7th-8th
24	Nun	נ	fish	Death	Scorpio	Watery	6th-7th	7th-9th
25	Samekh	ס	prop	Temperance	Sagittarius	Fiery	6th-9th	6th-8th
26	Ayin	ע	eye	The Devil	Capricorn	Earthy	6th-8th	3rd-6th
27	Peh	פ	mouth	The Tower	Mars	Iron	7th -8th	5th-8th
28	Tzaddi	צ	fish-hook	The Star	Aquarius	Airy	7th-9th	5th-6th
29	Qoph	ק	back of head	The Moon	Pisces	Watery	7th-10th	3rd-4th
30	Resh	ר	head	The Sun	Sun	Gold	8th-9th	6th-9th
31	Shin	ש	tooth	Judgement	Pluto	Fire	8th-10th	2nd-3rd
32	Tav	ת	mark	The World	Saturn	Lead	9th-10th	9th-10th

In both of the two Trees, the Geronese and Kircher Tree, the Tree of Life will appear with ten spheres. Sometimes an eleventh sphere will be seen. This hidden or invisible eleventh sphere is Da'at and is located above the sixth Sefirot Tiphareth or Tifereth, with its twenty-two interconnecting paths. On this image of the Tree is superimposed The Lighting Flash or Path of Flaming Sword. The Flaming Sword follows the downward course of the Sephiroth, and is compared to a Lightning Flash with its hilt in Kether/Keter and its point in Malkuth.

Other uses for the Tree of Life

As the field of Western Hermetic studies became more popular in the late Renaissance period the Kircher's formation of the Tree of Life was expanded. As Europe's interest in the older ideas of "pagan" philosophies grew they began to combine them with the Kabbalah, Christian, Hermetism and Gnosticism philosophies. These schools of study resulted in the birth of many esoteric initiatory movements such as the Rosicrucians Orders, the Golden Dawn, and the Freemasons, most having initiatory rituals to join.

Charles T. McClenachan (1828–1896) who was a 33° Freemason, was a prolific author on Masonic related issues. In his 1884 book called *The Book of Ancient and Accepted Scottish Rite of Freemasonry* he included a single page showing a Tree of life. On page 436 the following glyph of the Tree is shown with a single short paragraph discussing the "pillars" placement of said Tree.

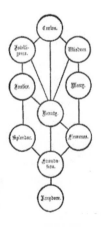

When viewing the diagram one will note the general configuration of the Tree follows that of the earlier Geronese Tree. One of the biggest difference is that there are only fifteen paths shown rather than the traditional twenty-two paths. McClenachan does not reveal any information concerning the origin of the Tree or about the configuration of the paths or why only fifteen paths. Another particularity of his Tree is the single diagonal path between 'Justice', passing through "Beauty" and terminating in "Firmness".

It appears this image of the Tree of Life used in McClenachan's book had previously appeared in an earlier publication by Albert G. Mackey (1807–1881). Mackey, a 33° Freemason, had images of the Tree in his book called *An Encyclopedia of Freemasonry Volume I*, published in 1873, eleven years prior to McClenachan's publication. In his book, Mackey devotes several pages (166–168) on the subject of the Tree of Life and the Sephirot placement. He gives a traditional description how the Sephiroth came about.

Kether, "the Crown," because it occupies the highest position. This first Sephirah contained within it the other nine, which sprang forth in the following order: At first a male, or active potency, proceeded from it, and this, the second Sephirah, is called, Chocmah or "Wisdom." This sent forth an opposite, female or passive potency, named, Binah or "Intelligence." These three Sephiroth constitute the first triad, and out of them proceeded the other seven. From the junction of Wisdom and Intelligence came the fourth Sephirah, called, Chesed or "Mercy." This was a male potency, and from it emanated the fifth Sephirah, named a Giburah or "Justice". The union of Mercy and Justice produced the sixth Sephirah, Tiphereth or "Beauty"; and these three constitute the second triad. From the sixth Sephirah came forth the seventh Sephirah, Nitzach or "Firmness." This was a male potency, and produced the female potency named Hod or "Splendor". From these two proceeded, Isod or "Foundation" and these three constituted the third triad of the Sephiroth. Lastly, from the Foundation came the tenth Sephirah, called Malcuth or "Kingdom", which was at the foot of all, as the Crown was at the top.[9]

---

9 *An Encyclopedia of Freemasonry Volume I*, Albert G Mackey, The- Masonic History Company, 1914, pg.37

But once again there is no description or explanation of the configu-ration of the paths. He does explain how the Sephirot relate to the human body with "Crown" or Kether being the Head, "Justice" or Geburah as the Left arm, Tiphareth as the "Chest" and Netzach as the Right leg. But why the one diagonal-l path from Geburah (Justice) though Tiphareth (Beauty), ending in Netzach (Firmness)? The answer appears to relate to only one possibility, the numerical value of the Sephirot.

Sephirot Number	Hebrew Name	Mackey's Name
First	Kether	Crown
Second	Chokmah	Wisdom
Third	Binah	Intelligence
Fourth	Chesed	Mercy
Fifth	Geburah	Justice
Sixth	Tiphareth	Beauty
Seventh	Netzach	Firmness
Eighth	Hod	Splendor
Ninth	Yesod	Foundation
Tenth	Malkuth	Kingdom

The Key to the un-explained path is the number 7. Seven is a very spe-cial number for initiatory ritualistic groups. Historians say many of the old spiritual groups had associated the number seven with the number of days, the number of known planets; there are 3 parts of the Soul, the Intellectual, Irascible and Epithymetic (desiring), and 4 most perfect virtues are produced. Just as there are three intervals—length, breadth, and depth, there are four boundaries in corporeal existence—point, line, superficies and solid. They also associated 7 with the number of steps or stages of initiation. The Persian Mystics of Mirtha described seven as the number of initiations, so did the Brahmas of India and the number of Egyptian Rites.

The number seven was also important to one of Masonry's oldest sym-bols, *Jacob's ladder*, which has seven steps leading to Heaven. It is also an important symbol of the Entered Apprentice Degree. A ladder of several staves or rounds of which three are illustrated to the candidate as Faith, Hope and Charity; the three theological virtues. In *The Book of Genesis* 28:10-13 it describes Jacob laying down:

[10] Jacob left Beersheba and went toward Haran.

[11] And he came to a certain place and stayed there that night, because the sun had set. Taking one of the stones of the place, he put it under his head and lay down in that place to sleep.

[12] And he dreamed, and behold, there was a ladder set up on the earth, and the top of it reached to heaven. And behold, the angels of God were ascending and descending on it!

It was felt this was so important that the early Masonic fathers included *Jacob's Ladder* in their rituals. It was officially introduced in Freemasonry in 1776 by Thomas Dunckerly (1724–1795) a Royal and Mark Mason. It is believed that Dunckerly may have gotten it from an earlier version that appeared around 1732 by the English Mason Matin Clare.

Esoterically the number seven is associated with the name J A H , a shortened version of Jehovah, was given to our universe because it represented the number 16, which in turn was composed of 3+4=7 and 4+5=9 (J=10, A=1, H=5). These two combinations are the 'two fundamental right angles of all geometry and the ones upon which most of our symbolisms are founded.' (6.)[10] It appears Mackey was hiding in front of us one of a core of Masonic symbolism-numbers. Other important numbers in Masonry are 3, 5, and 9.

The number 3 is the preeminent number for Craft Masonry. -There are three degrees; Entered Apprentice, Fellow of Craft and Master Mason. Other uses include the three virtues of faith, hope and charity. The third letter of the Hebrew alphabet gimel is the letter (G) as a Masonic symbol for God, the Great Architect of the Universe, the Grand Geometrician. The three principal officers, three original Grand Masters, three supporting pillars, three lesser lights and three greater lights, three movable and three immovable jewels, three raps and three in the 47th Problem of Euclid, just to name a few uses.

Five is significant for it represents the five senses, the five signs, the five-pointed star, the pentagon (five-sided figure), the five Points of Fellowship, and the hypotenuse of a right-angled triangle (the highest number in a five, four, three ratio.

The number nine is important as it represents the nine legendary figures who were the ideals of the Renaissance. The nine Muses of Greek mythology,

---

10 *Hermetic Masonry*, Frank C Higgins, Kessinger Publishing Company, pg. 39

the nine hells in Dante's Divine Comedy. Mathematically it is the last of the digits, and thus marks the end; and is significant of the conclusion of a matter. It is 3 X 3 = 9. Biblically it marks the completeness, the end and issue of all things as to man—the judgment of man and all his works. On the Tree of Life, it is the Sefirah Yesod of "Foundation". It is the foundation upon which all the material world is manifested. Yesod is the Sefirah of spiritual formation prior to its manifestation in the world of man, Malkuth or "the Kingdom".

A commonality of these numbers is that they are all odd numbers versus being even. They are very significant to Masonic Initiations and masonicly viewed as part of our mystic rites. It appeared Mackey wanted to emphasize these numbers as being important thus he outlined them within his Tree. By connecting them he reinforces the number seven, for there are seven Sephirot connected. It is the only path on his tree with seven connecting Sephirot, the others are five or six in number.

If one follows the path that Mackey drew starting at the foot of the first rung, that being the earth or "kingdom" the 10th Sefirah, then to the 9th "Foundation" up to the 7th Sefirah to the 6th Sefirah "Beauty" to the 5th "Justice", up to the 3rd Sefirah "Intelligence" ending or beginning in the 1st Sefirah "the Crown". Mackey has connected the primary sacred numbers of Freemasonry. He uses the 6th Sefirah, "Beauty" as his balancing point. For the sixth Sefirah is Tiphareth, symbol of balance and equilibrium. It is the point physically half way up the Tree separating the greater spiritual emanations from the lesser. It is the "heart" or "chest" of the "Perfect Elu". An "Elu" is a French word for "elected".

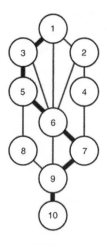

The first Sephirot, "Crown", is the "Head" of the "Perfect Man" while the tenth Sephirot is "Kingdom", or "earthly" point on the Tree. The sacred numbers of Masonry are thus balanced by the 6th Sephirot, 9th + 7th Sephirot on one side of the 6th Sephirot; and the 5th Sefirah and the 3rd Sephirot on the other side. These tenets of Freemasonry are brought down from the Divine (Kether) and installed in the Freemason's heart, represented by the sixth Tiphareth. These tenets mean nothing unless put into practice by the Freemason in the world he lives, the tenth Sephirot, Malkuth.

Figuratively it is thought the "Perfect Man" is pointing the way by which the initiate must travel for enlightenment. From the feet or Kingdom of reality, up into one's heart to THE ONE or Greater Architect. It is the same concept pictorially represented on the second Major Arcane Tarot card *The Magician*.

In this Key, *The Magician* (Initiate) points with his left hand to the source of all enlightenment (the Crown) and knowledge (Intelligence). He directs this energy downward through is heart (Chest) using is right hand to point of the w orld of reality. This world is symbolically represented by the cup, sword, pentacle, and wand on the table.

Mackey also discussed two other very important concepts of the Kabbalah and the Tree of Life. These were four worlds that Kircher had represented in his Tree of Life. They are:

Atziluth-world of emanation which is made up of Kether
Briah-world of creation, made up of Chokmah, and Binah
Yetzirah-the world of formation, comprising of Chesed,
    Geburah, Tiphareth, Netzach, Hod and Yesod
Assiah-the world of action which is Malkuth.

Mackey described them as:

These ten Sephiroth constitute in their totality the Atzilatic world or the world of emanations, and from it proceeded three other worlds, each having also its ten Sephiroth, namely, the Briatic world or the world of creation; the Yetziratic world or the world of formation; and the Ashiatic world or the world of action: each inhabited by a different order of beings. But to enter fully upon the nature of these worlds would carry us too far into the obscure mysticism of the Kabbala. These ten Sephiroth, represented in the parts of the body. Thus the Crown is the head; Wisdom, the brain; and Intelligence, the heart, which was deemed the seat of understanding. These three represent the intellectual; and the first triad is therefore called the Intellectual World.[11]

These four worlds of creation are some of the cornerstones of Kabbalistic creationism in that they try to explain the un-explainable in a manner that man can understand. He then continues to expound briefly on the triads on the Tree of Life that are mentioned in the Ancient and Accepted Scottish Rite's 18th °, Knight Rose Croix. Mackey describes the following:

Mercy is the right arm, and Justice the left arm, and Beauty is the chest. These three represent moral qualities; and hence the second triad is called the Moral World. Firmness is the right leg, Splendor the left leg, and Foundation the privates. These three represent power and stability; and hence the third triad is called the Material World. Lastly, Kingdom is the feet, the basis on which all stand, and represents the harmony of the whole archetypal man.

These are concepts that are once again discussed by Albert Pike, who was a 33° Mason and Supreme Commander of the Ancient and Accepted Scottish Rite of Freemasonry in the Southern Jurisdiction of the United States. In his book published in 1871 called *Morals and Dogma of the Ancient and Accepted Scottish Rite of Freemasonry* he too describes these worlds and presents his own version of the Tree of Life.

---

11 *An Encyclopedia of Freemasonry Volume I*, Albert G. Mackey, The Masonic History Company, 1914, pg. 770

Pike refers to the Kabbalah as a primitive tradition that "rests on the single dogma of Magism". This is the doctrine which changes the force of occult power which is the result of magic. The religion of Zoroastrianism originated from an older polytheistic faith called Magism. Pike went on to say the Ancients observed "equilibrium" through the physics of the universal laws. These laws were the result of the need for opposing forces being balanced by the will of God. Pike listed Stability and Movement, Necessity and Liberty, Justice and Love as a few examples.

Pike goes on to say the Kabbalah is the "foundation of all religions and all sciences".[13] He says the Sephiroth are the idea of Ternary shown as a triple triangle and circle. This Ternary is the balance and multiplied by itself to become the domain of the Ideal. He uses his Tree to represent this balance. He furthers his description of balance of opposites as male and female, Aleph and Binah respectively. Another example is the two columns of Boaz and Jachin. He states the Kabbalah explains them as "all the mysteries of the natural, political and religious antagonism". The Tree of Life is once again used as a visual symbol by which a deep philosophical concept is expressed.

THE PILLARS OF THE TREE OF LIFE
The Qabbalah teaches to not just look at the symbol before us but to see what is within that image. In this case, one can see the Sephirot form in groups. The most obvious are the grouping in vertical columns or Pillars.

---

12 *Morals and Dogma*, Albert Pike, Supreme Council of the Southern Jurisdiction, 1950, pg. 770
13 *Morals and Dogma*, Albert Pike, Supreme Council of the Southern Jurisdiction, 1950, pg. 769

Some refer to these pillars as "Pillars of Manifestation". They represent the positive, negative and center state of equilibrium. The concept of positive and negative does not refer to a "good" or "bad" aspect but to something like an atom with its protons, electrons, and neutrons.

The positive or masculine pillar is referred to as "The Pillar of Mercy"; the negative or feminine column is called "The Pillar of Severity" and the middle pillar is called the "Pillar of Equilibrium" or "Pillar of Mildness".

The Central column is headed by the Sephirot Kether or "Crown", and is associated with Hebrew Letter Aleph, "the breath", and the air element. It is a neutral pillar, a balance between the two opposing forces of male and female tendencies. Some teachings describe the Sephirot on this pillar as gender-neutral, while others say that the Sephirot vary in their sexual attributions.

The right column or "Pillar of Mercy" has the Sephirot of Chokhmah/Chokmah or "Wisdom". Metaphorically the "Pillar of Mercy", is associated with the Hebrew Letter Shin, the fire element, and the male aspect. The left column or "Pillar of Severity" headed by Binah or "Understanding" is associated with Hebrew Letter Mem, the water element and the female aspect.

Even though each pillar is given a sexual attribution, this does not mean that every Sephiroth on a given pillar has the same sexual attribution as the pillar on which they sit. In Jewish Kabbalah, of all the Sephirot only Binah and Malkuth are considered female, while all the other Sephirot are male.

The Pillars

Triads Represented on the Pillars

Supernal Triangle

As you further ponder the Tree you will notice the Sephiroth fall into a series of triadic groups or triangles. Each triad has one positive Sefirot, one negative Sefirot and a neutral one to act as a balance or reconciliation to the energies. The first triangle, located at the top of the Tree is referred to as the "Supernals" and is composed of Kether/ Crown, Chokmah/ Wisdom and Binah/ Understanding and 'Intellectual World', in Hebrew it is called Olam-Ha-Mevshekal. Another less common name is "The Intelligible World" which is still not a clear description of the essence this Supernal Triad represents. This is because it is the first point in which the "essence" starts to manifest itself. This "no thing" or Ain is the highest sphere which is represented by three veils above Kether and is the first of the veils. It is literally translated as "nothing", or simply "no"; it is "absolute emptiness", the opposite of existence, complete absence. The second veil below Ain is Ain Soph, is the middle of the three veils, and it proceeds from Ain by necessity. It is literally translated as "no limit". If there is nothing, then there are no boundaries or limitations; this is the limitless foundation — the eternal in its purest sense. The final one is Ain Soph Aur, the lower veil, situated closest to the Tree of Life, and it proceeds from Ain Soph as a necessity. It means 'limitless or eternal light'. Without any limitations, all things happen by virtue of the fact that there is no reason why they shouldn't. This triad is also referred to as one creative unit "Three-in-One" or "The One Head which has Three Heads". This triad is called the Supernal Triad because it points upward while the other two triads point downward focusing their energy downward toward mankind.

Ethical or Abstract Triangle

The second triad is composed of Geburah/ Severity, the negative Sefirot, Chesed/ Mercy, the positive Sefirot, and Tiphareth/Beauty the neutral Sefirot and is called the "Mediating Intelligence" or "Olam-Ha-Morgash" after the influence of Tiphareth. It is called the Ethical of Abstract Triangle and is the level of the Soul, the part of us that experiences a series of physical incarnations, and the conscious level of various higher beings. This triad is extremely import because it physically sits at the middle of the Tree.

Tiphareth is often referred to as the 'Christ-center' and is composed of the essences of love, justice and reconciliation.

ASTRAL OR MAGIC TRIANGLE

The final triad is called the "Material World", or "Olam-Ha-Vethau", though it is not truly a physical world in the sense of being a world of substance. It is more the part of the Tree were concepts have limits and boundaires placed on them and begin to form into existence which occurs in Malkuth/ Kingdom, which represents what is thought of as the physical world. This triad is made up of Hod/ Splendor, the masculine side, Netzach/ Victory, the feminine component and Yesod/ Foundation on the Middle Pillar. Hod and Netzach are described as "like unto the arms of God". In other words, it is as though God spreads His arms to help concentrate all the energies and forces into a point of existence, in this case creating something in the physical world. It is like giving flesh to an idea. The level of consciousness in the Astral Triangle equals the level of our everyday personality. It's far from perfection and it should be continually corrected as the Adept moves up and down the Tree and discovers and then revises the perceived realities and truths.

THE TREE OF LIFE'S WORLDS

According to Arthur Edward Waite who was a British scholar, mystic, occult author, and expert on esoteric matters, states the earliest known descriptions of the Worlds appeared in the *Masseket Atziluth* or *Treatise on Emanation,* written by Rabbi Isaac ha-Kohen (Cohen) (1013–1103) in the twelfth century and is the earliest literary product on Speculative Kabbalah. The four Worlds are described as:

Atziluth/Atzilut (אצי׳ל), — World of 'Emanation' is symbolically represented by Kether whose essence is the divine Fire. At this level, the light of the Ein Sof radiates downward and is united with its source, the Divine Chochma/Chokmah, and is the limitless flash of wisdom. It is related to the Chayah or Chaya, the level of the soul. This level communes with the Divine as He transcends the worlds. Here the soul's knowledge is not in the imminence of Divine attributes which identify the nature of the Divine energy manifested in Creation, but rather with knowing that God is not limited by the finite aspect of the Universe. Atziluth is manifested in the humanity as the individual's mind.

Briah/Beri áh/ Beriah (בריאל) — Represented by Chokmah and Binah–and is the Divine Water and called the World of "Creation". At this level, the first act of creation occurs coming out of nothing or the "no-thing". This is where the souls and angels have self-awareness, but without form and the Divine Binah, the intellectual understanding, predominates. Neshamah or Neshama is the soul parallel to Briah. The level of Neshama contemplates the manifestation of Divine energy in the world of Briah. This level of the soul's primary activity is to understand and is thus related to the human manifestation of thought.

Yetzirah (יְצִירָה)-World of "Formation" is made up of the Sephirot Chesed, Geburah, Tiphareth, Netzach, Hod and Yesod. It is the symbolic representation of the divine Air. The level of the soul assigned to Yetzirah is Ruach. The primary manifestation of Ruach is in the emotions, just as the primary activity of the six *Sephirot* of Zeir Anpin which includes the Sephirot from Chesed to Yesod, is in the world of Yetzira. In terms of Divine service this entails arousing the complementary emotions of love and awe of God. The love and awe of God is aroused by contemplating the divine energy which forms and maintains the world of Yetzirah. The human manifestation attributed to this is speech. For without the vocalizing of the manifested concept of God's great love it does not truly take form in the world.

Assiah/ Asiyah (עשיה) — is the World of "Action"– Malkuth/Malchut represent the Divine essence of Earth. On this level, creation is related to form and substance. This is where concepts become reality with existence based on form and limits. The Divine emotional Sephirot of Chesed to Yesod predominate. On this level creation is relegated to its physical aspect, the only physical realm and the lowest World, our realm with all its creatures. Nefesh is the lowest level of the soul and is assigned to Assiah and to man's manifestation of the process of action itself. Nefesh is also the lowest level of consciousness, is awareness of the physical body and the physical world, the world of Assiah, the world of Action. The Nefesh is in fact the life-force of the body, and it is precisely because of this it is the life-force of the body that the Nefesh has an awareness of the body. This physical awareness is a result of the enmeshing of the Nefesh with the body.

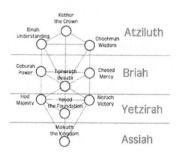

ADAM KADOMON — THE FIFTH WORLD

In the traditional Jewish or Lurianic system of Kabbalah, there is a mention of a fifth World called *Adam Kadomon,* meaning "primordial man" or Adam HaRishon the Biblical "first man", or Adam. It manifested itself at the Godhead level, which lies between the *Ein Sof* and the four lower Worlds. The discussion of creation was symbolically brought up in Lurianic doctrines where the act of *Ein-sof* was not to be that of revelation and emanation but one of concealment and limitation. Limitation is key in that the Limitless God placed some boundaries on Himself. Referring to Gesholm Scholem work *Kabbalah,* "When the primal intention to create came into being, Ein-Sof gathered together the roots of din (Judgment), which had been previously concealed within Him, to one place, from which the power and mercy had departed. In this way, the power of Din became concentrated. Zimzum (Contraction) therefore was an act of judgment and self-limitation."[14]. The very act of Zimzum is God contracting Himself to make something out of "no thing" of *Ein-Solf,* thus it is 'the entry of God into Himself'. Scholem goes on to describe that "creation" itself was a twofold activity of the *Ein-Sof* emanating itself followed by Zimzum; the Emanator acting also as a receptive.

---

14 *The Inner Meaning of the Hebrew Letters,* Haralick, Robert M., Jason Aronson Inc, 1995, pg. 141

The Lurianic approach to creation replaced the early work of Moses ben Jacob Cordovero, (1522–1570) aka RaMak, who's Cordoverian Kabbalah utilized the conceptual framework of evolving cause and effect. It is from the Infinite to the Finite and is the systemizing of the Kabbalah, with no real concern as to trying to explain the essence of Ein-sof. This is different in that it versus how God was thought of interacting with the whole concept of creation. For Cordovero, the Sephirot and the Five Worlds evolve sequentially from the Ein Sof. While for Luria, creation is a dynamic process of divine exile-rectification enclothement, where Adam Kadmon is preceded by the Zimzum which in turn is followed by the Olam HaTohu or The World of Tohu-Chaos and Olam HaTikun "The World of Tikun-Rectification" which are two stages in Lurianic Kabbalah, in the order of descending spiritual Worlds, called Olamot. They also represent two archetypal spiritual states, the first of "being" and the second of "consciousnesses". Their concepts of modern Kabbalah are based on Luria's interpretation of classic references in the *Zohar*.

One very important concept is that the implications of Tohu-Tikun present the underling concept of the origin of free will and the realm of Kelipah, Qliphoth (evil), caused by Shevirat HaKelim/Shevirah or "Shattering of the Vessels" of Tohu. Or even the very shattering of the Sephirot themselves, thus presenting the additional concept of spiritual and physical exile and redemption. The four Worlds link mankind with the Infinite, they also provide 'paths' that enable individual's soul to ascend in devotion or mystical states, towards the Divine. Each World provides a means for the soul's progress upward toward unity with or return to the Creator and redemption. This concept of redemption is key to Judaic concept of the use and reason for using the Tree and is an integral part of the Garden mythology. Adam Kadmon can also be thought of as the apex of Yod. It is related to the Yechida which corresponds to the level of soul called *Adam Kadmon*. Just as the sublime, pure and transcendent world of Adam Kadmon cleaves to and reflects the original Infinite Light (*Ohr Ein Sof*), so too does the level of Yechida. This is the essence of the soul which is naturally and immutably bound to the Holy One. It is related to man's will for at this level man opens his mind to the Divine Light.

Color and Its Importance

In most of today's depictions of the Tree of Life and its Sephirot one will see they are colored. The colors may vary depending on the depicter's perspective but they are generally very close. Color has been very important in exoteric work from as early as the eigth to sixth centuries B.C.E. when the *Shatapatha Brahmana* a Vedic Sanskrit was written. It is a sixth century text that describes a creation myth which is very similar to the Great Flood in the Bible including the use of primordial water. But it also gives a description of light and darkness, the separation of good and evil, and the explanation of time. The text describes in great detail the preparation of altars, ceremonial objects, ritual recitations, and the Soma libation, along with the symbolic attributes of every aspect of the rituals including the divinity of sound. For sound precedes color as in *Genesis* 1:3 And God *said,* "Let there be light, and there was light." For sound is vibration and vibration gives us color. The teachings of *Shatapatha Brahmana* provide the basis of the Oriental doctrine that states sound is the quality of Akasha, a Sanskrit word meaning "Aether" in both its elemental and metaphysical senses. Akasha in the Hindu philosophy dealing with the alchemy terms of quintessence which is the highest element in ancient and medieval philosophy that permeates all nature and is the substance composing the celestial bodies. In short sound precedes light. Within the Hindu teachings, they say "Through sound the world stands".

Shabda or sabda stands for word manifested by sound ("verbal") and such a word has innate power to convey a particular sense or meaning such as a verbal testimony. Sound is vibration and vibrations are color. Today science confirms what the ancients knew. Science has shown that varying velocities of light contain all the splendors of the universe. The velocities decrease from white light down though violet, indigo, blue, green, yellow, orange, and red to black. And white is the culmination of all color as all children have seen in the classroom experiment with the refraction of sunlight through a prism. It is these varying movements or vibrations that the eye senses as color.

Each Sefirah and eventually the pathways between the Sephirot are assigned a color and these colors/vibrations are sounds or musical notes.

It is believed that the doctrines of Shabda traveled to the Egyptians. The Egyptians then exposed the Greek initiates to their knowledge of the philosophic and therapeutic aspects of music. The Greeks supposedly took this knowledge and adapted it to their own mythology making Hermes the founder of the art. Plato, in describing the antiquity of these arts of music among the Egyptians, declared "that songs and poetry had existed in Egypt for at least ten thousand years". Plato went on to say they were of such an exalted and inspiring nature that only gods or godlike men could have composed them. In the Greek Mysteries, the lyre was regarded as the secret symbol of the human constitution. The body of the instrument representing the physical form, the strings the nerves, and the musician the spirit. Playing upon the nerves, the spirit thus created the harmonies of normal functioning, which, however, became discords if the nature of man were defiled.

Pythagoras, sometime between the fifth and fourth century B.C.E., is credited for the raising the art of sound and music to its true dignity. He did this by demonstrating its mathematical foundation. Even though Pythagoras, who was not a musician, is now generally credited with the discovery of the diatonic scale in music theory, which is a diatonic scale comprising of an eight-note musical scale composed of seven pitches and a repeated octave. Pythagoras is said to have first learned the divine theory of music from the priests of the various Mysteries into which he had been accepted. After many years of contemplation on harmony he discovered the key to harmonic ratios which are hidden in the famous Pythagorean tetractys, or pyramid of dots. The tetractys is made up of the first four numbers—1, 2, 3, and 4—which in their proportions reveal the intervals of the octave, the diapente, and the diatessaron.

Pythagoras related this harmony or music to the heavens and their observable movements which he referred to as spheres. He considered that the interval between the earth and the sphere of the fixed stars was considered to be a diapason or in the most perfect harmonic interval. Pythagoras calculated that the sphere of the earth to the sphere of the Moon was one tone. While the sphere of the Moon to that of Mercury, one half-tone; from Mercury to Venus, one-half; from Venus to the Sun, one and one-half tones; from the Sun to Mars, one tone; from Mars to Jupiter, one-half tone; from Jupiter to Saturn, one-half tone; from Saturn to the fixed stars, one-half tone. The sum of these intervals equals the six whole tones of the octave.

Sound and color was thus an important means of conveying many concepts of creation and the structure of how nature worked. As the Western Hermetic Mysteries continued to become popular these concepts became an integral topic of training and scholarship to the point that certain colors were associated with certain parts of the body such as:

Red which is C-natural is related to the zone of the head above the brows and the opening of the ears and due to its close proximity to the eyes. It is also associated with Aries.

As the student becomes involved with the deeper meaning and use of the Tree the relationship of color/sound/vibration will become more important and useful.

Angels and their role in Qabbalistic Mysticism
When studying any of the forms of the Kabbalah the student will find references to angels. Angelic lore has been part of the Kabbalah from the very beginning. Angels played a key role in the very earliest times prior even to the Talmud and the centralized Temple worship. Angels were a means to physically describe, at least in one's mind, the very essence of the attribute of God the worshipper was praying/meditating upon. Ancient sages believed that one duty of angels was to be messengers from and to God and thus sages were very interested in their various attributes of particular angels. And as students of the Kabbalah you should be aware of their symbolic existence and how their associated attributes come into play with the various Sephirot. As students of the Kabbalah remember that the concept of angelic lore is not the actual angel associated with the Sefirah but the personality represented by that angel, such as mercy, understanding or wisdom.

It should be noted that within the Hebrew Bible, the *Tanakh,* there are only three angels mentioned by name; they are Michael, Gabriel and Satan. The first two were mentioned in the *Book of Daniel* 10:13-21 and Satan in *1 Chronicles* 21:1. It is not until the *Book of Job* and *Zechariah* 3:1-2 that Satan was specifically mentioned as being an "adversary of God". For the Hebrews, the word mal'akh is the word for "messenger" both angelic as well as human. It was not until the term was translated into English that it become clarified to refer to angelic messengers.[15]

The Qabbalah and its teaching grew out of the teaching of the Jewish Mystic Kabbalah, which in turn was the codification of Jewish spiritual

---

15 *Kabbalah*, Gesholm Scholem, Dorset Publishing, 1974, pp.130

thought and lore. The Jewish belief in angels goes as far back as the *Book of Genesis*, where we read about angels calling out to Abraham at the binding of Isaac. Angels appearing in Jacob's dream, Jacob fighting with an angel, and many more accounts of angelic activity. Angels are then mentioned numerous times throughout the other books of the *Torah, Prophets*, and *Scriptures*.

According to Jewish tradition, an angel is a spiritual being and does not have any physical characteristics. The angelic descriptions provided by the prophets — such as wings, arms etc. — are anthropomorphic, referring to their spiritual abilities and tasks. As early as the thirteenth century Jewish angelic lore developed, as seen in the *Zohar* where many references to the importance of the Hebrew alphabet as a celestial code or blueprint for the cosmos are made.

Abraham ben Samuel Abulafia (1240–1291) is ranked among the most important Jewish mystics. He created a meditative system based on the Hebrew alphabet, which he called "knowing God through the twenty-two letters of the Hebrew alphabet". In his commentaries on *Sepher Yetzirah of Ashkenazi*, he called his Kabbalah "the *Kabbalah of Names*", that is, of Divine names. He said it was a means to reach what he called the prophetic experience, or "prophetic Kabbalah". In his writings, he expresses of his knowledge of prophetic Kabbalah, known as the unio mystica of the human and the supernal intellects, may be discerned. Adulafia was much less concerned with the theosophy of his contemporary Kabbalists, who were interested in theories of ten hypostatic Sefirot. He is said to have scoffed and described their work as worse than the Christian belief in the Trinity. Abulafia depicted the supernal realm, especially the cosmic Agent Intellect, in linguistic terms, as speech and letters. And the access and understanding of the universe and God can only come through the understanding of the secret meaning of the alphabet of flame, the Hebrew letters.

Among his writings on angels and prayer, Abulafia declared: "Look at these holy letters with truth and belief. It will awaken your heart to thoughts of godly and prophetic images." Adulafia even described how his students should reach these godly and prophetic thoughts. He advised: "Cleanse your body, choose a special place where none will hear you, and remain altogether by yourself in isolation. Sit in one place in a room...it is best to begin by night." These instructions can still be seen in tutorials instructions on meditation in many of the mystic Orders today.

Abulafia went on to describe a method the student can use to reach these divine inspired images. He instructs his students to "begins to combine letters, a few or many, reversing them and rolling them around rapidly, until one's heart feels warm". Those who carefully follow this technique, Abulafia assured, will eventually experience 'an abundance of saintly spirit, wisdom, understanding, good counsel and knowledge. The spirit of the Lord will rest upon them.' He added that angels would become the teachers of those who practiced his method with special devotion.

From the works and commentaries derived from studying the *Torah*, and the *Bible*, early initiates of the Qabbalistic Mysteries believed that its principles of creation of the universe were first taught by God to a school of His angels before the fall of man. The angels later communicated these secrets to Adam. With this knowledge man might gain an understanding of these divine principles to the point that humanity might regain its access to the symbolic Garden of Eden.

The Hebrew word for angel is "mal'akh", which means messenger, for the angels were believed to be God's messengers to perform various missions. Every angel is "programmed" to perform certain tasks; such as Michael who is dispatched on missions which are expressions of God's kindness; Gabriel, who executes God's severe judgments; and Rafael, whose responsibility it is to heal. The Angel Raziel was dispatched from heaven to instruct Adam in the mysteries of the Qabbalah. Other angels were assigned to provide knowledge to some of God's chosen. A few examples are the angel Tophiel was assigned as teacher of Shem, Raphael to guide Isaac, Metatron to work and help Moses, and Michael to provide David with Divine guidance.

Angels act as the conduit between the world of man and that of God. As messengers of God they also perform another very important duty as described in the sacred texts of both the Jewish and Christian tradition. They are described as providing a means for our prayers to reach to the "foot stool of God's throne". Other angels were created to report the deeds of man. In the words of our Sages: "He who fulfills one mitzvah, acquires for himself one angel-advocate; he who commits one transgression, acquires against himself one angel-accuser." These deeds are formed from the energies created through the intellectual and emotional acts upon both in the positive as well as the negative.

The Ancient Planets and their Influence on Man

The observations of the planets in the starry night has long been a fascination of man. All of the ancient civilizations, from the Chinese, Greek, Egyptians, Babylonians and Romans had theorized what these transitory objects were and how they affected their daily lives. The Seven Ancient Planets started with the five planets that can be seen with the naked eye, which are Mercury, Venus, Mars, Jupiter, and Saturn, sometimes, referred as "luminaries" because of their brightness. The Sun and Moon, rounded out the list to make a total of seven. With these observations came a realization, that when certain planets were seen in particular quadrants of the sky certain events did, or should occur. They observed the skies at the time of planting or harvesting of crops, migration of birds and animals, and the changing of the seasons of the year. These associations developed further as shamans, priests, and healers began to assign certain energies that would or could affect bodily energies and functions to specific planets. There are some variations as to which functions are associated with which planet depending on which source you use. Here is one list:

Sun — heart, spine, and general vitality
Moon — stomach, digestive system, female organs, lymphatic system
Mercury — brain, central nervous system, thyroid gland, five senses, hands
Venus — throat, kidneys, thymus gland, sense of touch, ovaries
Mars — muscles, head, adrenal glands, senses of smell and taste
Jupiter — liver, thighs, feet, growth, pituitary gland
Saturn — skin, hair, teeth, bones, the body's defenses, spleen

This is according to the early writings of Hermes Zoroaster (628–551 B.C.E.), a first century B.C.E. philosopher, who discovered that the movements of the planets had meaning beyond the basic laws of physics. He felt that if we understood the influences of these celestial travelers we could gain wisdom that could help us to direct our actions to successful conclusions. Later mystics and alchemists took this one step further to try to use this esoteric information as a tool to understand and possibly manipulate the laws of nature.

According to the *Sepher Yetzirah*, one of the initial functions of the seven double letters was to produce the seven planets:

Bet/Beth	Mercury
Gimel	Moon
Daleth/Delet	Venus
Kaph	Jupiter
Peh	Mars
Resh	Sun
Tav	Saturn

The seven double letters vary in how they are being pronounced, either hard or soft, depending on how the speaker varies their intake or expulsion of air. The seven planets are said to be in continuous movement, approaching or receding from the earth. The seven days, which were also the result of the double letters, in like manner change in time according to their relation to the planets. The seven apertures in man, another creation of the double letters, connect man with the outer world as the seven planets join heaven and earth. Hence these organs are subject to the influence of the planets, and with knowledge and understanding of how each planet influences each organ the nature of that organ could be understood.

From the *Sepher Yetzirah* the ten spheres are arranged in three pillars, which correspond to the three modalities in astrology: cardinal, fixed, and mutable. Understanding these attributes becomes important as the student expands their knowledge of the Tree of Life and its effect on their lives.

As the mystics, alchemists and scholars contemplated the planets and their effect on our physical world theories developed on how to use these energies or the knowledge of these energies to understand and thus manipulate nature.

The alchemists, in an attempt to symbolize the potencies and effects of the planets assigned each planet to a base metal.

Gold dominated by Sol ☉ ☿
Silver dominated by Luna ☽
Copper dominated by Venus ♀
Iron dominated by Mars ♂
Tin dominated by Jupiter ♃

Mercury (quicksilver) dominated by Mercury ☿
Lead dominated by Saturn ♄

One large pitfall for those first stepping upon the path upon seeing a list of physical materials, is feeling that they can use those physical metals to perform acts of alchemy such as seen in television and movies. These items, much like the elements of fire, water, and earth are symbolic representations of "other world" energies. It is important for students of the Qabalah to understand these basic energies associated with particular Sefirah as they expand their understanding and wisdom.

IX.

THE SEPHIROTH: AN
INTRODUCTION

I n 1620, Jakob Böhme born around, 1575 and died in 1624, was a German
Lutheran mystic and theologian. His name sometimes is spelled
Jacob Boehme or Behmen. He is remembered for writing *Mysterium
Pansophicum; A Fundemental Statement Concerning the Earthly and Heavenly
Mystery......* written around 1620. In the "Seventh Text" he describes a rev-
elation; "the second alphabet is the Hebrew, which reveals the mystery "of
the language of Nature", and names the tree with the branches and twigs".
This tree is believed to be the Tree of Life and the branches are the Sephirot,
which are each represented by a specific color. Often times there is a varia-
tion of the color, which A.E. Waite mentioned. Color was also discussed by
Rabbi Azariel ben Menachem (1160–1238), also known as Azriel of Gerona,
or Azriel ben Menahem, depending on your historical source. He was a
Spanish rabbi, born in Valladolid or Girona, in the autonomous region of
Castile and Leon about 1160. He distinguished himself as a philosopher,
Cabalist, Talmudist, and commentator. He was a pupil of Isaac the Blind,
who is regarded as the originator of the Cabala. In one of his Commentaries
on the Sephirot he placed particular colors to each Sephirot, yet these do
not agree with the colors given in the *Zohar*. Because of this variation there
has been a great deal of confusion as to the "true" color and thus which
vibratory note assigned to each Sefirah would be correct.

Each path and Sefirah has a Hebrew letter assigned to them and within these letters lies the "Secret Wisdom of Israel". This is not the secrets of the political State of Israel, but a metaphorical or esoteric meaning. Y'srael (a more correct transliteration) is said to be composed of 12 "tribes" of "Nomadic Wanderers". These "tribes" were continually in apparent conflict with each other. This concept of conflict is of importance as it relates to "the spiritual man" as described below.

The esoteric symbolism of the 12 tribes are that they are the 12 primary archetypes of the ego — or of the personality. They are 1) The Innocent, 2) The Orphan, 3) The Hero, 4) The Caregiver 5) The Explorer, 6) The Rebel, 7) The Lover, 8) The Creator, 9) The Jester, 10) The Sage, 11) The Magician, and 12) the Ruler. Even though the term "archetype" has its origins in ancient Greek, Carl Gustav Jung (1875–1961), who was a Swiss psychiatrist and psychotherapist, helped to place them into personalities which we recognize today.

There is no need to learn Hebrew for one to be able to walk the path of the Qabbalah, because the secrets of the Qabbalah or Secrets of Israel are not written in the Hebrew language but hidden in the Hebrew characters. One will need to know and understands the attributions of the twenty-two Hebrew letters and the Tree of Life before the secrets will be unveiled and revealed to those who understand their meanings. For the Hebrew letters are a magical language and is a means to preserve and transmit the practical secrets revealed is the Western Hermetic Qabbalah.

In 1860, Eliphas Levi, who was born Alphonse Louis Constant (, 1810 -1875), a French occult author and ceremonial magician who began to write *Historie de la Magie*. In *Historie de la Magie* he says: "The absolute hiero-glyphically science had for its basis an alphabet of which all the gods were letters, all the letters ideas, all the ideas numbers, all the numbers perfect signs."[16] This is a good summary about why there is so much written on the subject of the Sephirot.

Generally, the Hebrew letter and its corresponding number is the constant. The interpretations of what the names mean as well as the concepts/ ideas are as numerous as the scholars who profess esoteric information obtained from divine instruction. Each generation of writer/scholar adds their own interpretation of what their predecessor had revealed thus adding

---

16 *A Garden of Pomegranates*, Israel Regardie, Llewellyn Publications, pp. 39

to the accumulation of data concerning the Sephirot. Another reason for so many interpretations is that the individual Sefirah do not stand alone as a single entity but comprise all the other qualities of their fellow Sephirot at various levels. This adds to the complication of interpretations because a scholar may be more sensitive to certain aspects or qualities at the time of study. It is thought each Sefirah has the qualities of not only their primary emanation but also those of the Trees of the four worlds: Atziluth, Briah, Yetzirah, and Assiah. Another reason for confusion may be the individual Sefirah presents itself differently to each person, like the way we are seen differently by individuals whom meet us in a social gathering.

When meditating on the Sephirot it is recommended to alternate between visualizing them a singular unified system and as individual powers or clusters of powers. For the individual Sefirah are not single centers but integrally interlocked with each other. It is like trying to understand a forest. It is an essence made up of as many independent trees all integrally interlocked. To understand the Tree of Life one must understand its parts but those parts do not represent what the Tree is in its entirety.

Finally, the Sephirot are centers of the Divine's Infinite Light, but at the same time they act as screens or puffers of His immensely powerful radiant Light. Without these screens man's mind would not be able to comprehend its vastness. Without the screens it would be like trying to contain the oceans of the world in a single vase, it could not be done. So, the individual Sefirah act as a means for God's Infinite to be limited for man's limited understanding.

First Sefirah: Keter / Kether (כתר) "the Crown"

God-name:	Ehieh (I am) or Ehyeh Asher Ehyeh (אהיה אשר אהיה) (I am that I am)
Number:	1
Archangel:	Metatron
Order of Angels:	Chaioth he-Qadesh (Holy Living Ones)
Body Part:	Crown of the Head
Symbol:	Swirling Swastika, The Point, The Point within a circle, The Crown
Spiritual Experience:	Union with God
Color in Atziluth:	Brilliance
Color in Briah:	Pure White Brilliance
Color in Yetzirah:	Pure White Brilliance
Color in Assiah:	White Flecked Gold
Personal Chakra:	The Crown Chakra, Thousand Petalled Lotus

Kether is the topmost of the Sephirot on the Tree of Life as described in the *Sepher Yetzirah*. It resides as the topmost Sefirah of the Supernal Triangle above and between Chokmah and Binah. Chokmah sits on the right and Binah on the left, and is located above Tiphareth on the central pillar. There are usually three paths leading to it from three lower Sephirot of; Chokmah, Tiphareth, and Binah.

In the *Zohar*, Kether is called "the most hidden of all hidden things", and is completely incomprehensible to man. Human consciousness has no means to access Kether due to its incomprehensible spiritual essence. Although it contains all the potential for content, it contains no content itself, and is therefore called "Nothing", "The Hidden Light", "The air that cannot be grasped". And in Dion Fortune's *The Mystical Qabalah*, Keter/Kether is described as pure consciousness, beyond all categories, timeless, a point that crystallizes out of the Ein Soph, and commences the process of emanation that ends in Malkuth.

The name of God associated with Kether is Ehyeh Asher Ehyeh (אהיה אשר אהיה), the name through which He revealed Himself to Moses from the burning bush. I AM is the name of God. I AM is also one of the only two universally accepted literal translations of the word ehyeh as it occurs in *Exodus* 3:14. It can be identified in its context as a Divine name, and, because it is first person singular of the verb, can be identified as the name by which God is known to Himself; His Personal name.

Thus in *Exodus* 3:14a, where Moses asked what he should tell the Israelites he is told to tell them: ehyeh asher ehyeh which was God identifying Himself to Moses using His Personal name Ehyeh. God's response to Moses' is translated as: "I am Ehyeh. Tell the Israelites that Ehyeh has sent you to them."

METATRON (מטטרון) OR MATTATRON

The meaning of the name Metatron is unclear. It is thought that Eleazar of Worms (1176–1238) who is believed to have presented this name may have derived the name from the Latin word "metator", meaning "guide" or "measure". In the *Encyclopedia Mysthica*, Dr. Ilil Arbel states that the myths of Metatron are extremely complicated, and at least two separate versions exist. Dr. Arbel notes the first version states Metatron came into being when God created the world, and that Metatron immediately assumed his many responsibilities. The second claims that he was first a human named Enoch, who is the son of Jared (*Genesis* 5:3-18), the father of Methuselah, and the great-grandfather of Noah. Enoch is described as a pious, good man who had ascended to Heaven a few times, and eventually was transformed into a fiery angel. Some later books adopt the first version, some the second, and in other literature both are combined. There are even two versions of the name Metatron, one spelled with seven letters, the other with six, lacking the Hebrew letter "yod". The Kabbalists explained that the six-letter name represents the Enoch-related Metatron, while the seven-letter name refers to the primordial Metatron.

Even though there is a great deal of confusion as to the origins of Metatron he is still seen as one of the most important angels in the heavenly hierarchy. He is a member of a special group that is permitted to look at God's countenance, an honor most angels do not share. In the literature, Metatron is often referred to as "the Prince of the Countenance", other titles are "Angel of the Presence" and "World-Prince". He is also recognized as the heavenly scribe who records everything that happens in the ethereal achives or Book of Lives. Metatron is the first and the last of the ten archangels of the Briatic World or Archangelic World of Creations. He sometimes called the "Angel of Death" for he is said to transmit the orders of God to his subordinates Gabriel and Samael of which souls should be taken that day.

Adding to the confusion, Isidore Loëb (1839–1892), a French-Jewish scholar born at Soultzmatt, Haut-Rhin, France, contends that Metatron was a species of Demiourgos. Demiourgos are defined as a concept from the Platonic, Neopythagorean, Middle Platonic, and Neoplatonic schools of philosophy for an artisan-like figure responsible for the fashioning and maintenance of the physical universe, thus giving Metatron the role of maintaining the balance of the physical world. Another view is expressed by Gershom Scholem who writes that according to old traditions God took Enoch from earth to heaven transforming him into the angel Metatron, who was said to be a cobbler. And like a cobbler who using his awl to bind the upper portion of a shoe's sole to its lower section, Metatron used meditation to draw the stream of emanation down from the upper Sephirot to lower Sephirot; thus transforming profane actions into ritual action.

CHAIOTH HA QADESH, (היות הקדש)

Metatron is said to belong to the order of angels that resides in the Chaioth ha Qadesh, (הקדש היות) which means the Holy Living Creatures. The Chaioth ha Qadesh is part of a Christian angelic hierarchy as described by Pseudo-Dionysius the Areopagite (650–725 C.E.), also known as Pseudo-Denys, who was a Christian theologian and philosopher, originally credited for writing *Corpus Areopagiticum* or *Corpus Dionysiacum*, probably in Syrian. Later research revealed that the *Corpus Areopagiticum* or *Corpus Dionysiacum* was written as early as 500 C.E. by an unknown author. Another book credited to Pseudo-Dionysius is called *De Coelesti Hierarchia (On the Celestial Hierarchy)*, which is a work on angelology, written in Greek. In *De Coelesti Hierarchia*, Pseudo-Denys attempts to organize the angels into several orders which he called "Angelic Choirs". Metatron belonged to the Order/Choirs of Chaioth ha Qadesh which is the highest of the nine orders of angels. It is called the Order of Seraphim; whose primary responsibility is to be the caretakers of the divine throne. The Seraphim (singular form "Seraph") are mentioned in *Isaiah* 6:1-7 where they are described as the highest angelic class who serve as the caretakers of God's throne and continuously shout praises: "Holy, Holy, Holy is the Lord of hosts; the whole earth is full of his glory!" According to *Isaiah* 6:2, the Seraphim have six wings: "with two he covered his face, and with two he covered his feet, and with two he flew".

Metatron is also described in many texts as the receiver of the prayers, sacrifices, and/or meditations of the people of Israel. It is said as the Shekinah receives the offering from the faithful, she carries them to the footstool of Metatron who receives them for the God Almighty. The Shekinah, Shechinah, Shechina, or Schechinah (שכינה), is the grammatically feminine Hebrew name of God in Judaism. She is said to be the receiver of the offerings and is often described as 'the Shekinah Glory Entering the Tabernacle to receive the prayers' of the people.

Second Sefirah: Chokmah/ Chochmah/ Hokhmah
(חכמה) "Wisdom"

God-name:	Jehovah or Jah-eternal
Number:	2
Archangel:	Ratziel/ Razeil/ Razeel/ Rezial/ Reziel/ Ratziel, and Galizur.
Order of Angels:	Auphanim—Wheels
Body Part:	Crown of the Head-practically the right hemisphere of the brain
Symbol:	The Phallus, The Inner Robe of Glory, The Standing Stone, the Straight Line, The Uplifted Rod of Power
Spiritual Experience:	The Vision of God Face to Face
Color in Atziluth:	Pure soft Blue
Color in Briah:	Grey
Color in Yetzirah:	Pearl Grey Iridescence
Color in Assiah:	White flecked Red Blue Yellow
Personal Chakra:	The Ajna Chakra, behind the center of the forehead

Chokmah, or "Wisdom", the second of the ten Sephirot, is the first power of conscious intellect within Creation. Chokmah appears in the configuration of the Sefirot at the top of the right axis, and is part of the Supernal Triangle. Being at the top of right axis it forms the head of the Pillar of Mercy and is called the Supernal Father. In its fully articulated form, Chokmah possesses two partzufim or Divine personage, visages, face, form or configuration. The first or higher partzufim is referred to as Abba Ila'ah ("the higher father"), whereas the lower partzufim is referred to as Yisrael Saba ("Israel, the Elder"). These two partzufim are referred to jointly as Abba "the father" or "supernal father".

Chokmah gives the soul of man the power of intuitive insight, and it often appears as a flashing lightning across what symbolizes man's consciousness. The higher partzuf or Abba Ila'ah is associated with the process to spontaneously extract such insight from the superconscious realm, whereas the lower partzuf of Yisrael Saba is associated with the power to subsequently direct it into consciousness.

When trying to determine the underlying truth of some aspect of life one needs to seek the "wisdom" of Chokmah for it implies the ability to look deeply into that aspect of reality and abstract its conceptual essence till one succeeds in uncovering the essence of that truth as to be the axiomatic truth. These seeds of truth can then be conveyed to the companion power of Binah for the sake of intellectual analysis and development or 'understanding' of that ultimate truth.

Chokmah is the primary or beginning force in the creative process, as it is said in the *Torah*: "You have made them all with Chokmah." The first word of the *Torah*, Breishit, "in the beginning (God created the heavens and the earth)", is translated as "With chokmah (God created...)". Because Chokmah is so close to the God Head, it is said that during intense prayer of meditation, Chokmah acts like a magnet pulling your upward and transforming your human self into the divine.

RATZIEL—THE WILL OF GOD

The name Ratziel is translated as the "Will of God", as is represented by the sphere of Chokmah. The Archangel Ratziel is the ruling power below the first emanation of God, Kether. Ratziel is another of the Godlike Archangels, (Metatron being the other) and has no specific day of the week assigned to him. As such, he can be easily called upon at any time. Ratziel belongs to the angelic order of the Auphaneem. Ratziel can appear in many forms, but, more often, this being is seen as pure energy or light. It is said the Archangel Ratziel comes to you when your wisdom has grown to a point where your energy can be increased to the next level of meditation or prayer. His visitations are said to occur at night, with his recipients perceiving a surge of white like energy.

One of the main legends concerning the Archangel Raziel is that God gave the Secret Knowledge or Holy Secrets to him and for that reason the Hebrew word "Raziel" means "Secret of God". And with this Secret Knowledge God gave Raziel the mission to be the transmitter of secrets to those who seek it especially "through the Kabbalah".

In the *Zohar*, it is said that Raziel is the angel in charge of Chokmah (Wisdom). This legend says Raziel is credited with writing the *Sefer Raziel HaMalach* or *Sefer Raziel HaMalakh* (ספר רזיאל המלאך), (the *Book of Raziel the Angel*). This is a medieval Practical Kabbalah book of magic which was primarily written in Hebrew and Aramaic, but surviving also in Latin translation, as *Liber Razielis Archangeli*. The *Razielis Archangeli* is a thirteenth century manuscript produced under Alfonso X, who was also known as Alphonso X, Alphonse X, or Alfons X (1221–1284). He was called "the Wise" and was the King of Castile, León and Galicia from 30 May 1252 until his death. In the *Book of Raziel the Angel* it claims to explain divine secrets about both celestial and earthly knowledge. This knowledge was obtained from the Angel Raziel according to Jewish tradition. Raziel stood so close to God's throne that he could hear everything God said; Raziel then wrote God's secret insights about the universe down in the *Sefer Raziel HaMalach*. The Angel Raziel began the book by stating: "Blessed are the wise by the mysteries coming from the wisdom." Some of the insights that Raziel included in the book are that creative energy begins with thoughts in the spiritual realm and then leads to words and actions in the physical realm.

Also according to legend, Raziel gave Adam and Eve the *Sefer Raziel HaMalach* after they were expelled from the Garden of Eden. But other angels were so upset that Raziel had given Adam and Eve the book, they cast Raziel's book into the ocean. Eventually, the *Sefer Raziel HaMalach* washed ashore, and the prophet Enoch found it and added some of his own knowledge before he was transformed into the archangel Metatron. The *Sefer Raziel HaMalach* then passed on to the Archangel Raphael, then to Noah, and to King Solomon. This is according to the legend which probably began near the time of Alfonso X publication.

AUPHANIM —WHEELS

The Auphanim are the whirling forces, described as "wheels within wheels with many eyes". They are associated with Merkabah/Merkavah mysticism, also known as Chariot mysticism, which was first seen in some of the early schools of Jewish mysticism, c. 100 B.C.E.– 1000 C.E. Merkabah lore is centered on visions such as those found in the *Book of Ezekiel* Chapter 1, or in the hekhalot ("palaces") literature, concerning stories of ascents to the heavenly palaces and the Throne of God. The main corpus of the Merkabah literature was composed in Israel in the period 200–700 C.E.

Auphanim is also described as the second heaven which is the area of the stars and planets (*Genesis.* 1:14-18), and some say is also the abode of all supernatural angelic beings. To the ancients, the area of starry heavens seems to be in eternal motion which was similarly said to describe the wheels of God's throne, thus the concept of cyclic action as a source of inexhaustible power through motion. This power is the reflection of God's limitlessness, and "The heavens declare the glory of God; and the firmament shows His handiwork." *Psalm* 19:1.

Third Sefirah: Binah/ Beri'ah/ Briyah, or Briah (בינה) "Understanding" (also known as Olam Briah, Olam Briah, (עולם בריאה) literally World of Creation) is the second of the four celestial worlds in the Tree of Life of the Kabbalah

God-name:	Jehovah Elohim-God and Goddess
Number:	3
Archangel:	Tzaphkiel/Zadkiel
Order of Angels:	Aralim—Thrones
Body Part:	Crown of the Head-left hemisphere of the brain
Symbol:	The Vesica Piscis, The Cup, The Chalice, The Outer Robe of Concealment
Spiritual Experience:	The Vision of Sorrow
Planet:	Saturn
Color in Atziluth:	Crimson
Color in Briah:	Black
Color in Yetzirah:	Dark Brown
Color in Assiah:	Grey flecked Pink
Personal Chakra:	The Ajna Chakra, behind the center of the forehead.

Binah, or "Understanding", is the third of the ten Sephirot, and the second conscious power of intellect in Creation. According to the *Bahir* is described as "The third utterance". The "understanding" or more precisely "intuitive understanding" or the ability to contemplate implies the ability to examine the degree of truth or falsehood inherent in a particular idea. Thus

Binah acts as a reflection to the ideas or energy coming from Chokmah's "Wisdom". Binah is the processing center of knowledge revealed by Archangel Raziel. This is expressed in *Job* (12:11 and 34:3) as: "the ear examines words". The ear, the organ of hearing, is associated with Binah. "Hear, O Israel..." (*Deuteronomy* 6:4) which means "Understand....". The initial letters of the phrase "the ear examines words" spell "emet", meaning "truth".

Binah is associated with the feminine or the Great Mother. The *Bahir* states: "For you shall call Understanding a Mother." The conception of Binah, from Kether and Chokmah, creates the Supernal Triad or first triad of the Tree of Life. The first triad is the bearer and giver, of the divine intellect. As the bearer or giver Binah is often credited with giving birth to the lower seven Sephiroth.

Binah appears in the configuration of the Sephirot at the top of the left axis, or head of the Pillar of Severity. Binah is also associated with the concept of tzelem Elohim which translates to The Image of God or image of the Holy Spirit. Theologians as well as the common man have long tried to describe what God looked like. No matter who you ask everyone has their own concept of what the Creator looks like; this comes from the left hemisphere of the brain attempting to contemplate or understand the wisdom which has been revealed through Chokmah. And since each of us has a different level of understanding of the wisdom given us we each have our own concept of what God should look like.

Like Chokmah, Binah possesses two leaves of partzufim: the higher of these is referred to as Imma Ila'ah or "the higher mother", and the lower partzuf is referred to as Tevunah meaning "comprehension". These two partzufim are referred to jointly as Imma or "the mother".

Binah is associated with the power of conceptual analysis and reasoning, both inductive and deductive. The partzuf of Imma Ila'ah is associated in particular with the power to grasp and comprehend the insights as given by Chokmah, whereas Tevunah represents the power to fully assimilate these insights into ideas in one's consciousness.

The word Binah derives from the root "bein" which means "between". The power of Binah is to distinguish and differentiate between ideas. This ability allows for the formation of "an" idea out of the chaos of limitless and inexhaustible nothingness that pours forth from the Onesness to the limited brain of man.

The union of Chokmah, the "father" and Binah the "mother" is continual, and is referred to in the *Zohar* as "two companions that never separate". This union is necessary for the continual recreation of the world, beginning with the birth of the seven attributes of the heart, which are 1) Loving Comforter, 2) Faithful Comforter, 3) Untiring Comforter, 4) Wise Comforter, 5) Safe Comforter, 6) Active Comforter, and 7) Ever Present Comforter. They also correspond to the seven days of Creation, from the womb of Great Mother, Binah. This concept is further revealed with the use of Gematria, the Assyro-Babylonian system of numerology that was later adopted by Jews, which assigns numerical value to a word or phrase, in the belief that words or phrases with identical numerical values bear some relation to each other. This can be seen when the union of Chokmah, whose numerical value is 73, and Binah, whose value is 67, are added together to make 140. The number 140 is the sum of square of all the numbers from 1 to 7. This reflects the source of all the 7 attributes of the heart (days of Creation), the 7 "children", in their ultimate state of perfection (a square number represents a perfected state of being) in the mind of "father" and "mother".

TZAPHKIEL ZAPHKIEL (לצקפיאל), JAFKIEL/ JAPHKIEL/ ZADKIEL/ZAFCHIAL/ ZAPHCHIAL/ ZAPHIEL OR ZELEL

The name Zadkiel means "the righteousness of God". As you can tell from the multiple spellings of names Zadkiel there is a great deal of confusion as to Zadkiel's identify and function. According to some sources, Zadkiel is the angel of Jupiter because he is the ruler of the sign of the Zodiac. According to the *Zohar* Zadkiel is one of the two chieftains who aid the Archangel Michael when he goes into battle. He is also one of the seven archangels presiding next to God. One of his most common identities is the Archangel who prevents Abraham from sacrificing his son Isaac to God. Overall Zadkiel is known as the angel of mercy, memory, benevolence and the chief of the order of dominions. The dominions are the first realm of beings that God gave executive free will to manage the day to day functions of the universe.

Another key aspect or duty for Zadkiel is that he is being the "keeper of the Records of Evolution". These records are often referred to as the "Memories of God" or the Cosmic Akashic Records. H.P. Blavatsky referred to the Akashic as a Sanskrit word for "sky" or "Aether", and as the "indestructible tablets of the astral light". Many mystics believe these "tablets" are the compendium of mystical knowledge supposedly encoded in a non-physical plane of existence known as the astral plane, and that these "tablets" record both the past and future thoughts and actions of humanity. Because of this the "tablets" are often referred to as a source of meditation as to present and future actions of humanity and in particular to individuals who are seeking answers. They are the same "tablets" portrayed on the Paul Foster Case's and Waite-Rider Tarot Card "The High Priestess".

HIGH PRIESTESS

Zadkiel is considered the Archangel of the Archetypal Temple and the source of the formations of mystical groups who have emanated from the Great White Lodge. This is the same supernatural Lodge through which the Great White Brotherhood works to spread spiritual teachings through selected humans such as H. P. Blavatsky, Alice A. Bailey, Paul Foster Case, and Aleister Crowley to name a few.

ARALIM—THRONES

The Aralim are the order of angels that dwell in Binah and are called the Thrones. They are the strength and stability of Binah. The Archangel Zadkiel /Tzaphkiel is head of the Aralim angels. As the guardian of the Akashic Records, he is responsible for watching of these records for they are where all things that were done, and all thing that will be, are recorded.

The "thrones" are also known as Ophanim and are described in *Daniel* 7:9 as unusual looking even compared to the other celestial beings. They appear as a beryl-colored wheel-within-a-wheel, their rims covered with hundreds of eyes.

SATURN

Like all the Seven Ancient Planets, Saturn is associated with one of the "interior stars". These "interior stars" are the centers of the forces that drive our singular personalities. The energies present in Binah are linked to the Saturn-like influences in astrology. The energy of deriving from Saturn invokes understanding, but only through patience and time. This understanding is not an open book but rather veiled, requiring the individual to apply their own energy in search of the answers. Saturn does not demand any more than what the individual is capable of giving. Binah is often perceived as dark or black because all colors are hidden within black. The color black veils the divine glory until time and understanding reveal it. This sphere is the place to seek the understanding of situations that have been difficult and obscure. It is a place of answers, but not until the time is right.

THE ABYSS

Whenever studying the Tree of Life the reference to "The Abyss" will appear. It is physically located on the Tree below the Supernal Triangle of Kether, Chokhmah and Binah. It is often referred to as the Great Abyss. One of the earliest sources for the Abyss comes from the *Bible*:

> "And the earth was without form, and void; and darkness was upon the face of the deep."
>
> *GENESIS* 1:2

The Abyss is mentioned several times in the *Zohar* as being the place that was the receptor for the several failed attempts at creation before the present one; these attempts failed because mercy and judgment were not balanced, and the resulting detritus of these failed attempts, the broken shells of previous Sephiroth, accumulated in the Abyss. Because the shells (Qlippoth) were the result of unbalanced rigor or judgment they were considered evil, and the Abyss became a repository of evil spirits not dissimilar from the pit of Hell into which the rebellious angels were cast, or the rebellious Titans in Greek mythology who were buried as far beneath the Earth as the Earth is beneath the sky.

Fourth Sefirah: Chesed / Khesed / Hesed (חסד),
"Loving-kindness", "Kindness" or "Love"
"Mercy"

God-name:	El --God the Almighty One
Number:	4
Archangel:	Tzaphkiel
Order of Angels:	Chasmalim—The Brilliant Ones
Body Part:	Right Arm
Symbol:	The Solid Figure, Tetrahedron, Orb, Wand, Pyramid, Scepter, Crook
Spiritual Experience:	The Vision of Love
Planet:	Jupiter
Color in Atziluth:	Deep Violet
Color in Briah:	Blue
Color in Yetzirah:	Dark Purple
Color in Assiah:	Deep Azure, flecked with Yellow
Personal Chakra:	The Anahata or Heart Chakra

Chesed, or "Mercy", is the first Sefirah of the Formative World whose attribute is to assign action to the intellect. Chesed receives all the Holy Powers from the Supernals and its symbol is the prism. According to the *Sefer ha-Bahir*, Chesed is the Sefirah through which God manifests its absolute and unlimited benevolence and kindness.

Chesed goes by many different names; it is also known as Gedulah (גדולה) which translates as "strength" or sometimes "power". Other titles are "Din", "Justice" and "Pachad", "Fear". The Sefirah Chesed represents the process of expansiveness and the point of creation and formalizing the building of form. This in contrast to Gevurah which stands for the restraint and preservation of form. This is where intelligence comes to shape, is tested, broken down and formed again until a shadowy image of that intellect is established. The actual concrete expression of that form or intellect or idea does not occur until Malkuth, the physical work, where it takes conscious being in the terms of the individual's reality.

Chesed can be viewed as a pool full of the energy of abundance. This is where one seeks the energy to start new endeavors such as starting a new job or new school, or any new phase in one's life. Chesed also provides the application of the laws of nature as it pertains to the reality of the individual's wants versus needs.

The following of the natural laws as they pertain to the individual leads to obedience to your inner spiritual self. One of the goals of working with the Qabalah is reaching "equilibrium" with what "is above" and the need for the self to be at harmony with the universe. For this harmony will eventually be followed if you want to manifest abundance in every aspect of your life. The real esoteric purpose of Chesed in the mystery schools was to amplify and bring out the spiritual quality of obedience from within the student/aspirant. After this spiritual quality is properly cultivated and the laws of abundance activated, all things from life will flow to the aspirants. For this reason, Chesed has often been seen as a sphere of acquiring wealth or luck. However, the real truth is that it was the adept's strict following to their holy inner self that lead them to manifest these things in their lives.

Tzadqiel/Chasmalin-The Brilliant Ones

The Order of Angels called Chasmalin or Hasmalim are, according to Jewish lore, high ranking angels such as Cherubim and Seraphim. Chasmalin means the Brilliant ones who support the Throne of God and are fiery by nature. With their fiery natures they bind the various parts of the cosmos together as whole. They also provide the universe with great abundance, joy, and hope coupled with the power of laughter. The Chasmalin are led by the Archangel Tzadqiel. He is the Angel of benevolence, abundance, mercy, and memory. Tzadqiel and his order of angels are especially helpful to those in time of need. Tzadqiel's duty is to direct all things to their best state of being. If asked Tzadqiel will direct you, but he will also test you. Tzadqiel will never lead you from the path of Righteousness so long as you wish to learn, before this path may not be an easy one. But even though Tzadquiel will test you, he will not present you with any barrier beyond your ability to overcome.

Jupiter

Jupiter is described as "temperate" because its sphere lies between the cooling influence of Saturn and the burning power of Mars. Because of its "temperate" nature it brings no destructive extremes to threaten vitality, and is thus defined as "warming and moistening", an active combination of qualities that draws things together in harmony to support increase and growth. Because of its nurturing nature, Jupiter is known as the "Greater Benefic", its essential nature being fertilizing and creative. Through its prolific influence, it is known as the Lord of Plenty, a symbol of prosperity that offers a ready supply for our physical, material, mental and spiritual needs.

Jupiter is a liberal planet with a relaxing influence. Being calming in nature, it seems to take away our awareness of limitation, filling us with confidence, optimism and a joy for living.

Fifth Sefirah: Gevurah /Geburah, (גבורה)
"Severity"

God-name:	Elohim Gebor-Almighty God
Number:	5
Archangel:	Sammael/Kamael/Chamuel
Order of Angels:	Seraphim—Fiery Serpents
Body Part:	Left Arm
Symbol:	Pentagon, Five Petalled Rose, Sword, Spear, Scourge, Chain
Spiritual Experience:	The Vision of Power
Planet:	Mars
Color in Atziluth:	Orange
Color in Briah:	Scarlet Red
Color in Yetzirah:	Bright Scarlet
Color in Assiah:	Red Flecked Black
Personal Chakra:	Throat Chakra

Geburah is the sphere that helps to break down false, or no longer relevant forms or ideas so that new perspectives or ideas can be formed. This is extremely important to humanity in its efforts to evolve to higher planes and concepts of Truth. This was seen by the ancients as when after the creative effort of God, there was a scrutinizing of the results and modifications to correct for any excrescences or defects. This concept of re-examining is repeated in the microcosm of man. The energies of Geburah are never used to destroy that which is essential and eternal, only what is necessary to allow for growth and renewal at a higher level. For Geburah is the center of movement and changing, this action creates the power of destruction and rebirth. Geburah is continually in motion and change and is never satisfied with any status quo. Geburah always is seeking new ideas to replace the old. Because of this, Geburah is often sensed as having unstable and imbalanced energies and thus unnerving to those who dwell on its essence. But once the Aspirant/student leans how to use the energy of Geburah can help to shape and mold them to a more perfect form. The aspirant will understand that by destroying what is unnecessary, such as breaking addictions, i.e. drugs, foods or even nail biting, and honing that which is important, it will lead to a purposeful change and awakening of inner and outer strength. At the Soul level, Geburah is the archetype of Will and Power, and represents Judgment, Might and Strength. Energy, discipline, and planning are needed to bring our Soul's ideals into being.

Geburah also teaches that it is important to be flexible in our ways and allow for the ebb and flow of energies. If energies are blocked, they will find an outlet by bursting through in an uncontrollable way. It is better to allow the natural flow of energies, but in a way that we can control and direct. It is through Geburah that we learn the right use of power and energies symbolized by the Red planet, Mars, by awakening our inner and outer strength in order to achieve purposeful change. This is the fulfillment of purpose, as directed by our Higher Self, through motion, through doing.

SAMMAEL/KAMAEL/CHAMUEL/SAMAEL/SAMIL

Samael means "Severity of God" and is an important archangel in Talmudic and post-Talmudic lore. It is often seen in a negative light as a figure who takes the role as an accuser, seducer and destroyer. Because of this action of destruction of the old he is also regarded as both good and evil. It is said that he was the guardian angel of Esau the twin brother of Jacob, who were the sons of Isaac and Rebekah, and the grandsons of Abraham and Sarah. Samael is also sometimes identified as being the angelic antagonist who wrestled with Jacob, and also the angel who held back the arm of Abraham as he was about to sacrifice his son. Samael is also known as the Prince of Strength and Courage.

Samael is often confused with Satan due to the book *Ascension of Isaiah* authored sometime late first century AD to the second half of the second century AD by an unknown Christian author. It is felt that the current form of Ascension *of Isaiah* was a Christianized version of an older story of the Vision of Isaiah, who was a prophet said to have lived in the 8th-century B.C.E. Kingdom of Judah. The Vision of Isaiah describes an angel-assisted journey, prior to the events of the first part of the book, by Isaiah through the Seven Heavens.

According to Talmudic texts, Samael is a member of the heavenly host with often grim and destructive duties. One of Samael's greatest roles in Jewish lore is that of the angel of death. He remains one of the Lord's servants even though he appears to want men to do evil. As a good angel, Samael resides in the seventh heaven, although he is declared to be the chief angel of the fifth heaven, and is listed as fifth of the archangels of the world of Briah.

SERAPHIM-FIERY SERPENTS

Literally meaning the "burning ones", or "flaming ones", because they are the closet beings to God, and are said to be aflame with the love of God. The word seraph is normally a synonym for serpents when used in the Hebrew Bible. A passage in the *Book of Isaiah* (*Isaiah* 6:1-8) used the term to describe fiery six-winged beings that fly around the Throne of God as a choir crying "Kadosh, Kadosh, Kadosh" or "Holy, Holy, Holy". This throne scene, with its triple invocation of holiness is called a Trisagion. The Trisagion, which is Greek for "Thrice Holy", is sometimes called by its opening line *Agios O Theos*, which comes from this crying of "Holy, Holy, Holy" and forms the basis for the standard hymn of the Divine Liturgy that is practiced in most of the Eastern Orthodox, Oriental Orthodox and Eastern Catholic Churches.

Seraphim are also seen as angels of love, light and fire. They are the highest order of the choirs and serve God as caretakers of his throne. Their love for God is expressed by their continual chanting of kadosh so the whole Earth is full of His Glory.

MARS

Nothing remains stagnant on the Tree of Life. Like a real tree, it is alive with energy. In the case of the Divine Tree the energy flows both from its roots and from its highest point. The Sephirot act as centers for these energies. Geburah, symbolized by Mars, is having a destructive dry nature. Mars is a planet of action, and is the center that causes change due to that perceived destructive energy. It is where forms are tested and reworked. Where misconceptions are corrected and new paths developed allowing the Adept to discern every expanding horizons of reality.

Mars should not be feared; it is the source of passion, drive and determination. It commands you to stand up, be noticed and get things done.

Those who enter the path do so to improve and change themselves and this is the source of that energy to break down the old fences, and old karmas and open paths for new forms to develop.

Sixth Sefirah: Tiferet /Tifaret/ Tifereth/ Tyfereth/ Tiphareth (תפארת) "Adornment", "Beauty", "Harmony"

God-name:	Jehovah Aloah va Daath-God made manifest in the Sphere of the mind
Number:	6
Archangel:	Raphael
Order of Angels:	The Malachim—the Kings
Body Part:	Upper Torso—particularly the Heart
Symbol:	Lamen, Rose-Cross, Calvary Cross, Truncated Pyramid, Cube
Spiritual Experience:	The Vision of the Harmony of Things
Planet:	Sun
Color in Atziluth:	Clear Rose Pink
Color in Briah:	Yellow
Color in Yetzirah:	Rich Salmon Pink
Color in Assiah:	Golden Amber
Personal Chakra:	Heart Chakra

Tiphareth is the Sphere of Beauty, and the Perfect Equilibrium. It is the gateway to the high spiritual plane of existence of Universal Mind, or the Self. The transition from the Astral to the Causal Plane is as dramatic as that between Physical and Astral (See below the description of Planes). It requires the development of a subtler aspect of the Body of Light, so the soul may experience that level of awareness. The Causal Body is where the Ruach or life-breath of man, nephesh or moral soul takes form.

Located on the Middle Pillar of "Mildness" or "Equilibrium" it is a place of balance and transformation between Kether and Malkuth where ascending and descending influences meet. It is the equivalent of the Sun in our physical solar system in that it rests in the very center of our Universe with all our planets orbiting it. So Tiphareth sits at the center of the Tree of Life and all the Sephirot revolve about it. Tiphareth is at the transformation point between the physical manifested world symbolized by Malkuth and the un-manifested primal energies of Kether. Because of its location many religions believe it represents the height of spiritual ambition, and it is often referred to as the "Christ Center".

Tiphareth is also referred to as the Lesser Countenance and is in the place where Kether, the Greater Countenance is reflected. Tiphareth is also seen as reflecting The Supreme Mysteries into the Lesser Mysteries of humankind's world.

Tiphareth represents the halfway point on the continuum of spiritual development. It indicates the ability to direct one's base energies from the outside world of daily activities to the inside spiritual/mystic world and hold it there. One contemplates the "radiant form" internally. Self-Realization opens the beginning of the path to God-Realization. In the *Sefer ha-Bahir* it states: "Sixth is the adorned, glorious, delightful throne of glory, the house of the sixth to come. Its place is engraved in wisdom as it says God said: Let there be light, and there was light."

To Kabbalists the importance of Tiphareth is further enhanced through the fact that it is unique amongst the Sephirot as it is connected to all the other Sephirot, except Malkuth, via the subjective paths of the unconscious. Tiphareth acts as a crossing point for all the energies to pass through thus potentially changing the polarity of each from male to female, positive to negative and so forth. This reversing of polarity adds to the greater mystery of the Sephirot and how they interact with each other. The law of conservation of energy and mass tends to corroborate this — in all cases of energy transmutation, a sacrifice is necessary so a new form may be born.

PLANES
Late in the nineteenth century the Neo-theosophy of Annie Besant and C. W. Leadbeater replaced Blavatsky's "Higher Manas" principle with the "Higher Mental" or "Abstract Mind" versus the Lower Mental, "Concrete Mind" or Causal Body. The equivalent cosmic plane is the Causal Plane. Arthur Edward Powell (1882–1969), who was a Theosophist who studied the works of Besant and Leadbeater provided a series of books on each of the subtle bodies.

1. *Physical Plane*: Tiphareth represents the Vision of the Harmony of Things, and is the point on the Tree of Life of maximum equilibrium. The Cube is a magickal symbol for Tiphareth.

2. *Astral Plane:* The second plane of creation. Its medium is concrete emotional energy. It is where our consciousness is focused between lifetimes and when we're finished with the physical plane. A contemplative life in harmony with spiritual principles becomes the primary ritual. The magical images for Tiphareth include a magickal or divine child; a resplendent king, and a sacrificed God. These represent stages in the Mystery of Death and Rebirth. Tiphareth also corresponds with the Egyptian god, Osiris. Initiation on the path to God-Realization turns one's attitudes upside-down.

3. *Causal Plane:* The third plane of creation. Its medium is concrete intellectual energy. In the Causal, the Vision of Harmony indicates that all spiritual progress comes through the principle of Love. It implies the highest ethical standards in both behavior and thought. Thus psychology can express in words what mystics experience through intuition. Syntaxic Mode includes meditative Tantric sex, creativity, alpha states, etc. During times of intense meditation students often feel, for the briefest of moments a sense of Ecstasy; this is the result of their spirit ascending to the lowest influence of Tiphareth's energy and then falling back on the path they had climbed much like the myth of Icarus flying too close to the sun.

4. *Akashic Plane:* The central, neutral plane of creation that interconnects the other six. It is here that all knowledge of the universe is recorded. This includes everything that has ever happened and is often depicted as a Great Book of Life. This is very similar to the "Scales" that Anubus, in Egyptian myth, uses to "weigh the heart" to see if their lives where upright or not. An important difference is that the records show events exactly as they were experienced, so the information in them begins raw—it is not clarified, understood, and assimilated until a consciousness takes responsibility for doing so. With this knowledge comes wisdom on how to correct or modify one's future actions because of clear understanding of the past. Once this knowledge is fully assimilated, it is stored on the Akashic Plane.

5. *Mental Plane*: The fifth plane of creation. Its medium is abstract intellectual energy, emphasizing truth. The infinite soul who incarnated as Lao-tzu taught from this plane.

6. *Messianic Plane*: The sixth plane of creation. Its medium is abstract emotional energy, emphasizing love. The infinite soul who incarnated as Jesus taught from this plane.

7. *Buddhaic Plane*: The highest plane of creation. Its medium is pure or abstract kinetic energy. We experience the buddhaic plane just before fully refocusing our awareness in the Tao. The infinite soul who incarnated as Buddha taught from this plane.

RAPHAEL—GOD HAS HEALED

The name of this archangel (Raphael — "God has healed") does not appear in the Hebrew Scriptures, and only appears in the *Septuagint* and then only in the *Book of Tobias*. The *Septuagint* is the most ancient Greek translation of the *Old Testament*. Here Raphael first appears disguised in human form as the travelling companion of the younger Tobias, calling himself "Azarias the son of the great Ananias". It is a book of scripture that is part of the Catholic and Orthodox biblical canon, pronounced canonical by the Council of Carthage of 397 C.E. and confirmed for Roman Catholics by the Council of Trent held in 1546.

Originally Raphael was called Labbiel, translated from "He" the Hebrew word "raphe" to mean "healer", "doctor" or "surgeon". He rules the angels of healing and is often depicted with an image of a serpent. According to the *Book of Enoch* 1, Raphael is "one of the four presences set over all the diseases of all the wounds on children of men". He is credited to be the angel God sent to cure Abraham of the pain of circumcision.

Other legends placed Raphael as one of the three angels, Gabriel and Michael being the other two, who visited Abraham as described in *Genesis* 18:2. A second legend places Raphael visiting Noah after the flood to give him a special 'book' of healing, some claiming this to be the *"Book of the Angel Raziel"*.

God placed Raphael as the regent of the Sun, chief of the Order of Virtues, which were originally identified as chastity, temperance, charity, diligence, patience, kindness, and humility. They were latter modified by the Catholic catechism, and what became known as the seven Christian Virtues. The four cardinal virtues, from ancient Greek philosophy, are prudence, justice, temperance or restraint, and courage or fortitude. The three theological virtues, from the letters of *St. Paul of Tarsus*, are faith, hope, and charity or love. These were adopted by the Church Fathers as the *Seven Virtues*.

Raphael is also said to be the guardian of the Tree of Life in the Garden of Eden. He is one of six angels of repentance and an angel of prayer, love, joy, light, science and knowledge, and the protector of Isaac.

His appearance is similar to a seraph in that he is said to have six wings but also belongs to the cherubim, the dominions and the "powers". The "powers" being the first order of angels created by God whose job is to protect the world from being taken over by demons. The "powers" reside between the first and second heavens and acts as a barrier to protect against the devils. On an earthly level the "powers" protect men's souls from evil and act as God's avenger of evil in the world. The musical spelling of Raphael is RPAL which is tones of D C E F#. Gemini is its astrological sign and Discrimination is its function. Orange is its color.

THE MALACHIM—THE KINGS

Malachi is a plural form of the Hebrew word mal'ach, and means "angels" or "messengers". They are considered to be healers and life-bringing agents under the Archangel Raphael. He is part of the Four Elemental Kings and the Sphere of Elements.

Element	Elemental Beings	Ruling Archangel
Earth	Gnomes	Uriel
Water	Undines	Gabriel
Air	Sylphs	Raphael
Fire	Salamanders	Michael

These Four Elemental Kings of the World are a powerful group of four guardian angels of the borders of the world, dwelling in the heart of the astral world. They govern over the spiritual elements of Wind, Water, Earth and Fire and watch over the forces of nature. They are also referred to as:

The Four Elemental King
The Four Invisible Lords
The Four Angels

THE SUN

The Sun is one of the oldest symbols and representatives of the Divine. The sun has been revered both as a god and goddess depending on the region. Some examples of sun worship are: Arabian-Malakbel, Turkish-Kogash, Canaanite goddess Shapash, Egypt-Ra, and Greek goddess Alectrona and god Hellos. It is believed that the ancient Hebrews worshipped Yahweh as a Sun God as early as the eighth century B.C.E. According to the *Book of Kings*, King Josiah is described dedicating offerings to sun at "the entrance to the house of the Lord". In the *Book of Job,* we find God reiterated as the power behind the sun, as at 9:7, which refers to him "who commands the sun, and it does not rise; who seals up the stars..."

In *Ezekiel* 8:16 he is telling the Israelites to continue to worship the sun:

"And he brought me into the inner court of the house of the LORD; and behold, at the door of the temple of the LORD, between the porch and the altar, were about twenty-five men, with their backs to the temple of the LORD, and their faces toward the east, worshipping the sun toward the east."

The sun is light and is the Celestial Sun, called Tiphareth, the Resplendence or Magnificence, and because of the resplendent, magnificent whiteness of its Light, its immensity is recognized in its further designation as "Greatness". This is the Central Sun, the symbolic center of the entire universe, visible only to the spiritual or subjective sight, never to the natural or objective vision.

In Lurianic Kabbalah, the sun is described as the Astral Suns which move precisely around their respective planets that they control, illuminate and sustain. The Rouach Elohim (Breath of God) that brooded over or "moved upon the face of the waters" was held by the alchemists to have been Light from the Celestial Sun shining thereon. The star symbol within the Sephirot Tiphareth, in its upright, proper position represents the principle of good, when inverted it represents the evil principle. The five-pointed star seen on the disk of Tiphareth is the flaming pentagram of the Kabbalists and of the Magi of the Orient. It was the glorious Star of Bethlehem that was the Celestial forerunner of the Christian "Light of the World".

This great Celestial Luminary possesses the dual properties of Light and Fire, but in absolute equilibrium and perfect harmony. This perfect harmony embraces the rays of the Light, and the "chemistry" of the Fire. It is this harmony in the blending of the rays that produces the resplendent, magnificent white of which we have spoken as the characteristic of the Celestial Sun, and which justly gains the appellation. The sun as supreme among all of the celestial bodies. As a solar deity, god or goddess, it is a sky deity who represents the Sun, or an aspect of it, usually by its perceived power and strength.

In the Christian view of the Cabbala, Tiphareth is a very special Sefirah. It is said that this is where "extraordinary events happen with Tiphareth". Chokmah, the Cosmic Christ, is a universal force, beyond individuality, personality, and the ego. According to the Cabbalist this Cosmic Force is the redemption that can save a human being only if it is individualized and humanized. This process occurs in Tiphareth, where the Cosmic Christ manifests and converts Himself into our own particular, individualized Inner Christ. The Inner Christ must undergo within us the entire life, trials, and drama that Jesus lived publicly.

The Tree is used by the Cabbalist to represent the symbolic paths that lead back to the Absolute. And only through great work and practice can the Adept find their way back to the Inner Christ.

Seventh Sefirah: Netzach (נצח)
"Victory", "Eternity", "Perpetuity", "Endurance"

God-name:	Jehovah Tzabaoth-Lord of the Hosts
Number:	7
Archangel:	Haniel
Order of Angels:	Elohim-Gods and Goddesses
Body Part:	Right Leg
Symbol:	The Lamp, The Girdle, The Rose
Spiritual Experience:	The Vision of the Harmony of Things
Planet:	Venus
Color in Atziluth:	Amber
Color in Briah:	Emerald
Color in Yetzirah:	Bright Yellow Green
Color in Assiah:	Olive flecked Gold
Personal Chakra:	The Solar Plexus

Netzach, or "Victory", is part of the "tactical Sefirot" with Hod and Yesod, meaning that their purpose is not inherent in themselves, but rather as a means for something else. The Tactical Sephirot process the impulses coming from above, but taking the impulses from the opposite side of the Tree. Netzach modulates Gevurah, and Hod modulates Chesed. More important to the student is that the "tactical Sefirot" are the centers that are focused on man and are accessible to us through work and persistence. As we work with the various paths leading to these lower Sephiroth through meditation we work with the symbolic energies represented by these spheres.

Netzach's planet is Venus, and like the Goddess Venus she represents love, sex, and passion. Netzach is not the action or movement of these virtues, for Mars is the activator. But with these emotions comes sufferings and disappointments. But as we go through these hurts we are told we are made stronger by the experiences. Two questions arise with this statement: First, how long does it take the individual to process the personal hurt and disappointment? And second, and most important, "What did we learn from that experience?" The last question is the most important for if we do not learn from what has happened we tend to repeat it with the same results. This is where Netzach comes into play for it is the center where the energies to analyze these experiences can be processed.

Understanding the attributes of Netzach and Hod gives us a new perspective on understanding what is happening in the world around us. Through these Sephiroth we no longer need to merely look at an act at face value, and attempt to understand it as such, but we must look at it also in terms of "a means to an end". This 'means to end' is the learning portion of the equation that helps us reach that all important equilibrium of Tiphareth.

Netzach is "endurance", the fortitude, and patience to follow through on our passions. It is paired with Hod as the righteous attributes related to group interactivity; with Netzach being leadership or instigator, it is the ability to rally ourselves to a cause and motivate us as individuals to act, thus causing change; while Hod is community, the ability to do the footwork needed to follow through on ideas and make them happen. Netzach is identified with the right leg or foot when the Tree of Life is portrayed on the human form, while Hod is the left leg or foot. It is the center to help restore equilibrium if it is being lost but sometimes this restoration or change causes the individual to feel a sense of uneasiness until the new direction comes into focus.

This process happens many times as we grow and because of this Netzach is often associated with the idea of long-suffering, endurance and patience. For with change often pain and suffering occurs, but with patience the individual does endure and hopefully grow.

In summary, these Sephirot mark a turning point. Whereas the first two groups of Sephirot deal with the Creator's intrinsic will, and what it is that He desires to bestow upon man, these lower Sephirot are focused on man and his world of perceived reality.

HANIEL/ANAEL/HANAEL/ ANIEL

Haniel is called the "Grace of God", and is often included in lists as being one of the seven Archangels. This list includes Gabriel, Michael, Raphael, Uriel, Raguel, Remiel, and Saraqual. This list of Archangels does vary depending on the source and religious background. In the Catholic tradition they are: Michael, Gabriel, Raphael, Uriel, Jegudiel, Raguel, and Selaphiel. While in the Eastern Orthodox tradition, only mention three archangels, which are Michael, Raphael, and Uriel. But in the Coptic Orthodox tradition the seven archangels are named Gabriel, Michael, Raphael, Suriel, Zadakiel, Raguel and Aniel.

Haniel is generally associated with the planet Venus and he is also the Archangel of the Sefirah Netzach. The name Haniel probably derives from Hebrew hana'ah, "joy", "pleasure" which are qualities associated with Venus. The suffix "el", denotes "God". Archangel Haniel is also called the "glory of the grace of God". She is an angel of principalities and in that role, she is the caregiver of all nations on earth. She is empowered with a great deal of wisdom and strength and can directly impact human affairs. According to lore when one calls upon Haniel she can change the hearts and minds of world leaders to bring about significant changes for the benefit of humanity.

Haniel is the Chief of the Order of Principalities or Rulers and is one of the seven angels of the Creation. They are part of what is called the Third Order, or order of ministering angels. The angels of the Order Principalities are shown wearing a crown and carrying a scepter. Their duties also include carrying out the orders given to them by the Dominions and bequeathing blessings to the material world. They are the educators and guardians of the peoples of the realm of earth.

ELOHIM—GODS AND GODDESSES

The Hebrew word *Elohim* has multiple meanings. The best known is being the Hebrew name of God. When used in the singular form it refers to the God of Israel. As an Order relating to Netzach it refers to the diversity of God's appearance to humanity. This concept is the basis of much mythology in which the god and goddess take form to represent the various aspects of God. This is the same as an individual woman is being a sister/mother/lover/cousin or a grandmother. Each title has its own personality as seen by others but all are aspects of the same person. So are the "pagan" gods and goddesses the result of the creative images formed in this Order.

VENUS

The planet Venus represents the refinement of the senses, the arts, mystical love, desire, and earthly relationships. She was considered to be the feminine goddess of love and beauty just as her counterpart, Mars (Geburah), was thought of as the masculine god of war, strife and action or movement. These two archetypes complement each other perfectly and work as a polarity, manifesting a tension of the masculine and feminine. It is believed that until a person can bring both of these forces into conscious awareness and learn to balance and accept them fully, he or she cannot be a complete individual. Venus symbolizes the central function of judging and evaluating the emotions expressed in the psyche.

Venus is associated with the element of copper which in turn is associated with the powers of touch and speech, balanced feelings and ascending mind. The key here is the balancing feeling which is the union of the feminine and masculine components of the individual. It is the balance of symbolic male/strength and the symbolic female/softness. Through this balance, a greater awareness of others and a responsiveness to the "feelings" of those around you. As this balance occurs the individual begins to exercise free will, unencumbered by buried emotions, addictions, impulses, and instincts. This allows for the unconditional love towards others and a love that embraces all creation, is totally accepting and without discrimination or judgment.

Eighth Sefirah: Hod (הוד)
"Glory", "Majesty", "Splendor"

God-name:	Elohim Tzabaoth—God of Hosts
Number:	8
Archangel:	Michael
Order of Angels:	Beni Elohim-Children of the Gods and Goddesses
Body Part:	Left Leg
Symbol:	Names and Versicles, the Apron
Spiritual Experience:	Vision of Splendor
Planet:	Mercury
Color in Atziluth:	Violet—Purple
Color in Briah:	Orange
Color in Yetzirah:	Red—Russet
Color in Assiah:	Yellowish Black-flecked White
Personal Chakra:	The Solar Plexus

Hod is the eighth Sefirah and acts as a staging point for the formation or molding of energy into images that have boundaries and outline. It is the taking of all-encompassing energy and placing limits on it so that it can be formed into something the human mind can conceive. It is the center for the establishment of language, symbols, and other creative functions of the mind. Hod, with its center for language is important since the whole concept of ceremonial magic is predicated on the control and manifestation of oral vibration that is the word, which is concentration of energy into language.

Hod is the realm of ideas and communication, of magic, and of creating the skill to manifest and un-manifest things at will. It is sometimes called the Perfect or Absolute Intelligence, for if what is manifested in Hod is true, then they are the means by which man is able to glimpse the Supernal Regions of his very being.

Because of the energy of this sphere it is well suited for acquiring knowledge and wisdom of any scientific or concrete physical nature. More importantly it is the place to go to find or touch our inner God. The Beni Elohim's primary responsibility is the transmission of knowledge of the universe to unite man with God. And because of this Hod is a great place to uncover deception and to find the truth of things. The light of God here is powerful enough to illuminate all falsehoods. This use of Hod can be of great benefit to the Adept for it is a great place to acquire the energy of discovery. Knowledge will seek out knowledge and open more and more doorways for the Adept, if you are patient and observant. One must be careful because with knowledge comes power and if this is not used correctly it could be harmful to the seeker.

These creative forces find balance in Yesod, foundation, the world of the unconscious, where the different energies created await expression in the lowest world of Malkuth, the Kingdom.

MICHAEL/MIKHAIL

Michael, meaning "who is as God" comes from the Chaldeans, a nation that ruled the lands in the far southeastern corner of Mesopotamia from the tenth to sixth centuries B.C.E. Michael is venerated as one of the greatest angels in all three of the tribes of Abraham; the Jews, Christians and Muslims. He is considered the Chief of the Order of Virtues or Strongholds, chief of the Archangels, prince of the Presence and the angel representing repentance, righteousness, mercy and sanctification as well as ruler of the fourth heaven, and conqueror of Satan.

The "Virtues" or "Strongholds" primary duty is to supervise the movements of the heavenly bodies in order to ensure that the cosmos remains in order.

Michael is mentioned throughout Biblical history. He is credited with staying Abraham's hand from slaying his son. It is also mentioned that

Moses "saw him in the burning bush appearing before the Shekinah". In the *Talmud,* he is recognized by Sarah as one of the three men who Abraham entertained.

Michael's musical notes are: MIKAL G# F A# E F#. He is associated with Sagittarius and the action of Wrath and Vibration. The color Blue is Michael's color.

SEVEN HEAVENS

According to the *Talmud* the Seven Heavens, with their governing angels' are:

1. *Vilon* (וילון) also called "Araphel": The first Heaven, governed by Archangel Gabriel, is the closest of heavenly realms to the Earth; it is also considered the abode of Adam and Eve.

2. *Raqi'a* (רקיע): The second Heaven is dually controlled by Zachariel and Raphael. It was in this Heaven that Moses, during his visit to Paradise, encountered the angel Nuriel who stood "300 parasangs (an Iranian unit of measurement equating to around 3 miles) high, with a retinue of 50 myriads of angels all fashioned out of water and fire". Also, *Raqi'a* is considered the realm where the fallen angels are imprisoned and the planets are fastened.

3. *Shehaqim* (שחקים): The third Heaven, under the leadership of Anahel/Haniel, serves as the home of the Garden of Eden and the Tree of Life; it is also the realm where manna, the holy food of angels, is produced. The *Second Book of Enoch*, meanwhile, states that both Paradise and Hell are accommodated in *Shehaqim* with Hell being located simply "on the northern side".

4. *Ma'on* (מעון): The fourth Heaven is ruled by the Archangel Michael, and according to *Talmud Hagiga* 12, it contains the heavenly Jerusalem, the Temple, and the Altar.

5. *Makhon* (מכון): The fifth Heaven is under the administration of Samael, an angel referred to as evil by some, but who is to others merely a dark servant of God.

6. Zebul (זבול): The sixth Heaven falls under the jurisdiction of Sachiel.

7. *Araboth* (ערבות): The seventh Heaven, under the leadership of Cassiel, is the holiest of the Seven Heavens because it houses the Throne of Glory attended by the Seven Archangels and serves as the realm in which God dwells; underneath the throne itself lies the abode of all unborn human souls. It is also considered the home of the Seraphim, the Cherubim, and the Hayyoth living creatures, living being described in the *Book of Ezekiel*.

BENI ELOHIM—CHILDREN OF THE GODS AND GODDESSES

The Angelic Order of Beni Elohim is barely mentioned in the *Bible* except that it is a Divine Order. The Qabalists describe it as "units" of divine consciousness that provide man with the ability to be aware of God's presence. They are the force that gives form of all the divine images of the gods and goddesses that humanity has developed that allows us the ability to perceive the divine in its many aspects. They literally take on the shapes of Gods and the Goddesses so that we can perceive and understand the Divine and its workings. Thus Michael, which means "Perfect of God" or "He who is like unto God" has the cosmic task is to help to reveal the great complexity of the universe. Michael performs his task by engaging our rational mind with the powers of analysis, so that we can contemplate the divine cosmos.

MERCURY

Mercury is the physical planet associated with Hod. It is closely related to the Earth and Venus and with this association is on a psychic level associated with the abstract mind and the Mysteries of Hermes. The tradition of Hermes is that of enlightenment and Hod is the sphere of esoteric philosophy and magic. Mercury helps us to look upon the current situation, to interpret and determine the significance of events and to relate the old and the new, the past and the future through the light of the present.

Mercury, the star of conflict and cunning, is also the major planet of relationships, for it governs and 'engineers' the interplay between our Earth and its conditioning constellations. Conflict occur in relationships because of how they reactions of emotions to eachother, both positive and negative that occur in all relationships. Cunning in that it helps us develop skill, cultivated and cumulative intelligence, imitative, caution and ambition. Mercury helps to illuminate the mind and mediates between the soul and the personality.

Mercury is the expression of the dual aspect of the mind as it mediates between higher and lower. The mediation falls into two stages; the use of the concrete mind as the mediator within the personality, conditioning the personality life, analyzing and distinguishing between the self and the not-self and emphasizing the "me and thou" consciousness as well as that of the personality and its environment. This ability to designate between the "me and thou" is essential in developing meaningful relationships as well as lending clarity to one's own personality.

Ninth Sefirah: Yesod (יסוד) "Foundation"

God-name:	Shaddai el Chai—The Almighty Living God
Number:	9
Archangel:	Gabriel
Order of Angels:	The Holy Kerubs
Body Part:	Genitals
Symbol:	Perfumes and Sandals
Spiritual Experience:	Vision of the Machinery of the Universe
Planet:	Moon
Color in Atziluth:	Indigo
Color in Briah:	Violet
Color in Yetzirah:	Red-Russet
Color in Assiah:	Citrine Flecked Azure
Personal Chakra:	The Sacral Chakra

Yesod is the ninth of the ten Sephirot, and the sixth of the emotive attributes within Creation. Yesod is associated with the soul and its ability to contact, connect and communicate with outer reality, represented by the 10th Sefirah, Malkuth. The foundation (Yesod) of a building is its 'grounding,' its union with the earth, the physical world of humanity's reality.

Because Yesod is associated with the procreative organs it is the foundation of generations to come. The power to procreate is the manifestation of infinity within the finite context of the created human being. Yesod is the "small" and "narrow" bridge between the infinite potential of procreation that flows into it and its actual manifestation in the progeny of man. When working with these energies the student must understand the potency and how it can be transferred to the physical personality.

For this reason, the Sefirah of Yesod is identified in the *Torah* with the tzadik (righteous one), as is said: "and thetzadik is the foundation of the world". In particular, this refers to the one, perfect tzadik of the generation. Hasidic Jews adhere to the belief that there is a person, the perfect personality that is born each generation with the potential to become Messiah. In the very body of the tzadik, is where the finite and limiting of time and space occurs, God's infinite light and creative life force becomes manifest. Here God allows His limitless and infinite energies to begin to take physical form with all the boundaries of the laws of nature imposed upon it. The tzadik procreates on the spiritual plane as well as on the physical plane.

The fundamental nature of Yesod is that of interface; it interfaces the rest of the Tree of Life to the Sefirah Malkuth. The interface is bi-directional; there are energies coming down from Kether, and echoes bouncing back from Malkuth. Our own senses have the same characteristic of being a bi-directional interface through which we experience the world, in that we are continually adjusting our viewpoint of the world as we test our past experiences and intuitive knowledge against what our five senses are telling us.

The magical image of Yesod is of "a beautiful naked man, very strong". The phallic symbolism evident in the Magical Image of Yesod should not be confused with the external sexual organs but rather the inner force of intense energy that is often referred to as the Serpent Fire, Kundalini, or Prana. These are the reproductive energies that allow us to generate or regenerate our worlds on all levels of the Tree. Yesod continually tests and corrects the patterns we formulate with our ability to create mental images by projecting them into the field of reality in the sphere of Malkuth. If our imagery is based on error, disharmony or imbalance occurs which results in us becoming aware of the need for more work to free ourselves from succumbing to the errors in the collective consciousness.

The self-conscious controls the formative aspects of Yesod. We tend to hold on to the safe old views of the world with which we feel comfortable. It takes a conscious effort to direct the energies of the self-conscious to develop new 'enlightened' perspectives of the world.

As we develop these new views or habits we become aware of different goals with our Higher Self, which in turn cause a disharmony until the personality adjusts to its new role or image. This whole concept of new ideas-disharmony–new self-image–new ideas is a circle event that repeats itself throughout our lives.

GABRIEL

The name of Gabriel means "God is my strength" is of Chaldean origin and was unknown to the Jews prior to their captivity in Babylon around 597 B.C.E. Gabriel is described as possibly the only female angel in that she sits on the left hand of God. She is described as having 140 pairs of wings and is the governor of Eden, and ruler of the cherubim.

The Cabbalists identify Gabriel as "the man clothed in linen", as per *Daniel* 10:5-21. Gabriel helps people see the connections between everything in creation. It is taught by the Kabbalists that Gabriel is in charge of souls and also in charge of the Moon. According to Kabbalists, the Moon is considered to be the dwelling place of souls that have not yet been bound to physical bodies. Gabriel is also viewed as one of the main assistants of the Angel of Death. Gabriel gives insight through dreams, scrying and will usually give this insight through visions instead of a voice. But that does not mean the voice is not heard through some insight. Gabriel brings Divine wisdom and promotes the psychic abilities. And Gabriel is associated with both the Moon, and the element of water. Gabriel's stone is moonstone.

When meditating on the levels of the Tree, Gabriel is on the second rung of the meditation ladder; the first is Sandalphon, then Gabriel, Mikal/Michael and then Metatron. In the world of spiritual magic Gabriel is very important and any student should understand the concept of the Four Archangels of the Quarters; even though there are various names and attributes given to the four archangels the basic concept is still there. In *Revelation* 7:1 they are described as:

> "Four Angels" = Michael, Raphael, Gabriel, Uriel
> "Four Corners" = South, East, West, North
> "Four Winds" = East Wind of the Morning, West Wind of the
>   Evening, North Wind of Midnight, South Wind of Noon

In other esoteric literature, the following descriptions are given to the "Angels of the Four Corners" as they pertain to the elements:

Michael, Guardian Angel of the North, Elemental Angel of Fire
Raphael, Guardian Angel of the East, Elemental Angel of Air
Gabriel, Guardian Angel of the West, Elemental Angel of Water
Uriel, Guardian Angel of the South, Elemental Angel of Earth

Other aspects of the Four Angels are associated with nature:

Michael, Angel of the East Wind and/or Morning Wind
Raphael, Angel of the West Wind and/or Evening Wind
Gabriel, Angel of the North Wind and/or Midnight Wind
Uriel, Angel of the South Wind and/or Noonday Wind

These concepts are raised here because it is through Yesod that much spiritual magic is performed and all students will need to know the strengths and weaknesses of each of these angels and how those strengths and weakness apply to their own personality. The musical notes attributed to Gabriel are: GBRIAL G# E D F# E F#. It is part of the Higher Octave of Mars and Pluto. Its action is that of Regeneration and Rebirth. This is an archangel of action and is associated with Red-C natural.

HOLY ORDER OF KERUBS/ KERUBIM/CHERUBIM
Cherubim are described as the guardians attached to the throne of God as a protective barrier to guard His Holiness, and to the Garden of Eden to guard the Tree of Life.

Cherubim are described as living creatures. Each has four faces, as well as four wings. Their feet are straight feet, and the soles of their feet are like the sole of a calf's foot; and they sparkle like the color of burnished brass. Cherubims have the hands of a man under their wings on their four sides. Their wings are joined one to another; they do not turn when they go, they all go straight forward. They have the face of a man and the face of a lion on the right side, and the face of an ox and an eagle on the left side (*Ezekiel* 1:5-12). Cherubim first appeared in the Hebrew text in the *Apocrypha* in their full angelological development.

The cherubim have four primary responsibilities. First, they are the guardians of Paradise, they protect the gates from any unworthy souls entering. Second the Protective Bearer of the Throne of God. They are most often depicted as residing either side of the door to the Holy of Holies or on the lid of the Ark of the Covenant. They are described as two cherubim of gold, on the two ends of the "mercy seat". They are described as issuing the breath of God which many times came in the form of a deadly cloud that smote the unworthy. The cherubim shall stretch forth their wings on high, covering The Covenant as described in *Exodus* 37:7-9.

At the center of the mystery are the two cherubs. The *Zohar* teaches that the symbolic meaning of the cherubs is that they represent the union of opposites; they are a synonym for the unity of consciousness. This unity allows for the solidifying of concepts, to images, to our conscious and physical reality. The Cherubim are also said to bestow the gift of knowledge to those who are worthy. This may be a clue for the student to peruse since the Sefirah of Yesod is the sphere were energies are taking form and knowledge is key to enlightenment whose source is Binah and ultimately the higher knowledge of Da'at, the eleventh hidden Sefirah.

Finally, the cherubim also symbolically help God to move about as described in *Psalm 18:10* where The LORD GOD rode upon a cherub, and did fly; and He was seen upon the wings of the wind.

THE MOON

Yesod holds a special place in the development of the spiritual and physical world of man. It is here where the divine energies from the higher Sephirot become manifested in forms that man's mind can fathom and understand. If we say that Tiphareth is like the sun with its brilliance being so intense that we cannot look directly at it then the Moon, Yesod is the reflected brilliance that man can look upon.

The fascination and worship goes back prior to the great histories of Egypt, Babylonia, India and China. Moon worship is founded on the belief that the phases of the Moon and the growth and decline of plant, animal, and human life are related. Astrologically the Moon represents the principles of flux and response, assimilation and reflection of what has been. The Moon was frequently equated with wisdom and justice, as in the worship of the Egyptian god Thoth and the Mesopotamian God Sin.

According to the earliest writing of the Assyrians (2500 B.C.E. to 605 B.C.E.) and Chaldeans (tenth and sixth centuries B.C.E.) the Moon was worshipped as the supreme deity. Originally this deity took the feminine form which was closely related to cycles and fertility. As time went on the goddess often found herself taking a secondary role to a male counterpart which was probably the result of stronger male priestly orders. These male orders theoretically developed and spread during the Indo-Aron migrations of the Bronze Age. This in itself may only be a simple explanation, for the goddess cults may have stepped aside on their own and turned inward to protect their secrets and their rites, thus preserving their secrets from the profane. The worship of a moon-deity became very important to all the great civilizations of the 'fertile crescent' because of its relationship to agricultural cycles. Like all deities, the Moon-deity developed a cult following with its own rituals, occult teachings and priestly elite. Some of the ancient goddesses were: Anunit, who later was known as Ishtar originated in Babylon; Bendis who was the wife of the Greek god Sabazius (early fifth century B.C.E.); Isis the powerful Egyptian goddess, and Sefkhet the wife of Thoth.

In Egyptian mythology Thoth was venerated throughout Egypt as a true deity who in some manifestations was the Moon itself and in others was the guardian of the Moon. He is known as the lord and multiplier of time; the celestial scribe, as depicted on the walls of tombs and in the *Book of the Dead,* where he is depicted as asking questions of the souls of the dead about their deeds in life before their heart is weighed against the feather of Maat. He is credited as the inventor of writing and of all wisdom and the patron of secrets, magic and scribes. He is a teacher of man, the messenger of the gods (and thus identified by the Greeks with Hermes) and the divine record-keeper and mediator.

Thoth's appearance is often with the head of an ibis holding a scribe's palette and stylus. He was also shown as a full ibis, or sometimes as baboon. Thoth is worshipped widely throughout all of Egypt; his cult center was Hermopolis. In Egyptian mythology, the *Ogdoad* (in Greek means the eightfold) were eight deities who were worshipped in Hermopolis during what is called the Old Kingdom, the third through sixth dynasties, dated between 2686 and 2134 B.C.E. The concept of an *Ogdoad* is important to the Cabbalist because it introduces the concept of duality and is integrated in the Gnostic systems of the early Christian era, and was further developed by the theologian Valentinus, also spelled Valentinius; 100–160, who was the best known and for a time most successful early Christian gnostic theologian.

The *Ogdoad* consisted of eight deities arranged in one of the earliest dualistic portrayal of the Divine presence, the four female-male pairs: Naunet and Nu, Amaunet and Amun, Kauket and Kuk, Hauhet and Huh. The females were associated with snakes and the males were associated with frogs. Apart from their gender, there was little to distinguish the female goddess from the male god in a pair; indeed, the names of the females are merely the female forms of the male name. Essentially, each pair represents the female and male aspect of one of four concepts, namely the primordial waters (Naunet and Nu), air or invisibility (Amunet and Amun), darkness (Kauket and Kuk), and eternity or infinite space (Hauhet and Huh).

These four concepts represent the primal, fundamental state of creation. These pairs represented the balance or equilibrium of the universe. Unfortunately, like life the myth, their interaction ultimately proved to be unbalanced, resulting in the rising of a new entity. When this entity opened, it revealed Ra, the fiery sun, inside. After a long interval of rest, Ra, together with the other deities, created all other things as depicted in Egyptian lore.

Later the Greeks identified their own god Hermes, with Thoth and the enormous body of Egyptian traditions developed and alluded to stretching back into the impenetrable past.

Hermes Trismegistus (Ancient Greek "thrice-greatest Hermes"; or the Latin: Mercurius ter Maximus) is the purported author of the Hermetic Corpus, a series of sacred texts that are the basis of Hermeticism. He is often represented as the syncretic combination of the Greek god Hermes and the Egyptian god Thoth. In Hellenistic Egypt, the Greeks recognized the congruence of their god Hermes with Thoth. Subsequently the two gods were worshipped as one in what had been the Temple of Thoth in Khemnu, which the Greeks called Hermopolis.

Both Thoth and Hermes were gods of writing and of magic in their respective cultures. Thus, the Greek god of interpretive communication was combined with the Egyptian god of wisdom as a patron of astrology and alchemy. Because of this association, Thoth/Hermes has become an important part of modern hermetic studies.

Tenth Sefirah: Malkuth or Malchut (מלכות)
"The Kingdom"

God-name:	Adonai Malekh or Adonai ha Aretz-Lord of Earth
Number:	10
Archangel:	Sandalphon
Order of Angels:	The Ashim—Souls of Fire
Body Part:	The Feet and Anus
Symbol:	Altar of the Double Cube, the Equal-Armed Cross, the Magic Circle, The Triangle of Evocation
Spiritual Experience:	Vision of the Holy Guardian Angel
Planet:	Earth
Color in Atziluth:	Yellow
Color in Briah:	Citrine, Olive, Russet and Black
Color in Yetzirah:	Citrine, Olive, Russet and Black flecked with Gold
Color in Assiah:	Black rayed with Yellow
Personal Chakra:	Muladhara-The Root Chakra

Malkuth, or the "Kingdom", appears at the bottom in the configuration of the Sefirot on the middle axis, directly beneath Yesod. It draws its influences/energies from all the Sephirot above. This Sefirah represents the whole of the physical world, not just what any one particular person is conscious at the present time. Malkuth is the sphere of the physical elements and Kabbalists still use the four-fold scheme which dates back at least as far as Empedocles (490–430 B.C.E.), who was a Greek pre-Socratic philosopher and a citizen of Agrigentum, a Greek city in Sicily. Empedocles' philosophy is best known for being the originator of the cosmogenic theory of the four Classical elements. The four elements correspond to four readily-observable states of matter:

solid — earth
liquid — water
gas — air
plasma — fire/electric arc (lightning)

The four colors traditionally used for Malkuth are citrine, olive, russet, and black, representing the four-fold division of the Elements, the Four Worlds, and the other four-fold schemata that are intrinsic to the Qabalistic teachings.

Malkuth is often called the inferior mother because it's the ultimate manifestation of form as opposed to the Great Mother, Binah, who is the beginning of all form. As the tenth and final Sephirot it is sometimes called the "Gate" because when we pass on and leave this life on Malkuth we transcend this mortal coil only to pass through the Gate of the higher realms described in the teaching of the Qabalah.

Malkuth has many titles referring to the Gate which include the Gate of Death, Gate of the Shadow Death, Gate of Tears, Gate of Justice, Gate of Prayer, Gate to the Garden of Eden, Gate of the Inferior Mother, and the Bride and the Virgin. These plus numerous other titles indicate that Malkuth represents a definite stage of spiritual development or a portal that one must transport through. The concept of Death or Shadow Death obviously describes one's entry and exit from the physical world but more importantly to the student the death of old ideas and the birth of new ideas or perspectives of one's place in the physical world.

Malkuth is often associated with the four classical elements of Greek philosophy: fire, air, water and earth. The elements themselves are further considered to represent energy, gasses, liquids and solids; power, will, intuition and strength; and destiny, spirit, life and inanimate matter. Malkuth is therefore usually depicted as the Cross of Equated Forces, divided into four equal quarters, colored russet, citrine, olive and black. As the only sphere of the Tree grounded into physical reality, Malkuth is the only stable Sephira because of the balance of the four classic elements.

Malkuth corresponds to thetzelem Elokim the "crown" of the pro-creative organ (the corona in the male; the labia in the female), or to the mouth. This concept relates back to the *Sepher ha Zohar* describing that each person shall be known for the Tree they produce. Jehovah Elohim (the union of El and Elah Yam, god and goddess of the sea); that is, the heavenly father (the creative energy in the cerebral spinal fluid) and mother (the creative energy in the genitalia fluid); "garden", the lower, Shekinah, which is the feminine Hebrew name of God in Judaism, And the heavenly mother called the Kundalini; "in Eden in the Sephiroth Malkuth"; "Adam", the middle column (Yesod, Tiphareth) of the Sephirothic tree; from which was formed in Malkuth, his wife, and who being his delight should never be separated from him.

The *Zohar* goes on to say Elohim said, Let the earth bring forth grass, the herb yielding seed, and the fruit tree yielding fruit after his kind, whose seed is in itself, upon the earth: and it was so. (*Genesis* 1:11)

The "earth" is Malkuth and the "Bring forth grass" is to bring forth the generative forces that remained dormant and hidden until their *sexual alchemical manifestation*. This last italicized phrase is the key to the student, for in Malkuth the student will plant their Tree/grass which is the source of the energies that will give the emphasis to travel up the various paths of self-development. Problems occur when this sex-energy is manifested only in the physical form and the results often are disastrous because the sex-energy is often used for self-gratification and in the world of Assiah while ignoring the creative potential of Beri'ah. Many great alchemists/mages met their downfall when these sex-energies began to manifest in such a maner as to over power them and versus the creative growth energies.

Malkuth corresponds to the mouth in that it is often referred to as the "source of speech" in so far as the power of creation is the word which is the medium of self-expression. This refers back to the creative sex-energies and how they are used to manifest the physical world of the person to the outer world. Speech, which is the result of action, is what allows one to exercise their authority, dominion or kingship (Malkuth literally means kingship) to the world.

SANDALPHON

According to rabbinic lore, Sandalphon is the twin brother of Metatron. According to other traditions Sandalphon is said to be actually Elijah after Elijah was transported to heaven in a burning chariot. Sandalphon is the Archangel that acts as the Guide or Intelligence of the planet Earth. As the Guide, he helps those spiritual seekers to see what the physical world *should* become through persistent applications of spiritual principles in ordinary life.

One of Sandalphon's duties is to be the protector of unborn children. Sandalphon is designated "the left-hand feminine cherub of the Ark". In the liturgy for the Jewish Feast of Tabernacles, he is credited with gathering the prayers of the faithful, making a garland of such prayers, and then "adjuring them to ascend as an orb to the supreme King of Kings". Like the Archangel Michael, Sandalphon carries on a ceaseless battle with Sammael (perhaps Satan), the angel of evil and good. Sammael is often depicted as the great serpent with twelve wings and is considered the destroyer of the solar system.

The Ashim-Souls of Fire

The Ashim are the rank of angels assigned to Malkuth. It is the task of the Ashim to fashion and bind together physical matter. The name Ashim means "soul of fire". They are often said to be a special class of messengers for the Divine. Our Qabalistic scholars believe that the Ashim are human souls and not angels at all. Therefore, if their function is to bind physical matter, this would make them Magi, or practitioners of what the world calls "magik" and because of this are often referred to or called upon in ritual work.

The Earth

Personal consciousness and the interaction of the senses with the physical universe all fall within the realm of Malkuth. Its planetary symbol is the Earth, but it is very important to note that the sphere is not the physical universe itself. Solid matter — reality — is the product of all ten spheres and twenty-two paths, rather than just one. Malkuth then is not reality as such, but it is the portal through which reality is given form; the mother, rather than the child.

The planetary sphere of the Earth should be viewed not as the planet but what Malkuth is, "the kingdom". Like story book kingdoms this is our individual reality as we perceive it at this moment with our five senses. It is the result of our experiences and viewed with the flavoring of how we discern it on our own psyche. And since our senses are often, like our taste and sight, different than every other person, so is our "kingdom" even though the physical space is viewed by many. It is the task of the student to learn to clarify his or her 'kingdom' through the opening of their psychic spiritual senses by pulling the energies from the Tree and incorporating the enlightened visions into their worlds.

THE UNIFIED ONE-DA'AT THE HIDDEN SEFIRAH

When studying the Tree of Life there is often depicted an eleventh sphere referred to as Da'at. It is not a Sefirah like the first ten but the incorporation of all the Sephirot.

Eleventh Sphere: Da'at, Da'ath, or Daas (דעת)
"Knowledge"

God-name:	Conjunction of Jehovah and Jehovah Elohim
Number:	11
Archangel:	The four Archangels of the Cardinal Points,
	Michael—the South
	Gabriel—the West
	Uriel—the North
	Raphael—the East
Order of Angels:	Silver Serpents
Body Part:	Soul
Symbol:	The Condemned Cell, The Prism, The Empty Room,
	The Sacred Mountain, A Grain of Corn, The
	Absence of any Symbol
Spiritual Experience:	Vision across the Abyss
Color in Atziluth:	Lavender
Color in Briah:	Silver Grey
Color in Yetzirah:	Pure Purple
Color in Assiah:	Grey flecked with Yellow
Personal Chakra:	The Vishuddi or Throat Chakra

Da'at is often referred to as the pseudo-Sefirah because it is not thought to be a true Sefirah but an accumulation of all the other ten Sephirot. It first appeared in writtings toward the end of the thirteenth Century. Da'at is the location (the mystical state) where all ten Sephirot in the Tree of Life are united as one. Visually it is shown above the sixth Sefirah of Tiphareth on the middle pillar. In Hermetic Qabbalah the notion of an Abyss is often discussed that, lying between the three supernal Sephiroth of Kether, Chokhmah, and Binah, and the seven lower Sephiroth (see diagram below). The idea of a gap or cleft in the Tree of Life is visualized in the path of the Lightning Flash down the Tree of Life, where then one finds that it makes the jump from Binah to Chesed, thus reinforcing this idea of a "gap" or "gulf" which has to be crossed. This notion of an Abyss is extremely old and one of the earliest sources for The Abyss comes from the *Bible*:

"And the earth was without form, and void; and darkness was upon the face of the deep."

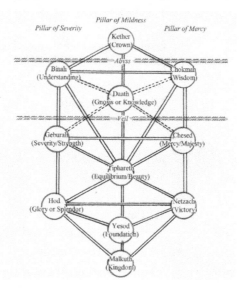

Another mention of The Abyss comes from the *Zohar* where it describes that there were several failed attempts at creation before the present one; these attempts failed because mercy and judgment (e.g. force and form) were not balanced, and the resulting detritus of these failed attempts, the broken shells of previous Sephiroth, accumulated in The Abyss. Because the shells called Qlippoth were the result of unbalanced rigor or judgment they were considered evil, and the Abyss became a repository of evil spirits not dissimilar from the pit of Hell into which the rebellious angels were cast, or the rebellious Titans in Greek mythology who were buried as far beneath the Earth as the Earth is beneath the sky.

In the Sphere of Da'at, all Sephirot exist in their perfected state of infinite sharing. Da'at is the external manifestation of Kether as revealed through Chokmah and Binah. The three Sephirot of the left column that would receive and conceal the Divine Light, instead share and reveal it. Da'at is thus known as ruach ka-kadesh or Divine Inspiration. Because all

Sephirot radiate infinite self-giving Divine Light, it is no longer possible to distinguish one Sephirot from another, thus they are one. Though the Divine Light is always shining, not all humans can see it because they are not open to its presence as symbolized within Malkuth. The perception of change can only occur in Malkuth. Humans who become self-giving like the Light become able to see it, and for them the benefits of Da'at's light seem "revealed". However, humans who remain selfish cannot see it, and for them its benefits seem "hidden".

Da'at is associated with the human soul and with the powers of memory and concentration, powers which rely upon one's "recognition" of, and "sensitivity" to, the potential meaningfulness of those ideas generated in consciousness through the powers of Chokmah and Binah. This sensitivity itself derives from Da'at's connection to the superconscious origin of the soul. For when the powers of Chokmah, Wisdom and Binah, Understanding are combined, Da'at or Knowledge is attainted and the Temple is built. This the same Temple that is referred to as the "Temple within each of us". Without Divine wisdom, understanding there is no Knowledge to build our Temple of spiritual enlightenment.

According to Hasidic thought Da'at operates on two levels: the higher level is referred to as Da'at Elyon or the "higher knowledge". It is also called the Da'at hane'elam or "the hidden knowledge", and serves to secure the continuous bond between the two higher powers of intellect–Chockmah and Binah. The lower level, is referred to as Da'at Tachton or "lower knowledge". It too has a second title of Da'at Hamitpashet or "extending knowledge", and serves to connect the intellect as a whole with the realm of emotion, thereby enhancing one's determination and resolve to act in accordance with the essential truths that one has integrated into consciousness. These terms are derived from the Kabbalistic Sephirot: Kether (above conscious Will) and Da'at (conscious Knowledge), considered two levels of the same unifying principle; the first encompassing, the second internalized within the person.

In the *Zohar*, it describes this level of Da'at as "the key that includes six". The "key" of Da'at opens all six chambers (attributes) of the heart and fills them with life-force. Each of these six chambers, when filled with Da'at, is referred to as a particular dei'ah or "attitude" of the soul.

THE FOUR ARCHANGELS OF THE CARDINAL POINTS

> Michael—the South
> Gabriel—the West
> Uriel—the North
> Raphael—the East

There are really no God Name, Archangels or Order of Angels tradition-ally assigned to Da'at since it is not considered a Sephiroth. The God name assigned to it is considered a synthesis of the God names of Chokmah and Binah and the Supernal Triangle which includes the reflected energies of Kether. One way for the student to deal with Da'at is dealing with The Cube of Space where the four Archangels represent the four vertical faces of the Cube. According to the *Sepher Yetzirah* the Cube represents the manifested universe. The Cube is a symbol of the physical embodiment and is the vehicle for the one's self-expression.

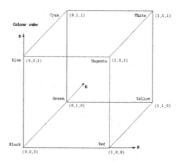

This symbolic representation is important to the student/adept for it is a balanced representation or symbol to meditate on which would possibly be a source of spiritual enlightenment. The archangels would be focal points to concentrate on to help in that enfoldment.

Some schools of thought feel it is not wise to work in this sphere until after assuring that one's personal foundations have been balanced and/or awakened. This is important for if one is does not have at least one school of thought mastered the act of bouncing to multiple schools weakens the student's ability to access any energies cleanly. This could result in chaos and confusion, at the least.

SILVER SERPENTS

The "Angels of this Sefirah" are a kind of Seraphim but without the flaming aspect associated with the Seraphim of Geburah. To those who have clairvoyant tendencies these angels often appear as silver serpents with golden tongues that are said to produce "Incandescent Knowledge".

X.

PATHWAYS OF THE
TREE OF LIFE

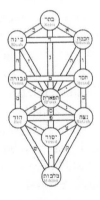

Tree according to Athanasius Kircher (1602–1680)

W hen looking at an image of the Tree of Life the student will note that each of the traditional ten Sephiroth are connected by "pathways" or "channels". Each of these pathways usually have a Hebrew letter associated with that specific path. According to this cosmological text, God created the universe. Inorder to understand this concept in terms of the Tree of Life and the "path-work" one should have a basic understanding of the histories of the Hebrew letters. There are several interpretative views as to how the letters came to be.

According to one translation of the first paragraph of the *Sepher Yetzirah:*

In thirty-two wonderful distinguishing paths of wisdom did Jah, Jehovah Tzabaoth, the Creative Powers of Life, King of Eternity, God Almighty, Compassionate and Merciful, Supreme and Exalted, Who is Eternal, Sublime, and Holy is His Name, decree and create His universe by means of three kinds of Characters: Numbers, Letters, and Words: ten circumscribed Sephiroth, and twenty-two fundamental signs; three Mother, seven Double, and twelve Simple Letters.

LINGUISTICAL AND PALEOGRAPHIC HISTORY OF THE HEBREW LETTERS

Like history itself there are many theories as to how the Hebrew alphabet developed. In fact, the English word "alphabet" comes from the Jewish term *Alef Beit*, which are the first two letters of the Hebrew alphabet. Most biblical scholars believe that the characters of the Hebrew alphabet were the result of the cultural blend with the Phoenician peoples. It is believed that the Semitic languages in the Levant (modern Syria and Lebanon) developed around 3750 B.C.E. with the blending of several of the tribes of the area as the result of conquest of territories and/or trade. There have been repeated attempts to link the Hebrew alphabet to the traditional theory of the Hebrew tribes being in Egypt or Babylon but with little true scientific success.

The reason for this scientific uncertainty is that the oldest known forms of these letters come from a time that had been preceded by a long period of development, during which the characters themselves may have undergone important modifications. It may also be said with a certain amount of probability that the alphabet did not possess from the beginning all the characters that it now contains. With this theory, it is felt the letters probably developed out of need as a way to identify near-by things such as items of the daily life of a nomadic people.

The Hebrew alphabet contains no vowels but often the letters take the form of graphemes or even hieroglyphic in nature as they crudely depict the item described such as vav (ו) which means "hook". These names, as well as the order of the letters, certainly existed at least one thousand years B.C.E., for they were known when the Greeks adopted their alphabet from the Semites. At this point the alphabet must already have undergone local variations among the different earlier versions. There is some thought that these variations consisted of differences in which letters belonged to various sequences.

The Creation of the Hebrew Alphabet

According to Merkavah or Merkabah/Merkavh mysticism (or Chariot mysticism) which is an early school of Jewish mysticism practiced around 100 B.C.E.–1000 C.E., the creation of the letters was centered on visions such as those found in the *Book of Ezekiel,* Chapter 1, or in the hekhalot ("palaces") literature. These sources concerned stories of ascents to the heavenly palaces and the Throne of God. Within these rabbinic narratives were legends that the letters were the result of God creating the universe and had hidden meanings. The most important of these early treatises, possibly from the second century AD, which describes the process of creation is The *Book of Creation (Sepher Yetzirah).* According to this cosmological text, God created the universe by 32 mysterious paths consisting of 22 letters of the Hebrew alphabet together with ten Sefirot comprised of ten primordial numbers/powers, associated with the attributes of God. The *Sepher Yetzirah* asserts that all of these letters play an important role in the creation of the cosmos:

> "By means of the twenty-two letters, by giving them a form and shape, by mixing them and combining them in different ways, God made the soul of all that which has been created and all of that which will be. It is upon these same letters that the Holy One (blessed be He) has founded his high and holy name."

The 32 paths concept became popular in the western world when English editions of the *Sepher Yetzirah* where made available. According to the Jewish tradition, the 32 Paths of Wisdom concept is derived from the 32 times that the name "Elohim" is mentioned in the *Book of Genesis,* specifically in Chapter One. As the secret understanding of each letter became available the true extent of complexity of the single letters and their combinations came to light. And with this knowledge came a great deal of scholarly comment of how and when to use the power of these letters. Each letter was assigned many meanings and values.

MYSTICAL CREATION OF THE HEBREW ALPHABET

In time the significance of each letter developed and with this attempts to establish each letter's relationship to mystical concepts grew. Each Hebrew letter originaly had only a numerical value attached to it. This expanded to include a color signifier, musical note, astrological sign and alchemical element as well. This expansion of attributes became more apparent as the Kabbalah moved from a strictly mystical Jewish process to the world of the non-Jewish thinkers and mystics. Though you will find some variations to them they hold fairly true in the Qabalistic world. Also note that each letter has a Gematria Value assigned to it.

MYSTICAL ASPECT OF THE HEBREW LETTERS

Gematria is based on the concept that each letter has a "mystical" value assigned to the correspondences of its meaning. Gematria is thought to have come from the Assyro-Babylonian system of numerology which was later adopted by Jews that assigns a numerical value to a word or phrase in the belief that words or phrases with identical numerical values have some relation to each other or have some relation to the number itself as it may apply to a person's age, or the calendar. Gematria became a key to "the Magical Language" of the Qabalah. The other two are Notariqon and Temurah.

Notariqon/Notarikon is a Hebrew word, derived from the Latin notarius, meaning "shorthand writer". It is a Kabbalistic method of analyzing and constructing Hebrew by the use of acronyms. This method can be used to analyze a word by treating it as an acronym for a phrase or sentence that may contain a secret Kabbalistic meaning.

When the term **Temurah** is used **by** Kabbalists are referring to the rearranging of words and sentences in the *Bible*, to make new phrases revealing some secret meaning. It was believed that by doing this they could derive the esoteric substratum and deeper spiritual meaning of the words.

THE HEBREW LETTERS

This is the key to the mystery of the sacred letters.
Fix thy mind on the object set before thee by any letter.
And hold thy thought to meditate thereon.
Then shall the inner nature of that object
Be made known to thee.[17]

There are twenty-two Hebrew Letters that comprise what is often referred as the "alphabet of fire". The basic shape of each of the twenty-two letters is Yod. If one looks at the basic form of the letter Yod one will see it appears to be a single flame ׳. Yod as the spark or first aspect of the Hebrew letters has a numerical value of ten and has a common meaning of "hand". It also means handle, movement, place, strength, and share. It is the energy of intelligent consciousness projecting an unbridled pulsating energy to Aleph into physical manifestation. This is Spirituality.[18] And even though Yod is the smallest of letters it represents the hand of the craftsman who creates all the other letters. Yod is the flame, which in Hebrew is "esh", a feminine noun. If Yod is the unbridled energy that bursts into manifestation and is thought to be the basis of the very spirituality of man, then the concept of *Shekinah*, the feminine aspect of God, is also associated with the Jewish conception of the Holy Spirit. This concept of male and female aspect of God or "Dualism" is probably the result of the Jewish exiles coming in contact with Zoroastrian religion of the Persian Empire.

This brings us back to the Hebrew Letters themselves being the "language of fire" as stated in the *Torah* when it says "My words are as fire". They are the creative energy of the world. It is said that "Holy One" organized the letter energy intelligences into form, with the last letter first (Tav), activating their spirit as the He created the Universe. The learning of the letters is not a rote memory an exercise but a process of spiritual growth. Learn and understand the meaning of the letters, from their construction to their relationships with their neighbors.

---

17 *The Book of Tokens*, Paul Foster Case, Builders of Adytum, 1983, pg. 51
18 *The Inner Meaning of the Hebrew Letters*, Haralick, Robert M., Jason Aronson Inc, 1995, pg. 141

ALEPH

Aleph is most often viewed as the first letter of the alphabet.

Gematria Value:	1
Color:	Yellow
Musical Note:	E
Signific:	Bull/Ox
Astrological Sign:	Uranus
Alchemical Element:	Air
Roman Equivalent:	A

According to Jewish lore the *Torah* begins with the letter *Beth;* it is the second letter of the Hebrew Alphabet because *Aleph* was given a greater honor. That honor was to begin the Ten Commandments as the opening letter of the word — "I am the Lord, your God". *Aleph* means "Ox", but what kind of animal is an ox? It is an animal of pure power that once domesticated is a greater helper of humanity. It is the animal that provides strength and fortitude that allows man to accomplish many magnificent tasks that he could not do alone. The ox helped man move from the "wanderer" to the "cultivator of lands". This is not just a physical feat but a spiritual one as well. When we can tame the unruly passions and desires we can begin to sow the seeds of enlightenment.

Aleph has the energy intelligence force of the air, fire and earth. Each of these elements, when spelled in Hebrew begin with the letter *Aleph;* it is the force that forms. It is timeless and beyond measure and beyond understanding for it is the creative transcendent force of creation. This energy intelligence of *Aleph* cannot manifest itself for it has no boundaries and needs the limits of formation from its sister and brother letters to manifest itself.

BETH

ב

Gematria Value:	2
Color:	Yellow
Musical Note:	E
Signific:	House
Astrological Sign:	Mercury
Alchemical Element:	Mercury
Roman Equivalent:	B

Jewish Lore says that *Beth,* which corresponds to the number two, begins the *Torah* for a very important lesson. It teaches us that there are two worlds. The first is "this world" and the second more important one is the "world to come". It reminds us that our current physical life is only a precursor to a more important world or next life. The *Zohar* teaches that where *Aleph* is the image of the male principle *Beth* is the image of the female principle.

Beth is the container, the former of boundaries or walls—the house of manifestation. The house is the place where we are. It is a place we have built that reflects our creative view of our existence. It is our understanding of the Temple of God and how we as individuals relate to it. The house is where we develop our personalities and defines who we are in relation to others and the world. It defines our physical, emotional and spiritual being. The house symbolizes the energy intelligence force of the "archetype of all containers or vessels". For without it we are nothing.

GIMEL/GIMMEL

ג

Gematria Value:	3
Color:	Blue
Musical Note:	G #
Signific:	Camel
Astrological Sign:	Moon
Alchemical Element:	Silver
Roman Equivalent:	C/G

Gimel is the camel, the provider of transportation, a means to leave one place to go onward. It symbolizes a spiritual need to leave ones "house" and travel onward to complete the Great Work. It is a task not asked of us but we must be willing to do ourselves. The Great Work (magnum opus) is as *Thelema* defines it as "the spiritual practice leading to the mystical union of the self with the ALL".

As the third letter its numerical value is three. It signifies the combining of the male, *Aleph*, with the female, *Beth*, principles to make a third perfect energy, *Gimel*. In the fifteenth century, Jewish scholars of the Maharal of Prague or the MaHaRal, explained that Gimel signified the capacity to act as a neutralizer. It was the equilibrium that balanced the feminine and masculine engeries, thus "uniting them into a lasting and more wholesome unit". It is by establishing this "wholesome unit" that the Divine light can reveal itself. This is not done as a single, stationary place but through movement and growth. That is why we may wish to be "a temple" of the Divine, but this temple needs to be able to grow and nourish the Divine light so it can shine forth. This can only be done by growing or moving forth the creative energy.

DALETH/DALET

ד

Gematria Value:	4
Color:	Green
Musical Note:	F #
Significh:	Door
Astrological Sign:	Venus
Alchemical Element:	Copper
Roman Equivalent:	D

According to *The Bahir*, there is a debate about how a camel become a door and then a window? *The Bahir* relates that a camel is unquestionably a means of exchange which cannot do other than produce the opporitunity for one's to flourish and expand one view of the world and its ever-changing vistas.

According to Rabbi Yitzchak Ginsburgh's (1944–), book *The Alef Beit*, published in English in 1995, *Daleth* is viewed as "the poor man". The position of the letter silhouettes a man bowed as if receiving charity from a rich man. It teaches us that as the face of *Daleth* is not perceived and thus a secret so too we must give charity in secret. For charity is not to honor the giver for giving but for those to receive and be nourished.

Rabbi Kaplan explains in his translation of *The Bahir* that the letter ד consists of two lines, one vertical and the other horizontal. The vertical line connects Chokmah (Wisdom) with Binah (Understanding). The vertical line connects Wisdom with Love. The Divine, which Wisdom represents its highest form, gives its Love freely and without reason. This *Daleth* is the door, the entranceway by which we humbly enter into realization of God's dwelling place.

This door represents the entranceway by which our own degree of consciousness of the Divine is expressed. It is up to us to determine how open that door for this Divine consciousness to manifest Itself.

HEH

$$ה$$

Gematria Value:	5
Color:	Red
Musical Note:	C
Signific:	Window
Astrological Sign:	Aries
Alchemical Element:	Fiery
Roman Equivalent:	E

Heh ה appears to be an archway with three walls and the center open. The three walls represent three dimensions of the physical world: breadth, height and depth. The open face of the letter indicates that God gives or allows man free choice. Man is free to obey or to disobey God's will. The window is open to allow us to choose our life. The important thing is that window is open to go through in either direction. This openness symbolizes God's willingness and readiness to forgive and welcome us back into His Divine grace.

The letter energy intelligence of ה is closely related with the "power of being" for it is the root to "be". And from ה we learn the Divine expresses Itself so we can experience as a Divine manifestation. For God brings the creation of the universe through *Heh*. Another key to this is that ה can be seen as symbolizing the "three garments, the means of expression of the soul". The garments are thought, speech and action. Thought and speech are the two connected lines while the single vertical line is action. This is because action is the key to enlightenment. If one only thinks and talks about the act of enlightenment without putting it into action, there is no transformation to higher planes.

Heh is also symbolic of man's ability to repent for his transgressions against the Divine. This is symbolized by the small gap in the letter ה. This gap also is the shape of the opening of man's eye. "It enables us to see how to do according to the Will of the Holy One."[19]. The letter can also be seen as the single line representing the letter intelligence for the physical existence and the

19 *The Inner Meaning of the Hebrew Letters*, Haralick, Robert M., Jason Aronson Inc, 1995, pg. 79

material world. The right side would represent the Divine. Thus ה links the physical to the spiritual, or the Divine manifestation in the world of Malkuth.

Vav

ו

Gematria Value:	6
Color:	Red-Orange
Musical Note:	C #
Signific:	Hook
Astrological Sign:	Taurus
Alchemical Element:	Earthly
Roman Equivalent:	V/U/Y/W

In the *Zohar Vav* ו is called the letter of truth, because it is straight and upright and suggests honesty and truth. It is shaped like a nail, and is the Hebrew word for hook, peg or nail. It is also used to "join" concepts together as well as a prefix that can place that concept in the present or future depending on how it is placed. Thus ו letter energy is to connect and or unify. This connection or unification unites the present with the past and to the future. It is the symbol of the eternal for it can encompass all time in a unified stream.

This unification transcends the contrasts of life. It unifies the left and right columns of the Tree of Life, it transcends the opposites of good and evil, male or female; it is the equalizer. This is important in dealing with the day to day ups and downs of life. When we think we are wronged we need to look deeper into the situation for God's hand only brings goodness. It is our job to learn to look for the good in everything that happens. There is a reason, a lesson, which we need to learn. When we lose this connection to the Divine the contrasts of life taint our interpretations of our world thus causing confusion, pain and chaos.

Vav's ו numerical value is six. The physical world is held together, as if nailed, to the spiritual aspect of the world. The six directions or boundaries to our reality are: 1) north, 2) south, 3) east, 4) west, 5) above, and 6) below. These are all held in place, according to *The Bahir*, by ו.

ZAÏN

ז

Gematria Value:	7
Color:	Orange
Musical Note:	D
Signific:	Sword
Astrological Sign:	Gemini
Alchemical Element:	Airy
Roman Equivalent:	Z

The letter *Zaïn* ז, means "sword" or "weapon" as represented by its very configuration. It is also a symbolic representation of the concept of "sustenance" and "armament", for by the sword or spear man can gain his sustenance. Spiritually it reflects the "straight light" through the crown or top of the head, for it is the light returning in its manifested form. It is the symbolic representation to student of the Divine light that is the sustenance by which the student grows. The fact that is in the form of 'weapon' indicates that obtaining this sustenance will require a struggle. The struggle is usually with old ideas that have formed an opaque view of the world.

The "sword" is a two-fold instrument, one of causing chaos or second an instrument to assure peace. How we use the "sword" is our choice. We can put ourselves in situations where love rules or situations where chaos becomes the destroyer. The concept of destroyer is not always bad, for by destroying old, false concepts, we can open ourselves up to new ideas and concepts. It is like plowing a field, we clear the field of old growth to allow for new ideas to spring forth. The important thing is the student needs to become wise enough to discriminate and to recognize the consequences of each choice made.

When the student is in unison with the Divine essence of ז it becomes a tool of the Divine judgment. It is not a judgment of punishment but one of nourishment and sustenance. For this nourishment allows for the ascendance to higher levels of purity. When the letter energy is associated with path work it can be the symbolic tool to clear and open the channel that it represents.

CHETH

ח

Gematria Value:	8
Color:	Orange-Yellow
Musical Note:	D #
Signify:	Fence
Astrological Sign:	Aries
Alchemical Element:	Watery
Roman Equivalent:	H

The letter *Cheth* ח is similar to the letter *Heh* ה shape except that the upper left hand corner is closed. This suggests that if a person becomes steeped in sin and impurity, this could lead to the closing of the door to repentance. It teaches that when we fall from the path our "eye" is closed to the Divine's glory. One scholar suggests that ח consists of two spears ו with a roof over them. The Rabbi suggests this represents man's banishment from Eden and he now has to balance the two ו's in order to have shelter. The first ו represents passive trust, while the second 'the sustainer' of his world.

Cheth has a numerical value of eight. In Rabbi Ginsburgh's book, *The Hebrew Letters* (1992), he teaches that eight means the Divine essence in physical reality. This concept was built on Rabbi Munk's concepts presented in *The Wisdom in the Hebrew Alphabet* (1988) that life is that which contains the Divine essence. This allows for the transcendence in the limitations inherent in the very circumstances of the physical existence. This allows for the spirit of man to go from his earthly boundaries to those of the higher realms.

God gave us a gift of free will. With this gift we sometimes think we stumble and make "poor decisions". In reality God's covenant with us allows these "poor decisions" to become beneficence from God to help us perfect our ways and become more perfect and holy before God. For each "poor decision" provides a lesson to be learned. The ability to see and understand the cause and effect of the "poor decision" is the Great Lesson of life. We often get confused with thinking our values and expectations are God's desire for us when in reality it just our own selfishness.

TETH

Gematria Value:	9
Color:	Yellow
Musical Note:	E
Signify:	Serpent
Astrological Sign:	Leo
Alchemical Element:	Fiery
Roman Equivalent:	none (Romans did not have a sound)

The *Zohar* states "its good is hidden within it" referring to the formation of *Teth* ט being inverted. Because it is inverted it symbolizes hidden, inverted good. The physical appearance of the letter resembles a container. The first time *Teth* appears in the *Torah's* in *Genesis* 1:4: *God saw that the light was good*. *Teth* ט symbolizes the union of the groom and the bride and their consummation the conception of their union. And when viewing the letter with this concept it resembles a female's uterus waiting for the groom to inseminate it with the life force of creation. Spiritually the small opening in the container provides an opening for the Divine light to flow and share its goodness with the world. The numerical value of *Teth* is nine, the same as the nine months of pregnancy. And like pregnancy of old, the joy is hidden until its birth.

Upon meditating on *Teth* the student is preparing an understanding and place to encourage the Divine light to enter. The container could be viewed as one's soul or temple. By meditating upon your temple and assuring it is ready to receive the Light from up high the student is acknowledging several things. First and foremost, there is a greater being and second the need to share in the Divine's light. By preparing for this insemination of light the student is opening the way for growth and understanding.

YOD

ז

Gematria Value:	10
Color:	Yellow—Green
Musical Note:	F
Signify:	Open-hand
Astrological Sign:	Virgo
Alchemical Element:	Earthy
Roman Equivalent:	I/J

Yod ז is the smallest and simplest of letters. Because of its small size, it symbolizes humility and represents the metaphysical or spirituality. It is the letter by which all the other letters of the alphabet begin. It is the single point of creation, a creation of all that is to come. It appears to have no component parts like its sister letters. Yet upon closer examination the *Yod* has a small top point that is directed to heaven, like a figure pointing to the sky. The *Yod* also has a small tail pointing downward towards earth. These two points are united in the middle. The *Zohar* teaches that the upward point is the Sefirah Kether, the middle is Chokmah and the tail is the Sefiroh Binah or Understanding. It is the small suspended point in *Teth* ט which represents the spark of good hidden in *Teth* ט. It symbolizes the very spark of the creative force. Its numerical value is 10 and means the hand of man. It also can mean handle, monument, place, strength, share or portion.

    Yod's energy intelligence consciousness is that of projecting the unleashed pulsating bullish power of *Aleph* א into the physical world of manifestation. Through its power and strength, it provides boundaries and limitations to the formative creation allowing us to perceive its existence.

    Yod ז, means "hand", and from our hand we can create our world, like a carpenter creates a table using his hands to manipulate his tools to create or manifest a physical object. The hand can facilitate our own illness or it can help to provide our healing both on the physical, emotional and spiritual levels. It is by the hand of God that God delivers the plagues on Egypt and it is by the hand Moses saves the people of Israel by parting the Red Sea. The hand is an instrument of great power and guidance. It is by the hand we soothe our loved ones, ease a baby's fears and tears. It is by the hand that a parent guides the child on their path. It is through the use of our hands that we manifest our spirituality both to others and to ourselves. No matter how much meditation and prayer the student practices that feeling of quiet, peace and focus only brings us to the doorway of our spirituality. For through our actions we manifest our goodness and spirituality.

Kaph/Khef/Kaf/Caph

Gematria Value: 20
Color: Violet
Musical Note: A #
Signify: Closed-hand
Astrological Sign: Jupiter
Alchemical Element: Tin
Roman Equivalent: K

Kaph has two forms, the singular form of כ with a numerical value of 20, and its final form of ך with a value of 200. When the letter *Yod* י is spelled out its Gematria Value is 20, the same as the numerical value of *Kaph*. This indicates that *Kaph* is responsible for the holding and letting flow of the divine light of *Yod* which is spiritual energy which abides within the container.

Kaph means "closed hand". This is symbolic of closing around or providing walls by which the Divine manifestation can be delineated. According to some archeologists when our ancient breathen built their temples to their gods they did not actually enter them to worship, but worshiped outside of the actual temple buildings. The temples themselves were places were the god heads could manifest or place perimeters to their unbounding spirits. Thus the 'closed hand' puts walls around the very Divine light to which we are attempting to connect. For as men we need a place, a tabernacle, a holy of holies, to go and commune with God. Though the temple is in the external physical world the real temple is within each of us. It is this internal temple that the student and later the Adept builds and maintains. It is in the temple that we attempt to shed our consciousness of our physical reality of confused and unworthy inclinations and concepts.

These unworthy inclinations and concepts are the result of our misinterpretations of the realities which were built of concepts laced with chaos and tainted interactions with our physical world. We offer up our consciousness in hopes that the "atonement" for our misinterpretations will provide fertile ground for new views and concepts, in other words enlightenment, to flourish. It is hoped the "crowning achievement" of our work is to see the glory of God wherever we go versus the entanglement of Chaos.

LAMED

ל

Gematria Value:	30
Color:	Green
Musical Note:	F #
Signify:	Ox-goad
Astrological Sign:	Libra
Alchemical Element:	Airy
Roman Equivalent:	L

Lamed ל is the only letter of the alphabet that ascends above the "upper bound" script line when writing the letter. For this reason, it is often said to symbolize the "King of kings" or "tower soaring in the air". ל, when used as a prefix can mean, to, unto, into, toward, during, by, of, with, within, each, every, or belonging, just to name a few. The one important aspect is that ל provides a direction association or connection in the physical world of one item with another. The root meaning of Lamed "to teach, learn, study or become familiar with". The energy intelligence of Lamed is the action of learning, teaching, and purpose.

This whole concept of learning or becoming familiar with is preparing us to learn to control the movement of active energies. For the student to progress this ability to control the energies aroused by use of the magical alphabet they must "conjure" to the awakened state. In Alchemy, there is always the story of the alchemist or his student conjuring a spell only to be consumed by what is conjured into reality. This is somewhat of an overstatement of what will happen if the student does not control the energy they are working with but still a real danger. One of the purposes of working with the energy and/or intelligence of the letters is for bringing the secret value of it down from the higher realms to the world of action. This is not just an intellectual learning but a learning that transforms the fiber of our being to have a greater desire for a stronger connection with Godliness. With this connection to the Godliness comes a learning that for every action, desire, thought, and expression there is a purpose.

Even this connection to the purpose does not give us a total understanding. For we may gain an intellectual understanding of the purpose, but if we do not extend it to our very heart and make it part of us it is useless. For one may gain Wisdom but not the Understanding of the Great Work. This learning must extend through the realms of Atzilut, Briah, Yetzirah and Asiyah. If it is not manifested in the realm of Asiyah it is not truly learned. For if the learning does not become transformed in the heart it does not become part of our Self and will not last. This deep understanding of true learning that of incorporating it into our heart, is the action for a "sacred purpose" of life.

Mem

Gematria Value:	40
Color:	Blue
Musical Note:	G #
Signify:	Water
Astrological Sign:	Neptune
Alchemical Element:	Water
Roman Equivalent:	M

The form of the letter *Mem* מ has a finger pointing upward to indicate God's sovereignty over all His creation. The remainder of the letter indicates a bent posture in humble recognition of His great mercy and our less than perfect ways. Mem also has a final form, as represented by closed bottom line ם. The final forms, value is 600 while the singular value is 40. Mem's letter energy intelligence is the bringing of physical existence into time and conditional physical being in a perfect and completed state. In a prefix form Mem מ can mean from, out of, away from, part of, or because of.

In order receive this perfection and completeness of this world that was created by God we must lift our eyes upward toward the God of Creation. This is not a single act but one that must be continual in order to receive His gifts.

In Robert Haralick's book *The Inner Meaning of the Hebrew Letters,* he states that words that begin with Mem מ and ends with the final form ם teach a great deal about its hidden meaning. The single form with its open bottom indicates to us that from below we can perceive God through the functioning of the universe. The final ם is closed. This alludes to fact that ultimately God remains unknowable and hidden.

Nun

נ

Gematria Value:	50
Color:	Blue-Green
Musical Note:	G
Signify:	Fish
Astrological Sign:	Scorpio
Alchemical Element:	Watery
Roman Equivalent:	N

The letter *Nun* נ is formed to represent a "bent-over" vessel. It is that of the "bent-over servant". In the final form *Nun* נ is an extended *Vav* descending below the line as the "unbounded servant". It symbolizes the power of submission. The value of *Nun* נ is 50 and the value of the final form of *Nun* נ is 700. Depending on which form of the letter is used in the word meaning of *Nun* it could be sprout, spread or propagate. The second meaning of words ending in the final form will be decline, decadent or cause to degenerate. Because of this twofold interpretation, it symbolizes a pulsating power. The power of growth, of blossoming, and spreading followed by a phase of decline and degeneration. This again is followed by a new flourishing, like the seasonal phases of nature.

This pulsating energy of growth and then decline teaches us that as we tread the path of enlightenment we will learn many ideas and concepts but they will change with new concepts replacing them. It is the same with our perceived concept of truth and reality. They will change as we uncover deeper understandings of existence in all the various worlds of creation. For as the light shines brighter in a darkened room our understanding of our place in that room ever changes and the light grows, revealing what once was in darkness.

SAMEKH/SAMEK

Gematria Value:	60
Color:	Blue
Musical Note:	G #
Signify:	Prop
Astrological Sign:	Sagittarius
Alchemical Element:	Fiery
Roman Equivalent:	X

According to Kabbalistic tradition the form of ס symbolizes the wedding ring placed by the groom on the pointing or index finger of the bride. It is the form of circle inside a square, the final *Mem*. The pointing finger of the bride points to the future within the coming world. The root meaning of *Samek* is to rely on, trust in and be supported, just as symbolized by a marriage between two people. But the deeper meaning is that of "laying hands on", the hands of spiritual annointing.

This relates to the spiritual support that can be found in *Samek*'s secrets. This spiritual support comes from God's never ending graciousness. When the letter energy intelligence of ס is combined with other letters it results in adding supportive energy to that letters energy intelligence. Such as when *Samek* is combined with *Kaph* כ it results in a container for support.

This combining of energies is a key of working with the individual Hebrew Letters and the energies they represent. By the very combination or placement of the letters it strengthens or reveals aspects of the prime letter that may not have been realized when studied alone.

AYIN

ע

Gematria Value:	70
Color:	Blue-Violet
Musical Note:	A
Signify:	Eye
Astrological Sign:	Capricorn
Alchemical Element:	Earthy
Roman Equivalent:	O

It is said that *Ayin* "does not speak. It only sees. Close your eyes. Open your mouth. Now try to see". This phrase is very important for it differentiates the unenlightened who only see with their physical eyes and those who use their inner eye. For the reality seen with the physical eyes is not the true reality but that made from our emotions, desires and thoughts of what we perceive as reality. This refers to *Ayin*'s meaning of eye or insight. The numerical value of *Ayin* is 70. The energy intelligence of *Ayin* is that of projecting the flow of energy into existence, thus allowing the formation of energy to become part of consciousness.

According to Rabbinic teaching the formation of *Ayin* is that of having two eyes that are attached to a pipe that faces toward the left. Our left side is our heart. This shows that our insights and consciousness come from what we see and influence our decisions and interpretations of our world. We must learn to use our inner eye to see the Godliness that is brought into existence for it is often concealed. This Godliness is kept hidden and waits to be revealed to us as we gain insight and consciousness of its existence. For the unknowing will wander through life, often viewing the same as the initiated, but not seeing the true beauty of God's hand.

The world often seems full of conflict and contradiction and the whole idea of God's Divine presence seems far away. But by connecting to God through the use of our intuition and insight we rise above this cloud of disharmony. As this occurs we start to manifest an internal reality of peace, tranquility, balance and unity. This is the true essence that we often call an external reality. Those who reachthis can be seen in our world as those who are calm in the face of chaos and discord.

PEH/FEY/PE/PEY

Gematria Value:	80
Color:	Red
Musical Note:	C
Signify:	Mouth
Astrological Sign:	Mars
Alchemical Element:	Iron
Roman Equivalent:	P

Peh פ can be seen as a mouth with no eyes. Because it is a *Yod* י'supended in a *Kaph* כ it represents the spiritual quality of wisdom that is contained within the vessel for its practical realization. With this practical realization comes productivity and accomplishment. *Peh* is related to the words: mouth, speech, saying, command, opening, entrance, and border. *Peh's* פ singular value is 80 and its final form ף is 800.

Everything that happens, no matter if it is physical, mental, emotional or spiritual can only be transformed into action by passing from the one Divine reality to that of our physical reality. This action passes through the "entrance" of the formative to physical reality. For the formative is within the vessel of *Kaph* and is expressed by the letter energies that *Yod* is the first to make. It is through this transformation that it is made possible for the student to change, grow, and enter a higher state of consciousness and a higher state of being.

TZADQIEL/TSADE/ZADI/TZADI

Gematria Value:	90
Color:	Violet
Musical Note:	A #
Signify:	Fish-hook
Astrological Sign:	Aquarius
Alchemical Element:	Airy
Roman Equivalent:	none (Romans had no use for the "sh" sound)

Peh פ immediately precedes the letter *Tzaddi* צ in the Hebrew alphabet for a very specific reason. It teaches us to guard one's mouth from slander, gossip and foul language. For to reach a higher state of tzadik one must have control of comes from the mouth. The state of tzadik refers to the personalities in Jewish tradition that are considered righteous, such as Biblical figures and later spiritual masters.

The numerical value of *Tzaddi* צ is 90 and the final form ץ has a value of 900. There are several words associated to *Tzaddi* צ such as righteousness and humility. These are very important in that the command of God as it is to our true will to be righteous and humble. For Jewish tradition teaches that we should be humble and charitable to our neighbors. As students of the Kabbalah it reminds us that even though we feel that we are well along the path of enlightenment we are only neophytes in the greater scheme of God's plan. For if we lose our humility and righteousness we lose the true understanding of the Work. For the Work and accomplishment of the true student are not for public proclamation but to be kept silent and close to the student's heart.

QOPH

ק

Gematria Value:	100
Color:	Violet-Red
Musical Note:	B
Signify:	Back of the Head
Astrological Sign:	Pisces
Alchemical Element:	Watery
Roman Equivalent:	Q

Qoph ק is made with two distinct strokes of the quill. The lower mark on the left side symbolizes man "calling God". The upper mark is "HE whispering very softly" to see if we are really listening to His words. Its letter energy intelligence is that of growth and holiness. It is the pulsating energy of ק that elevates man above the animals in that man can act in ways to create sacredness and holiness to glorify God's existence in all that he does. For it is said a wise person is one who is in tune with the very spirit of God. The Piel form, referring to intensive action, associates the following words with *Qoph*: put in state of holiness, sanctify, consecrate or to set apart as holy.

By using the energy of this letter in combinations with other letters, the second letter's energy is engorged with the pulsating energy of *Qoph*. This action helps to sanctify the action toward that of sacredness and holiness. In meditation, it would empower the act of meditation to higher and more sacred nature. This is another example that when understanding and tapping the individual letters they cannot be done in isolation. The Hebrew letters are alive and interact with their neighbors. This is one of the secrets of alchemy, how to combine the mystical powers of the language of God.

RESH

Gematria Value:	200
Color:	Orange
Musical Note:	D
Signify:	Head/Face
Astrological Sign:	Sun
Alchemical Element:	Gold
Roman Equivalent:	R

The letter *Resh* ר symbolizes man and human intelligence. This is based on the Qabalistic meaning of the Hebrew letter *Resh*, which is attributed to the "Collective Intelligence". The meaning of ר is head. The top is the profile of a man's head and the downward stroke is the profile of the spinal column. Other meanings attributed to the Hebrew spelling of *Resh* are poverty and principal. The energy intelligence assigned to its cosmic container, thus symbolizing that man's head holds the whole concept of what the cosmos comprises.

The cosmos container is a vessel of contexts. On the cosmic level this means every action, reaction, and every expressed statement that has been brought into existence by action of energy into manifestation. The situation that this manifestation creates is limited by our own interpretation and will of limitation. This can be seen easiest in the expression of anger resulting from a situation. We can react with extreme violent actions or on the other end of the spectrum accept the situation and move on. The context or experience is not determined by the situation but by our experience and what is learned by that experience.

This teaches a fundamental lesson that needs to be learned before we gain control of our primal passions. There is a reality and an illusion of reality. The outer reality which we sense with our outer sensory receptors makes up the illusionary reality. Once these senses are received in the "head" we assess the phenomena and create a reaction. That reaction and the view justifying that reaction is manifested in our "head" and becomes the reality in our world. That reality is ours alone and may not be shared by others in the same situation. For others interpret their sensory input and evaluate based on their life storage of contexts.

Our cosmic container is also a recipient of our channeling from the higher realms; it is a gateway to the upper worlds. This gateway connects our lower world with the higher world of the Divine. It is said that it opens the very gates of Heaven allowing for our lower world to be showered with the Divine light and understanding of God. From this Divine light comes the tools that helps us view the illusions of the outer world with greater clarity, understanding and acceptance.

SHIN

Gematria Value:	300
Color:	Red
Musical Note:	C
Signify:	Tooth/Fang
Astrological Sign:	Pluto
Alchemical Element:	Fire
Roman Equivalent:	S

The letter *Shin* ש has the appearance of an open mouth full of teeth. This teachs us to symbolically chew and break down the energy sources enabling us to think, speak and to do. The waste products of this action are expelled or released in the process of breathing and other bodily functions of discharge. This process is repeated continually to replenish the energies our body and soul consume on both the physical and spiritual level, as we tread the path of life. For as we move forward we learn to evaluate our environments, physically, morally, intellectually, and spiritually with newly acquired pro-spective. We learn, and then do, based on that learning we change ourselves in a hopefully continual spiral upward. This cosmic nourishment feeds the student's consciousness with the energies to see with clearer vision to help dispel the fog of chaos and misinterpretation.

This spiral climb upward to higher levels is not smooth. The student, and even the Master Adept will continually meet with resistance. This resistance is not from external sources but from inside of us. It is a continual struggle that yields temporary defeats but glorious successes as well. It is these successes that keep the student, and the Master Adept is a student as well, working onward. For these successes are revealing of the Divine light which lights the path through the darkness of Chaos and over the great Abyss of Ignorance.

The letter energy intelligence of שׁ is fire and flame. This fire burns and destroys the old and allows for change. This fire produces heat and light which are both useful to the student IF governed and controlled properly, but can burn the unsuspected. For the occultists this flame, when governed and controlled is one of the goals of alchemy. On the reverse side many unprepared occultists loose themselves when this flame symbolically and spiritual explodes in them, generally resulting in a destructive, uncontrolled surge in their passions. This surge of their passions often results in destructive vices taking control of their worlds both physically and spiritually.

Tav/Tau

Gematria Value:	400
Color:	Blue—Violet
Musical Note:	A
Signify:	Mark/Cross
Astrological Sign:	Saturn
Alchemical Element:	Lead
Roman Equivalent:	T

Tav ת is the seal of the cosmic administration. It combines the imaginative powers of the subconscious with those of the liberating powers of change. It is the limiting power of our imagination that places boundaries on the infinite enrgy of the very Life Power itself. Tav ת also implies security, guaranty, and pledge for it is the seal of completion of the Great Work. It is the balance and equilibrium of that completed Work of creation of the Universe.

The energy intelligence of Tav is that of the physical projection of existence from the great cosmic Life Power. When ת is spelled out in Hebrew letters it has the meaning of mark, sign, line, musical note and/or label. In Aramaic it means again, further and more. It is a sign by which something is made known. It is a mark of completion. Not one of a completion that is hidden but one that's existence is known to all who wish to see.

The "True Law" meaning of ת is that of the Divine Dance. It is dance of the consciousness of the appearance, the physical world, which is below, with that which is above which is the essence, or spiritual world. This "True Law" is in continual movement, fluctuation, or oscillation. As we change our knowledge so changes our view point of our own world. This is the True Law in action as it transforms our heart to one of goodness. From this knowledge comes wisdom which again causes more change that leads us to reach higher and higher levels of unifying perfection and closeness to the Divine.

FINAL LETTERS

There are five Hebrew letters called "finals" which are used to denote the end of a word. They are sometimes called "sofit" which is pronounced "so-feet".

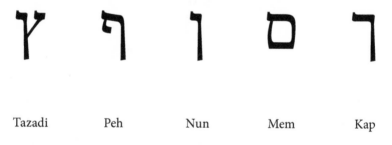

| Tazadi | Peh | Nun | Mem | Kap |

Their numerical values are much different from their single form and must be recognized for their Gematria Values.

| 900 | 800 | 700 | 600 | 500 |

HISTORY AND DEVELOPMENT OF THE
32 SECRET PATHS OF WISDOM

The 32 paths we associate with the Tree of Life developed over time. The names and to which Sephiroth the paths were attached varied by school and interpretation. The oldest commentary that was exclusively devoted to the 32 paths of wisdom is credited to Joseph ben Shalom Ashkenazi, an early Spanish kabbalist who lived in the 1300's. He equates the paths to the 32 times that God is mentioned in *Genesis*. He does not directly associate the paths with the Sephiroth but rather with forms of transcendental awareness. One translation of Ashkenazi's work identified the paths as:

1. Mystical Consciousness
2. Radiant Consciousness
3. Sanctified Consciousness
4. Settled Consciousness
5. Rooted Consciousness
6. Transcendental Influx Consciousness
7. Hidden Consciousness
8. Perfect Consciousness
9. Pure Consciousness
10. Scintillating Consciousness
11. Glaring Consciousness
12. Brilliant Consciousness
13. Unity Consciousness
14. Illuminating Consciousness
15. Stabilizing Consciousness
16. Ending Consciousness
17. Consciousness of the Senses
18. Consciousness of the house of Influx
19. Consciousness of the mystery of all Spiritual Activities
20. Consciousness of will
21. Desired and Sought Consciousness
22. Faithful Consciousness
23. Sustaining Consciousness
24. Apparitive Consciousness
25. Testing Consciousness

26. Renewing Consciousness
27. Palpable Consciousness
28. Natural Consciousness
29. Physical Consciousness
30. General Consciousness
31. Continual Consciousness
32. Worshipped Consciousness

It should be noted that the original diagrams of the Tree of Life had the ten Sephiroth with 22 lines connecting them to make the 32 paths of wisdom.

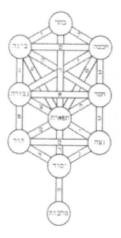

Even after Isaac the Blind died, his commentaries on the *Sepher Yetzirah* continued to stimulate Cabalists throughout Spain. Though there are numerous versions of the Tree a general consensus developed around accepting what became known as the Geronese Tree. This version came about in Gerona, where the Cabalists began to consolidate their ideas as to the names and location on the Tree of the 10 Sephiroth.

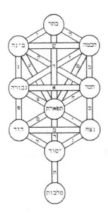

The psedo-sephira, Da'ath, became recognized early in the thirteenth century by Joseph ben Abraham Gikatilla (1248– after 1305) who was a Spanish kabbalist, and a student of Abraham Abulafia. This psedo-sephira was a culmination of all the Sephiroth and was seen as the total of "Knowledge". This additional "sphere" or "center" was placed on the middle column above Tiphareth.

As the Tree of Life is symbolic of the scholar's interpretations of the written description of the relationships of the Sephiroth to each other, the structure of the pathways and Tree is always in flux. Elijah ben Shlomo Zalman Kremer, known as the Vilna Gaon or Elijah of Vilna, or Elijah Ben Solomon, (1720–1797) was a Talmudist, and Kabbalist. He was born in Vilnius, capital city of Grand Duchy of Lithuania. His view of the Tree moved Yesod upward and lettered the 22 paths according to the principle of the "mother" letters on the horizontal paths, the "doubles"; on the vertical paths and the "singles" on the diagonals.

During the late fifteenth century and sixteenth century the lure of the Tree began to spread with Johannes Gutenberg's invention of the moveable type press somewhere from 1439 to 1450, allowing for a greater number of books to be produced. During this time of spread of works dealing with cabalistic magic, Guillaume Postel (1510–1581) who was a French linguist, astronomer, Cabbalist, diplomat, professor, and religious Universalist, translated the *Portae Lucis, Sepher Yetzirah* and *Zohar* into Latin. By doing this the Christian scholars had much greater access to these important works.

One such Christian scholar was a German Jesuit priest Athanasius Kircher, S.J. (sometimes erroneously spelled Kirchner; 1602–1680) a seventeenth century German Jesuit scholar and polymath, who published around 40 major works, most notably in the fields of Oriental studies, geology, and medicine. He wrote much about his concept of the 32 paths comparing the Hebrew letters to those of Latin equivalents. Like all authors, he assigned various meanings to them.

Kircher assigned the first ten letters from Aleph to Yod to the ten angelic ranks. He also assigned the seven known planets to specific letters which in turn were assigned to pathways. They are:

Lamed	Saturn
Mem	Jupiter
Mem (final)	Mars
Nun	Sun
Nun (final)	Venus
Samekh	Mercury
Ayin	Moon

This original assignment of planets was totally different than the traditional assignments. This may have been Kircher's attempt to hide what he thought was the "esoteric" knowledge it revealed by using a "blind", which was common practice with the early Cabalist writters. Kircher later modified his assessments of the plants to be closer to what the others had determined from the *Sepher Yetzirah*. What he did do that has influenced future Qabbalalists was to associate Air rather than Earth to Aleph, Shin with fire and Mem with Water. Another quirk was that he placed a face on the Sun which still can be found on many Tarot cards today. His revised assignments are:

Beth	Sun
Gimel	Venus
Daleth	Mercury
Kaph	Moon
Peh	Saturn
Resh	Jupiter
Tau	Mars

Most important was how Kircher drew his Tree. He modified the connecting paths or channels, by removing two of them from the upper portion of the Tree and adding them to the lower part connecting Malkuth to the two outer parallel pillars. This version is the one most scholars have adapted as the "accepted" version of the Tree of Life and its paths when studying the Qabbalah.

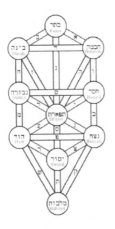

WALKING THE PATHWAYS

The pathways on the Tree of Life are the channels that connect the energy sources, Sephiroth, and are packed with much archetypal imagery and symbolism. The pathways vary according to which scholar's work is being used. I will attempt to give a summary of the associations attributed to the *Golden Dawn* including the Tarot card associated with that path. As mentioned earlier the Sephiroth themselves are centers of energy and wisdom and should be seen as separate but connected sources of study. The 22 paths are channels to be used to derive access to these centers.

Please note that all the comments concerning the explanation of the Intelligence are from the *Golden Dawn* "Knowledge Lectures" Regardie, "Concerning the Tree of Life", *The Golden Dawn*, v. I, 191-198.

PATH 11 *ALEPH*

1 (Kether)—2 (Chokmah)
Scintillating Intelligence
>The Eleventh Path is the Scintillating Intelligence because it is the essence of that curtain which is placed close to the order of the disposition, and this is a special dignity given to it that it may be able to stand before the Face of the Cause of Causes.

Spiritual Significance: Air
Tarot Key: The Fool
Meaning: Ox
Esoteric Title:
>Spirit of Aether—The element of spirit goes by several names, the most common being spirit, ether or aether, and quintessence, which is literally Latin for "fifth element". There is also no standard symbol for spirit, although circles are common. Eight-spoke wheels and spirals are also sometimes used to represent spirit.

Path Color: Bright Pale Yellow
Related Sound: E-Neutral

PATH 12 *BETH*

1 (Kether)—3 (Binah)
Intelligence of Transparency
>The Twelfth Path is the Intelligence of Transparency because it is that species of Magnificence called Chazachazit, the place whence issues the vision of those seeing in apparitions.

Spiritual Significance: Planet Mercury
Tarot Key: The Magician
Meaning: House
Esoteric Title: Magus of Power
Path Color: Yellow
Related Sound: E-Neutral

PATH 13 *GIMEL*

1 (Kether)—6 (Tiphareth)
Uniting Intelligence
> *The Thirteenth Path is named the Uniting Intelligence, and so called because it is itself the Essence of Glory; it is the Consummation of Truth of individual spiritual things.*

Spiritual Significance: The Moon
Tarot Key: The High Priestess
Meaning: Camel
Esoteric Title: The Princess of the Silver Star
Path Color: Blue
Related Sound: G#

PATH 14 *DALETH*

2 (Chokmah)—3 (Binah)
Illuminating Intelligence
> *The Fourteenth Path is the Illuminating Intelligence, and is so because it is that Brilliant One which is the founder of the concealed and fundamental ideas of holiness and of their stages of preparation.*

Spiritual Significance: Planet Venus
Tarot Key: The Empress
Meaning: Door
Esoteric Title: The Daughter of the Mighty Ones
Path Color: Emerald Green
Related Sound: F#.

Path 15 *Heh*

2(Chokmah)—6 (Tiphareth)

Constituting Intelligence

> *The Fifteenth Path is the Constituting Intelligence, so called because it constitutes the substance of creation in pure darkness, and men have spoken of these contemplations; it is that darkness spoken of in Scriptures, Job xxxviii.9. "and thick darkness a swaddling band for it".*

Spiritual Significance: Aries (Cardinal Fire)
Tarot Key: The Emperor
Meaning: Window
Esoteric Title: Sun of the Morning, Chief Among the Mighty
Path Color: Scarlet
Related Sound: C Natural

Path 16 *Vau*

2 (Chokmah)—4 (Chesed)

Triumphal Intelligence

> *The Sixteenth Path is the Triumphal or Eternal Intelligence, so called because it is the pleasure of the Glory, beyond which is no other Glory like to it, and it is called also the Paradise prepared for the Righteous.*

Spiritual Significance: Taurus (Fixed Earth)
Tarot Key: The Hierophant
Meaning: The Magus of the Eternal
Path Color: C Sharp

PATH 17 *ZAIN*

3 (Binah)—6 (Tiphareth)
Disposing Intelligence
> *The Seventeenth Path is the Disposing Intelligence, which provides Faith to the Righteous, and they are clothed with the Holy Spirit by it, and it is called the Foundation of Excellence in the state of higher things.*

Spiritual Significance: Gemini (Mutable Air)
Tarot Key: The Lovers
Meaning: Sword or Armor
Esoteric Title: The Children of the Voice;
                        The Oracle of the

Mighty Gods
Path Color: Orange
Related Sound: D Natural

PATH 18 *CHETH*

3(Binah)–5 (Geburah)
House of Influence
> *The Eighteenth Path is called the House of Influence (by the greatness of whose abundance the influx of good things upon created beings is increased), and from the midst of the investigation in arcana and hidden senses are drawn forth, which dwell in its shade and which cling to it, from the cause of all causes.*

Spiritual Significance: Cancer (Cardinal water)
Tarot Key: The Chariot
Meaning: Fence or Enclosure
Esoteric Title: The Child of the Powers of the Waters;
                        Lord of the Triumph of Light
Path Color: Red-Orange
Related Sound: C #

PATH 19 *TETH*

4 (Chesed) — 5 (Geburah)
Intelligence of all the activites and Spiritual beings
> *The Nineteenth Path is the Intelligence of all the activities and spiritual beings, and is so called because of the affluence diffused by it from the most high blessing and most exalted sublime glory.*

Spiritual Significance:	Leo (Fixed Fire)
Tarot Key:	Strength
Meaning:	Snake
Esoteric Title:	The Daughter of the Flaming Sword
Path Color:	Yellow-Greenish
Related Sound:	E Natural

PATH 20 *YOD*

4 (Chesed)-- 6 (Tiphareth)
Intelligence of Will
> *The Twentieth Path is the Intelligence of Will, and is so called because it is the means of preparation of all and each created being, and by this intelligence the existence of the Primordial Wisdom becomes known.*

Spiritual Significance:	Virgo (Mutable Earth)
Tarot Key:	The Hermit
Meaning:	Hand
Esoteric Title:	The Prophet of the Eternal, Magus of the Voice of Power
Path Color:	Green-yellowish
Related Sound:	F Natural

Path 21 Kaph

4 (Chesed) — 7 (Netzach)
Intelligence of Conciliation
> The Twenty-first Path is the Intelligence of Conciliation, and
> is so called because it receives the divine influence which flows
> into it from its benediction upon all and each existence.

Spiritual Significance:	Jupiter
Tarot Key:	The Wheel of Fortune
Meaning:	Fist
Esoteric Title:	The Lord of the Forces of Life
Path Color:	Violet
Related Sound:	A Sharp

Path 22 Lamed

5 (Geburah) — 6 (Tiphareth)
Faithful Intelligence
> The Twenty-second Path is the Faithful Intelligence, and is
> so called because by it spiritual virtues are increased, and all
> dwellers on earth are nearly under its shadow.

Spiritual Significance:	Libra (Cardinal Air)
Tarot Key:	Justice
Meaning:	Ox Goad
Esoteric Title:	The Daughter of the Lords of Truth; the Ruler of the Blance
Path Color:	Emerald Green
Related Sound:	F Sharp

PATH 23 *MEM*

5 (Geburah) — 8 (Hod)
Stable of Intelligence

> *The Twenty-third Path is called the Stable of Intelligence, and is so called because it has the virtue of consistency among all.*

Spiritual Significance:	Water
Tarot Key:	The Hanged Man
Meaning:	Water
Esoteric Title:	The Spirit of the Mighty Waters
Path Color:	Deep Blue
Related Sound:	G #

PATH 24 *NUN*

6 (Tiphareth) — 7 (Netzach)
Imaginative Intelligence

> *The Twenty-fourth Path is the Imaginative Intelligence, and it is so called because it gives a likeness to all the similitudes which are created in like manner similar to its harmonious elegancies.*

Spiritual Significance:	Scorpio (Fixed Water)
Tarot Key:	Death
Meaning:	Fish
Esoteric Title:	The Child of the Great Transformers; the Lord of the Gate of Death
Path Color:	Green-Blue
Related Sound:	G Natural

PATH 25 SAMEKH

6 (Tiphareth) —9 (Yesod)
Intelligence of Probation
>*The Twenty-fifth Path is the Intelligence of Probation, or is Tentative, and is so called because it is the primary temptation, by which the Creator trieth all righteous persons.*

Spiritual Significance:	Sagittarius (Mutable Fire)
Tarot Key:	Temperance
Meaning:	Prop
Esoteric Title:	The Daughter of the Reconcilers, the Bringer Forth of Life
Path Color:	Yellow Blue-Greenish hue
Related Sound:	G #

PATH 26 AYIN

6 (Tiphareth) —8 (Hod)
Renovating Intelligence
>*The Twenty-sixth Path is called Renovating Intelligence, because the Holy God renews by it all the changing things which are renewed by the creation of the world.*

Spiritual Significance:	Capricorn (Cardinal Earth)
Tarot Key:	The Devil
Meaning:	Eye
Esoteric Title:	The Lord of the Gates of Matter; the Child of the Forces of Time
Path Color:	Indigo
Related Sound:	A Natural

Path 27 *Peh*

7 (Netzach) — 8 (Hod)
Active Intelligence

> *The Twenty-seventh Path is the Active or Exciting -Intelligence and is so called because through it every existent being receives its spirit and motion.*

Spiritual Significance: Planet Mars
Tarot Key: The Tower
Meaning: Mouth
Esoteric Title: The Lord of the Hosts of the Mighty
Path Color: Scarlet
Related Sound: C Natural

Path 28 *Tzaddi*

7 (Netzach) — 9 (Yesod)
Natural Intelligence

> *The Twenty-eighth Path is called the Natural Intelligence, and is so called because through it is consummated and perfected the Nature of every existing thing beneath the Sun.*

Spiritual Significance: Aquarius (Fixed Air)
Tarot Key: The Star
Meaning: Fish Hook
Esoteric Title: The Daughter of the Firmament;
                            the Dweller between the Waters.
Path Color: Violet
Related Sound: A #

PATH 29 QOPH

7 (Netzach)—10 (Malkuth)

Corporeal Intelligence

> *The Twenty-ninth Path is called the Corporeal Intelligence, so called because it forms every body which is formed beneath the whole set of worlds and the increment of them.*

Spiritual Significance:	Pisces (Mutable Water)
Tarot Key:	The Moon
Meaning:	Back of the Head, Ear
Esoteric Title:	The Ruler of Flux and Reflux, The Child of the Sons of the Mighty
Path Color:	Crimson (Ultraviolet)
Related Sound:	B Natural

PATH 30 RESH

8 (Hod) — 9 (Yesod)

Collecting Intelligence

> *The Thirtieth Path is the Collecting Intelligence and is so called because Astrologers deduce from it the judgment of the Stars, and of the celestial signs, and the perfections of their science, according to the rules of the resolutions.*

Spiritual Significance:	Sun
Tarot Key:	The Sun
Meaning:	Head
Esoteric Title:	The Lord of the Fire of the World
Path Color:	Orange
Related Sound:	D Natural

Path 31 *Shin*

8 (Hod)–10 (Malkuth)
Perpetual Intelligence
> *The Thirty-first Path is the Perpetual Intelligence; but why is it called? Because it regulates the motions of the Sun and Moon in their proper order, each in an orbit convenient for it.*

Spiritual Significance:	Fire
Tarot Key:	Judgment
Meaning:	Tooth
Esoteric Title:	The Spirit of the Primal Fire
Path Color:	Glowing Orange Scarlet
Related Sound:	C Natural

Path 32 *Tau*

9 (Yesod) — 10 (Malkuth)
Administrative Intelligence
> *The Thirty-second Path is the Administrative Intelligence, and it is so called because it directs and associates in all their operations the seven planets, even all of them in their own due course.*

Spiritual Significance:	Planet Saturn
Tarot Key:	The Universe
Meaning:	Tau Cross, Equal Armed Cross
Esoteric Title:	The Great One of the Night of Time
Path Color:	Indigo
Related Sound:	A Natural

Using the 32 Paths of Wisdom

In the beginning, it is said all the souls of humanity resided under The Throne of God. When a mother was impregnated God sent one of His angels to implant one of these souls in the new baby. When the child emerges, it cries, not out of pain but because it realizes it has a long journey back to God. This journey is mapped out by the Tree of Life and its 32 Paths. These paths contain numerous clues that once read and understood give us the Wisdom to progress farther up the Tree of Life toward a reunion with God. In like manner, it allows or points us toward the quickest path to this reunion and that is the straight path of the Middle Pillar. The problem is that we have the proverbial map but often get lost trying to understand and most importantly see the sign posts that will led us to the straight path upward and back to the Divine.

Another way to look at the Paths is that they represent the stepping stones to the first stages of mysticism. This mysticism is the psyche opening of the student's unconscious awareness. The Paths have many symbols represented on them from the Hebrew Letters themselves, Tarot cards, numbers, even scents, colors, musical notes, symbols, animal totems, herbs, stones and plants. This allows the individual to seek or relate to any number of items depending on their affinity. For we all have different elements that speak to us. Some are very musically inclined, while others relate closer to colors or astrological signs. No matter what the student's affinity is there is a sign post for them.

No matter which Tree of Life diagram one uses the student should have it close at hand for visual identification. This is extremely important when working the paths of Wisdom. One must engage as many senses as possible, including all forms available to the eye: color, form, and prospective. There are numerous courses, and books concerning how to meditate and use the symbols associated with path work. The student will know which one is best. As it is said 'listen to your heart' and you will not go astray.

Most schools of study suggest when working with the Paths of Wisdom the student should start a Malkuth, the symbolic Earth and move upward. With that here are some suggestions of what may be obtained from each of the paths. Remember these are only suggestions and one's own perspective may or may not be greater than what is described.

THIRTY-SECOND PATH

This is the path that leads from the outer physical world to the inner world of the psyche. It is the first step to our self-awareness. Without understanding the relations between the consciousness and the unconscious the student cannot leave the physical world to start the journey. It is the first stage of mysticism offered by the Administrative Intelligence. It is here the symbol of *Tau* (cross) represents the four Elements, and the four esoteric Worlds. The Administrative Intelligence opens the access to the Seven Ancient Planets which correspond to the seven "interior stars" or Chakras.

THIRTY-FIRST PATH

Here we journey from the physical world of Malkuth to the realm of the mind, Hod. Here the mind begins to develop its relationship with the Astral Plane. According to the *Golden Dawn* this is the path that leads to resurrection and rebirth. Like all aspects of path work it is based on balance or equilibrium. In this case, the resurrection is based on the relationship of the opposite path *Qoph*. *Qoph* relates to the physiological rebuilding of the body by being exposed to the heightened energies within the paths. Paul Foster Case, founder of the *Builders of Adytum*, described this process "as the building of the Master's Body". It is the path where the magical arts and the sciences come together.

THIRTIETH PATH

This path is said to join the realm of the unconscious with that of the rational consciousness. Here is where the student learns to use the mind. Like the Thirty-First Path each relate to the practice of awakening and expanding the mental powers as part of the Astral World. It is the Path of activating the personality by use of the intellect versus the passions. It is here where the aspirant attempts to cultivate clearer vision to identify the pitfalls that result from previously misconceptions of the physical, mental and emotional world.

TWENTY-NINTH PATH

The Twenty-Ninth Path connects the physical world of Malkuth with the realm of instinct, feelings, instuition, and imagination represented by Netzach. This is often one of the first Paths that is considered terrifying and disquiting. It is here the aspirant learns to control the powers of physical instincts and sexual urges, because here the aspirant comes face to face with their phantoms in the deepest corners of their unconscious. They must deal with and conquer the illusions and misconceptions of their lives that reside "in the back of their heads" (*Qoph*). It is said those who succeed on this path grow their powers of 'bewitchment and casting illusions'.

TWENTY-EIGHTH PATH

This Path, as implied by its name Natural Intelligence deals with all the forces of nature beneath the Sun. One lesson the aspirant must learn is there is no distinction between what we traditionally call natural and that which is often called supernatural. It is learning to open the eye to all things not just what we were taught. The name *Tzaddi*, which means hook, is the symbol of meditation and often it is said that the fish hook is used to fish in the waters of Mem which is the symbol of consciousness. Here is where we learn to go beyond our comfort zone and experiment with our meditation and imaginative visualizations by casting our hooks in the Universal Sea to seek the understanding of the processes of life and death in the worlds above the physical.

TWENTY-SEVENTH PATH

This Path often seen as the equilibrating Path of the Personality in that it connects the reasoning process represented by *Hod* with the intuition-desire nature of Netzach. It is here the aspirant learns to adjust and rebalance these processes to allow for growth of new ideas. It is the destroying of old ideas, prejudices, and self-images that we have used to shield ourselves from others as well as ourselves. The lesson is learning to let go of these old ideas so new ones can appear. This Path is ruled by Mars which is often thought as the god of destruction and war. Mars helps destroy the old ideas. But it is also the symbol of action, movement, and the force of change which is needed to allow for growth.

TWENTY-SIXTH PATH

This is the Path that prepares us to face the obstacle which stands in the way of universalized mystical consciousness. This is represented by the old fear of the devil. Aspirants must realize this fear is due to their current lack the light of enlightenment. As I have taught students it as though standing on the threshold of dark and forbidding room. But once you turn the light on it turns out to be your bedroom. It takes light to see the truth and The Devil symbolizes that falsehood of the dark unknown. For Qabalists they must penetrate this unknown before they can know the Higher Principles of the Self.

TWENTY-FIFTH PATH

This Path forges a direct route up the middle pillar between the personality and the Individuality or Higher Self. This is where oppositions are brought into harmony. This Path is governed by the Great Mother, the *YHVH Elohim* of Binah. It is here the aspirant feels the give and take of inner energies which the aspirant must gain mental control over and learn to consciously manipulate these inner energies. These energies are symbolized by the interchange of Fire and Water. This ability to unite symbolic Fire and symbolic Water is one of the secrets of alchemy. When the Personality is brought in contact with these inner energies it gives birth to the Divine Child which is symbolized by Tiphareth or the human incarnation of illumination.

TWENTY-FOURTH PATH

This is a key Path that connects the Pillar of Mercy with the central Pillar of Consciousness of Equilibrium. It is governed by *Nun*. The Twenty-Fourth Path forms a link between Psychological triangles represented in Netzach with the Ethical aspects of Tiphareth. This is where the personality learns to face the death of the ego or small self. Where the aspirant learned to face the fears of the Devil in the 26th Path; and the fear of losing self-identity in the 25th Path, the fear of death is confronted in the 24th Path, thus opening and preparing of the soil for the rebirth of the true Adept shown by the symbolic reaping and sowing in the Death Key.

TWENTY-THIRD PATH

This is the Path of *Mem* or the Path of Water, the letter Mem being one of the three Maternals. The Fool is Air and Judgment is Fire. Through the baptism of Water, the aspirant continues refinement and development of a moral and ethical code that should govern the aspirant's use of the alchemical powers.

TWENTY-SECOND PATH

The Twenty-Second Path is called this "because its spiritual values are increased and all dwellers on earth are nearly under its shadow". This Path is part of the Moral or Ethical triangle, and as part of this triangle it further deepens the awareness and understanding of what the karmic effects are of our actions. For every action, there is a consequence.

TWENTY-FIRST PATH
According to the *Sepher Yetzirah*, this Intelligence is directly connected to riches and poverty and this is where the aspirant will have to determine if riches are necessary for one's satisfaction in life. This Path continues to expand on one's perspective of life itself. It is here one learns to use the Occult as a means to learn the nature of Wisdom.

TWENTIETH PATH
This Path represents the self-sustained original beginning of manifestation. The letter *Yod* is assigned to this Path. It is symbolic representation of the first flame. Fable says that this is the first letter of the alphabet of flame from which all other letters are derived. In other words, *Yod* signifies the first dynamic principle of creation. For each Hebrew letter is the word of God creating the universe. It is the seed of all creation. It is from here the aspirant brings Wisdom to birth.

NINETEENTH PATH
This Path is assigned to the letter *Teth*. It is the Path of the serpent power. In the West, the serpent is often associated with evil, but it is actually a symbol of rebirth and growth. This shedding of the old skin allows for it to grow and be as a reborn creature. This concept is extremely important to the aspirant for the individual must continually shed the old ideas to allow for enlightened growth and rebirth.

EIGHTEENTH PATH
The most important aspect of this Path is seen in the Tarot Key, The Chariot. One must closely observe an often over-looked aspect symbolized in the Key. This is that the charioteer is guiding his chariot with no visible reins. The message here is that this Path is that of Spirit and this Spirit is behind all form. It is the mind that directs the charioteer and his world forward. The form must be directed toward the One. Another lesson to be learned is represented by the two moons on the shoulders of the charioteer. One

moon represents the severe aspect of reality, while the other represents the benign. This shows the two faces of reality when it is formed into existence.

SEVENTEENTH PATH
As the Divine Energy surges across The Abyss into the lower realm of manifestation, stable dualities are formed. One of the primary goals of the Great Work is a "marriage" of the dualities of manifestation, and the return to a primeval state. Thus this Path is often seen as the way back to the Garden of Eden by consciously dealing with the inner Sun and Moon, uniting them by the Spiritual Self, under Mercury; the planet ruling Gemini—the Twins.

SIXTEENTH PATH
This Path is assigned to the Triumphal or Eternal Intelligence. This Path is where we are able to place life within the context of spiritual eternity. This is a Path of revelation and insight, the initiator of the very mysteries of being and becoming.

FIFTEENTH PATH
As the aspirant nears the top of the Tree and creation the window of creation is opened and one comes face to face with the Vision of God. This window gives a glimpse into creation and all its mystery and awe. One of the mysteries of this Path is that it connects to Chokmah, which means Wisdom, which primary quality is maleness, but Chokmah is a female noun. This concept is revealed through the use of Gematria where the numerical aspects of the letter are divulged. *Heh* is one of the "Holy" letters, mentioned twice in the name of God, (*Yod, Heh, Vau, Heh*). And being the only letter used in God's name the very gender of the letter must be considered important even though the gender of the Hebrew noun of Wisdom is seldom discussed.

FOURTEENTH PATH
The Path of Chokmah is called the Illuminating Intelligence implying the brilliance of Chokmah illuminates everything passing through the Door (*Daleth*), which is The Empress. This Path is the base of the Supernal Triangle which connects the ultimate and firstness of Chokmah with that of the ultimate Great Mother, Binah the Mother of ideas. Because this Path has no connection to the lower Tree and nature it has no relationship with

the physical form. It is a path of causation, not effect; it is the doorway by which all of nature can be manifested to form and function.

THIRTEENTH PATH
This is the first path from the Supernal Triangle to the Ethical Triangle of the actual. The Cabalists point out this is the direct path that God the Father (Kether) reaches to God the Son (Tiphareth). The Tarot Key, The High Priestess is assigned to this Path. This Key represents the Divine Feminine and thus by travelling this Path the aspirant may rediscover the divine feminine in its purest and virginal form. For within this Key she holds the manuscript of life itself, which holds of the secrets of past, present and future.

TWELFTH PATH
This is the Path leading from the One Pure Source of All to that of the Great Mother. The tarot key assigned to this path is The Magician. To the Qabalists and to the Alchemist this Key represents the First Matter or the Philosophic Mercury. The Magician contains the seed-thoughts of transformation, healing, miracles, and seership and is often referred to as the Mercury-Hermes figure. He also represents one of the most important mottos of the Adept, which is "To Dare, To Desire, To Know, To Be Silent".

ELEVENTH PATH
The Eleventh Path is the beginning of the journey to Malkuth. It is the beginning of creation through all its manifestations. It connects the Hidden Intelligence of Kether's black fire, to the Illuminating Intelligence of Chokmah in all its brilliant illumination. It is the Path representing the first translation of energy towards matter. It is the purest of energies prior to any formation. As the Adept steps upon this Path he learns that "what is Above is Below" and is plunged back to the Thirty-Second Path just as Icarus and his journey toward the sun sent him uncontrollably back to Earth (Malkuth).

Path work is essential to knowing and understanding any of the forms of the Kabbalah. It is up to the student to take it upon themselves which way to start upon the path. It is not easy and has many internal and external barriers. But these barriers can be overcome, though perhaps not on the student's personal schedule. Just remember there is always a reason and more importantly a lesson to be learned at each and "every barrier".

XI.

THE TAROT DECK

A BRIEF HISTORY OF THE TAROT

There has been a great deal written as to the origin of the Tarot Deck. There are several sources claiming that the first playing cards were introduced to Europe around the late fourteenth century by the Mamluk Sultanate, which was located in Egypt. This deck of cards had similar suits as the early Tarot Decks, containing the suits of Swords, Staves, Cups and Coins or Pentacles. The first Tarot Decks known have been documented from the area of Milan, Ferrara and Bologna in northern Italy around 1430 to 1450. Later additional trump cards were added to the common four-suit pack. These were called *carte da trionfi*, triumph cards. As other cards were added they eventually became known simply as trionfi, which became 'trumps' in English. The earliest literary evidence of the existence of *carte da trionfi* comes from a written statement in the court records in Florence, in 1440. The oldest surviving tarot cards are from fifteen fragmented decks painted in the mid-fifteenth century for the Visconti-Sforza family, who were the rulers of Milan from 1447-1624.

SOME EARLY KEY PLAYERS IN THE TAROT MYSTIC

There are many fine publications chronicling the history of how the Tarot deck came to be what we see today. Here is a very brief mention of some of the key players and their contributions.

ANTOINE COURT DE GÉBELIN

In 1781, Antoine Court, who changed his name to Antoine Court de Gébelin (1725–1784), produced his interpretation of the Tarot. He was a former Protestant pastor who wrote a large essay including his *Le Monde Primitif, Analysé et Comparé Avec le Monde* Moderne ('The Primeval World, Analyzed and Compared to the Modern World"), Volume viii, in 1781. Within his essay there was a chapter on the Tarot. According to de Gébelin he had saw an immediate insight that the Tarot Deck held the secrets of the Egyptians. He had no formal training in deciphering the Egyptian hieroglyphs, but deduced that the Egyptian priests had distilled the ancient *Book of Thoth* into these images. He claimed, with no real historic proof, that this information was brought to Rome, where they were secretly known to the popes, who brought them to Avignon in the fourteenth century, whence they were introduced into France.

LOUIS-RAPHAEL-LUCRECE DE FAYOLLE

Louis-Raphael-Lucrece de Fayolle (1727–1804) was a French military man and a lieutenant in the King of France's bodyguard. In Gébelin's chapter on the Tarot there was 30 of the 60 pages identified as coming from an anonymous author called M. le C de M.***. This person was later identified as Louis-Raphael-Lucrece de Fayolle, Comte de Mellet. The Comte has by some accounts been associated with being a Freemason. The essay, published in 1781 by the Comte de Mellet is responsible for the mystical connection of the Tarot's 21 trumps and the Fool with the 22 letters of the Hebrew alphabet. An essay appended to this gave suggestions for cartomancy or fortune telling by interpreting a random selection of cards. Within two years of this publication the fortune-teller known as "Etteilla" (Alliette) published another book on the technique for reading the tarot. The practice of tarot reading was born. One well known reader was 'Etteilla', was the pseudonym of Jean-Baptiste Alliette (1738–1791), who was a French occultist who first popularized tarot divination to a wide audience in 1785. He was the first professional tarot occultist known to history who made his living by card divination

The work that Louis-Raphael-Lucrece de Fayolle began was instrumental to many future occultists such as: the French occultist Eliphas Levi (1810-1875); Gérard Anaclet Vincent Encausse (1865–1916), also known by his esoteric pseudonym Papus, a Spanish-born French physician, hypnotist, and an individual who helped to popularizer occultism, he is also responsible for founding the modern *Martinist Order.* The American Paul Foster Case (1884–1954) who in the early 20th century authored numerous books on occult tarot and Qabalah as well as founding the *Builders of the Adytum.*

THE MODERNS

The Hermetic Order of the Golden Dawn, was an esoteric order founded in Great Britain and was active from the later part of the ninteenth century until the early part of the twentith century. From this Order four major decks emerged that formed the backbone of the majority of Tarot decks used today.

They were: The Waite-Smith Tarot, The Thoth Tarot, The Golden Dawn Tarot and the *Builders of the Adytum* or BOTA Tarot. Each of these decks can be linked to four men who were instrumental in bring them to birth, respectively: Dr. Arthur Edward Waite; Aleister Crowley; Samuel Liddell MacGregor Mathers and Dr. Paul Foster Case.

DR. ARTHUR EDWARD WAITE

Arthur Edward Waite (1857–1942) was a British poet and scholarly mystic who wrote extensively on occult and esoteric matters, and was the co-creator of the Rider-Waite Tarot deck. Waite is credited for being the first to attempt a systematic study of the history of western occultism—viewed as a spiritual tradition rather than as aspects of proto-science or as the pathology of religion. Waite is the author of two supportive works; the *Key to the Tarot,* which was republished in expanded form the following year, 1911, as the Pictorial Key to the Tarot, a guide to Tarot reading. The Rider-Waite-Smith tarot was notable for being one of the first tarot decks to illustrate all 78 cards fully, in addition to the 22 major arcana cards. Golden Dawn member Pamela Colman Smith (1878–1951), also nicknamed Pixie, illustrated the cards for Waite. This deck was first published in 1909, and it remains in publication today.

It is known that the inspiration for this deck was partly provided by Sola-Busca Tarot, the oldest known complete deck of 72 cards from Northern Italy, dated to around 1491.

The Sola-Busca Tarot was exhibited in the British Museum in 1907 and it is believed Waite got his inspiration from this deck. Aleister Crowley developed his deck as a divinatory tarot deck and had it painted by Lady Frieda Harris under Crowley's instructions. Marguerite Frieda Harris (1877–1962) was an artist, and had studied Rudolf Steiner's Anthroposophical teachings. Rudolf Joseph Lorenz Steiner (1861–1925) was a noted Austrian philosopher, social reformer, architect, and esotericist. The *Anthroposophical Society* was founded in 1913 by members of the Theosophical Society in Germany, most centraled around the works of Rudolf Steiner. Harris was aged 60 when she was introduced to the occultist Aleister Crowley. Crowley referred to this deck as *The Book of Thoth* published in 1944 in a limited number of only 200 volumes.

Crowley viewed his cards as not just a deck of cards but as living beings. He professed that the student of the Tarot would learn the gifts of the cards only after a slow and temperate use of them.

> *Each card is, in a sense, a living being; and its relations with its neighbors are what might be called diplomatic.*[20]

This is a very important phrase and should be taken to heart by any student who attempts to understand what the Tarot is or could become. For whichever deck the student chooses this concept of them being a "living being" should be remembered. This also relates to how the cards interact when they are used in divination, for each card relates to it's their neighbor in a card 'spread' and is the key to reading the secrets within.

Like so many developers of specific Tarot Decks, Crowley attempted to modify the standard base Waite-Rider deck, adding to or rearranging certain names and attributes to come within accordance with their teachings. In Crowley's case his Deck was based on his earlier book published in 1904, *Liber AL vel Legis*. This book is the central sacred text of *Thelema*. And according to Crowley's biography it was written down while Aleister and his wife Rose were honeymooning in Cairo, Egypt. According to Aleister he was contacted by two discarnate entities named Aiwass or Aiwaz. From these entities, he dictated instructions to his new bride Rose Edith Crowley. However, there are three chapters he claimed were largely written in the first person by the Thelemic deities Nuit, Hadit, and Ra-Hoor-Khuit respectively, rather than by Aiwass or Aiwaz.

As stated, Crowley renamed several of the trump cards as well as the minor arcana cards. He also assigned or rearranged the astrological and Hebrew letters assigned to many of the cards.

---

20 *The Book of Thoth*, Crowley, Aleister, Samuel Weiser, Inc., Seventh Printing 1981, pgs. 47-48

Waiter-Rider Deck	_Thoth Deck_
I: The Magician	I: The Magus
II: The High Priestess	II: The Priestess
VII: Strength	VIII: Lust
X: Wheel of Fortune	X: Fortune
XI: Justice	XI: Adjustment
XIV: Temperance	XIV: Art
XX: Judgement	XX: Æon
XXI: The World	XXI: The Universe

He also altered many of the other card names so they would correspond to the symbols represented in Crowley's *Book of Thoth,* so it is important that those studying the other more common decks be alert to these differences.

SAMUEL LIDDELL MACGREGOR MATHERS

S.L. MacGregor Mathers was one of the founding members of the *Golden Dawn*, in 1888, together with Dr. William Wynn Westcott and Dr. Robert William Woodman. The *Golden Dawn* became one if not the primary source of spreading the concept of the Tarot to English speaking countries. According to Robert Wang, author of *The Qabalistic Tarot* (1983) there is only one reference for the origin of the *Golden Dawn Tarot*[21], it is referenced in the autobiography of an Irish artist and poet Ella Young (1867–1956). She stated that she was invited to MacGregor Mathers' home and saw "some large illustrations of Egyptian Gods" on paper. They made up a mosaic on paper. When asked about them MacGregor Mathers claimed that he had done them in one night. The papers were brought to the Order's headquarters and made into the rough version of a Tarot deck. Later Mrs. Mathers completed the deck by painting the missing cards.

Mathers also wrote a short book about the Tarot around 1888, around the same time he was involved in founding the *Golden Dawn*. In this book, he presents his own understanding and his knowledge of the history of the cards. It included his ideas on the "Gringonneur" deck. According to history in 1392, Jacquemin Gringonneur was paid to paint three decks of cards for King Charles VI of France (1380–1422). These were probably playing cards, not tarot. He also commented on Court de Gébelin's deck for at the time

---

21 *The Qabalistic Tarot*, Wang, Robert, Samuel Weiser, Inc., Third Printing 1992, pg. 12

Gébelin's deck was still viewed as a great prophecy to much of the European world. Mathers in his text also informs his readers that Tarot is a game. This may have been a "blind" for the Tarot become a very important tool in the teachings of the *Golden Dawn*. As the aspirant advances they are exposed to additional aspects of each card as they advance up the pathways of the Tree of Life.

In the *Golden Dawn* deck the trumps are essentially in the same order as that of the Tarot of Marseille. This Tarot deck was probably invented in northern Italy in the fifteenth century and introduced into southern France when the French conquered Milan and the Piedmont in 1499. There are two crucial differences. Firstly, "The Fool" is placed at the head of the Trumps — following the example of de Gébelin. Secondly, "Strength" is assigned to Leo and the letter Teth, and "Justice" is assigned to Libra and the letter Lamed. Now it so happens that in the Knowledge Lectures of the *Golden Dawn* these two trumps were actually renumbered as 8 and 11 respectively. However, the Cipher Manuscript, although it adjusted the astrological and Hebrew attributions of the two trumps, kept the old numbering system.

Paul Foster Case

Perhaps Paul's greatest contributions to the field of occultism were the lessons he wrote for associate members of Builders of the Adytum. Paul's approach to developing his deck differs from Waite who was hampered because according to Waite he had taken an oath of silence in the *Golden Dawn*, while Paul side stepped the same oath he had taken. He did this by affirming that he discovered the "attributions" associated with the Tarot on his own. These attributions included a wide range of fields including cosmological, astrological, numerological and schematic as they are found on the Cabalistic Tree.

After several revisions by Case, Jessie Burns Park (1889–1964) could produce his revised Tarot Deck. The *BOTA* deck was based closely on the Rider-Waite deck, except that it was printed in black and white. Case chose this with the intention that the student learn by coloring in the deck themselves. Case felt that by having the student coloring their own deck they would internalize and personalize the individual cards. In his instructions he gives details as to how and what exact colors the cards should be colored along with instructions as to the importance of each symbol, number, Hebrew letter and color. He also instructed that the margins be colored.

These outer margin colors were associated with the astrological signs that each Key was assigned.

Case's Tarot Keys are composed of pictorial and geometrical symbols. He taught that these symbols are the natural "language" of the subconscious mind, a language older than any human tongue, a language from which all modes of human speech have been derived. He felt that we thought in pictures, not in words, and this pictorial language, common to the whole human race, is the means whereby the subconscious mind may communicate to us the higher knowledge reflected from the superconscious levels of the True Self.

CHOOSING AND USE OF TAROT CARDS

Over the years there have been dozens of types of Tarot Cards developed and offered by an ever increasing number of schools of esoteric study. They are usually developed to express an idea or concept but most importantly to pique the internal interest of individuals. For in today's mass marketing and multimedia world there is a greater desire to attach new members than in the past when aspirants had to be "introduced" to a particular school, often by a sponsor.

When choosing a deck, the student should listen to their inter-self and choose a deck that "speaks to them". This may take several attempts but will eventually pay off. Remember a Tarot deck is a personal tool and not something that is shown to others. Many students have several decks that they use. They have a specific deck that is used to do divinations for the public, while reserving a specific deck for their own use and meditation, thus not exposing their personal deck to the energies of others. For as a true student starts their study and use of a specific deck their personal energy is transposed into that deck. Thus your working deck should be handled and stored with respect, and even a form of reverance, for it is your book of knowledge. Many suggest storing one's deck in a natural material such as silk, or a natural wood box, versus a synthetic material such as a plastic container or a polyester material.

As there is such a diversity of individuals, so there is a diversity of decks. A name of some of these decks are: Medicine Deck, Motherpeace Deck, Cat People Deck, Lovecraft Tarot, Ator Tarot, Haindi Tarot and any number of decks called Templar Tarot.

USE OF YOUR TAROT

Often potential students are drawn to Tarot cards out of curiosity. These individuals usually are seeking Tarot cards out as a potential form of divination. This often is the result of a personal crisis or of trying to solve a personal problem by seeking an "answer from the beyond". In other cases, some seek out Tarot decks just for "fun".

The more serious seeker often starts as a selfish personality that is unhappy in their selfish chaotic world they have created for themselves. At the time this is usually not how they see their life but they came to realize it after some time as they look back on their lives. They then see their world is one of chaotic thinking and immature emotions or turmoil due to what is perceived as a world over which they have no control. Still others are seeking something greater than themselves. These are often the same individuals who have not found answers to internal questions from established institutions offered from mainstream society.

Those dedicated students or seekers that are serious about gaining a clearer insight to their lives often search out what are called "alternative" groups or societies. These groups offer an "alternative" approach to viewing one's place in the greater universe. As the neophyte begins their study they are often presented a specific Tarot deck as a tool to aid them in their studies. The very act of seriously seeking out some way of changing the chaos of life, to one with a direction, is often the first indicator that the individual is truly ready to seek enlightenment. The Tarot thus can be a very useful tool to finding this path of enlightenment. Remember though there are many paths to enlightenment. As one travels down their path, like in life, one will see something new and different every time, depending on one's mood, sight and desire.

Many students who consider themselves serious students of the Tarot feel that the memorization of every detail of a specific card is essential to obtaining the knowledge contained within the card. The fact is the various portrayals of the cards act as stimulation of the inner subconscious mind. This can be done by the individual colors, shapes, symbols, Hebrew letters, or numeric assignments; or combination of them.

The Keys are just that- "keys" to open up the potential of what can be. This is usually done by connecting to the inner aspects of the symbols presented on the Key. The colors and texture of the work magnify the essence of the symbol. This only occurs if the person viewing the symbol can identify with that particular symbol. That identification is the door to the potential that it holds.

When seeking your preferred cards also consider if they were produced as a tool for evoking thought or just a game of divination. The former often support information as to internalizing the energies derived from the use of the cards, while the latter often are surrounded with some "deep mystery" that only the greatest of Masters know—but will 'give you the ability to see into the past, present and future'.

You will know which is correct, for even the beginning student will recognize and understand that the principles presented are based on practical occultism which is hidden in the hearts of all men. Remember be TRUE TO ONESELF, if it feels right it is generally right.

Numbers as Symbols

Pythagoras said the number was a "great and perfect and omnipotent, and a principle and guide of divine and human life'". He went on to say "a number is order and limitation, and alone makes the cosmos possible, by numbers nature moves, and to understand numbers is to be the master of nature". This concept has been a basic tenet of occultism and one of the cornerstones of Hermetic Qabalah.

Paul Foster Case went so far as to describe what he considered the meaning of numbers as symbols. He considered the number as a symbol to greater understanding of the Tarot and its relationship to order.

No-Thing. He considered "0" to be the undifferentiated Power preceding all manifestation. He said this Power was free of quantity, quality, mass or any limitations.

Beginning. This is first true number for "0" is no-thing.

Duplication. This is symbolic of repetition, wisdom and science, opposition and polarity, succession, sequence and separation.

Multiplication. This number symbolized increase, growth, expansion, amplification, productiveness.

Order. Regulation, management, supervision, control, command, dominance.

Mediation. This is the middle of the series of numbers, intervention, adjustment, and reconciliation.

Reciprocation. It represents interchange, response correlation, cooperation, harmony.

Equilibrium. Or the result of equilibrium, mastery, poise, rest, conquest, safety, security.

Rhythm. Vibration, pulsation, flux, involution and evolution.

Conclusion. The "closing together", union of elements.

He went on to say "10" was the symbol of embodiment, of the Kingdom, and of Law in action. It is combination of the feminine "0" with the masculine "1".

COLORS AS SYMBOLS

Colors have many attributions assigned to them as well. The one major aspect of colors is they evoke emotions in the person who is immersed in the colors. These emotions can evoke overt physical responses such as joy, laughter or even on the other end of the scale, anger or depression. Colors can also evoke very subdued changes in the mind as to how it "feels" about what it is viewing—a sort of "like" or "dislike", acceptance or rejection of what is being seen. Modern science has "discovered" or "rediscovered" colors as very powerful tools to modify behavior. An example is the use of passive colors in prisons and bright colors in hospitals, especially children's wings.

Colors are associated with the planets and musical notes as well. When comparing the 'emotions' associated with colors compare those same colors to the planets and what attributes were associated with the gods and goddesses that the ancients assigned to them. For often times, depending on the culture, the emotion evoked is subjectively associated with the deity. A modern example is in the Roman Catholic Church's icon of the Virgin Mary. She is often clothed in blues, which are generally related to water and nurturing feelings.

COLORS

Red: Excitement, energy, passion, love, desire, speed, strength, power, heat, aggression, danger, fire, blood, war, violence, all things intense and passionate, sincerity, happiness (Only in Japan)

Pink: Symbolizes love and romance, caring, tenderness, acceptance and calm.

Yellow: Signifies joy, happiness, betrayal, optimism, idealism, imagination, hope, sunshine, summer, gold, philosophy, dishonesty, cowardice, jealousy, covetousness, deceit, illness, hazard and friendship.

Blue: Peace, tranquility, cold, calm, stability, harmony, unity, trust, truth, confidence, conservatism, security, cleanliness, order, loyalty, sky, water, technology, depression, appetite suppressant.

Purple: Royalty, nobility, spirituality, ceremony, mysterious, transformation, wisdom, enlightenment, cruelty, honor, arrogance, mourning, temperance.

Orange: Energy, balance, enthusiasm, warmth, vibrant, expansive, flamboyant, demanding of attention.

Green: Is symbolic for Nature, environment, healthy, good luck, renewal, youth, spring, generosity, fertility, jealousy, inexperience, envy, misfortune, vigor.

Brown: Earth, stability, hearth, home, outdoors, reliability, comfort, endurance, simplicity, and comfort.

Gray: Security, reliability, intelligence, staid, modesty, dignity, maturity, solid, conservative, practical, old age, sadness, boring. Silver symbolizes calm.

White: Reverence, purity, birth, simplicity, cleanliness, peace, humility, precision, innocence, youth, winter, snow, good, sterility, marriage (Western cultures), death (Eastern cultures), cold, clinical.

Black: Power, sexuality, sophistication, formality, elegance, wealth, mystery, fear, evil, unhappiness, depth, style, sadness, remorse, anger, anonymity, underground, good technical color, mourning, death (Western cultures), austerity, detachment.

PLANETS
Sun: Helios
> Orange, gold, deep yellows.

Moon: Selene—sister of Helios
> White, pearl, opal, light, pale blues; iridescent and silvery hues.

Mercury: Hermes
> Insofar as Mercury can be said to have any appropriate colors of its own, slate color, spotted mixtures. Most authorities agree that Mercury generally assumes the color of that planet with which it is in nearest aspect.

Venus: Aphrodite
> Sky—blue to pale green, lemon yellow; and tints in general as contrasted to colors.

Mars: Ares
> Red, scarlet, carmine.

Jupiter: Zeus
> Royal purple, violet, some blends of red and indigo, deep blue.

Uranus: Roman god of the Universe
> Streaked mixtures, checks and plaids like Joseph's coat 'of many colors'.

Neptune: Poseidon
> Lavender, sea-green, mauve, smoke-blue and possibly peculiar shades of gray.

Pluto. Hades
> Luminous pigments, in unusual shades containing a large percentage of red

THE MAJOR ARCANA

The 76 cards of a traditional Tarot Deck are broken into two types of cards. The first is called the "Major Arcana" which generally consists of twenty-two individual cards or "Keys". The second is comprised of 54 "Minor Arcana" cards. The Major Arcana are considered to be the most important cards because they represent the deeper, more meaningful aspects or spiritual component of life, while the Minor Arcana are often viewed as "amplifiers" to the Major Arcana. This is not a hard and fast fact and often depends on the person doing the divination.

0—THE FOOL

The Fool is the first Card of the Major Arcana. The number associated with it is 0. The Key represents the way in which the Absolute Power presents itself to the minds of man. It represents the concept that nothing can be positively affirmed. The Hebrew letter is Aleph meaning "bull" or "ox". Aleph is the symbol of creative power and is the symbol of the taming of nature as represented by the bull being domesticated to become the ox, the plower of fields and aid to man.

Breath is extremely important and is symbolized by the Fool. It is the first aspect of life a newborn does. It is the sign of Air. The Fool is shown at the beginning of his journey with no boundaries and unlimited potential. The sun rising up behind him represents the beginning of his journey. He is facing north-west, the direction of the unknown. He is looking upwards, toward the sky, or Spirit. He is about to step off a cliff into the material world which is open to his creation. He has all the tools and resources he needs in the bag on his staff to create his world but at this stage the bag is not opened yet. The white rose in his left hand represents purity and innocence. He has a guardian in the little white dog who will protect him throughout his journey but who will also push him to learn the lessons the Fool came here to learn. The mountains behind the Fool represent the realms of Spirit that he has just left and will spend his life trying to regain.

There will be a short paragraph of "key" or "prime" words associated with each Key. They are generally used when using the cards for divination. A student of the Tarot should be aware of them because they describe actions or emotions associated or stimulated by that Key. When using a Tarot Deck for divination the deck is shuffled and a hand is 'spread'. If a card appears upside down or 'reversed' it could denote a negative action. The student of Tarot should realize this is an aspect of the card. There is a duplicity of everything and this needs to be understood. Just as a sword is an offensive as well as a defensive tool.

Some Key words associated with The Fool are: Beginnings, fresh start, hope, innocence, free spirit, blind faith, and spontaneity. If the card appears Reversed during divination the key words would be: Naivety, foolishness, perils, recklessness and risk taking.

1—The Magician

This Key represents initiation—the beginning or inception of processes. It symbolizes the bringing "down" of ideas to the material world, as represented by the table. The Magician is associated with the planet Mercury and carries with it skill, logic, and intellect. The number of the Magician is 1, the number of beginnings. This is the first step in the practical work of occultism. The Magician is the bridge between the world of the spirit and the world of humanity. His right hand holds a staff raised toward the sky and his left hand points to the earth. The right hand is the "receptive" or "receiving" hand while the left is the "giving" or "becoming" or "formation" hand. He takes the power of the Universe, and channels it through his own body and directs it to the physical plane. Above the Magician's head is the symbol of eternity and around his waist is a snake biting its own tail, another symbol of eternity. His magical table holds all four suits of the Tarot, each of which represents one of the four primordial elements of the alchemists — earth, air, fire and water. These symbolize the appropriate use of mind, heart, body and soul in the process of manifestation. They also represent the idea of combining special sounds and ideas in the proper way to produce extraordinary results. It is often referred to as "the power of the word". The Magician's robe is white, symbolizing the purity and innocence found in the Fool but his cloak is red, representing worldly experience and knowledge. In the bed of flowers at his feet this duality is repeated in the mix of pure white lilies and thorny red roses.

This Key, as its number figuratively represents, a pointing to a center, or concentration of formative energies.

When this Key is viewed prime words are: power, skill, reality, illusion, concentration, action, resourcefulness. If reversed during divination: Manipulation, poor planning, latent talents.

2—THE HIGH PRIESTESS

HIGH PRIESTESS

Where Key 1, the Magician, represents controlling the powers of the sub-consciousness, Key 2, The High Priestess represents the act of subordination of the objective mind versus the self-consciousness of Key 1. The home of our memories and experiences is the subconsciousness. The High Priestess symbolizes the universal subconsciousness by the scroll or book she holds. It is the half-revealed and half-concealed Torah, representative of the exoteric and the esoteric teachings and higher knowledge. It is from this scroll the true Adept hopes to gain access to these records which contain all the discoveries that were, are and will be.

The High Priestess is also known by mfallen angelsany names such as Persephone, Isis, the Corn Maiden and Artemis. All relate to the Moon. She sits at the very gate before the great Mystery, she sits between the darkness and the light, represented by the pillars Jachin and Boaz that stood at the door of Solomon's temple, a metaphor for the temple of our being. The pomegranates on the tapestry are sacred to Persephone. They are a symbol of duty because Persephone ate a pomegranate seed in the underworld which forced her to return every year. The blue robe the Priestess is wearing is a symbol of knowledge and the beginning of the subconscious that flows out and continues through many of the Keys. She is wearing the crown of Isis symbolizing the Triple Goddess. The solar cross on her breast is a symbol of balance between male and female. In her lap she holds "The Scroll of Knowledge". The moon under her left foot shows her dominion over pure intuition. The palm indicates fertility of the mind and the cube on which she sits is the earth.

Key words are: Intuition, Higher powers, mystery, mystic, initiation, intuition, and the subconscious mind. Reversed: Hidden agendas, and the need to listen to inner voice.

3—THE EMPRESS

THE EMPRESS

♃   ♀

The Empress's key word is Multiplication and is attributed to the number 3. It is the act of increasing "creative imagination" in one's mental life. The Hebrew letter Daleth means "door" and for the Qabalists is the symbol for entrance or passageway. Also a door is a feminine symbol representing rebirth. Daleth represents the feminine organ of generation and the alluvial soil at the mouth of rivers, which we name as deltas. This is the same as the fourth letter in the Greek alphabet Δ delta, and it is also one of the oldest symbols of deity. This is a very important concept that should be remembered, that the earliest symbol of a deity, is the triangle, which is also feminine symbol and meansing door or pathway.

The Empress is the archetypal Earth Mother, the Anima, the Feminine Principle, Demeter, Freyja and the Goddess of Fertility. The Empress is ruled by Venus, the planet of love, creativity, fertility, art, harmony, luxury, beauty and grace.

The main feature of this card is the Empress herself, a full-figured woman with blond hair and a peaceful and calm aura about her. On her head she wears a crown of stars, showing her connection with the mystical realm of angels and fairies. She is dressed in a patterned robe of pomegranates, symbolic of fertility, and is seated upon a luxurious array of cushions and flowing red velvet with the symbol of Venus emblazoned upon it.

The Empress is surrounded by a beautiful, lush forest with a stream running through it, demonstrating the Empress's deep emotional connection with Mother Earth and life. This is the same stream that started from the robes of the High Priestess. She is portrayed sitting with a sense of peace while surrounded with the trees and the water which give her the rejuvenated energy from nature. This can be especially important in today's world of high stress. In the foreground, golden wheat springs from the ground, reflecting abundance from a recent harvest.

Key words are: Fertility, femininity, beauty, creativity, nature, and abundance. The reversed card represents the key words: Creative block, dependence on others.

4—THE EMPEROR

The Emperor is the complement to the Empress, but where the Empress symbolized "multiplication", the Emperor represents "order". Other concepts represented would system, regulation, management and supervision. It is the clarification of self-conscious ideas leading to the activity of reason. He is the Masculine Principle, the Animus and the Patriarch. He represents power and authority. The noun of emperor means "he who sets in order". The Emperor is linked to The Empress for without her manifesting power which brings forth forms The Emperor would have nothing to supervise.

The Emperor has a long, white beard, a symbol of his experience. As an archetype, it is common to see masculine figures of authority or father figures with long white beards. It suggests that this man has acquired years of wisdom and experience and he is worthy of listening to because he has seen first-hand the consequences of his actions. The Emperor is The Magician who has brought forth the ideas of reason to now be transformed from chaotic images to manageable thoughts and forms.

Behind his throne are barren mountains and the throne itself is decorated with four rams' heads, representing intellectual heights, determination, action, initiative and leadership. In the Case Key there is the river of sub-consciousness which can be viewed in the background. The ram is also a symbol of Aries, the astral ruler of the Emperor. In his right hand, the Emperor holds an Ankh, the Egyptian symbol of Life, and in his left is an orb representing the world over which he rules. The orange background and the Emperor's red clothing symbolize his passion and Mars' energy for action in life and the challenges it offers.

Important concept words are: Authority, father-figure, justice, structure, and solid foundation. While if appearing in reversed: Domination, excessive control, rigidity, and inflexibility.

5—The Hierophant

The Hierophant is known as the High Priest in some decks, and in others older decks The Pope. His attribution is the act of hearing which also refers to the Hebrew letter of Vav. He is the masculine counterpart to the High Priestess. He is the Emperor, for both are symbols of the "father". He is also known as Chiron, and the Shaman. The Hierophant is ruled by Taurus.

The Hierophant is represented by a religious figure, and traditionally shown sitting within a formal church environment or a place sacred to the theme of the specific Tarot Deck. He is wearing three elaborate vestments of his office that represent the three worlds. The crown he is wearing has three tiers to. His right hand is raised in benediction; the same hand the Magician has raised. While the Magician was taking raw power from the

Universe and manifesting it on the material plane, the Hierophant channels that power through what society can accept. The triple scepter is another symbol of his dominion over the three worlds. The crossed keys represent a balance between the conscious and subconscious minds and unlock the mysteries. Before him kneel two initiates. They represent desire and knowledge. Hierophant's task is to bring the two initiates under the yoke of self-consciousness.

Key Words: Divine wisdom, inspiration, stubborn strength, toil, authority, endurance, persistence, teaching, group identification, conformity, tradition, and beliefs. Reversed would be: Restriction, challenging the status quo.

6—THE LOVERS

THE LOVERS.

The Lovers present the idea of pairs of opposites including the special opposite of self-conscious and subconscious forms of mental activity. The most important lesson is that the universe shows in all details the power of love, which produces a harmonious balance between various pairs of opposites that which become manifested in order.

The planet Mercury rules the sign associated with the Lovers, which is Gemini. The two figures in the Lovers Card are blessed and protected by the angel Raphael, in the clouds above them. Angels, in general, represent the refinement of earthly desires. Raphael in particular is the angel of Air. One of the associations of Air is communication, necessary for a healthy relationship. The violet cloak on the angel represents royalty and dominion, a symbol of how important that discrimination leads to control of conditions.

The sun shines brightly over the couple, bringing warmth and security. The earth at their feet is green and fertile and suggests life and happiness. The five apples on the tree behind the woman represent the five senses, indicating how important sensual romance is to the woman. The snake in the fruit-laden tree behind the woman suggests the story of Adam and Eve, the fall of humanity from grace, and the temptations of the world. The snake is also a symbol of the senses as well as the serpent-power, the kundalini. The flames behind the man represent the flames of passion, indicating the primary concern of the man. There are twelve flames, representing the twelve zodiac signs, the symbol of time and eternity. The man looks to the woman, who looks to the angel, forming the triangle of deity once again. This triangle indicates the path of the conscious to the subconscious to the super-conscious, or from physical desire to emotional needs to spiritual concerns. The mountain is a symbol of attainment and realization, while the water is a feminine symbol, indicating balance between the two.

The key words are: Love, union, relationships, potential, challenge, opposites, values alignment, and choices. In reversed position: Disharmony, imbalance, and misalignment of values.

7—The Chariot

One of the most important principles of this Key is the power of the "will". To the occultist will is not the same as the proverbial 'strong willed or minded' individual. It is a thing of its own life, continually pulsating with the motivating energy of the universe. It is a power that is available to all of us. This is specifically seen in that the individual in Chariot does not control his pullers by brute strength but through the power of the mind, thus emphasizing the need to go through life not as a bull using the physical strength of the body but by the superconscious power of the mind. He controls through strength of will in the same way the Magician brings forth the powers from above.

The Chariot is associated with the astrological sign of Cancer. He sits within a canopy of six-pointed stars, representing the celestial influences of the four elements as they affect all external manifestations. The towers shown in background represent the true development of will-power. The crescent moons on the man's shoulders are outward facing to refer to the formative world. The symbols on his tunic are alchemical symbols, representing the spiritual transformation of man. The square signifies earth, a sign of strength of will. The laurel and star crown indicate the highest attainment of man in spiritual evolution. The wings on the Chariot represent inspiration and the Hindu sign of the union of positive and negative. The black and white sphinxes are the propounders of riddles and represent our senses as they measure and test our perceived manifested material world.

When the Key appears in the upright form it confers: Control, will power, ascent, victory, motivation, assertion, and determination. In the reversed form: Lack of control and direction, and aggression.

8—Strength

Under a golden sky, a woman gently pats a lion on its forehead and lower jaw. The woman gazes down at the lion with a peaceful smile on her face and appears to be successfully taming this wild beast. The fact that Strength is represented by a woman indicates that this card is not focused on pure physical strength. She has the infinity symbol above her head, the same symbol seen in the Magician. Her white robe is that of the innocent Fool, indicating a purity of spirit. The blue mountain in the background is the same phallic symbol seen in the Lovers. The lion is a symbol of our animal passions and desires. The lion itself is sticking out his tongue. Animals that are preparing to bite do not stick their tongues out. This lion is happy to submit and surrender to the woman. The woman overcomes the lion with a quiet strength that can only come from within. Her left arm represents mental effort, while the right arm represents physical effort. Her right arm is merely holding, while the left arm is exerting all the pressure. She wears a belt and crown of flowers and stands unprotected in an open green field. The crown on her head represents the fullest, most beautiful expression of nature and transient life. The sign associated with the Strength card is Leo.

Key words: Strength, courage, patience, mastery, submission, ego, control, and compassion. Reversed they would be: Weakness, self-doubt, lack of self-discipline.

9—THE HERMIT

The Hermit stands alone, as a symbol of adeptship and prophecy, at the top of a mountain with a lantern in his hand. Mountains typically symbolize achievement, growth, and accomplishment. The Hermit has attained his spiritual pinnacle and is ready to share his knowledge with others. He is looking down the path he has chosen yet lights his path as he continues the path of enlightenment, and he is committed to his goal of ultimate awareness. The star in the lantern is a six-pointed star which is the Seal of Solomon, a symbol of wisdom. The staff carried by the Hermit is the patriarch's staff, a symbol of the narrow path of initiation and an emblem of power and authority. It represents the Hermit's ability to use his isolation and the knowledge he has gained as a tool upon his path to reach even higher levels of awareness. The staff is in the Hermit's left hand, the hand associated with the subconscious mind. The snow at his feet represents the heights of spiritual attainment. He wears the grey cloak of invisibility. His secrets are not for everyone, only for those earnestly seeking them and those willing to climb the heights to wisdom. Astrologically The Hermit represents rulership, but also the exaltation of the planet Mercury, as well as the correspondence with Virgo. The number 9 signifies accomplishment, wisdom, the attainment of goals, as well as the search for truth.

The Hermit stands for many key concepts such as: Soul-searching, solitude, meditation, introspection, being alone, and the inner guidance that comes with calmness. In reverse it is: Isolation, loneliness, withdrawal.

10—THE WHEEL OF FORTUNE

The Wheel represents the "The Wheel of Ezekiel", *Ezekiel* 1:6, and is a glyph of perpetual motion. The Wheel of Fortune is highly symbolic. The angel in the top left corner is Aquarius, the eagle is Scorpio, the lion is Leo and the bull is Taurus. These are the four fixed signs of the Zodiac but all have wings signifying stability amidst movement and change. The book they each have in their hands is the Torah, representing wisdom. On the wheel itself are the Hebrew letters IHVH (*Yod Heh Vau Heh*), the unpronounceable name of God. Interspersed with these letters are TORA (read anti-clockwise) or TARO (read clockwise) which also translates to TAROT. The snake descending on the left side of the Wheel is the Egyptian god Typhon, the god of evil. The snake also represents the life force descending into the material world. The Anubis rising on the right side of the Wheel is Hermes, a symbol of intelligence, wisdom, ascending or our shadow selves. The Sphinx on the top of the wheel represents life's riddles. The middle wheel contains the alchemical symbols for mercury, sulphur, water and salt. These are alchemical building blocks of life and represent the four elements of power. The outer circle represents the material world. The eight spokes in the wheel represent the Universal radiant energy, as well as the eight Sabbaths of the year. The blue background represents wisdom. Growth is possible only by the principle of rotation, the continual movement of the wheel of time. The movement of the wheel produces energy that will manifest itself in the physical form-it is the root-matter which occultist refer to as the interior fire or "water" of creation.

The planet of this card is Jupiter, the mythical ruler of the gods. It is exalted in Cancer. Jupiter is the planet of opportunity, growth, success, and expansion. The number 10 is a higher octave of the number 1, empowering the qualities of the 1.

In the upright form it means: Good luck, karma, mutability, experience, life cycles, destiny, and a turning point. In reverse: Bad luck, negative external forces, and out of control.

11—Justice

Equilibrium is the basis of the Great Work.[22] Equilibrium only comes with the balance of two forces. For the Master Adept this is be in a state of immortality. For the student Adept it is a goal that is reached and lost again, the elusive elixir of life. The very Hebrew letter, Lamed, or ox-goad says it all. The ox-goad is used to keep the ox, us, moving forward, even when times are tough.

Justice is ruled by Libra and the card number is 11. Libra governs the kidneys; whose function is to maintain our blood in a state of chemical equilibrium. The figure of Justice sits in her chair, clothed in red, the Mars color-the color of action. This symbolically calls us to action, that we must progress on the path, not settle in one spot or level. She is holding a sword in her right hand and scales in her left. Her cape is green, the color attributed to Venus. She wears a crown with a small square on it representing well-ordered thoughts. Notice the clasp holding the cloak together. The square is the law protecting the circle and the eternal state of oneness within us all. The sword is double-edged, cutting both ways, signifying impartiality. It is point-up, signifying victory. The sword in her right hand also demonstrates the logical, well-ordered mindset necessary to dispense fair justice. The scales are in her left, intuitive hand, showing that logic must be balanced by the intuition. A little white shoe pops out from beneath her cloak, reminding us of the spiritual consequences of our actions. The purple cloth draped behind her signifies compassion and the grey pillars represent the constraints of the physical world.

The key words associated with Justice are: Justice, impartiality, mercy, decisiveness, fairness, perception, truth, cause and effect, and law. Reversed: Unfairness, lack of accountability, and dishonesty.

---

22 *Tarot Fundamentals,* Case, Paul Foster, B.O.T.A., Lesson 25. Pg.1

12—THE HANGED MAN

THE HANGED MAN.

The concept of Key 12 is related to the Law of Reversal. It emphasizes the concept that the adept needs to step away from popular beliefs and seek out what is not known to the masses. The letter associated with Key 12 is Mem, which means waters or seas and relates directly to the metaphysical "waters" referred to in esoteric texts. It is said for a student to understand this concept of "water" they must understand that like water, things are reflected upside down and must be reversed by the onlooker to truly see the picture.

The Hanged Man shows a man suspended, upside-down, from the living World Tree, rooted in the underworld and supporting the heavens. Given the serene expression on his face, it is believed he is hanging on the tree of his own will. His right foot is bound to the tree but his left foot remains free, bent at the knee and tucked in behind his right leg. His legs form the number 4, which refers to reason or in this case the reverse of reason. His arms are bent, with hands held behind his back, forming an inverted triangle corresponding to the number 3. The number 12 is a product of 3 and 4.

The man is wearing red pants representing human passion and the physical body, a blue coat for knowledge, and yellow shoes representing his high ideals. Around the Hanged Man's head is a bright yellow halo showing spiritual attainment, with the grey background suggesting invisibility, or in this case a false sense of invisibility. This is the card of ultimate surrender, of being suspended in time and of martyrdom and sacrifice to the greater good. This is the archetype to meditate on to help break old patterns of behavior and bad habits that restrict you. The ruling planet is Neptune, the planet ruled by inspiration and mediumship.

Suspension, obligation, serene, transfiguration, restriction, letting go, and sacrifice are key words, while in the reverse they are martyrdom, indecision, and delay.

13—DEATH

Whenever a discussion of Tarot comes up in the general populace the one card that elicits the most comment and fear is The Death Key and the number 13. But like so many things in the study of the occult there are multiple meanings even to the concept of death. As for the number 13, myth/tradition says this became an unlucky number because of its relationship to the date the Knights Templar were arrested by King Philip IV of France on Friday, the 13th of October 1307.

Man generally fears death because he does not know the meaning of the transformation, the dissolution of one form giving room for the birth of a new form. It is only when that form breaks down does the energy held in the old form is released to be able to reform in a new structure. The Death Key is thus a very important Key to the Adept for it signifies the breaking down of old ideas and the birth of new ones. In many depictions of The Death card it shows a giver of death reaping destruction but also it shows the rebirth or growing of new forms.

The Death card shows Death himself riding from north to south. From darkness of ignorance to the light of perfection. Death is portrayed as a skeleton, since the bones are the part of the body that survives death. When there is a skeleton depicted there are traditionally two anomalies in the skeleton. The first is an abnormal twist just above the pelvis and the second is another twist at the neck. The force represented by the skeleton must be twisted, or reversed in order to perform its highest function of rebirth. In the Keys where death is clothed the armor he is wearing indicates that he is invincible and unconquerable. The horse that Death rides is white, the color of purity. Death is therefore the ultimate purifier. All things are reborn fresh, new and pure. In the Case Key there is a small oval in the upper left corner symbolic of the egg of creation.

The banner that Death carries has a black background, indicating an absence of light. The white rose, on the other hand, indicates beauty, purification and immortality. In the background of the card, there is a rising sun, a sign of immortality. The sun appears to "die" each night but is reborn fresh and new every morning. The two pillars are guarding the gateway to the sun, symbolizing the knowledge needed to gain immortality.

Death is ruled by Scorpio which is ruled by Mars. Both death and inheritance are connected to the eighth house of the horoscope, the house assigned to Scorpio.

When the Key turns facing up key words would be: Endings, beginnings, change, rebirth, transformation, letting go, loss or gain, optimism, and transition. Reversed: Resistance to change, need for reassessment, and unable to move on.

14—TEMPERANCE

On the Temperance card stands a winged angel Michael, the angel of the sun and the element of fire. The angel has one foot on dry land, representative of the concrete manifestation of the material world, and one foot in the water, representative of the cosmic mind-stuff. In this position, she also represents the need to "test the waters" before jumping headfirst into unknown circumstances. Here she tempers the whimsical flight of the Fool who jumps without giving a second thought. The triangle inside the square on her robe represents the female being protected by natural law. This is sometimes shown as a seven-pointed star which too stands for mastery because of the skill required to form it out of a 360-degree circle. In her hands she holds two cups which she uses to mix water. The cups represent the sub- and super-conscious minds. This is the water of Mem and the doctrine of The Hanged Man. The water flowing between them is actually going from the lower cup to the higher one, signifying rising from a lower plane to a higher one. The temperate individual mixes the opposites and finds a balance in life by avoiding extremes.

The astrological sign is Sagittarius, the teacher of truth, enthusiasm, tolerance and beauty. Sagittarius also has to do with dreams, visions, religion and philosophy. Here there is a systematic formulation of ideas with a desire to verify them by obtaining knowledge. Sagittarius has to do with long journeys, the long path of the student-adept.

Upright: Balance, moderation, patience, equilibrium, peace, purpose, and meaning. Reversed: Imbalance, excess, and lack of long-term vision.

15—The Devil

The card of the Devil portrays a Satyr, a creature that is half man and half goat. In many myths, the goat was considered an unclean and lustful animal. However, the goat also symbolizes the scapegoat, the person or thing upon which people project the inferior side of themselves in order to feel better about themselves. Thus the Devil is the scapegoat we blame for our troubles in life.

The Devil is one of those feared cards that many see as evil. In fact, it has a very important concept to teach—Key 15 shows that bondage is an illusion. If one looks closely the chains that hold the two figures "bound" to the devil are actually made of paper. They represent that we often view ourselves bound to some concept or situation only by the illusion of misconception. When we view our worlds by conceptions and observations they are often false or ill interpreted due to the lack of clear knowledge or the misunderstanding of what we observed. But as the adept progresses he is able to break this bond of illusion and move forward.

The Devil has the wings of a vampire bat, an animal that sucks the life blood out of its prey. This is symbolic of what happens when we give full reign to the realm of our raw desires and misconceptions. We lose our vitality and life energy. The Devil has an almost hypnotic stare, bringing those who come near him within his power. His eyes are emphasized to draw our attention to that our own eyes, both physical and symbolic, often are the source of our deceptions. Above him is an inverted pentagram, signifying the darker side of magic and occultism. The inverted pentagram is a symbol of falsehood because it is never true that the Spirit can be dominated by matter. The eagle's legs and feet refer to Scorpio, which is ruled by Mars, which is exalted in Capricorn.

The man and woman wear tiny horns like those of the Satyr — they are becoming more and more like the devil the longer they stay chained to their misconceptions and fears. Both have tails — a further symbol of their animalistic or "lower" tendencies.

Upright: Bondage, addiction, sexuality, trial of strength, shadow, transformation, and materialism.

Reversed: Detachment, breaking free, and power reclaimed.

16—THE TOWER

This is the second stage of spiritual unfoldment, the awakening from the dream sense, from the nightmares of misconception and bondage to one of seeing a reality that is clear. Key 16 is a picture of destruction but more so the flash of lightning which is the flash of the superconsciouness. It is the breaking down of the old self which is symbolized by the tower, the barrier or shell we build to protect our inner self. The experience of spiritual unfoldment is a destructive process. The breaking or destroying all of the customary wrong thing and wrong action. The false sense of personal will and personal self-action must be destroyed for the greater powers to flourish.

The Tower shows a tall tower perched atop a craggy mountain. Lightning shows there is an active force at work in this phase of life. It strikes and flames burst from the building's windows symbolizing the reproductive force of Mars. People are seen to be leaping from the tower in desperation, wanting to flee such destruction and turmoil. The man represents self-consciousness, and the woman subconscious. The Tower signifies human error, and ignorance. The physical image of the Tower represents ambitions built on false premises. The lightning bolt breaks down existing forms in order to make room for new ones. It represents a sudden, momentary glimpse of truth, a flash of inspiration that breaks down structures of ignorance and false reasoning. Notice the lightning bolt is oriented left to right, from heaven to earth, and from Spirit to material. The falling figures correspond to the chained prisoners in the Devil card. They fall headfirst, because the sudden influx of spiritual consciousness represented by the lightning flash completely upsets all our old notions about the relations between subconsciousness and self-consciousness. It is time in the student's development where physical readjustment is often required before we can venture to higher levels of consciousness. The flames are actually the Hebrew yods. There are 22 flames, representing the 22 Major Arcana, for each letter begins with a yod. The gray clouds are the clouds of misfortune that rain on everyone indiscriminately. The ruling planet of this card is Mars, for the Mars force manifests itself in the driving power for all successful activity.

In a positive form it represents the key concepts of: Disturbance, release, upheaval, sudden change, and revelation. Reversed: The avoidance of disaster, and a fear of change.

17—STAR

Key 17 represents the third stage of spiritual unfoldment, revelation, the unveiling, disclosure and discovery. This discovery or revelation is a gift from Isis that is given not taken by the student. These revelations are above the physical awakening, more like revelations coming from the reasoning mind ONLY when it is completely stilled and the physical senses closed to stimuli. This is a time of deep meditation when we quest and seek for answers. This is represented by the Hebrew letter Tzaddi which means "fish-hook".

The Star card shows a blazing star symbolic of the fifth essence or Quintessence. The Quintessence is the material that fills the region of the universe above the terrestrial sphere. Key 17 shows a naked woman, Isis-Urania, kneeling at the edge of a small pool. The woman holds two containers of water. She pours the water out to nourish the earth and to continue the cycle of fertility, represented by the lush greenery around her. The other container pours the water onto dry land in five rivulets, representing the five senses. The woman has one foot on the ground, representing her practical abilities and good common sense, and the other foot in the water, representing her intuition and inner resources, and listening to her inner voice. Behind her shines one large star and seven smaller stars, representing your chakras. This represents a need to open your chakras and cleanse your aura. Notice all the stars have eight points. They also represent the seven alchemical elements or metals: 1) lead, 2) iron, 3) tin, 4) gold, 5) silver, 6) copper and 7) mercury. The bird in the tree in the background is the sacred ibis of thought, roosting in the tree of the mind. The astrological sign of the Star is Aquarius and the alchemical symbol for dissolution.

Revelation, hope, spirituality, guidance, renewal, inspiration, and serenity are some of the key words when the Key is in an upright position. Reversed: Lack of faith, despair, and discouragement.

18—THE MOON

XVIII – THE MOON

New relations are revealed to us in this fourth stage of spiritual unfoldment through the process of organization of evolutionary development. This is represented by the various creatures pictured in Key 18. From the lowly creature climbing from the sea of universal mind-stuff, to the wolf and then to the dog. Key 18 represents the alchemist's practice of producing higher, finer, and more sensitive natures to better perceive their work. This is done by the continual exercise of the imagination making clear and definite our desires and aspirations, for mental images are patterns which pass into our subconsciousness.

The Moon is the card of intuition, duplication, reflection, dreams and the unconscious. The Moon provides light as a reflection of the Sun, yet this light is dim, uncertain, and only vaguely illuminates our path as we journey toward higher consciousness. The pool at the base of the card represents the subconscious mind and the crayfish that crawls out of the pool symbolizes the early stages of consciousness unfolding. The crayfish is the force of Scorpio. This creature also represents the often disturbing images that appear from our inner depths, such as selfishness, and obstinacy. The wolf is the symbol of nature and the dog of Art. They represent the beginning of the path from the wild aspects of our minds to a tamer and more organized mind. The path leads upward, through the twin towers, and over undulating ground representing the ups and downs faced in the student's path toward adeptship. The two towers leading into the mountains in the distance are the boundaries we set between us and our emergence into the purer light. The astrological sign associated with this card is Pisces, which rules the feet and suggests our journey upon the path. Pisces further suggests the psychic, receptive and mysterious aspect of the work.

Illusion, mystery, psychic powers, anxiety, insecurity, obstacles, and subconscious are key words for Key 18. While in reverse: unhappiness and confusion.

19—THE SUN

Key 19 represents a new birth from natural humanity into spiritual humanity and is the fifth stage of spiritual unfoldment. It is the process of regeneration of one's spiritual identity. The new birth is both mental and physical.

At this point the Adept often finds a new way of living. This is often seen in moderation of desires and abuses. The Adept knows how to control the desires that rise from the various pathways and knows how and why. Diets often change in the Adept with moderation being the key. Key 19 has the Hebrew letter Resh assigned to it, it meaning is that it represents the head, which is the seat of government.

The Sun is an image of optimism and fulfilment, the dawn that follows the darkest night. The solar energy shines in us and our energy shines in the sun. As the source of all life on earth, the Sun represents the source of life itself. The child or children, depending on which deck being used, are playing joyfully in the foreground representing the happiness of our inner spirit when we are in tune with our truest Self. They are naked, having nothing to hide. They represent all that is innocence and purity, which childhood should be.

In the Waite Deck the white horse upon which the child rides represent strength and purity of spirit. The horse is without a saddle and is controlled without the use of the hands. This is a symbol of perfect control between the conscious and subconscious. The child holds an orange banner in his left hand, showing that control has passed from the conscious to the sub-conscious. The orange banner represents action and vibration, and the rays of the sun represent the same thing.

In the Case Deck there are two concentric circles which are symbol of the fourth dimension. It is the way of the spiritual man not the natural man. The inner circle is the spiritual circle of manifestation. Both children are of equal status even though the female is subjected to "the misunderstanding and misinterpretations of the masculine natural man". It is only after the adept is able to transcend the threshold to the fourth dimension that these misunderstandings are set aside with the knowledge of equilibrium.

The straight rays are action while the wavy rays represent vibration. The sunflowers in the background represent life and the fruitfulness of the spirit under the nourishment of the Sun. There are four sunflowers, representing the four suits of the Minor Arcana, as well as the four elements. The astrological correspondence to this card is the Sun, which rules Leo and governs the heart. It is exhaled in Aries in its highest form.

Life-giving, trust, fun, warmth, success, positivity, and vitality are the key words. Reversed: Temporary depression, and the lack of success.

20—JUDGEMENT

Key 20 represents the sixth stage of spiritual unfoldment which is when the personal consciousness is just on the verge of blending with the universal. Here the adept realizes that his personality of has nothing to do his physical achievements but is a manifestation of the self-consciousness and subconsciousness. The adept learns that the concept of personal separateness is an illusion and that he is part of the whole, the universe. An aspect of deity itself.

Shin, the Hebrew letter assigned to Key 20 is the last of the Mother Letters. It is formed by three tongues of fire rising from the fiery base. The sound of the letter Shin is 'shi' thus corresponding to the sound of the occult saying: "BE SILENT".

The Judgement card shows a number of naked men, women and children (not shown in this version) rising up from their graves, arms outspread and responding to the trumpet call of the archangel, Gabriel, who hovers high above them as the Moon and is the archangel of the Moon. Clouds surround the angel because the true nature of the self is veiled by appearances. The people are appealing to the angel, ready to be judged by the power of the Universe. They face inward to represent insight, the turning of the mind away from false reports of external sensations. In the background, there are huge mountains, or even tidal waves, which signify insurmountable obstacles and the impossibility of avoiding judgment. The ocean represents the end of the river that flows through the Major Arcana, starting with the High Priestess. Gabriel's banner is red on white, the same as the Magician's clothing. As with everything in life, the beginning is woven irrevocably into the end and the end eventually leads to a new beginning. The planetary ruler of this card is Pluto, the ruler of the underworld.

Key words: Judgement, rebirth, inner calling, evaluation, questions, and absolution. Reversed: Self-doubt, and refusal of self-examination.

21—THE WORLD

Key 21 is the final Key and represents the seventh stage of spiritual unfoldment, which is traditionally shown with the "dancer". She is the representative of the universal dance of Life. When the Adept turns inward, the innermost, center Self is the Eternal Dancer. This is the dance of true equilibrium for she is floating in a perpetual dance of life. The letter Tav is assigned to this card, which means "signature or mark". It is similar to the Egyptian letter Tau which is what they used to tally the depth of the Nile. This in itself may hold many deeper meanings that should be explored.

The World suggest "world-consciousness". It is the whole universe as the body of the I AM. When the Adept reaches this level they discover that the center of life and power at the heart of one's self is the same one Power which rules the universe of creation. It is the final path on the Tree of Life yet is the end and the beginning.

When viewing Key 21 the dancing figure is the center of the card. She dances in rejoicing for the completion of the journey and celebrating not only this completion but also the new beginnings it promises. The dancer has one leg crossed over the other, just like the Hanged man. She is, in a sense, his opposite, just as the Hanged Man, but in an upright position. As the Hanged Man looks infinitely inward, the dancer in the World card looks infinitely outward. Upon close inspection the dancer appears to be feminine but with legs that are masculine. She is shown as the World Dancer, i the Celestial Androgyne. In each of her hands she holds a wand or baton, representative of evolution and balance. The one in her right hand turns toward the right while the left one turns towards the left-perfect balance is met. She is surrounded by a thick, green wreath, symbolic of success, victory, achievement and accomplishment, and tied with the red ribbons of eternity. The red ribbons form the infinity symbol, representing the infinite rewards of positive effort in improving both ourselves and those around us. Within the laurel wreath are stars of light indicating attainment of enlightenment or cosmic consciousness.

The figures in each of the four corners of the World card are the same figures that appear on the Wheel of Fortune. Interestingly, the World card is very much associated with the Wheel of Fortune, reflecting the cyclical progression of time and the human experience. The four figures; a lion, bull, cherub and eagle, represent the four fixed signs of the zodiac—Leo, Taurus, Aquarius and Scorpio. These are symbolic of the four elements, four suits of the Tarot, four compass points, four seasons, and the four corners of the universe. And all are within the dancer's sight and power. The planetary ruler is Saturn, the symbol of time.

Destination, Completion, integration, balance, accomplishment, travel and wholeness are the key words. Reversed: Lack of completion, and the lack of closure.

THE MINOR ARCANA

The Minor Arcana consists of four suits: they are Cups, Pentacles, Swords and Wands. Originally the older Tarot Decks' Minor Arcana were quite simple. The Three of Cups actually only showed three cups. It was Pamela Coleman Smith, under the direction of A. E. Waite, who created the 56 suit cards which are part of the total 78 allegorical cards seen today. Each suit corresponds with a different element of life. There are fourteen cards in each suit including Ace through Ten and four Court Cards, the Page, Knight, Queen and King. These titles both of suits and cards often vary according to which deck the student uses. In the traditional deck the Suit of Cups relates to the element of Water and is representative of emotions, relationships, feelings and creativity. The Suit of Pentacles relates to the element of Earth and is representative of money, financial resources, material possessions, career and the physical realm. The Suit of Swords relates to the element of Air and is representative of power, rationality, the intellect, and thoughts. And finally the Suit of Wands relates to the element of Fire and is representative of inspiration, spirituality, ideas and energy flow. The numerical values of the suit cards are important giving esoteric meaning and substance to the specific card.

THE COURT CARDS

There are four Court Cards are, the Page, Knight, Queen and King. MacGregor Mathers described the court cards as not lying on the paths or Sephiroth but next to the Sephiroth. He was suggesting they were extensions of the Sephiroth qualities. The Minor Arcana are believed to represent relatively mundane features of life. In divination the court cards represent the people we meet.

Even though traditionally the Court Cards were Pages, Knights, Queens and Kings, there were variations. Sometimes different decks represented the four court cards as Princess, Prince, Girl, Boy, Woman or Man.

THE PAGES

The Pages can be of either sex, but are generally portrayed as being young or of adolescent age. They are generally message bringers of some news or information. The information will vary depending on which Page is represented. Some show action, others show different directions that one's attention should attend. This is sometimes symbolized by which way the Page is moving or looking in relation to the foreground depicted.

Page of Wands

The Page of Wands appears to be represented by a well-dressed young man who wants to address the listener with some important news. This scene indicates that much of the Page's creative energy is still very much only a potential or, at best, only an idea. He holds his staff upwards ready to hit the ground with it to get someone's attention. He will look to it be filled with confidence. His shirt is covered with the design of salamanders, a mythical creature that is associated with fire and transformation.

Page of Cups

The Page of Cups, like the Pages in all the suits, represents some sort of beginning or renewal. He appears ready to congratulate someone for something well done. The Page of Cups is dressed in a blue tunic with floral print as sweet and light hearted as a Spring day. The young man appears to be raising his cup for a toast or a drink, and instead is confronted with the ominous appearance of a fish rising out of his cup. The fish seems to be speaking to him, the fish symbolizes an idea in the imagination of the person. The Page of Cups indicates the surprising and unexpected nature of inspiration that comes to us from the realm of the unconscious and the spirit. Inspiration is seen to be something which comes upon us most unexpectedly and often in a manner which we do not understand.

Page of Swords

The Page of Swords shows a young man standing in the midst of rough terrain on a windblown hilltop. He holds his sword in both hands. The sky is filled with turbulent clouds and the trees in the background are obviously wind-blown, as is the young man's hair. The waters behind the Page are rough and the general feeling of this card is one of tumultuous energy. This is a card that indicates an advance notice to be vigilant of pending changes.

Page of Pentacles

The Page of Pentacles shows a young man who stands alone in a field full of beautiful freshly blossoming flowers. Behind him in the distance to his right is a grove of lush trees, probably fruit-bearing trees of some sort, and to his left lies a newly furrowed field which promises an abundant harvest. Like all other Pages, the Page of Pentacles is a card of new beginnings, of inspiration and the initial stages of a creative project or venture. Pentacles correspond to the alchemical element of earth, and in this sense the coin that the Page holds may symbolize the beginnings of sensual awareness not only in terms of money and its value but also in terms of the importance of health and other material needs.

THE KNIGHTS

The Knights too are messengers similar to The Pages, but unlike The Pages their message is about a long term condition or life process that is about to change for good or ill. The position of the Knight's horse indicates the speed of the process.

The Knight of Wands

The Knight of Wands is seen riding upon his horse, which rears up in the intensity of the Knight's quest for success in career, finances and love life. The Knight's face bears the determination of one bound to succeed. He is in constant motion which could mean a great deal of generosity and passion or conflict and rivalry.

Knight of Cups

The Knight of Cups is seen as a young knight, riding along on his white horse, holding a cup as if he is a messenger of some type. He moves slowly and may indicate a change coming but slower than you would like. The horse represents power, energy, and drive, and of course the color white is a symbol of purity, spirituality, and light. The Knight wears a cloak covered with images of fish, the symbol of the spirit, consciousness and creativity. His helmet and feet are winged, a symbol of an active and creative imagination.

Knight of Swords

The Knight of Swords shows a young man whose adrenaline seems to be pumping and appears to be throwing caution to the wind. He is armored, riding a powerful white horse, his sword is flashing, and in the distance a battle is being waged. The white color of the horse symbolizes the purity of the intellectual energy that motivates the rider. The horse's harness is decorated with images of butterflies and birds and the knight's cape is also decorated with birds. He charges forward with great momentum and apparently without any regard to the dangers he may encounter.

Knight of Pentacles

The Knight of Pentacles sits upon a heavy plough horse in the midst of a field. He is making no effort to move. In his hands he carries a single gold coin. His eyes reflect careful thought and consideration. The Knight is engaged in the often toilsome, routine efforts required to realize the dreams of his heart. He is looking to the future and building the foundations to support his dreams and his goals.

Queens

The Queens generally represent women in the manifested world. They represent an actual situation or life experience versus that of The Pages who are represented as messengers in life.

Queen of Wands

The Queen sits upon her throne that is decorated with lions which are facing in opposing directions; they are symbols of fire and strength. In her left hand and behind her are sunflowers, symbolizing life, fertility, joy and satisfaction. In her right hand is a wand which is beginning to blossom with life. In these positive aspects, the Queen of Wands represents fidelity, warmth, and sustenance. However, at her feet is a black cat, a symbol of the intuition. Black cats are typically associated with magic and occultism. The cat expresses the independent nature of this Queen and her interest in occult powers and the energy of magic.

Queen of Cups

The Queen of Cups is the Queen of the realm of emotions. She also deals with the skill of predicting life cycles. She is a beautiful, introspective woman who sits on a throne at the edge of the sea. In her hands, she cradles a beautiful cup with handles shaped like angels. The cup is closed, an indication that the thoughts of the Queen originate from the unconscious, from the depths of her own soul. Wearing a gold crown and silver robe, she is alone, sitting and staring at this cup, which she holds before her with both hands on the base. Traditionally she is associated with a married woman with children and being a good mother.

Queen of Swords

The Queen of Swords sits high on her throne with a stern look on her face indicating that no-one can fool her. In her right hand, she comfortably holds a sword pointed to the sky, and her left hand extends as if she has something to offer to others. She is used to getting her own way especially in matters of great importance. Behind her is a spring sky, different from the winter settings on most other Swords cards, and this has an emergence and growth quality to it. The sky is clear, representing her clarity of mind as she considers matters of the intellect. The bird above her head symbolizes the mind's ability to soar above day-to-day issues in order to arrive at appropriate solutions.

Queen of Pentacles
The Queen of Pentacles depicts a dark and powerful woman who sits upon a throne decorated with carvings of fruit trees, goats, angels, and other symbols of material success and sensual pleasure. The tree above her and the ground beneath her feet are rich with flowers and ripe plants of all sorts and she holds in her hand a single golden pentacle, which represents her material richness. Her greatest fault is her slowness to act due to being overly thoughtful before deciding to act.

Kings
Similar to the Queens who represent the female component, the Kings represent the male or a masculine component in the Court Cards. They represent a situation where there is a male involved. Generally, he is older and could be worldlier in his demeanor.

King of Wands
The King of Wands is contemplating the horizon. His throne and cape are decorated with the lion and the salamander, symbols of fire and strength. Traditionally he is thought as being a content married man, happy in his situation. He can afford to be generous and passionate, but there is a current of fiery temper that could flash up even though his exterior appears calm.

King of Cups
The King of Cups sits on his throne on a grey stone block, which seems to float calmly in the midst of a turbulent sea, and wears a necklace with a fish amulet. The fish is the symbol of spirit and creativity and represents the balance of the unconscious with the conscious. Behind him on his right, another fish jumps wildly from the tumultuous ocean, and, on his left, a ship sails steadily in the choppy ocean. The chaos does not affect him. The King of Cups does not repress his emotions and unconscious impulses, but has learned to accept and deal with them in the mature and balanced manner expected of his station in life.

King of Swords

The King of Swords sits upon his throne of command, holding a large upward-pointing, double-edged sword in his right hand, while his left hand rests gently upon his lap. On his left finger is a ring representing Saturn, symbolic of power and taking his responsibilities seriously. The King is a man dull and emotionless. He wears a blue tunic, symbolic of a desire for spiritual understanding, and a purple cape, symbolic of compassion combined with intellect. The back of his throne is decorated with butterflies indicating a transformation, crescent moons and an angel just near his left ear, positioned as if to give him subtle guidance. The sky is relatively clear with a few clouds, representing general mental clarity. The trees in the background appear motionless and reflect the stern judgment of the King.

King of Pentacles

The King of Pentacles is a card of worldly success, ultimate fulfilment, material satisfaction, and high ambition. The King is traditionally thought as someone who is accomplished in math and banking skills in the material world of business. He appears very regal and sophisticated. At his feet and all around him are vines, flowers, and plants of all sorts, representing the highest attainment of material success. In his right hand, he holds the scepter of his power and in his left he holds a golden coin, symbolic of his material influence. Behind him is his castle, a symbol of all he has built through his efforts and determination. The King is proud of his financial success and the achievements brought by that success.

Numeral Cards of the Minor Arcana

The Minor Arcana have many interpretations depending on the school or/ and their creator's interpretation of that specific card. The accompanying texts gives a traditional interpretation as to what was used in the "older" Tarot Decks. The images accompanying each card represent just a few of the types of decks.

Aces

Most Aces, of which there is one for each suit, are very similar. They generally show a hand emerging from a cloud. The card represents the number "1" and thus indicates "a beginning or early stage". Aces can also indicate in what season this beginning will start. This is generally symbolically shown in the card, many times as an astrological sign. Other times the background scene indicates which season of the year.

Ace of Cups
The Ace of Cups shows a hand holding a cup or chalice that is overflowing with five streams of water. The hand that appears from the clouds represents our consciousness of spiritual energy and influence. Radiating from the hand are rays which symbolize that you must always trust your inner feelings and your heart to lead the way. This is your inner self talking to you. The five streams represent the abundance and power of the spirit and the effect of spiritual energy upon our five senses. A dove holding a wafer or small disc in its mouth descends from above, signifying the incarnation and appearance of the spirit in the material world. Below the hand is a great sea covered with lotus blossoms, symbolizing the awakening of the human spirit. The cup has an upside down M or a W inscribed on it.

Ace of Pentacles
Like all Aces the Ace of Pentacles depicts a single hand with a pentacle coming out of the clouds. The clouds represent "heaven" and represents the primary element of the suit. In the Ace of Pentacles, the landscape is a rich garden with flowers, shrubs, a flowing creek and mountains in the distance, indicating prosperity, growth and wealth.

Ace of Swords
The Ace of Swords shows a hand, cloaked in white, holding an upright sword, symbolic of the mind and the intellect. At the tip of the sword is a wreath, indicating success and victory, and a crown, indicating mental clarity. However, the barren, mountainous landscape below the sword reflects the often cold nature of intellect and that knowledge is nothing but barren facts unless wisdom is applied.

Ace of Wands
In the Ace of Wands, a hand reaches out from a cloud, as if a spiritual opportunity or offering is being made, to grasp a wand that is still flowering, growing and developing. The leaves floating down with the wind signify material and spiritual progress and balance. In the distance on the

left, there is a castle that represents the promise of what opportunities may come. This card often is related to future events.

THE TWOS

Twos generally indicate involvement with another person. It is a time of waiting until more is revealed. They also indicate duality, the pairing of opposites and creativity not yet fulfilled.

Two of Wands

The man in the Two of Wands is holding a small globe and stands on the roof of a castle, looking out over a vast terrain to the right and an ocean to the left. The globe in his hands represents that the world is his oyster and there is huge potential if he can expand his horizons to encompass broader life experiences. The Wands signify enterprise, energy and growth. He understands how his ambition must grow and knows what must be done.

Two of Cups

The Two of Cups depicts a man and a woman supposedly exchanging cups in what appears to be a wedding ceremony. This is an example of balance. On the Two of Cups, the caduceus sends a positive message for new partnerships, and suggests that with honor, respect and balance, new relationships shall be rewarding. The card is a symbol of passion and fire energy suggesting that there may be a lot of sexual attraction between the people, although that may or may not be allowed to express itself. It also suggests a balance between spiritual and earthly love with caduceus standing for life's positive and negative qualities.

Two of Swords

The Two of Swords depicts a blindfolded woman who holding two swords. She sits before a sea filled with rocks and crags that present obstacles to ships which need clear passage. The blindfold shows that the woman in this card is confused about her situation and that she can see neither the problem nor the solution clearly. This indicates a stalemate or trouble ahead. The crossed swords are also symbolic of the need for a truce and the Suit of Swords indicates that the problem at hand needs to be resolved using logic and intellect. The waxing moon to the right of the woman shows a new beginning arising out of the solutions found for this problem.

Two of Pentacles
On the Two of Pentacles, a young man dances as he juggles two proposals. The infinity sign loops around the two Pentacles suggesting that he can handle unlimited problems in a sea of emotions. In the background, two ships ride the waves easily, cruising the ups and downs of life. The man seems to have a somewhat concerned look on his face, yet he dances with apparent abandon despite the turbulence of the sea behind him.

THREES
Threes indicate action with a group. They also indicate that there will be success after some delays. This delay may require patience on the part of the individual. For to act too soon may result in adverse results.

Three of Wands
On the Three of Wands, a man stands on a cliff, with his back turned, looking out over the sea to distant mountains and the unseen ship that has come in. From this height, he can see all that lies ahead and is aware of the impending challenges and opportunities. The three Wands surrounding him are firmly planted in the ground, reflecting his commitment to his future plans, even though there can be delays.

Three of Cups
The Three of Cups is a card of celebration, a possible engagement, graduation or accomplishment. Three young maidens dance in a circle with their golden goblets upraised in a toast of joy. Their arms reach out to each other and they connect through their emotions and their friendship with one another. Each woman in the Three of Cups has a wreath of laurel on her head. Wreaths of this type have long been a symbol of victory and success. A sweet smelling laurel wreath is also a symbol of protection, peace and purification and is a message that the favor of the Universe is upon us, and that we shall be the victor in this stage of our lives. At the women's feet lie various flowers, symbolizing joy, beauty, compassion and growth. The flowers remind us of the good times in life, the sweet smell of success, and the beauty that surrounds us if only we open up to its presence.

Three of Swords
The Three of Swords is a simply illustrated and graphic card with a difficult message. A heart, suspended in the air, is pierced by three swords. The heart is symbolic of emotion and beauty, while the piercing swords reflect the ability of logic and power to harm the physical body and the emotions of a person. The sky is heavily clouded and rain pours down violently, representing a grim moment in time.

Three of Pentacles
The Three of Pentacles shows a young apprentice working in a cathedral. In front of him stand two architects who are holding the plans for the cathedral. The apprentice appears to be discussing his progress so far with two architects and even though he is less experienced, the architects listen carefully as they value his opinion and his specialist knowledge. There is also an acknowledgement that this young man is an essential contributor to the completion of the cathedral and the architects want to make sure that everyone is on the same page.

FOURS
Fours indicate growth and fruition of ideas. It is setting the boundaires for ideas to clarify themselves and to allow them to be manifested in the physical world.

Four of Wands
In the Four of Wands, a couple dances beneath a welcome wreath, tied between four crystal tipped wands. The canopy of flowers on the four wands is also similar to the wedding canopy of the traditional Jewish ceremony and thus represents a time of fulfilment and satisfaction at the attainment of a goal. It is a card showing public relationships, skills and working with others. In the background stand another group of people, just in front of a large castle, also decorated in flowers. It appears as if a celebration is being held, perhaps as a homecoming or a celebration from within the castle. The four shows solidarity, prosperity, peace, abundance and happiness.

Four of Cups
The Four of Cups depicts a young man sitting under a tree lost in his own thoughts. He sits far away from others in what looks like deep contemplation

and meditation. In fact, he is so engrossed in deep contemplation that he does not appear to notice the cup being presented to him by an outstretched arm. A further three cups stand at his feet, symbolizing the world and its attractions but again, he pays little attention to these. In this sense, he indicates the need to look deep into our Self to discover the answers we seek. External influences can be distracting and may not lead us to the goal we seek even if those influences purport to be of a spiritual nature.

Four of Swords

The Four of Swords depicts the effigy of a knight lying upon a tomb but is not a card of death. The 4 of Swords suggests it is a time of retreat, or a sense of exile or a short-time banishment. The stained glass behind the statue depicts a woman and child together. One sword lies beneath the knight, symbolizing that there is only one key issue that is dominating your life at this time. Three further swords hang above him, pointing downwards.

Four of Pentacles

The Four of Pentacles shows a man tightly holding onto his pentacles or coins in a very defensive posture as though he were hoarding them for fear of loss. One pentacle is balanced on his head, one clutched between his hands, and two are securely placed underneath his feet. He is making sure that no-one touches his coins! And, he cannot go anywhere because his feet are busy holding the coins down. In other words, this man is so tied up with his possessions, that he cannot do anything else. Despite the fact the number 4 expresses solidarity and strength of purpose, there are indications of a lack of willingness to share.

Fives

Fives indicate change and fluctuation. They indicate material prosperity but with material prosperity comes spiritual poverty bringing a feeling of unbalance.

Five of Wands

In the Five of Wands, five men wave around their wands chaotically without any regard for each other and appear to be in direct competition with each other and engaged in conflict. This card is about strong competition. However, on closer observation, their wands are only raised and are not striking anyone. It is possible that they are actually enjoying themselves in this chaos with no real intent to harm anyone. The men wear different colored clothes to symbolize the various backgrounds and belief systems that are held by the world's populations.

Five of Cups

The Five of Cups is a card that signifies difficulty, loss, and the challenges of dealing with that loss. The figure in the card wears a black cloak in which he hides his face in apparent despair. At his feet are five cups, three of which have fallen and spilled onto the ground and the other two behind his back remain standing. He does not seem to notice these upstanding cups because he is so focused on the fallen cups instead. The two cups behind him untouched are full of promise. Ahead of him a powerful river flows between himself and a castle or home in the distance. To his right is a bridge that can lead him to the security of the house across the river. Despite the fact that this card has a strong indication of loss and tribulation, there is a positive aspect that must be considered. When things are bleak there is always promise of the positive.

Five of Swords

In the Five of Swords, a young man, with a look of contempt on his face, stares at his conquered enemies. He possesses five swords, most of which he has taken from the other people in the card. The other two figures retreat unhappily in distance, with a sense of sadness and loss. The sky is cloudy and tumultuous, indicating that not all is well despite the battle being seemingly over.

Five of Pentacles

The Five of Pentacles, like the fives in the other suits, portrays a situation of adversity. In this card, a destitute couple walk through the snow outside the stained glass of a brightly lit church window. The church is symbolic of providing spiritual comfort while helping those who cannot help themselves. The man uses a crutch because of his crippled leg and the woman attempts to cover herself with her threadbare shawl. Both appear to be living in poverty and with little or no possessions. This is a card about feeling destitute, lonely, and abandoned.

SIXES

Sixes indicate an adjustment in thoughts and attitudes. They also represent the ability to transcend difficulties. Sixes are balance and equilibrium. They are symbols of the middle path and often indicate a preferred path.

Six of Wands

The Six of Wands depicts a man wearing a victory wreath around his head, riding a white horse through a crowd of cheering people celebrating his achievement or leadership qualities. The white horse represents strength, purity, and the success of an adventure. The wand held by the rider also has a wreath tied to it, further emphasizing success and achievement. He is not afraid to show off to others what he has accomplished in his life so far, and even better, the people around him cheer him along.

Six of Cups

On the Six of Cups, there are six cups filled with white, five-pointed flowers. A young boy seems to smell one flower, offering this filled cup to another young child. The one child symbolizes the past and the other child symbolizes the future, and together they symbolize happy reunions with past friends or lovers. They share old pleasures with lots of nostalgia. In the background, there is an older figure walking away, symbolizing our worries leaving us to be locked in the turret. The house symbolizes comfort and security but the barren garden symbolizes the lost happier times of the past. Everything is bright yellow which indicates great happiness in this overall scene.

Six of Swords

The Six of Swords depicts a woman and a young child being rowed across a body of water towards a land that lies not too far ahead. The woman's head is covered, indicating sadness or loss as she moves away from something in her past. The water to the right of the boat is turbulent but the water to the left and near the land to which they are journeying is calm and steady. Although there is an indication of change or loss in the Six of Swords, and therefore a sense of moving away from something, there is also a sense of moving towards a more promising future. The sense that when the feeling of defeat occurs it might be best to run from the situation. The calm waters in the distance suggest that the woman and child are now moving away from turmoil and conflict toward peace and tranquility, even though they are both sad to leave behind their pasts. In the boat are six upright swords, symbolizing the power of a rational mind over the heart and the intuition.

Six of Pentacles

The Six of Pentacles presents an interesting situation—it shows a man dressed in a purple robe, symbolic of his wealth and status. In one hand, he holds a balanced scale, representing fairness and equality, and with the other hand, he feeds two beggars who kneel at his feet. Not only does this card reflect the state of being materially secure, it also suggests that you are able to use the abundance in your life for the benefit of others. The wealthy man shares his abundance so that stability is preserved.

SEVENS

Sevens denote a time of introspection and/or solitude. It is a time of developing the inner self through thought and meditation. It is a time of reflection. A time of slowing down to evaluate what is happening and what may happen if the individual contiues pushing forth without considering the consequences of their actions.

Seven of Wands

In the Seven of Wands, a man stands on top of a hill and is challenged below by opponents; he is protecting what he has. The man appears to be in a defensive position, fiercely retaliating against those who attack him and defending his higher position. This is done with energy and courage.

Seven of Cups

The Seven of Cups depicts an individual faced with the mysterious appearance of strange images from cups in a floating cloud. Clouds conjure ideas, dreams, thoughts, illusions, transitions and mystery. It makes the individual's head fill with hopes and desires. The various prizes appearing from the cups are a mixture of positive and negative visions. In some keys the cups each have a single item rising from them like a snake, representing wisdom and knowledge; a shrouded figure, representing the need for illumination; a human head, representing a companion for the conjurer; a tower, representing stability and power; treasure, representing abundance and wealth; a laurel wreath, representing victory or honor, and status; and a dragon, representing supernatural forces. In the Crowley and Waite decks the cups are empty. The seven of cups appear as gifts or prizes, many options, but are the choices real options at all or are they delusions of the imagination? This card hints of errors, illusion and illusionary success.

Seven of Swords
The Seven of Swords shows a man with a bundle of five swords in his arms. Two other swords remain planted in the ground just behind him. His expression exhibits a sense of over-confidence and mocking, as though he felt absolutely sure of his success in his ability to balance all the swords. This is a scene of potential unbalance and instability, not just the physical type but of the personality as well.

Seven of Pentacles
The Seven of Pentacles portrays a farmer taking a rest from the difficult work of harvesting his abundant crop. He has been laboring long and hard in his garden hoping for the successful crop. The foliage is full and the blossoms are out. It seems that his work has paid off. He gazes meditatively at the pentacles hanging from the rich greenery of the thicket in which he works and seems to be contemplating the value of his efforts. He is finally taking a break to admire his handiwork and the benefits of his labor. It is a time of reevaluation of his labors.

Eights
Eights represent changes to a more positive mind or status. Eight is a number of justice, judgement, material progress and good health.

Eight of Wands
The Eight of Wands shows eight blossoming wands hurtling through the air at a great pace. The flight of the wands can suggest change, new ideas, goals, careers, and travel. The background is clear, indicating that there is now little that stands in your way, and there is a beautiful river flowing freely and giving life to the landscape around it.

Eight of Cups
The Eight of Cups is a card of change and transition. The card evokes an immediate reaction of sadness and a sense of solitude. The figure in this card has turned his back on all he has accumulated or accomplished before. He is

walking away as though he wants to start over. He disappears by night into a barren and difficult terrain with only a cloak on his back and a staff in hand. The character in the Eight of Cups has lived and experienced life's joys and sorrows, finding what he thought was success only to find he is unfulfilled and empty inside. This individual has chosen to forsake the familiar and the comfortable in the pursuit of higher goals. He is embarking upon the spiritual journey because he has not found deep satisfaction in the things of the world, the things with which he is familiar.

Eight of Swords

The Eight of Swords shows a woman tied up, blindfolded, and surrounded by swords that act as a kind of prison or enclosure. It appears that there is no possibility of escape. She appears to being censured and restricted by her personal indecision. She appears isolated and alone as she stands in the midst of a barren, watery wasteland far from the town in the distance. The sky is grey and cloudy, indicating despair and a lack of hope. The woman's feet do not touch the water, indicating that the feeling of being restricted in the Eight of Swords is based on an intellectual assessment of the situation and not an emotional one. There is a path cleared before her, so there is actually a way out of this situation but her lack of true action may prevent her from seeing the correct path.

Eight of Pentacles

The Eight of Pentacles shows a young man laboring over eight coins, carefully etching out a pentacle shape into each coin. He has already successfully completed six coins, and has two more to go. This card reflects a time when you are focusing all of your energy on something and making sure it is as perfect as it can be. You are very engaged in what you are doing and determined to do a good job. It is time of small financial gains due to the continual effort of the project or job done.

NINES

Nines generally show a very great fundamental force such as executive force. It maintains its strength because it is on a firm base. The great force can be for good or evil. This is often hinted by two factors. The first factor is how the card appears when dealtf, this is what is called the "lay" or sequence of cards being revealed. The second is in what position the card appears, is it right side up or reversed.

Nine of Wands

The Nine of Wands shows a weary, injured man who holds a staff as though in a posture of final defense. He has fought the battle and won. He is protected by a number of wands behind him that appear like a wall around him. He appears drained and exhausted as he leans on his wand but he is ready to go to battle again for he is concerned with the welfare of others. He stands up for what he believes in and holds firm in those beliefs. The card indicates a return to health but the person must stand up for himself as well.

Nine of Cups

Traditionally shows a robust well-dressed man in front of nine cups. He wears an expression of true satisfaction on his face and his red head-dress symbolizes an active mind. Behind him is a wall with nine golden cups arranged in a structured, well-organized arch. The man enjoys success both materially and spiritually and represents that fulfilment realized.

Nine of Swords

The Nine of Swords shows a woman with her head in her hands, as though having a bad dream and sitting up in her bed. She appears to have just woken and is obviously upset, fearful and anxious following her dream. Nine swords hang on the wall behind her and the base of the bed is decorated with a carving of a duel in which one person is being defeated by another. The quilt covering the woman is decorated with roses and the outlines of astrological symbols.

Nine of Pentacles

The Nine of Pentacles shows a mature woman walking in the midst of a vineyard. The vines are heavy with grapes and golden coins representing the improvements she has made to her environment. A hooded falcon sits calmly on her gloved hand. There is a general sense of peace, satisfaction, and the fulfilment of a creative venture or personal investment. It could also mean that a possible inheritance could occur.

TENS

Tens generally show as a fixed, culminated, fixed Forces, which could be bad or good. It depends on how the activity is activated.

Ten of Wands

The Ten of Wands shows a man carrying a very heavy bundle of wands or sticks. He appears to be over-burdened with the weight, yet he knows he is not far away from the town he is walking towards. This card appears to indicate someone who is an overachiever, always taking on more than should be taken on by a single person.

Ten of Cups

The Ten of Cups and Ten of Pentacles are almost interchangeable. This card shows a loving couple united by the bonds of true, everlasting love. They not only have each other but all that they wish for in life as well, represented by the two children frolicking at their side and the small but comfortable home in the distance, surrounded by trees and water. A special moment is being shared. The symbols show a stability in the home, garden and the shared love of the individuals. A rainbow of cups is overhead, blessing the scene. The cups symbolize an abundance of heavenly gifts and the rainbow signifies the end of hard times and is also is considered to be a highly spiritual omen in many of the world's religions. It is a sign that the idyllic scene we see represented has been blessed from above and reinforces the idea that the achievement of perfect love is one sure way of experiencing the glory of the heavens here on earth.

Ten of Swords

The Ten of Swords shows a man lying face down with ten long swords embedded in his back. Swords are the symbol of what ultimate strife, hatred, and aggression can do. A red cape is draped over the lower half of his body, while his top half remains unclothed. The sky above him is pitch black and there is a general feeling of pain, loss, and misfortune. However, despite these ominous images, there are positive aspects to this card. The sea before which the body lies is still and calm and the sun is rising in the distance beyond the mountains, indicating that the darkness will soon be dispelled. Thus, each new beginning must come from an end, and with every defeat are sown the seeds of future victory.

Ten of Pentacles

The Ten of Pentacles is a card of culmination and final fulfilment. The card shows an aged, wise man sitting comfortably just outside an archway leading into a town. He is surrounded by his family and his dogs and wears a rich robe decorated with images of grapevines, crescent moons, and other symbols, all symbols of what he and his family have obtained. Behind the laughing couple under the arch, a young boy reaches playfully to pet one of the dogs. This card is a symbol of financial security, accomplishment, and comfort. This is a man who has accomplished a great deal during his life and is now finally able to rest in the satisfaction of knowing that what he has created will provide value and joy to others, even when he is gone.

The lesser or Minor Arcana are important in the use of the Tarot; it is a means of gaining additional knowledge on the path to personal enlightenment. By meditating on them they can open new doors to the inner self. In divination they are the adjectives and amplifiers in the process of divination.

THE MATURING OF THE TAROT

The concept and development of Tarot decks is not stagnant. It is a thriving activity where individuals are developing new or improved forms of existing decks. Tarot decks represent the symbols that are most pertinent to the time of their conception. Yes, there are some symbols that do transcend time such as the moon, images of death as a skeleton or fertility a sheaf of wheat. But as our world changes so do the symbols that are important to individual cultures, spiritual beliefs or mystical interpretations. Thus there are always "new and better" decks appearing.

Sometimes these decks attempt to relate to a concept of "older times". They try to attract significance to them by including ancient symbols from Egyptian, Druids or symbols from medieval legends. It is often stated or hoped these 'older pagan' symbols will wake what lays dormant in our subconsciousness.

Other times there are students of past masters of schools such as Aleister Crowley, A. E. Waite or Paul Foster Case, who feel they have found some symbol that was misused on these masters' work. In these cases, they modify these decks in attempt to clarify what is perceived as an error or forgotten symbol to improve their deck. Many of these decks never are seen commercially and are only used by the individual or a close-knit group of similar students.

As the number of decks increase the student needs to take care in choosing the one whose symbols and imagery best speak to them. For the Tarot deck is a tool for enlightenment and one needs the best tool for each one's work.

XII.

TREE OF KNOWLEDGE OF GOOD AND BAD

Now the Lord God had planted a garden in the east, in Eden; and there he put the man he had formed. The Lord God made all kinds of trees grow out of the ground—trees that were pleasing to the eye and good for food. In the middle of the garden were the tree of life and the tree of the knowledge of good and evil.

GENESIS 2:8-9

As in all dealing with the *Bible* there are those who question any given translation, especially the non-Latin based languages including the Hebrew translations. There is various version of 'Hebrew' translations due to the fact that ancient Hebrew only used consonants, with no vowels. It was primarily a verbal alphabet. Because there were only consonants, there were often words spelled using the same consonants. Since Hebrew is a verbal language there is a great need for the information written in Hebrew to also have a keeper of that information. This keeper or keepers literately memorize what the phrase means, often depending on the Hebrew letters to act as a cypher for what it means. Like any memory work, if one word is forgotten or mispronounced, whole meanings or translations can change.

In addition, Hebrew words can have many meaning such as the word *ra'* (Hebrew רַע) which has a male and female translation according to pronunciation. The female form could mean *bad, disagreeable, or malignant,* and in the male *bad, unpleasant, giving pain, unhappiness, misery: evil days (of trial and hardship).* Other translators say *ra'* is translated as *evil* but a more precise translation would be *dysfunctional.* The most common translation currently is "evil" but the use of "bad" is very common as well. Because of this one will often find a "wise" or "elder" nearby whenever any Hebrew text, such as the *Torah,* is read. He is there to assure the proper pronunciation, correct word, is verbalized.

Because of the variety of translations there has developed a great deal of debate as to what any one passage means. Since the writing of the *Pentateuch,* scholars have applied numerous interpretations to as what the "Tree of the Knowledge of Good and Evil" meant.

Most Biblical scholars agree this is not the origin of the tale of the Garden of Eden or the two Trees. There are many variations of this idyllic beginning of mankind throughout ancient cultures. Additional ones are becoming known as archeologists and anthropologist decipher additional ancient languages. Edward Waite, a British poet, occultist, writer of scholarly mystic, discussed the Trees mentioned in *The Book of Genesis,* in his book *The Holy Kabbalah,* published in 1929. Waite describes in one of stories concerning a creation myth. He writes about a time of 'pre-existence' of the earth when there was a revolt in Heaven of "many spirits" who planned to descend on the earth and take possession of it. God placed these spirits into two categories: the good He placed on the side of the Tree of Life and the evil on that of the Tree of "mixed knowledge".

This was a very simplified version of what Isaac Luria (1534–1572) stated when he described his World of Tohu or Chaos. According to Luria, there was a cosmic catastrophe in the Divine realm. At the time of creation, the Divine light poured into the first Sefirah, then downward to fill all the nine Sephirot below. All the Sephirot, or vessels, were close enough to the source of the Divine Light to contain the abundance of vitality. But due to the infinite amount of Divine Light pouring into a finite vessel the Divine light overflowed the boundary of the individual Sephiroth resulting in them being shattered. These Sephirot, which Luria called the Shevirat Ha-Keilm or "Shattering of the Vessels" consisted of the third Sefirah, *Binah* down through the other Sephirot to the ninth Sefirah, *Yesod.* The coarser fragments from the shattering fell down into our material realm. It is these Kelipot (shells) that fell into the material realm and were allowed to stay as impure energy fragments and were nurtured, allowing for troublesome spirits to exist. Luria thus gave us a view of creation in which everything did not evolve smoothly and orderly, but in chaos and shadows. This was not the first time the creation myth appeared describing trouble at the time of creation. The creation myths of the Canaanites, Persians and even Greeks, to name a few, had tales of the creation process occurring under chaotic and destructive influences.

THE BEGINNING OF THE CONCEPT OF GOOD AND BAD

Luria's works were an attempt to explain an issue that has been with mankind from the beginning of time. That is how to explain the break in what was thought to be normal and/or routine in nature. It is believed that when some disaster or abnormality occurred primitive man reacted to it in awe or fear. This is based on the same reactions modern man has to the disasters or strange events that occur today.

Archeologists, anthropologists and other scholars have surmised that the introduction of shamans, both female and male, came about as an attempt to interpret these abnormalities and to provide an answer to these strange occurrences. And like today, an explanation was generally not enough and an action to prevent it from reoccurring was demanded. In ancient times it was thought that some supernatural being had caused the problem and they would need to appease whatever was causing the disturbance to what was thought to be normal. "For humankind tend to psychologize' wrong doing, to find some (extrinsic) reason for it, but they refrain from psychologizing good deeds."[23]

For early humanoids, these chaotic phenomena could have been anything from assuring. Anything that would have interfered with a successful hunt, an easy birth, illness, or acts of nature such as lightning, storms and earthquakes would cause a great deal of stress in a world already full of the unkown. Since these disturbances were believed by anthropologists, to be viewed by these early humans as acts that were not part of the norm, the

---

23 *Tree of Life, Tree of Knowledge*, Michael Rosenak, Westview Press, 2001, pg. 141

peoples tried to understand what was causing these bursts of seemingly random chaos. One way of doing this was to personify the act, thus giving it a nature that could be understood. This personification often took the form of viewing the act as a spirit, and usually took on an animal or human form. With this personification they then could understand the spirit in human characteristics, such as the spirit being angry or troublesome. In time, those who became shamans, were the links to appeasing these spirits, and thus hopefully safeguarding the clan or individual. This provided a very important function in helping the individuals to cope with the unknown. It gave the individual, family or clan a means to understand the mysteries around them and place them into a perspective as it pertained to their world. In other words, it helped them to understand that there were things in their world that would hurt or disturb them. This in turn often led to these events as being labeled "bad or evil". And these "bad or evil" spirits were part of the greater scheme of life and they would have to accept them.

As time progressed names were attached to these various malevolent forces. In the British Isles they were called Gremlins, in China these disruptive spirits were believed to be dragons, and the Greeks had the harpies sent from Zeus. In Persia they had the "peri" or fairies, in the Middle East they had the Jinn, Djin or Jinnees. In the Muslim world they had tales of what they called "bad angels". Elsewhere throughout the western world there are myths and tales about the Kelpei, trolls, imps, nymph, sylph, undines and kobold. With each culture and time period in history, uniquely regional characters developed, each with their own specific names. An example is the Egyptian gods and goddess; there is Apopis (a maleficent serpent), Baal, and the goddess Sakhmet. The ancient civilizations of the Middle East associated the known planets with gods and goddesses; Venus-Ishtar, Jupiter-Marduk, Mars-Nergal, Mercury-Nabu and Saturn with Ninurta. The ancient Hebrew tribes had their Shedim-demons and se'irim or śa'ir–goat-demons. In addition, there were literally hundreds of major and minor household spirits. These household spirit, each developed their own personification. They were blamed or thought to cause potential harm if not appeased or honored. To do this individual families and cultures built altars, shrines, and temples. Prayers, amulets and gestures were invented as a means of protecting themselves and their world from the harm these spirits may cause.

It is speculated by anthropologists, that as these spirits, gods and goddesses developed as a whole sub-culture of individuals whose job was to help appease or "serve" these spirits as emissaries. These "servants to the spirits" developed their own personification adding to their stature as having special powers or connections to these spirits. They began to assign "holy sites" that were associated with specific spirits. As this happened, it is theorized priestess/priest orders attached themselves to these holy sites and or temples. With this perceived "power" which the common people gave them, as the "official" emissary to specific spirits, came the opportunity to misuse the trust they had been given by their fellow countrymen. Both individuals as well as various monarchs sought out these emissaries who seek out the wrath of a particular spirit towards an enemy. This enemy could be a 'husband stealing women', someone who owed you money or even an entire village or empire. Of course the sequence of the development is only a theory based on myths, tales, and interpretations of archeological sites.

As the belief in the world of deities, from major gods and goddesses, to Jinns, Gremlins, household "peri" to the "goddesses of birth", and the "reaper of the dead" became more entrenched the fabric of societies, so did the esoteric understanding and 'connection to' these spirits develop into cults and sects. Myths and stories were told about these spirits and their place in the universe and relationship to men and women, both young and old. It is not known which came first, the realization of "malevolent" forces, or their counter forces, those that protected the home, the traveler, and sailor, to name a few. What is known archeologically is a whole industry developed that took the form of small household shrines, amulets, rings and in larger urban centers' temples. Many of these small shrines, many with votive burners, even some with small shells and stones or even teraphim, Hebrew for idols, or household god(s), have been found on or near the entrance to the homes. To this day this custom of home altars is carried out in many parts of both the agricultural societies as well as in modern urban centers throughout the world.

The lives and habits of these spirits, gods and goddess often paralleled the individual culture they presided over. Their mystical lives were often woven into to the individual culture's myths of creation. The Babylonian or Mesopotamian myth of creation is typical of this incorporation of the struggle between the deities that caused chaos in the universe, and those that worked to maintain order in the cosmos and in nature. The Enûma Elisš or Enuma Elish is a Babylonian creation myth written on seven clay tablets around 1100 B.C.E. It describes this seasonal struggle between order and chaos. This epic told about Marduk, a god from ancient Mesopotamia and patron deity of the city of Babylon, and his struggle to become the chief god of the Babylonian people.

The seven clay tablets were found in the middle 19th century in the ruins of the palace of Ashurbanipal in Nineveh, northern Iraq. George Smith (1840–1876), was a pioneering English Assyriologist who first discovered and translated another famous flood myth called the *Epic of Gilgamesh*, one of the oldest-known written works of literature. George Smith first published these texts in 1876 in his book *The Chaldean Genesis*. Smith is credited for discovering this pre-biblical account of the flood in 1872. The tale parallels very closely to the later Biblical accounts in *The Book of Genesis*, causing some historians to conclude that the *Genesis* account was simply a rewriting of the earlier Babylonian story. There are many who disagree with this theory, saying the Biblical *Genesis* is unique in itself. But close study has revealed that there are too many similarities to deny any relationship between the two accounts. Scholars believe the Sumerian versions of the story predate the biblical account by several hundred years. Many biblical scholars believe that the Babylonian version may have been heard by the Jewish population and incorporated into the Hebrew mythos during their three exiles, 597 B.C.E., 587 B.C.E., and 582 B.C.E.

As the ancient story tellers and rabbis developed their culture's creation myth, they seem to have been influenced by those peoples whom they lived among. They surely would have heard their creation myths, relating to the struggle between good and chaos. According to rabbinic tradition, the *Torah*, of which Genesis is the first book, was given by God to Moses on Mount Sinai. According to a Midrash, or Jewish commentary, the *Torah* was created prior to the creation of the world and was the blueprint for the world's creation. According to the majority of Biblical scholars, the *Torah* as the *Pentateuch* was written while the Jews were in exile in Babylon around 600 B.C.E. and completed sometime around 400 B.C.E.

GENESIS

In the traditional account in *Book of Genesis* there are actually two versions of man's creation. Scholars attribute this to the probability of there having been several authors whose works were later combined into a single work. In the first part, *Genesis* 1:1 through *Genesis* 2:3, *Elohim*, the Hebrew generic word for God, creates the world in six days, starting with light and darkness on the first day, and ending with the creation of mankind on the sixth day. God then rests on, blesses, and sanctifies the seventh day.

In the second creation story, in *Book of Genesis* 2:4-24, it describes God, who is now referred to by the personal name of "*Yahweh*", creating the first man from dust and breathing a soul into him. God then places him in the Garden of Eden and creates the first woman from his rib as a companion.

It is believed the authorship of the *Book of Genesis* occurred sometime between 1440 B.C.E. and 1400 B.C.E. Traditionally, the author has always assumed to have been Moses. There is no conclusive evidence of this but it is believed Genesis was authored between the time Moses led the Israelites out of Egypt, and his death around 1273 B.C.E.

It is believed that this was about the same time that the concept of two trees in the Garden of Eden was developed. In Leon Kass's *The Beginning of Wisdom,* he discusses the *Tree of Life.* Kass' position was the Tree of Life originally offered deathlessness, but since man was not capable of the fear of death it was of little concern to him. He goes on to say the *Tree of Knowledge of Good and Bad* is the knowledge that comes with free choice. "As everyone knows, the human being indeed chose to disobey, never mind why. He (they) chose therewith the *principle of disobedience.*"[24] And to the leaders/Rabbis of a people who were trying to hold their people's identity together, this was especially important after the Jewish people had the center of their world destroyed, that being their great Temple in Jerusalem. And then being exiled to strange lands and customs, this was something that they believed could not be tolerated if the people were to remain as a people. Thus the concepts of "obedience" versus "disobedience" needed to be emphasized. For during this time one of the major concerns was the Jewish leaders maintaining the integrity of their people while facing the pressure of intermarriage with the local people.

The *Torah* was a means to preserve the cohesion of the Jewish people by outlining what and how the individual should behave from daily ritual to dietary practices. The leaders were aware there were many temptations in these strange lands. They saw the influence of the exotic customs both moral and religious, and how the pull to become part of the greater communities temped the refugees. The Jewish leaders believed they needed to keep their tribe's beliefs in place for the time of return to their Promised

---

24 *The Beginning of Wisdom,* Leon R Kass, Free Press, 2003, p. 65

Land. To do this they believed that their charges needed strong leadership and guidance, to keep them on the right path. In order to preserve their cultural and religious identities it appears they developed a series of myths/ stories to emphasize how the danger of the "Satan" was a continued threat to their spiritual welfare. In Judaism "Satan" is not a sentient being but a metaphor for an evil inclination — the *yetzer hara* (evil incarnation) — that exists in every person and tempts us to do wrong.

> It is believed that out of these cultural pressures the concept of a least two Trees in the Garden of Eden developed. Out of the ground the Lord God caused to grow every tree that is pleasing to the sight and good for food; the tree of life was in the midst of the garden, and the tree of the knowledge of good and evil.
>
> GENESIS 2:9

In the *Book of Isaiah*, which was believed to be written between 701 and 681 B.C.E., another concept of evil was discussed. In *Isaiah* 45:7:

> I form the light, and create darkness; I make peace, and create evil;
> I am the Lord, that doeth all these things.

According to Gershom Scholem, by this time evil has become part of life and is accepted as being the creation of the Divine. The concept of laying the responsibility of evil on the Lord goes back even farther to Solomon's time around 900 B.C.E. where in *Proverbs* 16:4 it says:

> The Lord hath made every thing for His own purpose. Yea, even the wicked for the day of evil

Scholem goes on to say this the oldest answer to the question of the origin of evil. It owes its origins to God's creation and activity.[25] Thus the idea of evil had moved from trying to explain the unusual to that of being part of the Divine's plan. It became not an abnormal act of nature but part of the natural order of life itself and needed to be explained and understood in that context.

---

25 *On the Mystical Shape of the Godhead*, Gershom Scholem, Schocken Books, 1991, pg. 57

THE TREE OF KNOWLEDGE OF GOOD AND EVIL

Since the act of evil now was part of creation itself, philosophers and theologians needed to place evil in the context that could be understood. By placing it in an ordered framework it took on an act of controlled manifestation, and thus could be understood in the greater scheme of life. With this understanding came a sense of acceptance and it took some of the fear of loss of control out of the situation.

The Swedish occultist, Thomas Karlsson (1972–) wrote in his book, *Qabalah, Qliphoth and Goetic Magic*, about the two trees, the *Tree of Life* and the *Tree of Knowledge*, being represented in two forms of the *Torah*. The Tree of Life corresponds to the *Torah* unknown to man which is emitting limitless amounts of life energy. This is the *Torah* that will become known during the Messianic Age. This Messianic age is characterized by a time of righteousness, justice and peace, and by the outpouring of the Holy Spirit and the restoration and renewal of God's people and of creation.

The *Tree of Knowledge* corresponds to what Karlsson calls the "common *Torah*" which is currently followed by the Jews today. He goes on to say that the Qabalists believe the two Trees represent the two sets of stone commandments given to Moses on Mount Sinai as described in Exodus. The first set of stone tablets that Moses brought down is destroyed when he sees the Israelites worshiping a pagan gold calf. This set represents the *Tree of Life* and freedom. Moses returns to the mountain to obtain another set of commandments. This second set is the *Torah* of laws to help govern the sinful Israelites through their struggles on earth and back to redemption. This is the set that has within it the representation of the *Tree of Knowledge*.

INTRODUCTION OF "EVIL"

In Vicki Noble's (1947–) book *Motherpeace,* she prescribes that prior to the Indo-Aryan invasion, sometime around 1500 B.C.E., the pre-eminent worship was to one form or another of the mother goddess. The mother goddess had many names; Bird Lady of Neolithic Egypt (3500–3400 B.C.E.), the Sumerian goddess Ninhursag, Asherah for Canaanites, Ashtarte for the Phoenicians, as well as Isis, Sophia, Aphrodite, Artemis, Demeter and Hecate, and Ishtar the goddess of Assyrian and Babylonians, to name a few. Professor Merlin Stone (1931–2011) and others hypothesized that with the invasion of the Indo-Ayran peoples around 1800 B.C.E. into present day

Levant. This migration of peoples includes the Sintashta culture according to archeologists. The Sintashta culture, also known as the Sintashta-Petrovka culture or Sintashta-Arkaim culture, was a Bronze Age archaeological culture of the northern Eurasian steppe on the borders of Eastern Europe and Central Asia, dated to the period 2100–1800 B.C.E. From the archeological records it appears these people were very warlike and considered to be one of the originators of the war chariot. Stone also felt there were incursions from the possible descendants of the Gravettian-Aurgnacian cultures, which were based in the Crimean Mountain region, descending from the north in waves to eventually dominate the tribes in the Near East sometime between 1500 and 800 B.C.E.

What Noble and Stone emphasized is that these invasions had brought their war-like gods with them. Stone speculated that these gods were those of fire and storm due to the area in which the invaders had came from, was a land of volcanoes. She goes on to say that the priestly tribe of the Hebrews, the Levi, were possibly one of these invading or dominating tribes called the Lewi. She feels that the Lewi and Luvians spoke an ancient language or group of languages of the Anatolian branch of the Indo-European language family. The two varieties of Luwian are named for the two different scripts that they were written in: Cuneiform Luwian (CLuwian) and Hieroglyphic Luwian (HLuwian). Their names derive from the material of volcanic eruptions. From their name comes the Sanskrit word *lauha*, defined as glowing redness. This is believed to be the basis of the image of the god on the glowing mountain described in *Exodus* when Moses returned with his "glowing face" (*Exodus* 34:29). This image of a glowing mountain was the Indo-European image of their male diety.[26]

These invading tribes came from a land of harshness and were a very domineering masculine culture who brought their cultural beliefs, which included ruling by total dominance. They were said to "rule by the sword" and this authoritativeness was used over all aspects of society including total dominance over women. This dominance went as far as devaluing the female to the point the female child was often left to die at birth. Over the centuries the worship of the mother goddess was suppressed to the point that the temples, cults, and priestesses were destroyed. This destruction of the 'pagan or heathen' religions continued with the Christian's destruction

---

26 *When God was a Woman*, Merlin Stone, Harvest Book, 1976, pg. 123

of sacred icons and literature as they attempted to follow the instructions in *Deut.* 12:2-3.

> You shall utterly destroy all the places where the nations whom you shall dispossess serve their gods, on the high mountains and on the hills and under every green tree. You shall tear down their altars and smash their sacred pillars and burn their Asherim with fire, and you shall cut down the engraved images of their gods and obliterate their name from that place....

This suppression of the importance became so drastic that in many of the Levant societies women were thought of as good only for sex and as "beasts of labor". It was during this period the family lines moved from matriarchal, were the child was identified by its mother, to the patriarchal line of succession, thus further moving women from their role as family head to one where they were viewed as possessions. The male gods started to populate the various pantheons; for example, the Greek's, Zeus with his thunderbolts, Egyptian God of War Auhur, or Atar as the Persian god of fire and heat, and Yahweh the Canaanite god of war, which later became the Jewish "Divine Warrior", late in the Bronze age.

Some theologians hint to the possibility that the writers of the *Pentateuch* or the first five books of the Bible wanted to emphasis their rabbinic dominance over women, and to place women in a position that they should be under the care of males both for protection and to control their sexuality so as not to pollute the purity of the male. The obsession on purity goes back to the earliest of discussions on how members of the Jewish community should live their lives. Stone goes on to say that prior to the dominance of male gods the concern of paternity of children was based on female-kinship and of matrilineal descent. In order to establish a certain knowledge of paternity ancient sexual customs had to be changed. These customs were believed to include the wide spread practice of "many women living within the temple complexes". While there they were involved in sacred sexual customs that blurred the knowledge of who the father might have been.

Stone goes on to suggest this custom had to stop. The Levite priests devised the concept of sexual "morality", and premarital virginity for women.

They also instituted the concept of marital fidelity for women, in other words total control over the knowledge of paternity.[27]

Talmud Bavli or Babylonian Talmud (Berakhot 21b–22a) provides an extended discussion where the closest male equivalent to female niddah, or menstruation, is severely restricted—a *ba'al keri* (a man who has a normal seminal emission) is treated with much less severity in that he may not utter words of *Torah*, and may not even enter the House of Study. While a woman would not be subject to the punishment of being "cut off" from the community for having sex with him, his punishment is nearly equivalent to that, since the House of Study was considered the primary location of importance, and if he was not permitted to utter certain blessings, it would make his life quite unworkable until he went to the ritual bath or mikveh. Thus the whole aspect of purity often centered on the women's niddah and the male's ability to contain his desires during this time. These fears are further enforced in the *Book of Leviticus* 15:19 & 24, 18:19 and 20:18, where the purity of the male is discussed, especially the males need to stay free of a women during niddah.

This fear of the power that a woman has over the male is extended into the symbolism represented in the myth of Eve in the Garden of Eden. The *Book of Genesis* contains two contradictory accounts of humanity's creation. The first account is known as the Priestly version and appears in *Genesis* 1:26-27. Here God fashions man and woman simultaneously: *"So God created mankind in the divine image, male and female God created them."*

The second account of Creation is known as the Yahwistic version and is found in *Genesis* 2:22. This is the version of Creation that most people are familiar with. First God creates Adam, then He places him in the Garden of Eden. Not long afterwards, God decides to make a companion for Adam and creates the animals of the land and sky to see if any of them are suitable partners for the man. God brings each animal to Adam, and ultimately decides that none are a 'suitable helper.' God then causes Adam to fall into a deep sleep and while the Adam is sleeping God fashioned Eve from his side. When Adam awakes he recognizes Eve as part of himself and accepts her as his companion. Not surprisingly, the ancient rabbis and priests commented on the two contradictory versions of Creation that appear in the *Book of Genesis* (which is called *Bereisheet* in Hebrew). They explained the

---

27 *When God was a Woman*, Merlin Stone, Harvest Book, 1976, pg. 161

discrepancy in two ways: First they explain that the first version of Creation described Adam's first wife, the "first Eve". Later she is referred to as Lilith. There is a myth or tradition that relates that Adam was displeased with this "first wife", so God replaced her with a "second Eve". This "second wife" is said to have met Adam's needs. The specifics of Adam's "needs" were not originally described. Again myth or tradition maintains that Lilith did not wish to be subordinate to Adam, feeling she was equal to him. During the medieval period this submissiveness referred specifically to the "missionary" sexual position denying the women's right to choose the position during copulation. Because of her refusal to submit to Adam she was chased or expelled from the Garden. To add to her "downfall" she became personified with all that is Evil. This tale, told by males, psychologically supported the concept of male dominance and that women have some "evil" tendency about them and that their sexuality needed to be controlled by males.

The story of Lilith was not something the Hebrews invented, it was adopted from the Sumerians. Sometime between 3000 B.C.E. and 2500 B.C.E., the ancient Sumerian culture was evolving from a matriarchy to a patriarchy. Around this same time the Canaanite's dualistic religious beliefs started to influence their neighbors. According to texts found around Ras Shamra (Ugarit, Syria) the world was in a continual struggle between the forces of life and death. Ba'al and his sister Anath represented the forces of life and death and were represented by the god Mot. To this day many Semitic based languages have mot as their word for death. The Hebrew word mot or mavet, in ancient Hebrew moth or maweth (מות) is currently used to denote death.

According to Canaanite mythology the newer gods, of which Mot was one, battled with the older god El. El was the "Name of God" which the Hebrew adopted to refer to their deity. The plural form of El is Elohim. "The plural can be used in Hebrew to indicate the magnitude of something without necessarily implying that there is actually more than one in the quanity."[28] This concept may have been part of the basis of the dualistic personification of the God of Abraham who had many faces or emanations showing both good and bad aspects.

As the patriarchy and its male gods evolved to overtake the reign of the Goddess, they first needed to sever the people's loyalty and beliefs in the

---

28 *When God was a Woman*, Merlin Stone, Harvest Book, 1976, pg. 161

Goddess. The many forms of the Goddess were extremely popular because she was often seen in a positive, matriarchal form that represented the earth, fertility, harvest, love and patience. They did this by demonizing the sexual power of women over men. And they rationalized by saying that since men had trouble subduing their own passions, it was not the male's fault but a force of 'evil' that was beyond the male's absolute control. Over the centuries the young maid Lilith became the symbol of the temptress, the one who first approached the men to take them to Innana's Holy Temple. Innana was the Sumerian Goddess of love, fertility and warfare. Innana or Ištar became, in the more patriarchal cultures, the embodiment of everything that was evil and dangerous in the sexual realm. She especially embodied men's worst fears concerning the sexual power of the feminine.

By 2400 B.C.E. Lilith, the Spirit of the Air, was distorted into a demon of the night who personified natural disasters such as storms and winds. Her image as a beautiful maiden who would neither release her lovers nor ever give them any real satisfaction. At the time there existed four classes of demons: First was the Lillu demons, who were vampires; Second the Lilitu or she-demons; Third the Ardat Lili and the fourth the Irdu Lili, who led female and male counterparts, dwelling in waste places, preying upon men and women by night and conceiving ghostly children. These demons haunted desolate places in stormy weather and were dangerous to pregnant women and to children.

In Jewish mysticism, Lilith was viewed as the moon that radiated its own light, and refused to yield to the sun. She was punished by only being allowed to reflect the light of the sun. In the *Zohar* she is described as leaving the Garden and taking Samael as her consort and from their union giving birth to numerous demons and evil spirits.

It was not until the time of the *Zohar* that a concept evolved that offered two ways for man to live as represented by the two different Trees. The Tree of Life represented a pathway to life in a place of paradise where those worthy could spend their days in bliss waiting for the resurrection and entrance into Heaven. The Tree of Knowledge represented the laws and rules by which man must live because of his separation from the true path.

THE DEVIL/ SATAN

When the discussion of evil arises the term often associated with evil is 'the devil'. The devil is often viewed as the personification of all that is evil.

The term "devil" derives from the Greek diabolos which originally meant an "accuser or traducer".

When the Egyptian Jews of the third century B.C.E. translated the Old Testament into Greek they used the word diabolos for the Hebrew word Satan. Satan was the angelic spirit whose main function was to test man's fidelity to God. Originally Satan was not evil but became associated with evil by his duties. He became further associated with evilness and badness by man associating the actions against deity with the reverse of pure and divine. When the Old Testament was translated into Latin the word turned from diabolos to diabolus or Satan. It should be noted that Satan is only one manifestation of the Devil. The Devil is the manifestation of hostile forces perceived to be out of our conscious control.

In the New Testament the concept of diabolos changed from an "adversary and tester" of man to that of an adversary to God. It was in Revelation that he was described as the "great dragon" who was cast from heaven and into earth "and his angels with him". The Devil or Satan became further demonized from the original Greek concept, that of the demon, which connoted "a guardian spirit or source of inspiration". This concept is important, especially when discussing those who "follow the Left Hand Path".

The concept of the Christian Devil has been attributed to the zealot hermits of the deserts who in the third and fourth century pieced together their concept of evil as that of a grotesque man who haunted their hallucinations and dreams. One of the better known hermits was Evangrius Ponticus (345–399 A.D.) a Catholic monk who exiled himself to the deserts of Egypt in an attempt to make amends for his own failures. His list of sins, based on his own life's failures were: gluttony, fornication/prostitution, avarice, hubris, sadness, wrath, boasting, and dejection. Ponticus' list was far from the first list of sins and excesses; Biblically there was the list traditionally associated with King Solomon in *Proverbs 6:16-19* and the *Epistle of Galatians 5:15-21*. The medieval Catholic Church patriarch added and refined the list of sins to contain "minor" venial sins as well as the more severe "mortal" sins. It was during these times that many of the sins that would later be the topic of heated sermons throughout Christendom took form. The Devil, as a creature enemy of God, was legalized and made part of official Christian mythology in 447 A.D., at the Council of Toledo, in Toledo, Spain.

Additional names for the Devil and his minions became popular during the discussions about and when Apocalyptic signs of Judaism and

Christianity would manifest to the world. This was the time which is often thought to be the centuries following the Jewish exiles, down to the close of the Middle Ages. Some of the names used, depending on decade and culture were;

Belial / Beliel–Was found in early Hebrew and Christian texts. Beliel was one of the fallen angels.

Mastema/Mansemat–Was a Hebrew angel of was called "the father" of all evil but yet subservient to God. Mastema is described as the Angel of Adversity or the Accusing Angel. Mastema works for God as a tempter and is God's executioner. He commands demons and evil spirits born of the dead bodies of giants and the offspring of other fallen angels who have mated with earthly women.

Azazel / Azazael or Azâzêl — According to tradition is said to be one of the chieftains of two hundred fallen angels who mated with mortal women. Azazel is said to have taught man how to make weapons and is credited with encouraging women to become vain by introducing cosmetics. The name tradionally means "scapegoat".

Samael or Samuel Sammael or Samil (Severity of God) is an important arhcangel in Talmudic and post-Talmudic lore, a figure who is accuser, seducer and destroyer, and has been regarded as both good and evil.

Semyaza /Samyaza / Semihazah, Shemyazaz, Shemyaza, Sêmîazâz, Semjâzâ, Samjâzâ, Semyaza, and Shemhazai — Semyaza is a fallen angel who is a "Grigori" Angel. Grigori is Greek for "watcher" and is associated with apocryphal Jewish and Christian tradition.

With so many names being associated with Satan and his devils a formal glossary was developed. This glossary included a description of the kinds of devils and was formulated and published by Michaelis Psellus, Michael Psellos or Psellus, who was a Byzantine monk, writer, philosopher, politician and historian. He was thought to have been born in Constantinople around 1017 or 1018, and is believed to have died around 1078, although it has also been maintained that he remained alive until 1096. Psellus' six varieties of demons appeared in a book by Francesco Maria Guazzo, aka Guaccio, aka Guaccius, who was thought to be born around 1570 and died early in the 1600s, the book is called the *Compendium Maleficarum* (*Book of Witches*) published around 1608 during the height of many European witch hunts.

Psellus was a member of one of the oldest of the Catholic Ambrosian orders, Ambrosians are members of one of the religious brotherhoods which at various times since the fourteenth century have sprung up in and around Milan and were also a sixteenth century sect of Anabaptist Ambrosians. The name Ambrosians is given to a sixteenth century Anabaptist sect, and also to various Catholic religious orders. The Ambrosians claim to have an immediate communication with God through the Holy Spirit. Basing their theology upon the words of the *Gospel of John 1: 9*, "There was the true light which lighteth every man, coming into the world". Because of this connection they denied the necessity of having any priests or ministers to interpret the Bible for them.

SIX VARIETY OF DEVILS

Fiery — These devils dwell in the upper air and will never descend to the lower regions of man's world until the Day of Judgment.

Aerial — These spirits dwell in the air around us. They can descend down to hell itself and are often visible to men due to their ability to form bodies out of thin air. With God's permission they can raise storms. These devils can be harmful to man because they can conspire for his destruction.

Terrestrial — These devils were cast out of heaven and sent to earth for their sins. They are said to live in the woods and forests and set traps for hunters. They also lay in wait to dwell in the fields and snare the unwary traveler. Other favorite haunts are in caverns. They are sometimes said to secret themselves among men.

Aqueous — These are the devils who dwell under the waters of rivers and lakes. They are said to be full of anger and are very deceitful.

They raise storms at sea and sink ships destroying life in the water. They take the form of women rather than men.

Subterranean — These live in caves and caverns of the mountains. Because of their mean dispositions they are the bane to those who work in caverns, mines and pits. They are known to cause earthquakes and winds and fires that shake and destroy homes.

Heliophobic — These devils hate the light and are never seen during the daytime. Once darkness falls they can form bodies. These devils cannot be comprehended by man because of their totally inscrutable personalities, described as having icy passions, malicious in nature, restless and they can be violent toward men with God's permission. They can kill men by merely breathing or touching them. These devils are so malicious they cannot be kept at bay by charms and are not friend to witch or man due to their hatred of light and the voices of men and noise itself.

As the concept and description of the Devil and Satan became more widespread his "being" became more popular with the common people. With this popularity the "evils" attributed to him increased. The devil was blamed for all kinds of misfortune, birth defects, and general "bad luck". This added to the increase of secular and spiritual preaching about the need to protect oneself from the "touch of the devil". This added to the devil frenzy giving to every increasing validity to the Devil or Satan existence in the natural world.

BIRTH OF THE TREE OF KNOWLEDGE OF GOOD AND EVIL

The concept of Tree of Knowledge of Good and Evil is most generally associated with the oral *Torah*, even though it is much older. The Tree of Knowledge has been around from very early in history, and it is often called by different names, but the concept is the same. These earlier ideas of the Tree of Knowledge are often linked to older ideas because each school of thought attempts to legitimize their current teaching by providing a direct link to older teaching. This occurs in some degree in Buddhism, Celtic Shamanisms, as well as the various cultures of the Middle Eastern and northern African origins. For the purpose of this book we will concentrate on the Kabbalistic viewpoint of history of the Tree of Knowledge of Good and Evil. When researching the teaching around the Tree of Knowledge there is generally a negative commentary associated with its followers. Mainstream writers state that those who follow the precepts of the Tree of Knowledge of Good and Evil are often those individuals who follow the Left-Hand Path (LHP). These scholars generally agree these individual are stepping the away from cultural norms and mores to follow this path.

Even though the concept of the Trees of the Garden of Eden have had a long history with the "Semitic peoples" it was codified for our purposes in the discussions in the oral *Torah*. "It is the oral *Torah* that determines a Jew's actual conduct."[29] Those who professed the teaching of the oral *Torah* believed that the life of the average Jew was one in which "free will" clouded their path to resurrection and redemption. This concept that the common Jew could not handle "free will" was deeply ingrained in their lives. It was even substantiated in the Pentateuch, in the story of Moses and the two sets of Commandments. The first set of Commandments were said to have come from the Tree of Life. Moses destroyed this first set upon returning to his people and seeing them worshipping the golden calf that Aaron had erected during Mose's absence. The second set Commandments was said to have come from the Tree of Knowledge. It was a stricter set of laws laying down the rules for a "sinful" people on how to return to God's grace through redemption of their "sinful" ways. The exact path to redemption has been the cornerstone of religions and religious debate ever since.

The *Zohar* is often credited with being the first written document discussing the Tree of Knowledge. But the whole concept of the two trees is greatly debated. Most writers agree the Tree of Knowledge was forbidden to man by God while the Tree of Life was not. It is often stated or inferred that the Tree of Knowledge, when once acknowledged and understood, and some sources "conquered", would be the only way for man to reach his divinity as is suggested in *Genesis* 5:1-2:

> This is the book of the generations of Adam. In the day when God created man, He made him in the likeness of God. He created them male and female, and He blessed them and named them Man in the day when they were created.

---

29 *When God was a Woman*, Merlin Stone, Barnes and Noble, 1976, pg. xvii

All this leads to the fact that even from the early stages of Jewish/ Christian mythology a component of esoteric or secret teachings was included. With the two Trees there was from the beginning a sencse of shadowy knowledge being kept from the common people. The common people may have known that there was more but were kept from it due to the implied concept they were not ready or able to understand its "true" meaning, *unless* they were initiated into the mysteries surrounding the secret knowledge.

THE "SHELLS" OF THE TREE OF KNOWLEDGE OF GOOD AND EVIL

The Qliphoth or "shells" that are represented on the Tree of Knowledge are historically attributed to be the creation of Jewish and Christian Qabalahists. Every Qlipha represents the anti-world or negative aspect of each Sefirah that it parallels on their respective Trees. One difference is that on the Tree of Life the Sefirah are populated with angels and their hosts, but the Tree of Knowledge's Qliphoth are reputed to be populated by demons and other demonic representatives. Like the Tree of Life, the Tree of Knowledge has numerous interpretations as to what is represented on the Tree. Here is one of those lists of the Qliphotic worlds with their rules, which is followed by most Left Hand Path followers of the Tree of Knowledge of Good and Evil:

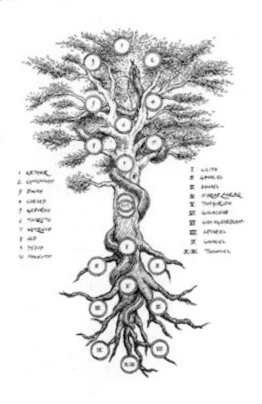

Qlipha	Demon Ruler	Sephira
Nehemo	Nehema	Malkuth
Gamaliel	Lilith	Yesod
Samael	Adarammelek	Hod
Hareh-Serapel	Baal	Netzach
Tagaririm	Belphegor	Tiphareth
Galab	Asmodeus	Geburah
Gamchicoth	Ashtaroth	Chesed
Sathariel	Lucifuge	Binah
Chaigidel	Beelzebub & Paimon	Chokmah
Thamiel	Satan & Molech	Kether

The above chart is from *The Kabbalah Unveiled*, translated by S. L. McgGregor Matters which in 1912. Another representation of the Qliphoths or husks is the chart below, attributed to the *Golden Dawn*, and which is another, often more accepted version of how the Husks relate to the Sephiroth.

	Sephiroth			Husks	
1	Kether/ Keter	Crown	1	Thaumiel-	The Twins of God
2	Chokhmah	Wisdom	2	Ogiel-	Hinders
3	Binah	Understanding	3	Satariel-	Concealers
4	Chesed	Mercy/Kindness	4	Gash'khalah-	Breakers in Pieces
5	Gevurah/ Geburah	Severity	5	Golachab-	Flaming Ones
6	Tiferet/ Tiphareth	Beauty	6	Tagiriron-	Litigation
7	Netzach	Eternity/Victory	7	Orev Zarak-	Ravens of Dispersion
8	Hod	Splendor	8	Samael-	False Accuser
9	Yesod	Foundation	9	Gamaliel-	Obscene Acts
10	Malkuth	Kingdom/Kingship	10	Lilith-	Woman of the Night

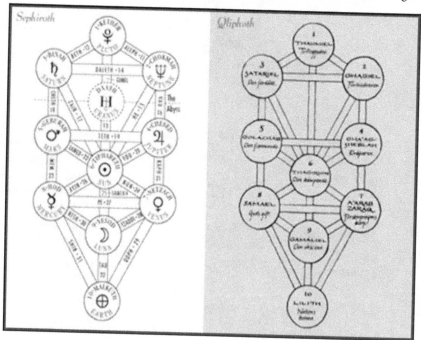

Sometimes the Tree of Knowledge is represented in a reversed fashion. This is done often as a pictorial representation of the concept that those who follow the Left Hand Path's philosophy is seeking the path down to "the Great Abyss", while others simply imply it is the reverse of "good".

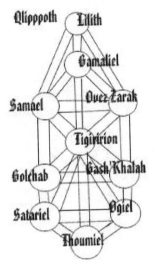

According to many who follow the LHP, in order to truly understand and gain the "knowledge" one must be able to gain mastery over the demon ruler to get the knowledge it possesses. This whole concept is potentially extremely dangerous to the Adept, for if the Adept's calling is flawed in any fashion the Adept may become a victim of the spirit being called. The danger, as so often played out in books about alchemists, is that the alchemist's ego gets the better of the alchemist's wisdom and the demon destroys the alchemist.

This knowledge is the same "apple" offered to humanity in exchange for "earthly pleasures". This angelic lore is reveled in *Genesis* 6:1-4 where it says:

When men began to multiply on the face of the Earth, and daughters were born to them, that the sons of God saw the daughters of men that they were fair; and took them wives of all which they chose.

These "Sons of God" or in Hebrew, the *Ben Elohim* or "fallen angels" were those whom God banned from earth. The myth goes on to say these *Ben Elohim* used temptation to attempted to mate or influence humanity by revealing some hidden knowledge in exchange for various favors.

XIII.

WORKING WITH THE
TREE OF KNOWLEDGE

The *Sod 'Ets ha-Da'ath, The Secret of the Tree of Knowledge,* was a work sometimes attributed to Rabbi Ezra ben Solomon of Gernoa (1160–1238), and by others saying the author was "anonymous". In this work the author points out that God did not keep Adam from the Tree of Knowledge but commanded that he could not eat of the fruit.

> But from the fruit of the tree which is in the middle of the garden, God has said, "You shall not eat from it or touch it, or you will die."
>
> GENESIS 3:3

God did not tell Adam he could not gather the fruit. But God did say about the Tree of Life: "eat, and live for ever". For the fruit would give Adam nourishment for both the body and the soul. But damage is caused to the soul, if the fruit contains damaging things, and things that stimulate the Evil Urge and diminish the soul in its rank and health...[30]

It is stated that the Tree of Life is from the eastern side of the Garden of Eden, while the Tree of Knowledge is from the northern side. From the Tree of Life light emanates into the entire world, while from the north Evil is present. In the *Bahir*, it says:

---

[30] *On the Mystical Shape of the GodHead,* Gershom Scholem, Schocken Books, 1991 pg.65-66

What is Satan? This teaches that the Holy One blessed be He has a quality whose name is Evil, and it lies to the north of God, as is written in the *Book of Jeremiah* 1:14: "Out of the north the evil shall break forth."

The Tree of Knowledge, since the time the Jewish lore was written, has been acquainted with Evil and Satan. And as the mythos of the Kabbalah grew, so did the discussions and debate as to how man related to this Tree. And as the Tree of Knowledge took form so did the various spheres of manifestation and the paths connecting them. Since the Tree of Knowledge in Kabbalistic terms is most often showed inverted, we will begin with the tenth sphere of manifestation and progress "downward".

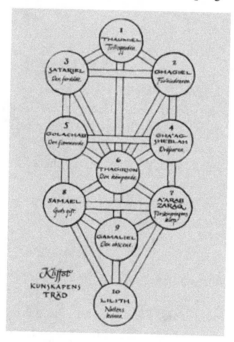

First Qlipha: Thaumiel-Duality of God/The Twin Gods

Anti-world to:	Kether
Demon Rulers:	Satan and Moloch
Satan:	Adversary
Moloch:	Name of an ancient Ammonite god
Magically:	Implosion of the Will
Associated With:	Black holes, the nothingness, parallel universes the dragon, the Eye, eternity and the infinite
Number:	1

THAUMIEL

Thaumiel is the anti or opposite of the Tree of Life's Sefirah Kether. It is often referred to as the shadow of Kether. Thaumiel represents the chaotic forces unleashed when this first Sefirah is not in balance. Where Kether represents unity of forces or energies, Thaumiel represents revolt and anarchy of these energies. Thaumiel is represented as a "double headed" demon, which is often shown with bat like wings. Prior to the "fall", these angels sought to become more powerful by adding an Aleph to their name. Because of their attempt to become like God they became known as the "Duality of God", an order of the lesser demons. In the lowest state of their "fall", they become "the Polluted of God". The cortex or outer form of the Thaumiel is called Cathariel, "the Broken" or "Fearful Light of God".

The ruler of Thaumiel is Satan. Satan in legend was the Chief of the angels, holding a position similar to that of Kether. According to Islamic legend, after God created man, Satan and his angels refused to bow down before Adam, and thus were condemned by God due to their arrogance. Satan became the representation of spiritual pride and arrogance.

Moloch has been known by numerous names, depending on the culture or religion of the time. He has gone by the name of Molech, Molekh, Molok, Molek, Molock, Moloc, Melech, Milcom, or Molcom. Many of these names derived from translations of ancient texts for the same deity. As a god he was worshipped by the Phoenicians and Canaanites. Moloch had associations with a particular kind of propitiatory child sacrifice by parents. There were even hints of these sacrifices occurring in Jerusalem; whether they were performed by the Hebrews themselves or by one of the cultural communities with Jerusalem, archeologists have not been able to verify. Some say the ritual site immediately south of Jerusalem called

Tophet, known in the Hebrew Bible as the Valley of the Son of Hanno, was a site was initially where apostate Israelites and followers of various Baal's and Canaanite gods, including Moloch, sacrificed their children by fire.

It is not known specifically when Moloch, the Canaanite Deity, became a demon or fallen angel or even when his name became synonymous with Satan.

Second Qlipha: Chaigidel/ Ogiel/ Ghagiel-Confusion / The Hinders

Anti-world to:	**Chokmah**
Demon Rulers:	**Beelzebub & Paimon**
Beelzebub:	**The Lord of the Flies**
Beelzebul:	**The Lord of the Heavens**
Paimon:	**One of the Kings of Hell**
Magically:	**The Magic Will formulated in word, signs that can Created other worlds.**
Associated With:	**Transexistential existence and supraexistential will**
Number:	**2**

Chaigidel is the Qlipha of Chokmah and the anti-world to the Sefirah of Wisdom, Chokmah. If wisdom is misused or flaunted it can result in great pride, stubbornness and egotism. It is the unwillingness to submit, the desire to make one's own laws and truth. But these shells can be material and illusory in their appearances.

There are two demon monarchs of Chaigidel: Beelzebub and Paimon. Beelzebub or Beelzebul, is the demon monarch of pride and second in power only to Lucifer, of whom Beelzebub is sometimes said to be an aspect. Beelzebub is not seen as a true leader of other demons but rather a guide. This Qlipha houses and energizes many of the greatest demons. It is also home to the Ghagiel (the Hinderers), gigantic demons with serpents writhing on their bodies.

BEELZEBUB

Beelzebub is proud, and craves the worship of humans more than any other demon. He fosters demonolatric cults in the world of humans wherever he can in the form of secret societies. He also strives to alter the monotheistic faiths, fostering pride and self-aggrandisation among the monotheists.

Those who would conjure Beelzebub should either be extremely confident in their power, or ready to offer him supplication.

PAIMON

Paimon is one of the Kings of Hell. Paimon is the demon king most obedient to Lucifer. They have a great gift for rulership, having a greater number of demons under their direct command than any other demon — ranging from one to two hundred legions, depending on the source.

Paimon is very tricky to summon. The conjurer must, in addition to drawing their seal, draw the demon's sigil properly while invoking the correct summoning commands. The Adept must face the correct direction (west or northwest, as it is commonly written) and make a suitable sacrifice. Failure to summon Paimon correctly may instead summon Amaymon/Amaimon or Amoyman, one of the kings of the four elements; it is said his breath would kill the conjurer if not given the proper respect.

Paimon is said to appear as a strong and beautiful androgynous youth riding on a swift dromedary. Paimon never appears alone, their coming is proceeded by a host of lesser demons in human form, playing trumpets, cymbals and a great range of other musical instruments. Sometimes they are followed by two other demon powers, Bebal and Abalam, each of whom command a number of legions of their own, and a skilled and daring conjurer may deliberately call up all three at once. Paimon has a strong and penetrating voice, and roars and rants on whatever subject is on their mind as soon as they arrive, until the conjurer persuades or compels them to answer questions. They demand that the conjurer answer their questions truthfully before they are willing to answer the conjurer's questions.

Paimon teaches their conjurer just about any skill. They also know many secrets, among them the mysteries of the earth, wind and water, of the human mind, as well as a great number of other things. Paimon gives good familiars, and can also raise up their conjurer to powerful positions in society, and bind other humans to the conjurer's will.

Third Qlipha: Sathariel/Satariel-Side of God/ The Concealer
Anti-world to: Binah
Demon Rulers: Lucifuge-One Who Flees Light
Knowledge: The "third eye" is opened of the great dragon
Power: Deeper magical sense

Magically:	**Magical will is united with principle of eternal Will**
Associated With:	**Wisdom, death, rebirth and roots of time**
Number:	**3**

Sathariel is described in the *Book of Enoch* as the seventeenth Watcher of the 20 leaders of the 200 fallen angels. The name is believed to be of Babylonian origin and a combination of shetar and el (God) with the name meaning "side of God". Sathariel is associated to ones who keep secrets and hide something.

The outer shell of Sathariel is called the order of Sheireil, "The Hairy Ones of God". This demonic order has been described in Thomas Karlsson's book *Qabalah, Qliphoth and Geotic Magic* as a black labyrinth of chaotic riddles, where Lucifuge reigns. When the magician reaches this final level he enters into the center of Hell itself. Others describe how the third eye is opened and darkness becomes light if ascension progresses through this order. The results are that the magician learns to see the light of Lucifer and becomes clairvoyant.

Lucifuge Rofocale is featured only in one text, the *Grand Grimoire*, a French handbook on black magic written in the 17th or 18th century. The *Grand Grimoire* is part of a series of black magic grimoires or texts, of which four are known; the least dark volume is the *Key of Solomon*, believed to date back to 1522. There is some question as to its exact publication. Some believe it could have been written some point after the eighteenth century. Still others believe it was part of a translation of *The Sworn Book of Honorius*, a thirteeth century text. *The Sworn Book of Honorius* was ostensibly published in Cairo by a person known as Alibek the Egyptian, he was also known as "The Red Dragon". This book contains instructions purported to summon Lucifer or Lucifuge Rofocale, for the purpose of forming a Deal with the Devil. The book is especially significant for its feature of a specific PACT between a magician and Lucifuge Rofocale for the purpose of securing the services of demons. Rocofale may be an anagram of Focalor, a demon named in the *Lemegeton*, a major grimoire. The *Lemegeton* also known as *Lesser Key of Solomon*, as well as the *Clavicula Salomonis Regisor*, an anonymous grimoire (or spell book) focused on demonology. It was compiled in the mid-seventeenth century, mostly from materials a couple of centuries older.

The *Grand Grimoire* states that if the magician cannot master a magic circle and a blasting rod for controlling demons, then a pact is necessary. A pact cannot be made with the three highest demons like Lucifer, Beelzebub, and Astaroth, but only with one of their lieutenants. It provides a Grand Conjuration for summoning Lucifuge Rofocale, who is a reluctant and obstinate spirit who must be forced to appear with the use of the blasting rod and threats of curses.

Fourth Qlipha: Gamchiroth / Gha'agsheblah/ Gash'khalah-Squandering Breakers in Pieces/The Smiters

Anti-world to:	Chesed
Demon Rulers:	Ashtaroth-Crowned Prince in Hell
Knowledge:	The "third eye" is opened of the great dragon
Power:	Erotic mysticism
Magically:	Consolidation of the Will
Associated With:	Power, balance, consolidation, nakedness, Forces of the warrior and pleasures of love
Number:	4

Gha'agsheblah is the highest Qlipha for it resides directly below the Supernal Triangle. It embodies desire, greed and possessiveness. It is all about the self-versus the self-existing and preservation and care of others.

Legend has it that in Hell, Gha'agsheblah is strongly present in the treasuries, granaries and slave-pens of the demons, as well as in their fields, slaughterhouses and presses. It is the refuge of Generators, those demons empowered by Gha'agsheblah, often appearing with feline aspects.

The Generators are demons of greed and desire. They take pride in their ability to create, refine, and breed. They also take a keen interest in the breeding of cambions, which are the offspring of demons and mortals. They tend to be beautiful and intelligent, and magically gifted. They also tend to be given to sin due to their uncontrolled desires and greed. The two chief Generators are Amaymon and Astaroth.

AMAYMON

Amaymon is a Prince of Hell, commanding 40 legions and taking refuge in Gamchicoth. He is also known as The Devourer. He often appears as a wolf with a serpent's tail, or as a man with the head of an owl, but his favored form is chimeric. A Chimeric is a mythical creature formed from the parts of two or more different animals. In the case of Amaymon, it appears with his hindquarters in the form of a giant serpent, the forequarters of a wolf, and the head of an owl. In any form, he has a fiery and poisonous breath which devastates anyone he breathes on, and quickly fills any chamber into which he is brought.

Calling up Amaymon is frighteningly easy, doing so safely is another matter entirely. If the summoner does not go through the proper steps of invocation, Amaymon will kill the summoner. Because of the ease of calling, Amaymon often materializes when a summoner incorrect attempts to summons other demons, especially Asmodai or Paimon.

Amaymon's greatest power is said to be the ability to devour and destroy all that is in his path. He may be called upon as a juggernaut of destruction, though he is more easily unleashed than sated. Amaymon also has drawn into him a vast trove of magical energy and bound souls, and may empower the greatest of spells if he so chooses. Surprisingly, Amaymon also has the power to end quarrels and reconcile former friends.

ASTAROTH

Astaroth is a Great Duchess of Hell. She commands 40 legions. She is a ruler of Gha'agsheblah/Gamchicoth. Astaroth and often appears as a crowned woman with angel wings. Others, such as A. E. Waite, who have drawn their knowledge from the ancient text *The Lemegeton,* believe that Astaroth as really a great Duke rather than a Duchess. When she appears as a female, it is often in the guise of a crone, with a haggard face. She may, of course, take a more pleasing form should it suit her purposes. She appears mounted on a draconic beast, holding a viper in her left hand. *The Lemegeton* has the viper in her right hand.

Astaroth was once a great angel, and unlike most other demons, she is openly bitter about her fall, claiming that she fell through no fault of her own.

Like most demons of Gamchicoth, Astaroth is sought primarily for her reservoirs of power, which she may lend to an aspiring magician. She also has great power over the element of water. Astaroth, whether seen as a male or female, has tremendous power and can inform the summoner about the past, present and future.

Fifth Qlipha: Golachab-Flaming Ones

Anti-world to:	Gevurah/Geburah
Demons:	Hepesimereth
	Phoubêl
	Sahu
	Tepsisen
Knowledge:	Learns to control and invert experiences of lust and suffering
Power:	Use of certain fire ceremonies, walking and eating burning coals;
Magically:	Birth of new magical will
Associated With:	Courage, fight, war, defense, power
Number:	5

Golachab is viewed as one of most brutal of the Qliphotic powers. It is said to be so brutal because it reflects the Sefirah Geburah, which is the wrath or punishing aspect of God. Golachab is a sphere of the arsonists, the flaming ones, the volcano, or those who burn in hell. Golachab emanates injustice and rage. It is the very identity of the core of Hell, embodying both the severe and divinely decreed banishment of the demons from heaven. Because of their banishment and feeling of defeat they developed their rage at this punishment, and with this rage they developed a willingness to destroy all of Creation and what it represents if necessary to tear down their prison.

Like Geburah, Golachab governs the magic of Hepesimereth, Phoubêl, Sahu and Tepsisem. He also governs over the human emotion of rage that the defeated feel, and the darkness of Hell. These demons' willingness to raise Babel and see it destroyed by fire from above, and the destruction of all things, is the nature of Golachab. The demon Asmodeus is attributed to Golachab and is traditional thought to be the result of a demon, Agrat bat Mahlat, a queen of the demons, who mated with King David. The name Asmodeus is translated to mean 'the one adorned with fire' and he is also called Samael the Black.

HEPESIMERETH

Hepesimereth is the embodiment of the very concept of nothingness. It permeates creation with defeat, emptiness, loss and despair and associated is with Aethyr. Aethyr, the fifth spirit or element of occultism, is a formless and invisible substance that pervades the cosmos. It is often associated with Erik, the Turkish god of death. The spirit is often felt in places of desolation such as abandoned cemeteries, abandoned houses, pits and mines and places where the land has been made unproductive due to the land being sown with salt.

Phoubêl

It is said, light cannot exist without darkness to define it, for without the contrast the other side will not be distinguishable. Phoubêl deals equally with both sides, darkness and light, and thus with vision, blindness, and irreconcilable conflict.

The Aethyr, a powerful demon of chaos is Lord of Strife. He strengthens Phoubêl, in that he promotes quarrels, conflict and discord. He appears alternately clad in noble splendor on the back of a lion or caparisoned in rags riding a gray horse.

Sahu

Sahu oversees such activities as archery, hunting, and herding. It is also found in the places that these activities are associated with such as the mountains, forests, grasslands, and other wild spaces.

He is said to appear as a giant, naked save for a belt and bow. His color ranges from blood red to forest green to basaltic black.

Tepsisen

Tepsisen gives rise to beauty and to its loss. It deals with youth and aging, and is intensely explored by those desiring immortality. Tepsisen appears as a middle-aged woman in red, a scarlet fire-sprite, or a swift horsewoman on a red horse.

Sixth Qlipha:	**Tagiriron/Thagirion-The Disputers**
Anti-world to:	**Tiferet/Tiphareth**
Demon:	**Bephegor-Lord of the Dead**
Knowledge:	**Mediate between the worlds above and below**
Power:	**Act as a mouthpiece for the lore of the shadow side. Power of discovery and ingenious invention**
Magically:	**Formulation and fulfillment of the true will**
Associated With:	**Working with Demons and communication**

with the higher-self, Power, success, long-life and Wisdom.

Number: 6

Thagirion and Tiphareth belong to the solar sphere or the mental level. This is the sphere where the adept comes in contact with their higher or lower selves, depending on which sphere they are working. This is also the level where the Adept comes in contact with their totem or daemon. Daemon are the benevolent or benign nature spirits. They are beings of the same nature as both mortals and deities, similar to ghosts, chthonic heroes, spirit guides, forces of nature or the deities themselves. On the negative side they are referred to as demons and provide instinctive illumination in which force, vision and action are united. On the positive side it provides intellectual illumination. The dark adept feels total power at this level as well as an unquenchable lust.

This sphere is dangerous for all White Adepts and the religious seeker because at this level the adept feels a sense of total benevolence which can become self-sufficient.

BELPHEGOR

Belphegor is the chief demon of the deadly sin known as Sloth, in Christian tradition. Belphegor originated as the Assyrian Baal-Peor, the Moabitish god to whom the Israelites became attached in Abel-Shittim. This was a failed settlement found in present day Israel, which was associated with licentiousness and orgies. Belphegor was worshipped in the form of a phallus. As a demon, he is described in Kabbalistic writings as the "disputer". When Belphegor is summoned, he can grant tremendous riches, the power of discovery and ingenious invention. His role as a demon was to sow discord among men and seduce them to evil through the apportionment of wealth.

Seventh Qlipha: Orev Zarak/A'arab Zaraq/
Harab-serapel- Ravens of Dispersion
Or Ravens of Death

Anti-world to:	Netzach
Demon Ruler:	Baal: Lord and Tubal Cain: Maker of Sharp Weapons.
Knowledge:	To be able to be "reborn" in the upper worlds.

Power: To invoke for victories in the battle of life.
Magically: Demon-Bhakri, eroto-magic, magical battles.
Number: 7

This is the sphere of dark emotions. These emotions lay deep in all Adepts, but are brought forth by A'arab Zaraq as well as the dark obscure instincts that lay deep within our primitive man. The demons associated with it are hideous, demon-headed ravens issuing forth from a volcano.

Blackness is the color associated with A'arab Zaraq and thus while the White Venus belongs to Netzach, the Black Venus or Venus Illegitima, the goddess of perversions, belongs to A'arab Zaraq.

In alchemy's four phases, nigredo belongs to the first stage, is associated with blackness, and means putrefaction or decomposition. The second stage of alchemy is albedo, attributed to whiteness, is the "washing away of impurities". The third sage is Citrijitas, and concens the yellowness and means "transmutation of silver to gold" or the "yellowing of the lunar consciousness". The fourth stage is rubedo, which is represented by redness and is associated with success or end of his great work for this is where the alchemistic color of red is associated with gold and the philosopher's stone which is the ultimate goal for the alchemist.

Bēlu/Baal/ Ba'al

There is Bēlu, a name seldom seen for it is known by a more common name found in the Bible as "Ba'al", which refers to Hadad, the lord over the assembly of gods on the holy mount of Heaven. The name Ba'al is alternatively used to refer to any number of local spirit-deities worshipped as cult images, each called Ba'al and regarded in the Hebrew Bible in that context as a "false god".

Baal was originally viewed in a positive mode. He was the god associated with fertility, which was extremely important to many ancient Middle Eastern communities, especially among the Canaanites.

To the Semitic people the term "Baal" was used in many ways but generally meant "master", "lord" or "owner". The name also referred to a local pagan god and to the land of Baal which was associated with the Canaanites. In some of the old texts the term 'Hadad' was used. Since the priests were the only ones to use the god's true name of Hadad, the common people used the name Ba'al. In either case it referred to a god of thunderstorms, fertility and agriculture, and the lord of Heaven. The bull was the symbolic animal of Hadad. He appeared bearded and often holding a club and thunderbolt while wearing a bull-horned headdress. With the development of monotheism Hadad was relegated to something evil as a false god.

With the rise of Christianity Hadad-Baal became a demon and was ranked as the first and principal king in Hell, ruling over the East. According to some authors Baal is a Duke of Hell, with 66 legions of demons under his command. As the reputation of Hadad declined he became known as Harab Serapel or the Ravens of Death, who were even rejected by their fellow demons. He was the outer form of Theumiel or "the fouled substance of God".

Eighth Qlipha: Samael/Sammael-The Poison of God/The Left Hand

Anti-world to:	**Hod**
Demon Ruler:	**Adrammelek-Powerful King**
Knowledge:	**Understand the functions of Existence.**
Power:	**To see the ethical rules that imprison our psyche.**
Magically:	**Master of magical works, formulas and auto-writing.**
Associated With:	**Journeys, intelligence, communications, healing, travel between worlds.**
Number:	**8**

Samael represents the barren desolation of a fallen and failed creation. The outer form is Theuniel, "The filthy Wailing Ones of God". In Jewish mythology, when Lilith, Adam's first wife, left the Garden of Eden she encountered Samael and mated with him producing all the demonic offspring to populate the desolation outside of the Garden. These demons symbolized all the fears, pains, and failed desires that haunted man's dreams.

Samael is seen as the great tempter both good and evil. He is the angel of death whom God sends to fetch souls. In rabbinic works Samael is seen as the Chief of the "Satans" or demons. Adramelech is described as the President of the Senate of the demons. He is also the Chancellor of Hell and supervisor of Satan's wardrobe. Adramelech is generally depicted in publications as having a human torso and head, and the limbs of a mule or peacock.

To Samael, Adrammelech is attributed. Like many of the early lesser pagan gods Adrammelech, was a sun god worshipped by the Phoenicians and Canaanites. Because Adrammelech was seen as a pagan god he was demonized in Jewish and Christian writings in an attempt to destroy his popularity amongst the common local people. Adrammelech was later associated with Moloch, the same god believed to be the center of a particular kind of propitiatory child sacrifice by parents.

As the Dark Adepts reach this level they will be able to tear away all the psychic censorships that darken our concepts of good and evil and right and wrong. Samael acts as the tempter offering the fruits of the forbidden knowledge that was denied to Adam and Eve in the Garden of Eden. "He also reveals the beauty of the world and points downwards, inwards, instead of up towards the kingdom of Heaven..."[31] This is the ultimate challenge—the acquiring of this knowledge, but at what cost? Without wisdom, knowledge seems to be the destroyer of individual. He destroys the Adepts' ability to denote their differences of moral and ethical choices as pertaining to magic by compromising the Adept's ability to see the true results of their desires and how those acts of magic will affect the magician.

Nineth Qlipha: Gamaliel- The Obscene Ones

Anti-world to:	**Yesod**
Demon Ruler:	**Lilith- "night creatures"/ "night Monster"/ "night hag"/ "screech owl"/dark lady**
Knowledge:	**How to remember and control dreams in the Astral plane.**
Power:	**Learn how to us sexuality for magical progression.**
Magically:	**Astral working, erotic dreams, and use of succubus and incubus**
Associated With:	**Dreams, imagination, art, astral travel, eroticism Witchcraft and paranormal abilities.**
Number:	**9**

Gamaliel is where Lilith personifies her shape as the ruling demoness of Gamaliel. This is the dream sphere and the dark side of Yesod and where Lilith secretively tries to control the world. Gamaliel is where the dark dreams reside, those dreams that man does not want to remember because

---

31 *Lords of the Left-Hand Path*, Stephen E Flowers, Inner Traditions, 2012, p. 90

they expose a view of himself he does not want to accept. This is the sphere of forbidden sexuality.

It is said that as the magician travels the worlds of Gamaliel he will be tempted to join into orgies with incubi and succubi. Thus the Adept must be cautious because he may have his energies "vampirized" and leaving an empty shell. What draws the Adept on to join these orgies is the knowledge that if the magician is strong enough, he or she can learn to release their soul during the periods of ecstatic states of mind.

The magician will need to be very cautious when working to summon any of the dark forces that haunt Gamaliel. For to lose control or attention to what is being done could leave the magician as an empty shell devoid of energy. If this happens the magician will have to seek others to draw their energy much as the mythical vampire seeks others for their blood.

LILITH

To Gamaliel, Lilith is attributed and "is the grand lady of all demons. The demons are sometimes considered to be the children of Lilith and are said to be the women who come to men in their dreams". She is associated with the dark side of the moon as commanded by God due to her falling from grace and being made lesser than the view of herself.

One description of the Biblical Lilith is that she has a body of a beautiful woman from the head to the navel, but from the navel down she is a flame. This represents Lilith's energy, according to Zoharic myths, from the resentment caused by the diminishment of the Moon as well as the dark and fiery side of night.

Besides the *Zohar* there are numerous descriptions as to the origins of Lilith. The Kabbalah has several myths. The principle one is the quaternion marriage. In such a marriage are two pairs, or couples: God and his indwelling spiritual feminine aspect Shekinah, above, and Samael the Devil containing Lilith, below. Here too the dualistic aspects of Zoroastrianism, good and chaos, can be seen. According to the earliest Jewish literature Lilith as evil. She evolved evil first the the diminution of the Moon, then was cast from heaven, and rejected by the 'first man' Adam as not having the feminine qualities appropriate to man. Lilith, like Samael, became something of a renegade, sent by God, to reign in the lower regions, in relative to humanity. Men experience her as the seductive witch, the death dealing succubus, and the strangling mother. For women she is the dark shadow of the Self married to the Devil. These descriptions were used to scare women into submissiveness by threating to identify her as a "Lilith" thus strengthening men's rule over women.

Tenth Qlipha: Lilith-Queen of the Night

Anti-world to:	Malkuth
Demon:	Naamah/Nehema/Nehemoth-Night Spector
Knowledge:	How to travel the dark tunnels
Power:	Open unknown pathways to unexpected places.
Magically:	Controlling the mundane existence to enhance Initiatoric work.
Associated With:	Kundalini, life forces and material Success.
Number:	10

The Qlipha called Lilith is the sphere of the "wild and carnal" desires. The *Zohar* calls her the "soul of the wild animals". Her name is associated with Lil the ancient Sumerian goddess of storms and hurricanes. She cannot be controlled by man and thus is often denied and considered an uncontrollable force or energy. She is seen as the destroyer of Earth by causing building to fall and the earth to shake.

Lilith is the mother of demons and the magician must seek her out to conjure up demons. This is not easy since Lilith's Qlipha is in the anti-world of the physical world Malkuth in aspects which man is not normally aware. She is the anti-force of the Shekinah and Gnostic Sophia.

NAAMAH

Naamah appears in the *Zohar* as one of the mates of the archangel Samael. She, along with her cohort Lilith, cause epilepsy in children. She has been called the daughter or younger sister of Lilith. She appears as a mighty queen dressed in jewels and precious garments. She is used as an intermediary by which magicians can call her to channel the dark unruly forces of the Qlipha. Naamah is sometimes attributed to the Egyptian goddess Isis and Nephthys, and possible is the same Naamah described as the sister to Tubal Cain. This is the same person mentioned in the Hebrew Bible, in *Genesis* 4:22, who was a descendant of Cain, the son of Lamech and Zillah, the brother of Naamah and half-brother of Jabal and Jubal.

PATHS ON THE TREE OF KNOWLEDGE

As in studying any of the information concerning the esoteric aspect of either the Tree of Life or the Tree of Knowledge there are many different interpretations is attributed to specific spheres, paths or channels represented on a specific Tree. When it comes to the paths, or 'tunnels' in the case of the Tree of Knowledge, the most often quoted information is from Kenneth Grant (1924–2011) and his *Nightside of Eden*.

KENNETH GRANT

One of the most influential writers concerning the Left Hand Path Grant provided a cornstone of information which later writers added to or modified as they developed their own schools of thought. Grant was an English ceremonial magician and prominent advocate of the Thelemite religion. He founded, with his wife Steffi Grant, his own Thelemite organization, called the Typhonian Ordo Templi Orientis, this was later renamed the *Typhonian Order*.

Grant's greatest contributions were his two Typhonian Trilogies. The first started in 1972 with *The Magical Revived*. This was followed by *Aleister Crowley and the Hidden God* in 1973, and *Cults of the Shadows* in 1975. His second work in his *Typhonian Trilogies* consisted of *Nightside of Eden*, 1977, *Outside the Circles of Time*, 1980 and his final work *Remembering Aleister Crowley* was completed eleven years later in 1991.

In his *Nightside of Eden* Grant discussed "the Tunnels of Set", conceived as a "dark side" of the Qabalistic Tree of Life. Grant made connections between this realm and the extramundane deities of H.P. Lovecraft's horror fiction. The following discriptions are based on his works which includes descriptions of the "tunnels" or "pathways".

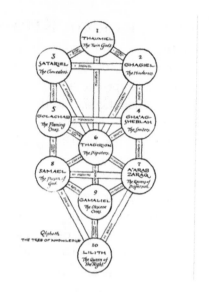

THE TUNNELS OR PATHWAYS ON THE TREE OF KNOWLEDGE

ELEVENTH TUNNEL-THAUMIEL (1) TO GHAGIEL (2)
Amprodias

The eleventh tunnel or kala is attributed to the element of Air. Kala is a Hindu reference to "hidden contents". Amprodias can be evoked by intoning its name in the Key of "E". Amprodias' number is 401, the same as Azoth. Both signify "sum and essence of all". It is the negative phase of the essence conceived as None and is the Void from which manifestation proceeds.

Its sigil is drawn as a pale yellow square on the ground with emerald flecked gold throughout it.

On the Kabbalistic Tree of Life, the tarot key The Fool is associated to Amprodias.

TWELFTH TUNNEL- THAUMIEL (1) TO SATARIEL (3)
Baratchial

The twelfth path or kala is attributed to the planet Mercury and its shadow masses in the form of Baratchial. The name Baratchial should be vibrated in the Key of "E". The number 260 is attributed to Baratchial, which is the number of Tiriel the Intelligence of Mercury. The number 260 also is the number for Tmira, meaning "concealed" or "hidden".

The sigil associated to Baratchial is yellow deeper than Amprodias' upon a vesica shaped plaque of indigo rayed with violet.

The Magician is the tarot on the Tree of Life that is attributed to Baratchial.

THIRTEENTH TUNNEL-THAUMIEL (1) TO THAGIRION (6)
Gargophias

This path is charged with the lunar kala. The name of its shadow-guardian is Gargophias whose name is 'howled' in regular repetitions in the key of "G" Sharp. 393 is the number associated with Gargophias and is a very important number to the Draconian Cult in Thelemic philosophy. It contains the number 39^2 and 93^3. It also has the numerical value of 3+9+3=15 which is the numerical value of Crowley's Atu XV, "The Devil". Other numerical references are 131 x 3=393 which is the number of Pan and Samael. This Samael is the same whosewife is Lilith the Elder, the Lady of the Darkness.

The sigil for Gargophias is drawn in silver on a black circle.

On the Tree of Life, the Tarot key for Garophias is The Priestess.

FOURTEENTH TUNNEL-GHAGIEL (2) TO SATARIEL (3)
Dagdagiel

The fourteenth tunnel is suffused with the kala of Venus, represented by the Whore. The name of its sentinel is Dagdagiel. She may be evoked by vibrating her name in the key of "F" Sharp accompanied by a crooning or lilting sound. The sigil of Dagdagiel shows the letter Daleth reversed and in the form of a gallows from which hangs an inverted triangle above the letters A V D on a vivid sky blue background, on a circle of bright rose, rayed with pale green.

55 is the mystic number associated to Dagdagiel and to Malkuth the power zone of the Earth.

On the Tree of Life, the Tarot associated to this tunnel is The Empress.

FIFTEENTH TUNNEL-GHAGIEL (2) TO THAGIRION (6)
Hemethterith

The fifteenth tunnel is illumined by the kala of the Star, and is the "dweller between the waters". The Guardian of this Pylon is Hemethterith who may be evoked by vibrating her name in the key of "A" Sharp. The mystic number of Hemethterith is 1054, the same as the Greek word Naos, meaning "ship" or "ark". She is also the material aspect of kala 13 the Virgin and kala 14 the Whore and represented by the seal of the Pentagram.

Her sigil is lurid red on a glowing red inverted triangle representing the intense sexuality attributed to her.

The Tarot key associated to her on the Tree of Life is The Star.

Sixteenth Tunnel Ghagiel (2) to Gha'agshebah (4)
Uriens

The 16th Path or Tunnel transmits the influence of the Tarot key, The Hierophant and its tunnel is sentineled by the demon Uriens who is evoked by vibrating his name in the key of "C" Sharp. Uriens is ruled by Air and is thus presided over by Satan the Prince of the Power of Air. The mystic number for Uriens is 395 and it relates to the 7 armed glyph of the Tree of Life as it has relevance to the world below the great Abyss.

His sigil is drawn of lines of flame on a brown square.

Seventeenth Tunnel Satatiel (2) to Thagirion (6)
Zamradiel

The 17th Tunnel transmits the influence of the Kabbalistic Tarot Key The Lovers. Its tunnel is guarded by Zamradiel who is summoned by evoking his name in the Key of "D". The number 292 is associated with Zamradiel and with TzRB, which is Hebrew for 'the Raven'. The Raven is the black bird of the Egyptian storm god Set. 292 is also the number Chazzar, the Cult of the Shadows. Choronzon, is a possible corrupted form of that name, and his astrological sign is Neptune, in addition he is the symbol of Atlantean Magic.

The sigil of Zamradiel is the color of new leather and I composed of a lunar crescent pierced by an arrow shot from a bow, both ends of which terminate in the letter G placed on visica of mauve.

Eighteenth Tunnel -Satariel (3) to Golachab (5)
Chatacith

The 18th Tunnel or Path is under the aegis of Cancer. He is called by evoking his name in the Key of "D" Sharp. This tunnel is sentineled by Chatacith. 640 is the astro glyph of the Holy Grail of Templar fame. KVS ThNChVMIM which means "cup of consolation" and is the cup which aids the Adept in on working on the Path of Cheth. The Holy Grail is like a two edged sword for the Adept, for it yields ecstasy and magical immortality. But if drank too often it is like a "vampire" for the cup will destroy the Adept by consuming the very essence it gives, plus more. In time the Adept will be consumed by the need to stay in the state of ecstasy, much like addictive drugs in the material world.

The sigil of Characith is painted in dark greenish brown on an amber-hued circle. The Tarot key associated with this tunnel on the Tree of Life is The Chariot.

NINETEENTH TUNNEL–GHAGIEL (2) TO THAGIRION (6)
Temphioth

Tunnel 19 is sentineled by the demon Temphioth whose number is 610. This number is the same as AThRVG meaning "lust" and "desire". Because of this Temphioth is associated with Crowley's Key 11, Lust, which is Key 8, Strength, in the Rider-Waite deck. It is also the numerical value of ChBRTh meaning "coupling point" and "place of junction". The predominant influence is that of the lion-serpent, Teth, a glyph of the spermatozoon, which is shown in the sigil in the shape of four vesicas colored in sharp greenish yellow hue upon a gray arrow shape on the ground.

The name of Temphioth should be vibrated in the key of "E".

TWENTIETH TUNNEL-GHA'AGSHEBLAH (4) TO THAGIRION (6)
Yamatu

The 20th Tunnel is under the domain of Yamatu whose name should be intoned in the Key of "F". His number is 131, the same as Samael. Samael is the name of the aspect of Satan or Set as the Guardian of the Threshold. This number is also the mystic number of Baphomet, the same one the Templars were said to have worshipped. Baphomet is often depicted as the "Satanic Goat". Its astrological association is with Virgo.

The sigil of Yamatu is a secret cypher of Set. It exhibits the inverted cross which signifies the downward passage or crossing into Amenta, the Egyptian word for underground. The sigil is yellowish green on a sliver of gray slate.

TWENTY-FIRST TUNNEL GHA'AGSHEBLAH (4) TO A'ARABZARAQ (7)
Kurgasiax

The 21st kala or Tunnel is dominated by Jupiter and is refracted into a Tunnel sentineled by Kurgasiax whose name should be intoned imperiously in the Key of "A" Sharp. The tunnel is represented by the 11th Key in the Thoth deck, Wheel of Fortune. It is the 21st Key in the Qliphoth deck called the Path of Caph. The mystic number associated with it is 315, the same as IShH, which means "to stand" or "stand out". IShH comes from the Egyptian word "As" meaning "secret part of the body", referring to the testicles.

The sigil of Kurgasiax shows as a horned (or crescent) sphere containing an equal armed cross mounted on a pole terminating in three caudiform appendages. It is depicted using rich purple on bright blue background on the ground. The image is rayed with yellow.

TWENTY-SECOND TUNNEL- GOLACHAB (5) TO THAGIRION (6)
Lafcursiax

The 22nd Tunnel is guarded by Lafcursiax. She responds to a prolonged vibration of her name in "F" Sharp. Her mystic number is 671 the same as the Law (ThORA). She stands at the "Gate" or "Wheel". 671 is also the number of Adonai, the Holy Guardian Angel. The traditional Tarot associated with this Tunnel is Justice.

Her sigil is a glyph of Unbalance. It is drawn in pale green on a rich blue ground and shows a pair of scales upset by a crooked demon with an inane countenance.

TWENTY-THIRD TUNNEL-GOLACHAB (5) TO SAMAEL (8)
Malkunofat

The 23rd kala is under the dominion of Malkunofat who lies in the depth of the watery abyss. He may be aroused by intoning his name in the Key of "G" Sharp. The 23rd Tunnel is the abode of the Deep Ones or the dragons of darkness. The sacred number of Malkunofat is 307, the same as VRIATz, which are the night demons of the second decant of Scorpio. Because of this this Tunnel has great sexual reference. 307 is also the number of LZRO, "to sow", again referring to fertility. His sigil is deep blue on an inverted triangle of sea-green blue.

TWENTY-FOURTH TUNNEL-THAGIRION (6) TO A'ARABZARAQ (7)
Niantiel
The 24th Tunnel is under the influence of Scorpio and guarded by Niantiel. The name of this Qlipha should be intoned in "G" in a manner suggestive of a bubbling cauldron of molten lava. The mystic number of Niantiel is the number 160. This is the same number for QIN meaning "the nucleus of the impurity". The Tarot associated to this Tunnel is Death Key.

The sigil of Niantiel is an image of Death with a five-rayed crown bearing a cross handled scythe beside the Cross of Set. It is colored in lurid indigo brown, like the color of a black beetle. It is on an equilateral triangle of greenish blue.

TWENTY-FIFTH TUNNEL-THAGIRION (6) TO GAMALIEL (9)
Saksaksalim
The 25th Path or Tunnel is the domain of Saksaksalim whose number is 300 and whose non-being may be induced to assume form by the vibration of a high pitched electric crackling sound in the Key of "G" Sharp. 300 is the numerical value of the letter *Shin* 𐤔, the triple fire tongued symbol of Chozzar. Chozzar is the disintegrating principle of anti-matter. Kenneth Grant recommends that ". . . the Golden Dawn symbolism of the 5° = 6° Grade . . . should be studied".

The sigil is bright yellow on vivid blue ground.

TWENTY-SIXTH TUNNEL-THAGIRON (6) TO SAMAEL (8)
A'ano'min
The 26th Tunnel is under the aegis of A'ano'nin those number is 237. His name should be intoned in a raucous and bleating tone in the Key of "A". This demon's Tarot Key is that of The Devil.

The sigil of A'ano'nin shows the Ur-Hekau, an Egyptian musical instrument, surmounted by the head of the priest and surrounded by the letters BKRN, which add up to its mystic number of 272.

When creating its sigil one uses black with an indigo colored inverted pentagram.

Twenty-Seventh Tunnel-A'arabzarq (7) to Samael (8)
Parfaxitas

The 27th Tunnel is under the aegis of Parfaxitas, whose Tarot key is the Tower. When invoking his name one should use a deep and imperious note of command in the Key of "C" and sound like thunder. 450 is his mystic number, the same as the "dragon", ThN. The feminine version is Tanith, which is the great dragon of the deep that manifests itself on earth as Babalon. She is the priestess of the Draconian Current. Grant recommends in his book *Nightside of Eden* that 'The formula of Parfaxitas is that of the VIII°⁺ O.T.O., which comports the assumption of astral animal forms for the reification of atavistic energies.' This pathway is said to be littered with hybrid creatures resulting from imperfectly performed magical operations by inexperienced Adepts.

The sigil of Parfaxitas depicts a Fortress with a door and two windows (eyes) superposed upon the letters SUE, the number of which is 71, which is the number of LAM. It is said the sigil shows the yoni-eyes, which at this point are yet mute and closely balance upon the Towers of Shaitan. Eyes of the Infinite, Negative source of all Positivity, the wise Adept should tremble at their terrible openings to come upon LAM's bidding—that inscrutable Guardian, angelic archetype. The sigil is drawn in bright red pigment on an emerald colored square.

Twenty-Eighth Tunnel-A'arabzaraq (7) to Gamaliel (9)
Tzuflifu

The 28th tunnel is sentineled by the demon Tzuflifu. When calling forth this demon invoke its name in the Key of "A" Sharp. Its sacred number is 302, the same as BQR, which means "to cut open" or "inquire within". BQR also means "to lighten", "to send lightning" as applied to the Great Serpent of the Gnostics. This Great Serpent is also known as the Serpent of Salvation by the Gnostics, as well as Lucifer, the Messenger of Light. They say Lucifer will liberate man, to show him his true situation and true destiny.

The sigil is drawn with white on a violet ground.

Twenty-Ninth Tunnel-A'arabzaraq (7) to Lilith (10)
Qulielfi

Tunnel 29 is under the influence of the moon and is the haunt of the witch typically represented by Hekt. The Egyptian goddess Kekt was depicted as frog-headed goddess, for the Egyptians believed the frog was the symbol of the life-giving power-goddess. She was the goddess who oversaw women, mid-wives, and others who helped women have babies. In terms of the LHP she is the Lady of Transformation. Qulielfi is the sentinel of the 29th Tunnel, and her number is 266 and her name should be intoned in the Key of "B". Her sigil is drawn in silver, "like slug slime".

Thirtieth Tunnel-Samael (8) to Gamaliel (9)
Raflifu

The 30th tunnel is under the guardianship of Raflifu whose name should be vibrated mellifluously in the Key of "D". 406 is this demon's mystic number. This is the same number as *Tau ת*, if it were spelled out in full. The mystic Tau is "the cross", the emblem of the dead, the symbol of "the crossing over".

The sigil of Raflifu exhibits the horned trident of Typhon (or Choronzon) flanked on either side by the axe or NETER sign and surmounted by a black sun in the arms of a crescent moon, drawn in rayed red upon an amber disc.

Thirty-First Tunnel-Samael (8) to Lilith (10)
Shalicu

The 31st tunnel is under the domination of Shalicu whose name should be vibrated in the Key of "C". 500 is the mystic number of this demon. 500 is the numerical value of Shr meaning "prince". This Tunnel is the Path of Evocation and Pyromancy (meaning divination by fire). This process is done with the fiery tongue that manifests itself in this Tunnel by Shalicu in the form of Choronzon. The sigil is colored using vermillion on an emerald ground. The Tarot key related to this demon is the Judgment Key.

Thirty-Second Tunnel-Gamaliel (9) to Lilith (10)
Thantifaxath

The 32nd tunnel is under the aegis of Thantifaxath, whose name should be called in the Key of "B" Sharp. This tunnel has the Tarot Key The Universe attributed to its location. The number 1040 is the mystic number, which is the same as the word temenos, which is the sacred precinct of a temple enclosure or court in ancient Greece. This path has a lot of symbolic similarities to this entranceway to "the temple" by which the Black Adept must pass. The sigil is a black triangle, though others say a diamond which is rayed with blue.

WHEN WORKING THE LHP TUNNELS

Kenneth Grant and others all agree that there is great danger in traveling through the Tunnels or Pathways of the Tree of Knowledge. Adept can fail in their attempts to navigate the channels of the Tree of Life with little real damage, except a misconception of the sexual-energy they activate. Generally, the failure to call on the spirits of the paths leads to the same effect as calling a name in an empty room. Nothing but echoes and disappointments.

When the aspirant or Adept calls on the demonic forces that are guardians of the Tunnels of the Qliphoths, real damage can occur. Forces unfriendly and chaotic can and will be released. They may take the form of nightmares, illuminations or at the worst a complete loss of the self. It has been suggested that Aleister Crowley, one of the greatest mystics in the twentieth century, lost much of his true Self to demonic forces that came for him in the form of excessive liquor, drugs and sexual practices. The Black Adept must be strong enough, and vested with the knowledge to call and most importantly control the demon guardians of the Tunnels they wish to travel. If they do not have this strength or even waver in strength, or knowledge there are chaotic consequences. The Black Adept must not succumb to the desires or powers found within these tunnels and lose their egos or self-consciousness. For when working with these forces there are many temptations and only the strongest Mages truly succeed on this journey for the esoteric knowledge offered on the Left Hand Path of Enlightenment.

XIV.

TRAVELING ON THE
SIDE OF THE LHP

LEFT HAND PATH TAROT

Like the Rider Waite Tarot Decks and all the variations of these traditional decks there are numerous varieties of decks that favor the LHP philosophies. Over time some of these decks have become popular with many, while others fade into the mists of time. Here are a few of the more popular decks, but not all.

THOTH TAROT DECK

The Thoth Deck was developed by Aleister Crowley over a five-year period between 1938 and 1943. This deck is often referred to as a divinatory deck first, versus the decks used by the Kabbalists, which are initially considered as instructional decks to path work. These decks have been used from the earliest times as divinatory as well but the Kabbalists, both Christian and Hermetic, have sought to use them as teaching tools for understanding the working of the Tree of Life. Crowley's deck was painted by Lady Frieda Harris (1877–1966) an English artist who met Crowley and began working under his instructions when she was 60 years of age. Crowley referred to his deck as The Book of Thoth.

Crowley wanted to incorporate all the various symbols he had learned from his studies, merging his knowledge of the sciences, philosophy and various occult studies. He used his extensive knowledge of symbolism and Egyptian mythology to develop a unique deck which was very different from the traditional Rider Waite variations. He also changed the astrological and

Hebrew letters assigned to his decks to support and emphasize his teaching from his earlier book, Liber Al vel Legis or Book of the Law, which he published in 1904. This book contained the basis for his Thelema teachings.

SHADOW TAROT

The Shadow Tarot is a divinatory deck evolved primarily due to the writings of Kenneth Grant. The primary source is from his book *Nightside of Eden*. Grant had a great knowledge and understanding of Crowley's work. It first appeared in Linda Falorio and Fred Fowler's book The Shadow Tarot Dancing with Demons in 1988. Their work produced paintings of 22 images of the Tunnels of Set—aligned with the 22 Major Arcana of the traditional Tarot.

The chart below shows the three decks and their major Arcana as they relate to each other.

Rider-Waite card	*Thoth equivalent*	*Grant's equivalent*
O: The Fool	O: The Fool	O: Amprodias
I: The Magician	I: The Magus	I: Baratchial
II: The High Priestess	II: The Priestess	II: Gargophias
III: The Empress	III: The Empress	III: Dagdagiel
IV: The Emperor	IV: The Emperor	IV: Tzuflifa
V: The Hierophant	V: The Hierophant	V: Uriens
VI: The Lovers	VI: The Lovers	VI: Zamradiel
VII: The Chariot	VII: The Chariot	VII: Characith
VIII: Strength	VII: Adjustment	VII: Baratchial
IX: The Hermit	XI: The Hermit	IX: Yamatu
X: Wheel of Fortune	X: Fortune	XI: Kurgasiax
XI: Justice	XI: Lust	XI: Lafcursiax
XII: The Hanged Man	XII: The Hanged Man	XII: Malkunofat
XIII: Death	XIII: Death	XIII: Niantiel
XIV: Temperance	XIV: Art	XIV: Saksaksalim
XV: The Devil	XV: The Devil	XV: A'ano'nin
XVI: The Tower	XVI: The Tower of War	XVI: Parfaxitas
XVII: The Star	XVII: The Star	XVII: Hermethterith
XVIII: The Moon	XVII: The Moon	XVIII: Quliefi
XIX: The Sun	XV: The Sun	XIX: Raflifu
XX: Judgement	XX: The Æon	XX: Shalicu
XXI: The World	XXI: The Universe	XXI: Thantifaxath

THE BLACK FLAME TAROT
In the 1960's there was a great upswing of interest in dark occultism. Out of this came the Black Flame Tarot. In 2000, Jennifer Chen, a 3° Priestess of the Temple of Set, began her designs for this Tarot. She combined her knowledge from various predecessors of Tarot Deck design including, Pamela Colman Smith's illustrations in the Rider-Waite-Smith Deck, and the geometrical forms of Frieda Harris's artwork for the Thoth Deck. Being a high ranking member of the Temple of Set she draws from her extensive knowledge of Setian inspiration concerning alchemical, astrological and other occult influences as well.

LUCIFERIAN TAROT
This version of the tarot was created by Michael Ford, founder *The Black Order of the Dragon* and *The Order of Phosphorus*. The deck is highly influenced by Ford's extensive work in the areas of Luciferian Witchcraft, and Left Hand Path magick. He is also highly versed in Yatuk-Dinoih or ancient Persian sorcery, Typhonian Magick, Hellenic — Near Eastern (Chaldean/Babylonian) Magick, Chaos Sorcery, Nocturnal Spiritual Vampyrism, just to name a few.

THE DEVIANT MOON TAROT DECK
This deck was developed by Patrick Valenza (1967–). According to Patrick he created the initial part of the deck when he was fifteen years old, but did not complete it until he was an adult. The symbolism in this deck comes from childhood dreams that carried over into adulthood. His imagery is somewhat dark in nature showing the images of factory smoke stacks, insane asylums, and abandoned buildings.

THE GOTHIC TAROT
In 2002 Joseph Vargo (1998–), a musician and gothic fantasy artist. introduced his Gothic Tarot Deck. It was taken from his existing works of dark gothic imagery, plus additional art created specifically for the deck. In 2007, Vargo co-wrote The Gothic Tarot Compendium, a detailed guide to understanding and using his best-selling Gothic Tarot deck.

NECRONOMICON TAROT

The Necronomicon Tarot is the product of Donald Tyson (1954–) author and artist of many esoteric based articles, and Anne Stokes. It is a completion of author Donald Tyson's trilogy that draws upon on the mythology created by H.P. Lovecraft, the occult and horror fantasy writer.

DARK FAIRYTALE TAROT

Another popular deck is The Dark Fairytale Tarot. It presents a darker side of the world of the fae. It takes elements of both the Rider-Waite and Thoth decks and blends them with lifelike medieval fantasy imagery.

ORGANIZATIONS ASSOCIATED WITH THE LEFT HAND PATH

There are a great many Orders, Societies, websites and groups a dedicated in one form or another to their interpretation of the theories and practices associated with the Tree of Knowledge and the LHP. Each proclaims and alludes to the fact their course study on the Draconian tradition and the Left Hand Path is the means for the advancement of the individual. Most of the groups are initiatory in nature but may not follow a "pathwork" framework for advancement in their particular Orders. Most of the sites are vague as to their historical sources but often name Aleister Crowley and his *O.T.O.* writing as being a source. I am only listing a few to give the reader a starting point for their own studies.

THE DRAGON ROUGE

The Dragon Rouge was founded by Thomas Karlsson (1977–) who is a Swedish occultist and esoteric author. He and six other magicians founded Dragon Rouge in 1989. It is a Left-Hand Path initiatory organization and a Draconian Tradition Order, led by Karlsson. Much of the material described concerning the qlipoths is based on Karlsson's book *Qabalah, Qliphoth and Goetic Magic*. In the summer of 2007, Karlsson held the first Swedish course ever in Western Esotericism at the Stockholm University. His personal influences include Sumerian mythology, Alchemy, Tantra, the Goetia, and the Qliphoth. The order is based on three main parts 1+9+1, one outer part which is open for all members, one inner part which contains an initiation system of 11 levels and finally the inner circle. In his above mentioned book he lists the steps as:

1. Litlith 1.0° The gate to the Unknown (LAMMASHTA/ NINHURSAG/LILITH)

2. Gamaliel 2.0°. (NANNA GATE) The Dark Dreams, Astral magic, Witchcraft. The Mysteries of the Dark moon. The Dark Goddess.

3. Samael 3.0°. (NEBO GATE) The philosophy of the left hand path. The wisdom of insanity. Yezidi magic. The dark side of the Chakras.

4. A'arab Zaraq 4.0°. (ISHTAR GATE) Luciferian Magic. The dark side of Venus. Eroto-mysticism and the path of the warrior.

5. Thagirion 5.0°. (SHAMMASH GATE) The illumination of the nightside.

6. Golachab 6.0°. (NERGAL GATE) Ragnarök. The activation of Surt/ Sorath. The magnetism of lust and suffering.

7. Gha'agsheblah 7.0°. (MARDUK GATE) The higher levels of eroto-mysticism. Preparations for the passing of the Abyss.

8. Satariel 8.0°. (ADAR GATE) The opening of the eye of Lucifer/ Shiva/Odin. The Drakon principle.

9. Ghagiel 9.0°. (SPHERE OF ENKI/ZODIAC/IGIGI) The lightening of the Luciferian star.

10. Thaumiel 10.0°, (SPHERE OF ENLIL/ Sphere of the Primum Mobile) The accomplishment of the promise given by the Serpent Divinity.

11. Thaumiel 11.0° (SPHERE OF ANU/TIAMAT) The Black hole. The step into new creation.

The Qliphothic Grade System is used by *The Dragon Rouge* with some of the working in the Simon Necronomicon. The whole foundation of the Walking in the Simon Necronomicon, which is based on the study of *The Simon Necronomicon,* is purported to have appeared in a book of magic written by an unknown author, with an introduction by a man identified only as 'Simon'. This 'fictional' story was introduced by H.P. Lovecraft (1890–1937), an American author of horror stories.

Entry into the Order can be done through their website.

THE TEMPLE OF ASCENDING FLAMES

The exact founding of this order is not given. They were "founded as a Gate to Draconian Current, arising from inspiration received from Lucifer and Draconian Gods, and in response to inquiries and expectations of those who wish to walk the Qlipothic Path of Spiritual Ascent", and claim not to be a "magical order".

Their primary goal is to provide guidance to those who seek illumination through the Flames of the Light Bearer and in the coils of Leviathan, those who are ready to descend into Qlipothic depths beneath the Tree of Life, travel through the pathways of Lilith, and step into the Void, the very Womb of the Dragon, in order to become reborn and arise as Gods incarnate.

The Secondary Goal is to empower the Adversarial Current of Lucifer who ignites the Ascending Flame and is the patron God of the Temple.

They do this by guiding their members through various aspects of this magical tradition and promoting Draconian magic as a self-initiatory path.

SACRED WOMEN LODGE O.T.O.

The *Sacred Women Lodge* was established in the Valley of Austin, Texas in 1993 in accordance to the rules and statutes of the *Ordo Templi Orientis U.S.A.* Like other orders their mission is to effect and promote the doctrines and practices of the philosophical and religious system known as Thelema. One of their projects is to provide information through an open source encyclopedia of Thelema and Magick. This site includes topics on Qabalah, astrology, yoga, godforms, biographies, and the works of Aleister Crowley. Their "goal is to make Thelemapedia the single best, most comprehensive source for information on Thelema and magick". It appears to be a great resource site, but like all public open-source sites one must verify the information given.

The Church of Satan

The *Church of Satan* was established in 1966 in San Francisco, California, based on Satanism and *The Satanic Bible*. The founder was Anton Szandor LaVey (1930–1997) born Howard Stanton Levey. LaVey was an American author, occultist, and musician and the Church's first High Priest, until his death. His book *The Satanic Bible* was published in 1969 and is the basis of La Veyan Satanism. This is a synthesized system of his understanding of human nature and the insights of philosophers who advocated materialism and individualism, for which he claimed no supernatural or theistic inspiration.

The Church has two levels of membership. The first is "Registered Member", which make up those members who are "loosely" affiliated with the Organization but are not actively involved. The second group is called the "Active Member". These are the individuals who take a more active role in the Church's organization, rituals and services.

After Anton Szandor LaVey's death, the role of High Priest was empty for some time. Finally, on November 7, 1997, LaVey's daughter Karla LaVey (1952-) with High Priestess Blanche Barton (1961–), known as Magistra Barton, took over the leadership. Barton eventually received ownership of the organization, which she held for 4 years. Karla LaVey ultimately left the Church of Satan and founded First Satanic Church.

Barton remained High Priestess until April 30, 2002, when she appointed Peggy Nadramia as High Priestess and assumed Nadramia's previous role of chairmistress of the Council of Nine.

Temple of Set

The *Temple of Set* is a left-hand path initiatory order founded in 1975. Initiates take the title "Setian". It was founded by members of The Church of Satan who left that group to start this new Order. The Temple of Set was consecrated in Santa Barbara, California during the summer solstice of June 1975. Michael A. Aquino (1946–), and his wife, Lilith, founded the new Order based on 'black magic' rituals that were inspirited by Aquino from *The Book of Coming Forth* by Night. According to Aquino in his 1975 book, *The Temple of Set*, the name of *The Book of Coming Forth by Night* is an "evident negation" of the name of the Ancient Egyptian *Book of Coming Forth by Day*, also known as the *Book of the Dead*. The book *The Temple of Set* is a very extensive dissertation on the theoretical aspects of Setian cosmology, philosophy, and magic.

The Order does not emphasize group work but that o the true self, or essence, is immortal, and Xeper, which is the ability to align consciousness with this essence. In other words, it emphasizes the individual's Xeper or self-realization and development. Because their work is based on the individual's own progress the Order sees that the individual member initiates himself and the Temple merely acknowledges this by granting the degree.
These degrees are:

The 1° Setian (First Degree) which is the initiatory Degree. The 2° is called the Adept Degree—they attain 'full membership' to the Order. Upon attaining the title 3°, the member may enter into the Priest or Priestess Order. The 4° is called the Magister or Magistra Templi Degree. Upon acknowledgment by a high priest or priestess that their skills are advanced enough they will be able to found their own school of magic. The 5° is a Degree that can only be awarded by the unanimous decision of the Council of Nine and by the approval of the high priest or priestess. If approved they will be known as Magus or Maga, depending on their gender. The 6° represents a Magus "whose Task is complete". This degree is held by a very select few in the Temple, although any fifth-degree member can assume the sixth degree based on his own assessment.

Some of the Orders within the *Temple of Set* are:
> *Order of Beelzebub*
> *Order of Leviathan*
> *Order of Setne khamuast*
> *Order of Trapezoid*
> *Order of Vampyre*
> *Order of Xnum*

THE ESOTERIC ORDER OF BEELZEBUB
According to their web site: "*The Esoteric Order of Beelzebub* is an Order within the *Temple of Set*. It took form during the Dog Days of Summer in XXXVIII AES, revealing a unique and multi-faceted approach to comprehending and connecting with the Black Flame."
In 1970, the text called The Diabolicon appeared. It is the sacred text describing the history of the universe from a satanic point of view. The

Diabolicon envisions a cosmos populated not by gods and goddesses, but by tangible races of higher beings and an energizing substance known as The Black Flame, which eventually becomes the "lever" for mankind's conscious evolution. This was a key source of inspiration in suggesting this unique approach to Setian initiation.

According to their philosophy there is a second, key statement within The Diabolicon which focuses on the ideas of essence, creative instance, and design. Beelzebub tastes of knowledge and recognizing the unbearable incompleteness of being, and demands more. Thus Lucifer names him Lord of the Flies, that he may "goad the infant mind to restlessness and invention".

Beelzebub further witnesses the Luciferian Exodus, following the Great Seraphic War, where the tribe of Daimons journey through the outer darkness to establish a new society called Pandemonium. This sounds very close to "Pandæmonium", the capital of Hell described by John Milton in his 1667 poem Paradise Lost.

FRATERNITAS SATURNI OR BROTHERHOOD OF SATURN

One of the older organizations in the "Brotherhoods of the Left" is the German magical order called Fraternitas Saturni or Brotherhood of Saturn. This Brotherhood was founded by Eugen Grosche (1888–1964), and four other occults. Eugen was also known as Gregor A. Gregorius and was an occultist and author in Germany. He was the chief founder of Fraternitas Saturni and was its Grandmaster from its founding in 1928 to his death in 1964.

The Lodge's major focus is on the study of esoteric principles, mysticism and magic. Their mission is the spiritual advancement of the individual using mental and ethical means. The individual advances through 33 different degrees as they become masters of esotericism and occultism.

Since the 1960's their degree system was expanded to contain five sections. The First is called "Label" or "Neophyt" section and is as follows: 0° Neophyt, 2° Scholasticus Verbi, 3° Scholasticus Vitae, 4° Frater/Soror, 5° Servus Juris, 6° Servus Templi, 7° Servus Ritus, 8° Gradus Mercurii, at which time the student is considered a "Journeyman" in the Order. They continued on with the 9° Servus Pentaculi, 10° Servus Tabernaculi, 11° Servus Mysterii. The second section is R + C Degrees. At the completion of 12° Gradus Solis, one is considered a "Master". Next comes: 13° Serus Selectus Imaginationis, 14° Servus Selectus Magicus, 15° Servus Selectus Elementorum, 16° Sacerdos Aiones, 17° Sacerdos Maximus, 18° Magus

Pentalphae, 19° Magus Sigilii Salomonis and the 20° Magus Heptagrammatos, which completes this section. The third section is "S. S. G." and starts with the 21° Magister Selectus Sapientiae, 22° Magister Perfectum Potestatum, 23° Magister Magnificus Pneumaticos, 24° Princeps Arcani, 25° Magister Gnosticus, 26° Magister Aquarii, the final Degree of this section. The next section is called "*Hochwürden*" and begins with the 27° called Groß-Komtur, 28° Groß-Kanzler and the 29° Groß-Inspekteur. The last section is called "*Hochwürdengrade*" and starts with 30° Magister Maximus Cados, 31° Magister Templarius, 32° Princeps Illustris Tabernaculi and ends with the Grandmaster as the 33° Gradus Ordinis Templi Orientis Saturnie.

As of 2011 *Fraternitas Saturni* have working lodges in Germany, Austria and Switzerland.

THE ORDER OF PHOSPHORUS (TOPH)

The Order of Phosphorus (TOPH) was founded in 2002 by Magus Akhtya Dahak (Michael W. Ford) an occult author of over 18 books concerning various topics on the darker aspects of rituals and their workings. He is also composer of dark ambient & ritualistic music, who is based in Texas. Some of his training comes from his membership in the Luciferian Witchcraft guild known as Coven Malefica. *TOPH* states they are not only a Luciferian order; "it is specifically an initiatory guild which is centered on Adversarial Magick and the self-determined shaping of the will and compelling change in the living world". Their approach to Luciferianism is that it is first a philosophy of training the mind (and will) to control and direct energy towards both short and long term goals.

TOPH has evolved with an initiatory structure which guides the self-motivated initiate to fashion and establish an inner spirituality. This is done with the initiate learning a clear understanding of symbolism, magick and utilizing the various grimoires to continually ascend (and descend) as the center of the Adversarial Current.

They present several key points as to how they feel Luciferiansm can awaken the consciousness that is 'deep-seated' in the individuals who they feel are blinded by mainstream religious faith systems. These are a few of their published beliefs:

First: Luciferian Magick begins within the mind, utilized via energy in the physical body and then into the spiritual realm via the unity of will, desire and belief. This must be done by the individual to tap into the dark recesses of primal power which lies within them.

Second: Luciferians embrace life in the here and now, understanding that your present and future is to be fashioned by your determined goals and realizing the practical steps necessary for this achievement. As a Luciferian one needs to utilize both the ideology and spiritual possibility in a challenging arena which over time ignites the spirituality of perception, understanding and result-driven insight.

Third: Luciferianism is a synthesis of the philosophy of the ancient, pre-Christian values of the strong of mind and body. They acknowledge that each person as an ability to accept knowledge. And by honoring those values they can contribute to the evolution of human potential, awareness of a spiritual reality (if this is in your perception) and seeking balance in both creative and destructive powers, symbols and desires within nature and the individual. They believe that Magick brings change according to the will; the powers of darkness motivate, challenge and transform the initiate. Ideology tests and affirms the individual's reality and over time will elevate you into a continually evolving divine consciousness.

And Fourth: Being your own god allows the individual i to not rely on or accept another master. You alone are responsible for your own life. And continual magickial rites will strengthen the temple of the individual mind-body-spirit.

The Order of Phosphorus is based on achieving various "Grades". The Order is guided by the Priesthood of the Adversary and the Council of Arezura. TOPH's High Priest and Magus is their founder, Akhtya Dahak (Michael W. Ford), who with others created another Order called the Black Order of the Dragon in 1993. TOPH initiates join as Grade 0° — Nahemoth and the Black Earth. After mastering the necessary skills of Lucificiarn magic one can pass to the Grade I° — The Blackened Forge of Cain. And finally Grade II°– The Witches Sabbat as Adepts of Algol.

The Order of Phosphorus does not limit the ways their students seek magickal skills. They believe there are numerous avenues to explore. TOPH initiates come from all different backgrounds and cultures, having many different magickal interests. TOPH is structured around the *Bible of the Adversary* written by Michael W. Ford, along with other works offering a structure of Luciferian initiation which is based around results rather than ego inflation.

The Order of Nine Angles (ONA; O9A)

According to members of the LHP associated groups, *The Order of Nine Angles* is one of most dangerous and extreme forms of Satanism functioning today. They were formed in England in the 1960's and were comprised of the merging of three neo-pagan temples called *Camlad, The Noctulians*, and *Temple of the Sun*. The current leader is David Myatt (1950–) who was also known as David Wulstan Myatt and Abdul-Aziz idn Myatt. He is a former British Muslim and neo-Nazi. He advocates The Numinous Way, which prescribes a "Way of Life" as being a life, in harmony with Nature and the Cosmos. And by doing this the individual will evolve oneselves and, after our causal death, transcend to another type of existence, in the "acausal".

Presently, the O9A is organized around clandestine cells called "traditional nexions", and these cells make up what they call "sinister tribes". The core mystical tradition of *The Order of the Nine Angles*, is the Seven Fold Way, also known as the Hebdomadry. This is essentially a hermetic system that defines itself as being deeply rooted in Western occultism, and provides a path to ascension that is exceptionally difficult in physical and psychic terms.

The seven stages of the Way are (1) Neophyte, (2) Initiate, (3) External Adept, (4) Internal Adept, (5) Master/Mistress, (6) Grand Master/Mousa and (7) Immortal. Yet unlike other degree-based systems, the ONA does not offer initiation to its students; rather, the students must initiate themselves through personal grade rituals of passage, and challenges. When they reach the fourth stage, called the Internal Adept, a more active commitment is required. This takes the form of the Adept living in complete isolation for at least one season, as well as being able to cycle, run, and hike considerable distances. Each grade thereafter requires increasingly difficult challenges, culminating in the 5th grade, called Master. Here the Master must undertake physical challenges comparable to a triathlon, as well as having developed/ learned several esoteric skills along the way. One of the most challenging aspects of the Seven Fold Way is the insistence on learning through adversity, known in Greek as pathei-mathos. This term comes from The Agamemnon of Aeschylus (written c. 458 B.C.E.), and can be interpreted, or translated, as meaning "learning from adversity, or wisdom arises from (personal) suffering; or personal experience is the genesis of true learning".

One of their goals is for their members to gain "real-life experience". They want their new members to experience something completely different from their normal life both to "aid the Sinister dialectic" and to enhance the experience of the Initiate. They ask them to do this for around eighteen months. They hope as they practice these new roles in life that the initiate has what they call a "transgression" into establishing new norms, roles, and develop new comfort zones in the "Sinister dialectic". "This extreme application of ideas further amplifies the ambiguity of satanic and Left Hand Path practices of antinomianism, making it almost impossible to penetrate the layers of subversion, play and counter-dichotomy inherent in the sinister dialectics." Of O9A.

Because of their rather radical beliefs, including human sacrifice for purpose of culling the social undesirables and promoting the rejection of ethical behavior, most other LHP groups have developed a rather "open animosity" towards this group.

The Order of the Nine Angels, use the term "nine angles" for several reasons. One is that they represent the nine emanations, and transformations, of the three basic alchemical substances (mercury, sulfur, salt) which occur in their occult and mystical use of Myatt's Star Game. In Myatt's history he describes how the Star Game came about.

The Star Game was developed in 1975 while I (Myatt) was in prison. My idea was to find a common and an abstract/symbolical means — possibly mathematical or employing symbolic logic — to represent the transformations, the processes, which I felt were common to, or which underlay, (a) the various personality types described by Jung, (b) the Jungian process of individuation, (c) the development and the stages of civilizations as described by Toynbee (the organic nature of civilizations), (d) the bifurcation of causal/acausal, and (e) what I at the time called "the flux of φ (acausal) and λ (causal) via causal time".

The nine angles also are in reference to their hermetic anados with its seven spheres and its two acausal aspects. There are also references stated that the O9A had borrowed from classical Indian traditions concerning the nine angled srivatsa, the ancient symbol, considered auspicious in India.

XV.

In Summary

L
ike all sciences, of which the esoteric mysteries are one, time results in change. As individuals study, mediate and debate different aspects of their craft or science, new ideas emerge. This change does not occur smoothly but in jerks and bounces. The study of the Tree of Knowledge is no different. The uses of the symbolism may change as of the result of cultural and political stress of society but the basics are there.

Those who follow the concept of the LHP generally view themselves as "mavericks" to the social norms at the time. With the freeing of restraints from the ruling institutions, government, church or ethics, more changes take place. Another major contributor is the blossoming of social media. With the ease of access to social communication any individual or group can expose their specific ideas to large numbers of people. If the idea has any appeal they have a possibility of attracting followers. It is said that when humanity is seeking enlightenment they search in places that at first look bright with promise but are lead further and further from the truth they seek. It goes on to say men accept all manner of theories, and attach themselves to outlandish sects and cults, while all the time believing, they are capable of distinguishing truth from falsehood.[32]

The most recent of the surge of LHP Orders, tools, and art occurred in the 1960's through to the present time. During this time the urge to

---

32 25th *Degree of the Scottish Rite of Freemasonry, "Kight of the Brazen Serpent or Sufi Master",* The Acient & Accepted Scottish Rite of The Southern Jursidition of the United States.

"break away" from conformity and the chains of the great institutions burst forth. Later as the internet and social media grew the ideas of the "radical", "unconstitutional" individuals burst on to the scene.

With this came a blossoming of groups, and LHP or dark Tarot. Often they were offshoots of dark fantasy electronic games and literature. No matter what their origin there are numerous versions available with more appearing all the time. Some relate to intitatory groups but many are extensions of the dark fantasy genre.

So like all things in the sciences of the esoteric world, have the strength to question, the passion of desire, and the patience of study, and enlightened wisdow will be yours.

Bibliography

A Bridge to Light, Dr. Rex R Hutchens, 33° The Supreme Council 33° of A.A.S.R. 2006

A Glossary to Morals and Dogma, Dr. Rex R Hutchens, 33°, The Supreme Council 33° of A.A.S.R. 1993

A History of the Occult Tarot 1870-1970, Ronald Decker & Michael Dummett Duckworth Overlook 2013

A New Encyclopaedia of Freemasonry, A. E. Waite, Wings Publishing 1970

A Practical Guide to Qabalistic Symbolism Vol 1, Gareth Knight, Helios Books 1969

Alchemy, E. J. Holmyard, Pelican Publishing 1968

Angels A to Z, Second Edition, Evelyn Dorthy Oliver & Jame R Lewis, Visible Ink Press 2008

Approaching the Kabbalah of Maat, Don Karr, Black Jackal Press 2013

Archetypes on the Tree of Life, Madonna Compton, Llewellyn Publications 1991

Early Islamic Mysticism, Kevin A Lynch, C.S.P., Paulist Press 1996

Esoteric Christianty, Annie Besant, Quest Books 2006

Essential Papers on Kabbalah, Lawrence Fine, NYU Press 1995

Gates of Light, Rabbi Joseph Gikatilla, Haper Collins 1994

Islamic Mysticism, Ibn al-Rawandi, Prometheus Books 2000

It's All in the Cards, John Mangiapane, Sterling Publication 2004

Judaic Mysticism, Avram Davis &Manuela Dunn Mascetti, Hyperion 1997

Kabbalah, Gershom Scholem, Dorset Press 1974

Lords of the Left-Hand Path, Stephen E Flowers, Inner Traditions International 2012

Motherpeace, Vickie Noble, Harper and Row 1983

Nightside of Eden, Kenneth Grant, Skoob Book 1994

On the Kabbalah and Its Symbolism, Gershom Scholem, Schocken Books 1996

Original Sinners, A New Interpretation of Genesis, John R Coats, Free Press 2009

Qabalah, A Magical Primer, John Bonner, Weiser Books 1995

Qabalah, Qliphoth, and Goetic Magic, Thomas Karlsson, Thomson-Shore 2012

Rose Croix, ACF Jackson, Lewis Masonic Publishing 1980

Sepher Yezirah, Rev. Dr. Isidor Kalisch, L.H. Frank & Co, 1957

Strong's Exhaustive Concordance of the Bible, James Strong, Hendrickson Publishing

The Bahir Illumination, Aryeh Kaplan, Weiser Publishing 1979

The Beginning of Wisdom, Reading Genesis, Leon R Kass, Free Press 2003

The Book of Thoth, Aleister Crowley, Samuel Weiser, Inc 1981

The Book of Tokens, Paul Foster Case, Builders of the Adytum 1960

The Cube of Space, Kevin Townley, Archive Press 1993

The Devil, Jeffrey Burton Russell, Cornell University 1977

The Early Kabbalah, Joseph Dan & Ronald C. Kiener, Paulist Press 1986

The Element Encyclopedia of Secret Societies, John Michael Greer, Harper Element 2013

The Encyclopedia of Cults, Sects, & New Religions, James R. Lewis, Prometheus Books 1998

The Encyclopedia of Witchcraft & Demonology, Rossell Hope Robbins, Crown 1959

The English Cabalah, Volume 1, William Eisen, DeVoress & Company 1980

The Essential Guide to The Tarot, David Fontana, David Baird Publishing 2011

The Golden Dawn, Israel Regardie, Llewellyn Publications 1998

The Hebrew Letters, Rabbi Yitzchak Ginsburgh, Gal Einai Publishing 1992

The Hermetic Qabalah, Paul A Clark, The Fraturity of the Hidden Light 2012

The Holy Kabbalah, A. E. Waite, University Books

The Inner Meaning of the Hebrew Letters, Robert M. Haralick, Jason Aronson 1995

The Kabbalah, Adolphe Franck, 1843 French Version-English 1926 1843

The Kabbalah Experience, Naomi Ozaniec, Watkins Publishing 2005

The Ladder of Lights, William G. Gray, Weiser Books 1968

The Mystic Quest, David S. Ariel, Schocken Books 1988

The Occult Philosophy in the Elizabethan Age, Frances A. Yates, Routledge & Kegan Paul 1979

The Other Bible, Willis Barnstone, Haper-SanFrancisco 1984

The Place of Enchantment, Alex Owen, The University of Chicago Press 1948

The Qabalistic Tarot, Robert Wang, Weiser Books 1983

The Rosicrucian Enlightenment, Frances A. Yates, Barnes and Noble 1972

The Secret Doctrine of the Kabbalah, Leonora Leet, Inner Traditions
    International 1999

The Tarot, Paul Foster Case, Builders of The Adytum 1947

The Tree of Life, Israel Regardie, Llewellyn Publications 2014

The True &Invisible Rosicrucian Order, Paul Foster Case, Weiser Books 1989

Three Books of Occult Philosophy, Henry Cornelius Agrippa of Nettesheim,
    Llewellyn Publications 1995

Tree of Life, Tree of Knowledge, Michael Rosenak, Westview Press 2001

When God was a Women, Merlin Stone, Barnes and Noble 1976

Zohar-Book of Splendor, Gershom Scholem,Schocken Books 1963

Zolar's Encyclopedia of Ancient & Forbidden Knowledge, Princeton Hall
    Press 1984

Index

CPSIA information can be obtained
at www.ICGtesting.com
Printed in the USA
BVHW071911250620
582143BV00003B/359